Mundane Governance

What is to be made of the outcry when newly issued recycling 'wheelie' bins are discovered to contain microchips for weighing and evaluating householders' rubbish? The angry accusations that speed cameras are generating excessive income for the government? The consternation at the measures taken by airports to heighten security in the wake of the increased threat of terrorist attacks? These increasingly widespread reactions to ordinary events and everyday phenomena share a common theme. They all embody concerns about the ways in which our lives are increasingly regulated and controlled in relation to ordinary objects and technologies.

This book takes these concerns as the starting point for exploring the ways in which relations of governance and accountability in contemporary life are organized around ordinary, everyday, pervasive objects and technologies. In contrast to the contemporary literature on governance, the book argues for the importance of examining how accountability relations are enacted on the ground in relation to mundane objects and technologies. In particular, it is crucial to understand how governance and accountability are implicated in the practical constitution of ordinary everyday objects and technologies.

The book argues that the key to understanding governance is to focus on political constitution at the level of ontology rather than just on the traditional politics of organization, structure, and human compliance. The term ontology is used here to draw attention to the social and cultural processes whereby the nature and existence of ordinary things come to matter. The argument is developed in relation to a wide variety of empirical materials drawn from three main areas of everyday life: waste management and recycling; the regulation and control of traffic (especially speed cameras and parking); and security and passenger movement in airports.

Steve Woolgar is Professor of Science and Technology Studies at Linköping University, and Professor of Marketing Emeritus at the University of Oxford. He was formerly Professor of Sociology, Head of the Department of Human Sciences, and Director of CRICT (Centre for Research into Innovation, Culture, and Technology) at Brunel University.

Daniel Neyland is Professor and Head of Sociology at Goldsmiths, University of London. He was previously Senior Lecturer in the Management School at the University of Lancaster, and Senior Research Fellow at Saïd Business School, University of Oxford.

Mundane Governance

Ontology and Accountability

Steve Woolgar and Daniel Neyland

OXFORD
UNIVERSITY PRESS

OXFORD

UNIVERSITY PRESS

Great Clarendon Street, Oxford, OX2 6DP,
United Kingdom

Oxford University Press is a department of the University of Oxford.
It furthers the University's objective of excellence in research, scholarship,
and education by publishing worldwide. Oxford is a registered trade mark of
Oxford University Press in the UK and in certain other countries

First published 2013
First published in paperback 2020

Published in the United States of America by Oxford University Press
198 Madison Avenue, New York, NY 10016, United States of America

British Library Cataloguing in Publication Data
Data available

Library of Congress Cataloging in Publication Data
Data available

ISBN 978–0–19–958474–1 (Hbk.)
ISBN 978–0–19–886444–8 (Pbk.)

Acknowledgements

Our thanks to ESRC (award no. RES-151-25-0029 'Accountability relations in networks of governance deploying mundane techno-scientific solutions to solve public problems') for supporting the project that forms the basis for the research reported here.

We are very grateful to the many participants who appear in this volume, who agreed to be interviewed, observed, and 'ethnographed'. They very generously gave up their time for us and happily agreed to reveal their mundane activities. We thank those who carried out mini-ethnographies of their airport experiences: Catelijne Coopmans, Terence Heng, Nyrie Palmer, Ju Min Wong, Faheem Mahmood, and Christian Toennesen. Thanks also to Elena Simakova (for her assistance with the airport research), James Tansey (for videotaping traffic lights), and Ju Min Wong (again, for helping out with the recycling surveys).

Over its long gestation, a very wide range of audiences and colleagues have suffered presentations of the materials in this book and made generous and helpful interventions. We thank them all, and especially Geof Bowker, Annamaria Carusi, Geoff Cooper, Catelijne Coopmans, Rob Hagendijk, C.F. Helgesson, Maja Horst, John Law, Javier Lezaun, Mike Lynch, Noortje Marres, Joao Nunes, Lindsey McGoey, Annemarie Mol, Randi Markussen, Katrina Moore, Tanja Schneider, Julie Sommerlund, Anna Sparrman, Nigel Thrift, Sarah Whatmore, and Sally Wyatt. Many former and present Oxford doctoral students gave energy and enthusiasm to the development of our ideas; thanks to Catelijne Coopmans, Elena Simakova, Julia Zamorska, Ju Min Wong, Christian Toennesen, Tarek Cheniti, Helene Ratner, Chris Sugden, Malte Ziewitz, Lucy Bartlett, and Fuz Dudhwala.

Science and Technology Studies at Oxford provided a stimulating environment throughout the period of research. Many thanks to the Said Business School and to Oxford's Institute for Science Innovation and Society (InSIS), its staff and students, Peter Healey, Anne Marie McBrien, Steve Rayner, James Tansey, Esther Vicente, and Sara Ward for providing an intellectual home for our endeavours. Thanks also for the support of former colleagues in Lancaster, perpetually in DOWT, and to Goldsmiths for providing new intellectual challenges.

Personal thanks for myriad different kinds of invaluable support to Jacqueline, Alex, Mados, Cesca, and Anna; and to Sarah, Thomas, and George.

Oxford
February 2013

Contents

Contents

Contents

List of Figures and Boxes

Figures

Boxes

1

Mundane Governance: A Profound Question of Political Philosophy?

Edward Stourton (Presenter, BBC Radio 4 *Today* Programme): *I suppose in a way, Paul Bessant, there's quite a profound question of political philosophy at stake here, which is the degree to which rubbish is something for which we should be expected to take responsibility ourselves and the degree to which it's something that we can simply offload on yourselves*

Paul Bessant (Chair of UK Local Government Association's Environment Board): *Heh heh yes that's absolutely right*

(BBC, 2006b)

1.1 Introduction

What is to be made of the huge outcry when hapless victims of local council policing are had up in court for using the 'wrong bin bag' or for depositing 'inappropriate materials' in a recycling container? Or the outrage when newly issued recycling 'wheelie' bins are discovered to contain microchips for weighing and evaluating householders' rubbish? The angry accusations that speed cameras are generating excessive income for the police? The establishment of courses for the 're-education' of drivers caught speeding? The hugely adverse reaction to government proposals to introduce road pricing schemes? The widespread sense of schadenfreude when major failures of traffic control systems, such as the break down of traffic lights, or the suspension of parking regulations, actually appear to improve traffic flow? The uproar at proposals to introduce identity (ID) cards containing individuals' biometric data? The protest at the extraordinary airport security measures introduced in response to the threat of terrorist attacks?

During the early years of the twenty-first century at least, these examples of reaction and concern are commonplace. And they share a common theme. In one way or another, they can all be said to express concerns about 'governance', that is, about the ways in which our lives are regulated and controlled. They are all the focus of questions about whom or what is accountable to whom (or what) for which kinds of behaviour. We might say they reflect consternation, and sometimes outrage, about changes in existing arrangements for governance and accountability. Of course, strong reaction to change is neither unusual nor surprising. But what is especially interesting about these examples is that such considerable concern about governance and accountability is focused on what seem to be very unremarkable objects and technologies. Across a very wide range of aspects of life, it turns out, concerns about the nature, manner, extent, and implications of governance and accountability, of regulation and control, all centre upon ordinary commonplace things.[1]

Indeed, the very level of concern and outrage in these examples articulates consternation about the degree to which our lives are being regulated and controlled by such mundane objects and technologies. It is a common experience that more and more different aspects and subcategories of objects are coming to prominence. Rubbish is no longer just rubbish, on the one hand it now comprises landfill waste and, on the other, recycling materials. Within the latter category, we witness the burgeoning of a bewildering variety of more and more fine subdivisions. We are greeted, on successive trips to the recycling centre, by further new subcategories of disposable materials. At the airport, we have to learn and understand a long litany of the kinds of containers, liquids, and other items, which can and cannot be carried in hand luggage. There seems to be an explosion of categories, which is all the more curious because it is happening to stuff about which we had previously given little thought. It used to be just stuff. Now we are required to develop knowledge and expertise about its apparently fine-grained qualities. And we need to keep up with what seems to be the continuous unpacking of typologies and further subdivision of categories.[2] Putting out the rubbish, just driving, going through airports, never used to be so complicated.

This introductory chapter sets the scene and provides the rationale for the research that forms the focus of this book. We consider a range of examples like those just mentioned—examples of apparently ordinary, everyday, pervasive objects and technologies that have generated intense concern, lively reactions and debates, and pervasive press and media attention. We use these narratives to identify some initial key characteristics of the phenomenon and to specify some preliminary questions about the place of ordinary everyday

---

[1] 'Ordinary' is used here as an initial working term; precisely what constitutes something or someone as ordinary will be explored in this and subsequent chapters.

[2] As we discuss in Chapter 3, the revision of these categories also occasionally includes the collapse of categorical distinctions.

things in governance. What are the processes and practices of governance associated with ordinary, everyday objects and technologies? What then are the key concerns about regulation and control in relation to ordinary objects and technologies? How can mere things implicate issues of governance and accountability?

We then use these preliminary questions as the basis for our evaluation (in Chapter 2), of the extent to which they can be illuminated by contemporary social science thinking about governance and accountability.

1.2 Narratives of Mundane Governance

This book brings concerns about governance into conjunction with perspectives in Science and Technology Studies (STS). Its aim is twofold: first, to suggest that STS inclined re-conceptualizations of objects and technology can offer new understandings of the nature and practice of governance; and second to assess which aspects of STS might most fruitfully achieve this.

It is the contention of the opening two chapters of this book that to get a handle on this question, we need to modify some commonly held assumptions about the nature of governance, accountability, and, indeed, mundaneity.

In this chapter, we take a first look at how ordinary objects and technologies are made to speak for politics. In this section, we ask where is governance in these examples? Who or what is rendered accountable and how? This leads us in Section 1.3 to trace out some initial analytic themes for the rest of the book. Section 1.4 then sets out the principles of research and investigation necessary to pursue our goal of respecifying ideas of governance, accountability, and the mundane—and which inform the discussion throughout the rest of the book. We end the chapter with an outline of the structure of the rest of the book.

1.2.1 The Omnipresence of the Mundane

Our first observation is that concern about apparently ordinary stuff is very widespread. Seen through the lens of much traditional social science, the kinds of ordinary phenomena we are looking at seem neither especially consequential nor important. Are these not trivial issues, objects, and events? Surely, things such as rubbish and parking are merely of parochial interest? The ordinariness of things such as wheelie bins and traffic lights seems a far cry from the supposedly more consequential topics that preoccupy much social and political science. They somehow seem much less important than questions about such matters as power, politics, globalization, climate change, global warming, energy conservation, geoengineering, financial crises, and war.

So it is surprising to discover in various media that coverage of supposedly trivial objects and practices is massive. We found print, online, and broadcast media awash with highly charged commentary, argument, debate, and outrage about rubbish bins, recycling containers, speed cameras, and so on. Local news sources seemed especially full of these stories. The letters page in the local weekly newspaper was regularly full of announcements, complaints, observations, debates, and recriminations in relation to the mundane. If there is a sense in which these objects and technologies are ordinary, the amount of attention they receive tells us they are pervasive in the public imagination. This in turn suggests we should perhaps question the assumption that such apparently ordinary things are lesser phenomena than, say, political power and global warming.

1.2.2 The Significance of the Mundane

Our second observation is that widespread attention to apparently ordinary stuff also involves stuff being accorded considerable significance. Thus, in much media treatment, stories about ordinary stuff are promoted as having significance beyond what we might traditionally think of as important political world events. For example, on Wednesday 20 April 2005 the daily national newspaper the *Daily Express* carried a photograph in the corner of the front page of the newly announced Pope, Benedict XVI. He is pictured, arms aloft, with the caption 'Pope Benedict XVI blesses the world'. This world news event is dwarfed, however, by the only other news item on the front page, which occupies three or four times as much space.

The headlines scream:

The £750,000 Speed Trap
That's how much was taken on one road in 2 months.
Can this robbery be justified?

The article announces that 'Angry motorists are to declare war on the Government's obsession with speed cameras. Tired of being an easy target to raise money, they are planning a go slow on one of the country's busiest motorways. Their frustration emerged as it was revealed that the latest speed camera scam had trapped 12,500 motorists in just two months—raising £750,000 in fines. Motoring organisations branded the cameras, which caught 200 drivers a day, as a "cash cow"'.

The example shows the relative newsworthiness of the ('robbing') speed camera. The space devoted to this familiar object seems to reflect the *Daily Express'* anticipation that readers will be more interested that they (*qua* motorists) are being taken advantage of (by 'the Government') than in the election of a new Pope. So news of the new pontiff takes second place to news about speed cameras. We thus see that not only are concerns about the mundane pervasive, they can also appear more significant than events of apparently global import.

1.2.3 The Morality of the Mundane

As part of its being accorded great significance, narratives about mundane governance are replete with moral charge. For example, in August 2006, the BBC Radio 4 *Today* programme carried an item on refuse (BBC, 2006b). In this item, passionate concern with such matters reflects the strength of feelings about what should and should not be done, to whom, and what and how. What is at issue is both the rationale for new moves and the reactions to those moves. In the case of recycling, the narratives of mundane governance make it possible to speak of the 'need' for recycling, and whether or not those responsible for recycling are 'doing well or badly'. For example, Dr Michael Warhurst, a representative of Friends of the Earth speaks of the variable performance of local councils. He is 'impressed by Richmond'—'they're you know apparently recycling 32 per cent which is about 10 per cent better than the national average at the moment', but regrets that some other councils are 'doing really badly'. Is the UK government doing enough? 'Not at all, we do still have really pathetic recycling compared with the rest of Europe. We have northern Belgium already recycling 72 per cent, that's 50 per cent more than we are managing here. The government needs to really make sure the councils know the best ways to recycle and the best ways to make sure the public know what to do'. Paul Bessant, Chair of the Local Government Association's Environment Board, talks about the 'need' for recycling and sets out the case for greater regulation of rubbish disposal. The days of the disposable society are coming to an end. We simply cannot any longer just chuck everything away. 'Because frankly the holes in the ground in which we've been putting this rubbish are filling up. In fact in a few short years there will be no more holes in the ground to put rubbish in.'

Responses to these measures exhibit considerable passion. An indication of the extent of concern is evident from stories of anger and resistance in relation to ordinary stuff.[3] For example, on 21 May 2006, the BBC Radio 4 programme *Broadcasting House* ran an item on 'rubbish rage' (BBC, 2006a). It features the 'bin men of London's Maida Vale, suffering from abuse on the doorstep.' The refuse collectors testify to being abused by householders, anxious that items should be taken away. The frustration and anger of

---

[3] Resistance and breakdown is examined in detail in Chapter 9.

householders is said to be about the complexity of rules. The media item links the anger vented on bin men to the kinds of rage associated with road rage, and air rage and, later on in the same item, to 'litter rage'.

One interesting aspect of this episode is the apparent incoherence of the rules about what can or cannot be collected. 'We actually take household refuse, anything that is not recyclable or garden waste, building material and furniture. We do not take any of that items. But they don't understand that we can not take these items.' So does this mean, for example, that they take garden waste or not? Is building material not recyclable, or is it household refuse? The ambiguity and confusion stem partly from the way the bin man describes the situation, but partly, perhaps, as we suggest in Chapters 3 and 4, from significant variations, both between councils and, over time, about what does or does not count as recyclable, and partly as a reflection of what householders have been used to for many years before recycling, namely the single refuse collection of (just about) everything thrown away by the household. The listener is left unclear about the rule and perhaps just a little bit sympathetic to the anger and frustration of the non-understanding householder. '…you try to explain it to them…' does not sound like it resulted in a very clear explanation. Unfortunately, the response to the reporter's suggestion that the complexity of rules may be responsible for the abuse is itself unclear:

> *Is it because the rules have got more complicated?*
> *Yes yes yes you know everyone's got rules you know and you've just got to abide by them.*

Dealings with ordinary stuff thus involve the setting and operation of rules, and the monitoring of behaviour in relation to those rules. As in the case of the speed camera illegitimately robbing motorists, considerable media attention was given to the prospect of sanctions being imposed on those who violate the rules of recycling:[4]

> *The union's report comes as an unemployed mother from Exeter is about to become the first person to be taken to court for putting non recyclable rubbish in her green recycling bin.*[5]

1.2.4 Irony, Incongruity, and the Exoticism of the Ordinary

These discussions about the moral order of governance—what should and should not be done with ordinary stuff—are populated by a litany of contrasts, nearly always contrasts between what could be done and what was in

---

[4] See also the detailed analysis of the 'wrong bin bag' episode in Chapter 2.
[5] *'38 year old Donna Challice denies the charge, saying passers-by must be responsible. But if she's convicted she could face a fine of £1000.'*

fact done. Particularly notable is the frequency of contrasts between treatments of the mundane in different locales. Much air time is given to the testimonies of listeners about the apparently amazing actions of local councils in their attempts to regulate and control. The stories are tied to experiences in specific geographical locales—what's happening in Scunthorpe, Cambridge, and Chichester. The doings of different councils in the UK are contrasted with each other and, often unfavourably, with the situation elsewhere, in Germany, Holland and Japan. These discussions bring together issues of comparison, contrast, and scale. Most strikingly, there is a strong sense of the exoticism of the ordinary, which turns on a recognizably familiar recitation of all the bizarre and different ways in which the same basic stuff—the rubbish—gets dealt with.

Similarly, a whole genre of stories about traffic regulation turns on the differences between what happens in different locales (see also Chapter 5). The axes of comparison and contrast range from local councils to governments and whole countries. This narrative feature of mundane governance is evident in many travellers' tales about the 'bizarre' doings in other places with regard to traffic lights (or the lack of them), or speed regulations (or the lack of them). Thus, for example, numerous examples of national/cultural differences in the operation of traffic lights (or the lack of them) are collected in a large corpus of YouTube clips posted by returning visitors to foreign countries (see Chapter 9).

In each of these examples, a key feature of the narrative is its depiction of different treatments of the same thing. In other words, the stories turn on an irony (in the technical sense): that waste, for example, is after all just waste and yet it is treated completely differently in different circumstances. As we explore in Chapter 2, this irony at the heart of narratives of mundane governance resonates strongly with an axiom central to much social science: that for any particular set of actions or behaviours in relation to phenomena, it could be otherwise. In the present case, the ironic juxtaposition is particularly marked because these are different actions in relation to the *same* ordinary, obvious, everyday (unremarkable, etc) objects: waste, rubbish, recycling, driving, speeding, parking.

1.2.5 Ironies of Mundane Governance as Social–Political Analysis

The ironic depiction of the regulation of ordinary stuff—the fact that 'the same thing' is treated differently in different places—directly supports another central feature of mundane governance. The insight that 'it could be otherwise' (indeed that it *is* observably otherwise, as testified through individuals' experiences, media stories, and travellers' tales) is crucially generative in opening a space for observation, comment, and analysis. The observation that it is or can be done differently, makes possible the question: why is it being done in this particular way here and now?

This in turn is crucial in establishing a central feature of these narratives: the depiction of ordinary technologies and objects as instruments of various prevailing social and political forces. The key apprehension is that ordinary stuff is not being treated ordinarily, or as it should. We have already seen, for example, how the tabloid story about the 'robbing speed camera' portrayed speed cameras as agents of 'the Government's' (unjustifiable) robbery. And in their dealings with the ordinary stuff of waste disposal, the characters we might call the operatives of governance—the council, the local authority, the municipality, the binmen, traffic wardens—can be portrayed as inept, often by reference to the supposedly superior way in which the same stuff is treated differently in other places, at other times, by other modes of government.

Our interest in this phenomenon comes at a time of much discussion about the nature of governance and at a time of concerns about increasing UK state regulation of social ('problem') behaviour. At the same time, recent years have been witness to complaints and concerns about overregulation and overgovernance. In this spirit, in December 2006, the BBC Radio 4 *Today* programme ran a listeners' poll on 'Which law would you like to get rid of?' Listeners were encouraged to nominate and vote for the most absurd, redundant law. Nick Clegg, then Liberal Democrat Home Affairs spokesman, proposed a 'wholesale repeal' of all the parliamentary acts responsible for unnecessary intrusion into the lives of ordinary citizens. In this spirit, Clegg singled out the proposed introduction of ID cards and the storage of DNA data. ID cards were said to be very expensive, intrusive, and unnecessary. Whereas it might be justified to keep details of those charged or arrested for wrong doing, to do so for thousands of others was to harass the innocent people of Britain. The complaint was that such measures amounted to unwarranted widespread interference into the everyday lives of law-abiding citizens.[6]

Two points are noteworthy here. First, the emphasis on the widespread impacts on everyday lives. The (alleged) problem is that large numbers of the population will be affected, when the appropriate target is only a minority of criminals and offenders. The complaint, in other words, is that these mundane measures are unnecessarily worldly. Second, it is striking, in this example, as in many other discussions and debates about mundane governance, that the technical capacities of the proposed technologies—ID cards and DNA data storage—are taken as given. That is, the complainant takes the

---

[6] Ironically since coming into government as Deputy Prime Minister for the UK coalition, Clegg has been party to a swathe of new regulations some of which appear to be designed to legislate into being greater freedom and choice (for example, in the Decentralism and Localism Bill) or introduce new forms of personal regulation (for example, through the Welfare Reform Bill). It seems that greater freedom can only be achieved through more regulation.

impact of these things as unequivocal. Their apparently self-evident effects are then tied into various negative consequences for 'people in Britain'. They are enrolled into a narrative about the inadequacies of government (in) action. The deficiencies of the government become the deficiencies of various agencies and institutions in dealing inappropriately with objects and technologies, which have self-evident impacts.

These examples share with many recent discussions of governance, as we shall see in Chapter 2, the same lack of serious critical attention to the role of objects and technology. In their focus at the level of institution and on the connection between structural form and effectiveness of governance, they overlook, or take for granted, the technical capacities of objects and technology. An important consequence is that many of these discussions tend to marginalize any doubts or uncertainties about technological capacity. In particular, as we shall argue in detail, a major weakness is that these discussions fail to take seriously what we call the ontological status of the object or technology in question. They tend to take for granted one or other version of what the object is, what it is for, what the technology can do, and so on.

So uninterrogated claims about the capacities of mundane objects and technologies provide the basis for arguments about the inadequacy of political action and/or the inappropriateness of regulation. The same kind of reasoning is evident in a more generalized form of social–political analysis, specifically the invocation of complaints about 'what is going wrong with our society'. It is notable that the period of our study coincided with the rise of new genres of complaining about everyday experiences, as popularized in the media. For example, *Grumpy Old Men* emerged as a highly successful UK television series, first broadcast on BBC TV in 2003. The programme adopted a conversational style format wherein a number of famous middle-aged men (actors, comedians, musicians, celebrities, sports commentators, and so on) talk animatedly about issues of modern life which irritate them, and give vent to their frustrations in relation to everyday objects and experiences.[7] Theirs is a kaleidoscopic assortment of pet hates, the vast majority of which focus on the mundane: packing, air travel, traffic calming, the proliferation of excessive road signs, automated call centres, overly-loud mobile phone conversations, insurance salesmen, the nanny state, handy flat-pack furniture, and so on.[8]

---

[7] 'Grumpy Old Men is a modern movement, a hitherto silent minority who see the world they have created, and are appalled. But now they are fighting back, no longer suffering in silence. This series of programmes is their manifesto' (BBC GOM Series 1 part 1 of 4; http://www.youtube.com/watch?v=_HWT9Mbxnk8&feature=relmfu).

[8] http://en.wikipedia.org/wiki/Grumpy_Old_Men_(TV_series). The original series spawned a series of subsequent programmes in the same format, including *Grumpy Old Women, The Grumpy Guide to Work, Grumpy Old Holidays, It's Grim Up North, My Appalling School Report, He Says, She Says,* and *The Meaning Of Life.*

NARRATOR: *And do our grumpy old men get phoned up at home while eating dinner by double glazing salesmen?*

BOB GELDORF: *I do and I tell them to fuck off.*

Companion books to the series were published and related publications appeared. For example, the pop comedy book *Completely Conkers: what drives you mad about modern Britain* (Jackson, 2009) features chapters about household waste collection (entitled 'Who's bin doing you a disservice?') and traffic ('Driving you round the bend') among complaints about the modern state of affairs in relation to political correctness in language use, excessive environmentalism, bureaucratic interference from Brussels, and so on.

Relatedly, we came across the view that such phenomena were not merely a source of irritation, but also indicative of a wider malaise in modern society. Thus, one of our informants offered the following comment when, in February 2007, a letter bomb exploded in the main UK Driving and Vehicle Licensing Authority (DVLA) centre in Swansea. Was it likely that the letter bomb was sent by a disgruntled motorist?

> *There will be a motorist bomber one day. Maybe me—having just been 'done' by the Orwellian-named 'Safety Camera Alliance' that snoops around the A303 making safe drivers at 82 mph into dangerous drivers as they jam on the brakes to try to get below 70 before speeding up to 82 mph again. I wouldn't mind if I accepted the justice of the cause, but I don't (AND I have a 'green' LPG car)...Grrr. And as for the extended 'congestion' charge zone...So I confess that my heart lifts each time that I see a necklaced or shot out speed camera the further west I drive.* (GP, 9/2/2007)

This respondent voices the unfairness of it all, by connecting the injustice of speed cameras, his own green credentials (driving an LPG car), and the outrage of congestion zone charging. The sight of vandalized speed cameras gives him heart and for him represents a 'heartfelt comment on the collapse of the social contract in modern Britain'. The agency of governance is Orwellian. And for this respondent, it is no surprise that the unfairness of several aspects of traffic governance gives rise to the destruction of a primary instrument of that governance, namely the speed camera. It is a natural and highly predictable reaction to excessive legislation. The unfairness of the politics makes the speed camera an understandable target.

1.2.6 Schadenfreude about Failures of Mundane Governance

We have seen that ironies in the differential or inappropriate treatment of ordinary stuff can give rise to invocations of social–political forces, protestations about excessive regulation, and declarations of a general societal malaise and/or the collapse of the social contract. We have also suggested how these quasi-analytic treatments of ordinary stuff depend on the uninterrogated acceptance of the supposedly given effects and capabilities of ordinary objects. It is perhaps no surprise then, that the subsequent disruption of these expectations can be a matter for considerable comment.

For example, in the course of countless discussions about the prospective introduction of UK national ID cards, media attention was given to a report of a meeting of the British Computer Society (*Computer Weekly*, 13 October 2005), that a large number of technical problems stand in the way of producing reliable systems for checking biometric data. On the question of fingerprinting alone, it was said, eating crisps could be enough to have a fingerprint rejected by the proposed scheme.

Crisps make fingerprints slightly oily, which will affect a reading, said a biometrics expert. Other issues which would also affect biometric readers: Would a fingerprint reader work reliably if it was positioned in sunlight? Would it recognise a surgeon with faded fingerprints from years of hand washing, or a bricklayer constantly handling rough bricks, or someone facially disfigured after a fire, or unable to manage an accurate iris scan after becoming blind?

Most discussions about the potential use of biometrics in ID cards portray them as unwarranted extensions of an already too intrusive form of government, and stress the prohibitive costs of their development and implementation and the likely disruptive effects of their deployment.[9] In this, the technical capabilities of ID cards are taken for granted. By contrast, this type of report highlights possible technical problems that might arise from ordinary situations and likely user characteristics. In particular, it turns out, or so it is said, that the smooth and potentially widespread operation of a sophisticated technology can trip over an occurrence as ordinary as sticky fingers. The incongruity between technical promise and ordinary circumstance is striking. And this in turn suggests that the very possibility of governance through ID cards is premised on an idealized, standardized normal citizen presenting him or herself to the technology under specific ('ideal') circumstances. Visions of prospective governance, in other words, configure a specific imagined user, which, in these stories, is brought into stark contrast with actual users.

We came across many similar stories of incongruities associated with the failed implementation of new technologies. For example, in 2008, the Scottish *Daily Record* ran a story about how a nuclear submarine had crashed off the Isle of Skye, causing £5 million pounds worth of damage and leading to the court martial of three senior officers. According to a 2002 MOD inquiry

---

[9] For example, through campaigning organizations such as No2ID and also in academic work, see LSE (2005).

report, only made public six years later, a major cause of the crash was the use of tracing paper, 'similar to that used by schoolchildren, which had been put over charts to prevent them being written on'.[10] The use of tracing paper was said to have obscured vital information, including symbols showing the strength of the current and contours of the sea floor. As a result, 'this led navigators to change course too early and head into water where the seabed was rising sharply'.[11] Media coverage delighted in the ironic contrast between the weighty technological sophistication of a '£300million sub' and ordinary common or garden tracing paper.[12]

Or again, media attention was excited in 2011 by the case of a student who was mistaken by police for a suicide bomber. 'STUDENT Goudarz Karimi was just hoping to get fitter when he went out for a quiet jog with a weight vest on . . . but the Iranian PhD student ended up being confronted by armed officers reacting to fears he could be a suicide bomber'.[13] Once again, the ironic juxtaposition between the putative suicide bomb and (what turned out to be only) a weight vest is what gives the story its appeal. The ordinariness and harmlessness of such objects is underscored by the additional claim that weight vests of this kind are 'used by the likes of Prince Harry'.

The failure or misapprehension of the presumed properties of ordinary objects is itself a newsworthy feature of narratives of mundane governance.

1.3 Some Initial Analytic Themes

Thus, our first look at mundane governance provides a flavour of the phenomena we wish to investigate. We have seen that the mundane is omnipresent, it is often given great significance, and its discussion is often highly charged. Accounts of the mundane are frequently characterized by a central irony: that the same ordinary stuff is treated differently in different circumstances. In these examples, the irony is important because it makes possible a form of social and political analysis of the ways in which ordinary stuff is treated: what circumstances lead to the same stuff being dealt with in one way rather than another?

For now, we note three main kinds of analytic issue that arise from our initial characterization of mundane governance. First, in all the examples so far,

---

[10] http://www.dailyrecord.co.uk/news/scottish-news/2008/05/23/tracing-paper-blamed-for-nuclear-submarine-crash-86908-20426393/

[11] *Daily Record*, n. 10.

[12] Cf http://www.dailymail.co.uk/news/article-1021173/Nuclear-submarine-5m-crash—trainees-plotting-course-tracing-paper.html

[13] http://www.oxfordmail.co.uk/news/9286990.Police_thought_student_was_a_suicide_bomber/?ref=mr

there is a strong sense that things could have been otherwise. This is the case in two ways. On the one hand, although the general phenomenon is often historically longstanding, each example manifests a particularly novel configuration of the problem. Thus, as already noted, the perception that rubbish used to be just rubbish, now gives way to a complicated typology of categories of recyclables and sorting behaviours. The literature on the history of traffic regulation reveals a whole series of unusual and seemingly curious ways in which speed has been monitored and regulated (for example, Emsley, 1993), of which the current organization of safety camera partnerships is a recent novelty. Fears about security and terrorism associated with travel are also longstanding, but take on a particular configuration in the modern management of passenger movement through airports.

Similarly, although the general phenomenon of mundane governance seems widespread, its particular manifestation is usually culturally and/or nationally specific. As already noted, contrasts between different systems of waste and recycling collection and disposal are a lively source of discussion and debate. The axis of contrast is both international and between different local council areas in the UK. It is less generally known that systems for monitoring speeding and other forms of traffic control vary markedly between different regions of the UK (see the discussion of Safety Camera Partnerships in Chapter 5). But there is evidence to suggest widespread differences internationally. For example, US states such as Iowa are characterized by lengthy arguments about the introduction of speed cameras and their possible infringement of civil liberties.[14] Airport authorities pay great attention to national differences and reputation in terms of passenger movement and security. As we show in Chapter 2, this general form of variation is key. Critics of governance exploit the fact that different agencies of governance deal with stuff differently. The irony of the contrast, say, between Richmond and other councils, between the UK and Japan, is all the more marked, in these accounts, because they are all taken to relate to the same apparently ordinary, common or garden, taken for granted, thing. This idea that these are all 'different' manifestations of the 'same' thing—is central to the ontological dynamics of the mundane.

Secondly, the fact that things could be otherwise emphasizes the point that we should resist the idea that there is anything obvious or 'natural', 'inherent' or 'given' about the capacities of the objects and technologies in question. We instead need to be alert to the processes whereby the capacities of these (and

---

[14] In Iowa, for example, arguments continue about the potential use of speed cameras, their civil liberty implications, and the extent to which supporting or opposing speed cameras might be a vote winner, see, for example: http://www.blogforiowa.com/2012/01/23/traffic-cameras-politics-and-civil-liberties/

other) entities are contingently enacted. We need to understand the ways in which, for example, 'soggy paper' becomes a non-recyclable (Chapter 3), the actions of a motorist become those of a speeding driver (Chapter 5), and departing airport passengers become constituted as either 'clean' or 'dirty' (Chapter 7).

Thirdly, and as a corollary of these preceding points, we observe the intriguing sense of politics that begins to emerge in these stories. It is not simply that politics is antecedent to objects about which there is contention. It seems more than that. It is not that politics swirls around, so to speak, the otherwise mute, obvious, objectively given things. Rather, one has a sense that the very character of the things is somehow intimately tied up with the politics, so that the appropriateness (predictability, blameworthiness, absurdity, etc) of political action is expressed in and through what, after all, the thing itself is. Politics stem from ordinary stuff. So the challenge for us is to articulate how politics work at the level of ontology—that is, in relation to the very nature of things. Can things 'have politics'? We begin to glimpse a sense in which, as the BBC presenter speculated at the start of this chapter, the governance of ordinary stuff might indeed be a profound question of political philosophy.

Taken together, these features of mundane governance give rise to a series of questions. How exactly can things as banal as rubbish collection have anything to do with the lofty problems of political philosophy? What exactly is the role of objects and ordinary technologies in these situations? What kinds of accountability relations are involved in networks of governance, which deploy mundane techno-scientific solutions to solve public problems? Moreover, if these manifestations of accountability and governance are widespread and yet, as we suggest, have been largely overlooked, what are the implications for our understanding of governance in general? To what extent and in what ways might a close examination of mundane governance contribute to rethinking the very idea of governance?

1.4 Principles for Researching the Mundane

It is clear that an understanding of governance and accountability in contemporary life requires a focus on ordinary, everyday, pervasive objects and technologies. In particular, a study of governance and accountability needs to understand how governance and accountability relations are enacted on the ground, in practice, in relation to mundane objects and technologies. Whereas, as we discuss in Chapter 2, governance and accountability have for the most part been addressed in terms of corporate and organizational structures—for example, the constitution of committees and of systems of reporting—we argue for the importance of examining accountability relations inside out, under the skin. An appreciation of governance requires us to understand how accountability and governance are mediated through material relations involving ordinary everyday objects and technologies.

In line with the discussion so far, certain analytic sensibilities are prerequisite for our exploration of mundane governance. Many of these derive from the multidiscipline of STS. These are discussed in Chapter 2 so here we briefly outline some of the main principles of our research. Our focus on the achieved ontological status of objects and technologies requires us to adopt a symmetrical, impartial perspective. This entails an analytic scepticism about the claims and uses involved. We try not to accept unthinkingly that one plastic bin bag is much like another. To aspire to this, we approach our research with a broadly ethnographic attitude. In one sense of the term, being ethnographic means intensive *in situ* participant observation among the natives to learn to see things from their point of view. We try to appreciate that for some people, for some purposes, and on some occasions, the difference between a council-issued sack and one bought from the supermarket is crucial. In the second sense of the term, we refuse merely to adopt (some of) the natives' point of view. We try instead to play down the exoticism of the Other. In particular, we try to stay attuned to a rarely emphasized feature of ethnographic research. Namely, that ethnography is not just an exercise in capturing and reporting back the natives' point of view—guess what weird things people think about bin bags! Nor is the main task to become accepted by members of the tribe under investigation—we struck up a really strong bond with the bin men! Rather, the task is to document and reflect upon the experiences of moving back and forth across cultural divides and perceptual boundaries, of being simultaneously an insider and an outsider, and of moving between the two. We take it that the analytical scepticism characteristic of ethnography can also be fruitfully brought to bear on the ethnographer's experiences and reflections.[15] The effort to achieve and maintain analytical scepticism was not without struggle. We made efforts to mundane-ize and to exotic-ize, to confront things with what they have become. But our aspiration to symmetry and impartiality involved frequent lapses, from which we can also learn.

How did we get to this point? We started with the question already mentioned: what kinds of accountability relations are involved in networks of governance that deploy mundane techno-scientific solutions to solve public problems? On the basis that mundane techno-scientific solutions have been comparatively overlooked in discussions of politics, we originally construed

---

[15] For stylistic purposes we sometimes use the 'I' character to refer to either or both our individual experiences and observations.

our study as a shift away from esoteric, high tech, headline grabbing, specialist new controversial technologies. By contrast with previous work on the (allegedly) world changing properties of internet technologies (Woolgar, 2002), we feared this shift in focus to the ordinary might seem rather trivial and inconsequential. As already indicated, however, and somewhat to our surprise, we found ourselves faced with what we might call the rise of the object—the explosion of categories and typologies of stuff, the intense public awareness of ordinary things, and their consternation about how stuff rules their lives. Our analytic objects may have moved down market, but the ordinary stuff in which we found ourselves immersed was none the less pervasive and headline grabbing.

Our argument is developed in relation to a wide variety of empirical materials drawn from three main areas of everyday life, the organization, behaviour, and activities associated with: waste management and recycling; the management and control of traffic, including speed cameras and parking; and the management of passenger movement through airports. In short, the book examines mundane governance in practice across three main substantive arenas—trash, traffic, and transit.

Our initial rationale for the choice of these three areas was to select mundane technologies at various stages of development. We imagined the cases would lie along a continuum between those now very widely deployed and those envisaged as routine applications of the future. Thus, waste disposal and recycling would entail established, routine, and fairly 'low tech' technologies. Traffic management, in particular speed cameras, would entail slightly 'higher tech' electronic systems, which are none the less fairly widely used. Security systems for airport passengers would involve more sophisticated monitoring systems, especially through the use of biometric ID cards, routine use of which is imagined in the future.

Although, as we hope to show, each case proved very fruitful, it quickly became clear that this rationale for their selection was not sustainable. Many features of airport passenger movement, for example the pervasive signage (referred to by those in the trade as 'wayfinding'), can be considered very low tech. The electronic components of speed cameras (safety cameras) were indeed routine and standardized in their design but, especially when contested by disgruntled drivers, were deemed unusual, invasive, and 'big brother'. And apparently ordinary waste and recycling collection containers provoked consternation and confusion, even before it was objected that local councils had secretly concealed electronic chips in the lids of wheelie bins. Clearly, what counts as mundane is far from straightforward; it can vary between situations, constituencies, and over time. More to the point, as we shall start to see in detail in Chapter 2, the achievement (we shall variously refer to construction, accomplishment, enactment, constitution, apprehension) of mundaneity comes laden with implications for governance and accountability.

So against our initial design to choose technologies at different stages of their evolution, no such clear cut distinctions survived our initial forays into the field(s). Our thoughts about classifying technologies according to different degrees of mundaneity, quickly tripped over the realization that mundane is a massively relative term. In retrospect the fate of our initial neat(ish) research design is itself informative and predictable. For it turns out that all the key terms in our initial formulation of the problem are themselves lively matters for debate and argument: accountability relations, governance, mundane. They all hang heavy with varying significance, interpretations, claims, and counter claims by all involved. And they are all tied to and implicate different sets of practices and procedure.

Each of the three areas of empirical focus requires the analysis of a range of social and technical entities (such as designers, developers, managers, objects, possible technologies, technologies in operation, and potential users) involved in accountability relations and governance in putative techno-scientific solutions to proposed public problems. So each area is intended as a multi-sited or 'mobile' ethnography (Hine, 2000: 64), which can be used to draw together such diverse research participants (for example, Hirsch, 1992).[16] Our procedure was to follow connections and links between objects, entities, individuals, groups, and agencies, crossing conventional boundaries. The advantage is that rather than predefining (or accepting given definitions of) the boundaries and linkages that make up the technology and its networks of governance, we consider when, where, and how objects and technologies are 'achieved', that is, how they are apprehended and experienced. For each area, we selected various starting points (for example, the development of regional Safety Camera Partnerships for the management of speed or safety cameras), followed the myriad connections (vehicle drivers, systems, engineers, and so on) emanating from these starting points and finally exploited these connections in our ethnographic reports, presentations, and publications. Our research included observational, interview, and document analysis as well as our own reflections on the process of transition and linkage, and this process in turn helped identify and recruit recipient audiences for our work. The research process was thus conceived as an 'experiential and engaged exploration of connectivity' (Hine, 2000: 61; cf Riles,

---

[16] Hirsch (1992) studies families' use, consumption, and negotiation of technologies in the home. Hirsch identifies himself as the key link between the families of his research, between the various sites in which the families operate, both within and between what Hirsch terms the public and private performances they offer in negotiating their understanding of technology.

2001), in which the connections and boundaries were up for analysis, not just the content or actions that occurred within those boundaries.

Our inquiry is organized around three broadly distinct areas of mundane governance, selected in the ways just mentioned. Yet the question arises, and particularly in light of our comments about the concurrent popularity of general modes of complaint about all manner of everyday matters, as to what extent these distinct areas share common features of mundane governance. We return to this issue in our concluding chapter. For now, it is worth noting that the three areas are sometimes linked in everyday experience. For example, one respondent made the following connection between trash (recycling) and traffic (parking):

> I was going into the car park the other night. As I drove in, another car was coming out. And I think this kind of thing is getting more common. He wound down his window and passed across his parking ticket to me so I could use it and save having to buy my own. It still had about an hour left on it I think. I thanked him and he said: 'Well the council keep saying they want us to recycle more, don't they!'

The anecdote conveys a sense of camaraderie as invoked between put-upon car drivers/parkers. The two drivers recognize each other as subjects of (local council) governance in the twin domains of waste management and traffic control. Or, for example, on the third (!) occasion during the course of this study that one of us was caught speeding (Chapter 6), it was noted that the offence took place while transporting waste materials to the recycling centre.

It would be easy to conclude that these kinds of intersecting experiences are the result of some mysterious overarching forces of governance. But our interest is not in this kind of account. Rather, we are interested (especially in Chapter 10) in how such commonalities are generated, sustained, achieve currency, and are used as sense making frameworks for ordinary experiences in relation to objects and technologies.

Our concern with the pervasive, omnipresent, ordinary, and mundane has a further methodological correlate, which, as far as we know, is not frequently discussed. This particular feature of our research has the curious consequence that many of the phenomena we wish to study are not merely omnipresent; they are unavoidable. That is, they do not exist merely as things and practices that we social scientists then topicalize and appropriate for research purposes. Instead, we ourselves are always and already constitutively part of these phenomena. This is obvious in the general sense that we as authors and researchers also happen to be recyclers, drivers, and airport passengers. It is also a fairly common ethnographic experience to find oneself, as we found ourselves, enrolled as social science research experts in carrying out surveys for our target organizations (recycling surveys for the local council; airport passenger surveys for our main airport field site). More interesting though is the way in which our constitutive presence actually generated many of the activities and events that we set out to study. Thus, for example, during the course of this research, one or other of us: was (as just mentioned) caught speeding; sent on a driver re-education course; became embroiled in a lengthy contestation of a series of parking tickets; flouted signs intended to prevent drivers entering a closed road; and caused considerable upset by brandishing a forbidden container of liquid on board an aircraft.

We consider the significance of these episodes in detail in ensuing chapters. For now, we note in advance that although this kind of constitutive involvement is reminiscent of Garfinkel's (1967) famous 'breaching experiments', designed to disrupt normal behaviour as a way of revealing the strength of the prevailing moral order, (almost) none of our own experiences were deliberate breaches. Instead, our interventions were as surprising to us as they were inadvertent.

1.5 Structure of our Argument

To what extent and in what ways do existing literatures on governance and accountability take account of the mundane? Chapter 2 critically assesses a range of literatures from the point of view of our interest in ontology, to help develop a way of respecifying concepts such as governance, accountability, and mundaneity, to refine the sense of ontology most useful to our inquiry, and to specify the research questions central to our task. This then forms the basis for our empirical exploration of the mundane in the ensuing chapters. Chapters 3 and 4 examine the ontologies of rubbish, waste disposal, and recycling. Chapters 5 and 6 look at ordinary objects and technologies in relation to the regulation of traffic, especially speeding and parking. Chapters 7 and 8 focus on the governance of passenger movement and on security issues in airports. Trash, traffic, and transit are the empirical foci of Chapters 3–8. As we set out at the end of Chapter 2, in light of a critical assessment of the relevant literatures, we use each of these central Chapters 3–8 to develop a different analytic theme in mundane governance.

Chapter 9 turns attention to disruption: the myriad kinds of resistance and breakdown associated with mundane governance. If, as we suggest, there has been a growth in the forms of governance organized in relation to ordinary objects and technologies, what new kinds of resistance does this engender and with what success? What happens when apparently smooth running systems of mundane governance break down? Resistance and breakdown are important because they can teach us about mundane governance in the breach. In this chapter, we examine some of the many forms of resistance and break down in mundane governance for what these tell us about the dynamics of its 'normal' operation.

Finally, in Chapter 10, we recap the central theoretical contributions of our work. We pull together the empirical findings across the different areas of our study to ask whether and in what sense we can adduce significant generalities about mundane governance.

2

The Wrong Bin Bag: The Situated Ontology of Mundane Governance

2.1 Introduction

This book argues for a new understanding of governance based on a form of ontological politics—the practices and processes whereby objects and entities are apprehended as things of the world, and whereby their identities and attributes give rise to relations of governance and accountability. The key to understanding governance, we argue, is to focus on political constitution at the level of ontology rather than just on the traditional politics of organization and structure.

In Chapter 1, we encountered the omnipresence and significance of the mundane. Our first look at the narratives of mundane governance suggested we need to pay close attention to the many different ways in which ordinary stuff is apprehended and understood, a heightened awareness that there is nothing intrinsic to the properties of ordinary phenomena, and a sensitivity to the ways in which the notion of politics is entangled with the mundane.

How then should we go about understanding regulation and control in relation to ordinary objects and technologies? In this chapter, we examine some of the resources available for making sense of mundane governance. We first consider some of the literature, which bears upon the interrelated concepts of governance and accountability, and assess the extent to which they can help us. We identify some features of Science and Technology Studies (STS) as the basis for developing an ontologically sensitive analytic framework. We then try out some general features of this approach in relation to one particular empirical episode—the wrong bin bag—to specify the main research questions to be addressed throughout the rest of the book.

2.2 Governance and Accountability

Governance is a very general and old problem, which admits a wide variety of treatments, and a wide range of ideas about social control and regulation. In recent years, governance and accountability have become key themes in discussions across government, public and private sectors, corporate and not for profit organizations, and academia. More and more institutions have used the term 'governance' to refer to aspects of the ways they manage, control, and regulate themselves. Concerns about the nature and effectiveness of government have prompted renewed consideration of the frameworks, organization, structures, and institutional forms that make government possible. Attention to governance is generally thought to be healthy, and to promise changes for the better. To demonstrate one's capacity to reflect upon and bring about changes in governance is reckoned to bring credit to one's organization.

Given the extensive range of interpretations of governance, let us distinguish between two main uses of the term.

2.2.1 Corporate Governance

'Governance' is commonly used to refer to proposals for the reform of existing organizational structures and processes. This sense of governance meaning organizational reform came to enjoy special prominence since the scandals and company crashes of the late 1990s and early 2000s. The problems included 'certain CEOs on the make, most non executives frozen out, shareholders too often treated like cannon fodder, lawyers and auditors duped', in the light of which 'a raft of new reforms and measures were designed to rebalance corporate governance, to bring back trust and integrity, and to lay down clear lines of accountability, to company boards, to shareholders, to governments and to international authorities' (Flather, 2006: 2). When speaking especially of private sector organizations, the phrase 'corporate governance' is used; when speaking of reform in government the equivalent phrase is 'public services reform' (for example, Benington, 2006). In both cases, governance reform is not just directed to the repair and prevention of illicit behaviour, but is also reckoned a means of improving organizational performance. Better governance means greater efficiency, productivity, and responsiveness to relevant 'stakeholders'.

In private sector organizations activities aimed at establishing or improving corporate governance tend to focus on the putative needs of shareholders. One rationale arises from the perceived distance between shareholders making investments in companies, and company boards, directors, employees, and so on, who are responsible for making something from those investments. Corporate governance is discussed as a framework for providing a means whereby those investing in organizations can receive information about what goes on in the organization and a certain guarantee that organizations will adhere to certain recognizable business standards (Blowfield and Murray, 2008). However, both functions of governance are noted as problematic. Precisely what kinds of information should be made available and the extent to which such information turns out to be trustworthy, reliable, and of good provenance, has become a matter of concern following a series of corporate scandals (for example, Enron, BCCI, Robert Maxwell). Discussions about the appropriate criteria for corporate governance have given rise, in the UK, to a succession of reports and codes (Cadbury 1992; Greenbury 1995; Combined Code 1998; Hampel 1998; Turnbull 1999; Higgs 2003; Revised Combined Code 2003).

A main assumption of these reports and codes is that changes at the level of organizational structure or legislation are a key determinant of changes in behaviour. However, many of these codes have been noted as having unintended consequences. First, at the centre of each report and code is a role designated for auditors. They are to be deemed responsible for carrying out independent, verified, and certified checks that organizations do indeed adhere to the latest code. It is an ongoing feature of each of the aforementioned corporate scandals (Enron, Maxwell, and BCCI), that immediately preceding the scandal, auditors have provided organizations with a clean bill of health. The Maxwell scandal, for example, revealed after many years of forensic work following the tycoon's suicide that Maxwell organized and helped to run thousands of front organizations through which money was constantly moving, that money was moved illegally, and that many of the organizations were running up huge, but mostly invisible, debts. Although the UK government had raised concerns about Maxwell's business from the 1950s onwards, it was only through his death and many years of investigation, that auditors drew together this complex picture. The response to this apparent demonstration of the limitations of ongoing (rather than forensic) audit, was a government report and an updated, more stringent code of corporate governance with a more central role for ongoing audit (for more on Maxwell, see Bower 1988, 1996).

Secondly, alongside a more central role for audit, each successive code is also said to be more stringent than the previous one. This stringency is also tied to corporate scandals. However, stringency is also said to have its unanticipated effects. For example, in the USA, the development of the Sarbanes–Oxley Act (2002) is said to have been considered so stringent (and the legislation so rushed) by some firms that they have sought to list their company elsewhere (Blowfield and Murray, 2008).

Thirdly, the logics of corporate governance appear to shift from private sector firms to publicly funded organizations without much translation.[1] For example, in proposing major changes to the ways in which Oxford University is run, there is much discussion of 'the future of Oxford's governance'. This turns out to refer to changes in 'the University's structures and procedures', including, for example, the 'difficulties of operating parallel University and College governance systems; and a concern that under present arrangements Council has too much business to give due depth of deliberation to every issue'.[2] Similarly, the 'governance changes' outlined in the BBC White Paper (2006) included the proposal that existing BBC Governors be abolished and replaced with two new bodies, the BBC Trust and a separate Executive Board. 'The Trust will be the voice of the licence fee payer, and will oversee the Executive Board. The job of the Executive will be to run the BBC's services. The responsibilities of each will be separate and clearly defined, eliminating any conflict of interests' (quoted in ALCS News, May 2006: 13).[3]

The literature on social and/or critical studies of accounting takes up the analytical theme of corporate structures and processes of governance. It comprises a broad array of studies of the multiple forms and effects of governance in the shape of, among other things, regulation, instruction, and professionalization. Governance is considered through forms of, for example, the professionalization of accounting (Hopwood, 1998) and attempts to get organizations to adopt transparency protocols (Gray, 1992). A problem for our purposes is that many of these approaches pay scant critical attention to the objects and technologies of governance. They tend either not to mention technology at all, or to conceptualize technology as an incidental player, a mere appendage to systems of government and power. For example, Hopwood characterizes audit firms of the past in terms of concerns with firms' 'identity, their products, their history, their corporate culture and their

---

[1] This is in line with the audit society thesis of Power (1997), which will be addressed in Section 2.2.3.

[2] http://www.ox.ac.uk/blueprint/2005-06/2906/01.shtml Notably, those proposing changes in the governance of large organizations often take the precaution of highlighting the need for extensive consultation. Democratic participation in fashioning governance is important. So much thought is given to planning an elaborate consultation process. The latter includes the publication of Green and White papers, distribution of email progress reports, and of newsletters and a folded colour leaflet ('A Brief Guide to Governance Reform') to all members of the University, and a series of open question time meetings http://www.ox.ac.uk/blueprint/2005-06/2906/12.shtml

[3] A striking feature of this focus on 'corporate' structural change in the public sector is that it offers the promise of procedural solutions that are largely indifferent to the particular substance of the organizational work. For example, systems of communicating decisions in a university context are not driven by a particular cognisance of the specific character of university research. Or again, it is not clear that splitting the responsibilities of BBC Governors is the solution most appropriate to the particular business of public broadcasting. This alludes to the deeper and more complex question about the extent to which structures of governance can (re)define what the core business of the organization actually is.

managerial needs' and contrasts this with an increasing focus on 'rules, procedures, standardised processes and manuals' (1998: 1). Questions about the nature and status of objects and technology are notably absent.[4] Instead, by focusing at the level of institution and on the connection between structural form and regulatory effectiveness, these discussions tend to overlook, or take for granted, the nature and technical capacity of objects and technology.[5]

2.2.2 Neo-Foucauldian Approaches to Governance

Recent arguments deriving from the work of Foucault offer a sense of governance, which falls outside and beyond (and yet retains interesting connections with) the specifically structural meanings of corporate governance.

Foucault (1966, 1967, 1977) leaves the precise role of technology (from houses, to prisons, to hospital beds) somewhat unspecified. But general features of the Foucauldian approach do lend themselves to a critical treatment of technology and government. For example, Foucault's (1966) *Order of Things* and (1967) *Madness and Civilization* are concerned with projects of order and ordering. Foucault's approach to order is particularly useful insofar as it enables us to open up to scrutiny what we take for granted about government and technology, our certainty about technical capacity and effects. As Rose (1999: x) points out, it is a central thrust of Foucault's work that we can question our present certainties—about what we know, who we are, and how we should act—by confronting them with their histories: this experience can prove more unsettling and provocative than either the exposure of empirical errors or the formulation of conceptual critiques. Rose goes on to say that the important point of this form of 'deconstruction' is not merely to reiterate the argument that something claimed objective is in fact socially constructed, but rather to show, for example, how 'certain constructions acquire the status of truth—through experimental procedures, demonstrations and other

---

[4] This is perhaps especially surprising in the light of claims about the transformative capacities of computational technologies.

[5] A separate literature not considered here deals with the governance of science and technology: the regulation and control of the conduct and application of science and technology. Earlier analyses in this tradition examined the 'social contract for science', for example, the extent to which state funding of science necessitates government monitoring of the effectiveness of that funding (for example, Guston, 1993; Guston and Keniston, 1994; Wolf, 1994). More recent work, argues that the products of technoscience are now hugely significant both politically and commercially; that technical controversies must be understood as political controversies (for example, Barry, 2001). This is both because 'science and technology permeate the culture and politics of modernity' (Jasanoff, 2004a: 1) and, more interestingly, because STS has succeeded in problematizing conventional assumptions 'that what is scientific or political can be straightforwardly identified and ring fenced' (Irwin, 2008: 583). Yet despite its appeal to the entanglement of politics with science and technology, this literature tends to construe politics as being *about* technology, rather than, in the sense we explore below, politics being *in* technology.

interventions, through the production of effects and the reflection on effects, through the rhetorical deployment of evidence and logic and so forth' (Rose, 1999: x; cf Latour and Woolgar, 1979).

In the later work of Foucault, these concerns with government and truth become subsumed under technologies of governmentality. For British Neo-Foucauldian authors governmental technologies should be ana-lysed as 'the complex of mundane programmes, calculations, techniques, apparatuses, documents and procedures through which authorities seek to embody and give effect to government ambitions' (Rose and Miller, 1992: 175). For these authors governmentality involves four principal ele-ments. First, there is work done to produce the truth of any particular subject of government; 'a kind of intellectual machinery or apparatus for rendering reality thinkable in such a way that it is amenable to political programming' (Rose, 1996: 42). The production of truth in this way ren-ders the world governable and individuals calculable. Second, this produc-tion of truth also involves the production of the immoral. For example, the emergence of urban governance can be understood in terms of managed (im)morality: 'Observations of these immoral subjects inscribed in a pleth-ora of pamphlets, programmes, demands, solutions, tracts, scientific inves-tigations, bureaucratic documentation, commissions of enquiry, medical reports, and the like focused upon the dangers that life in towns posed to the moral and physical constitution of subjects' (Osborne and Rose, 1999: 743). Third, liberty was to become regularized, indicating: 'a new modality of government, which works by creating mechanisms that work "all by themselves" to bring about governmental results through the devo-lution of risk onto the "enterprise" or the individual (now to be construed as the entrepreneur of his or her own "firm") and the "responsibilisation" of subjects who are increasingly "empowered" to discipline themselves' (Ferguson and Gupta, 2002: 989). Fourth, managed liberty requires tech-nologies of government, which are: 'not a matter of the implementation of idealised schema in the real by an act of will, but of the complex assem-blage of diverse forces, . . . techniques, . . . devices . . . that promise to regulate decisions and actions of individuals, groups, organisations in relation to authoritative criteria' (Rose, 1996: 42). This enables government 'at a dis-tance' (Osborne and Rose, 1999: 751) and 'the "power of the state" is a resultant, not a cause', of these technologies (Rose, 1996: 43). That is, gov-ernment carries on in and through the actions of individuals who regulate their actions in line with available rationales of the collective, in a kind of enforced, managed, and assessed liberty.

Within these four elements, neo-Foucauldian authors engage with tech-nology as a metaphor for government. For example, research into the emer-gence and growth of disciplines such as psychology and psychiatry, uses the term 'technologies' to refer to 'the technical assembly of means of judgement (clinical examinations, tests, examinations, assessments with their associated norms and normativities); the techniques of reformation and cure (pedagogic, physical, therapeutic, punitive); the apparatuses within which intervention is to take place (design of prisons, classrooms, equipment, the connection of these into larger assemblages such as schooling and health visiting)' (Rose, 1999: xi).

A strength of these Foucauldian inclined approaches for our purposes is that whole systems can be considered as technologies implicated in a form of governance. They can do so, as Rose (1999a) makes clear in the subtitle to his book *Governing the Soul* by way of *The shaping of the private self*. Rose treats in extensive detail the varied ways in which we come to think of ourselves as persons adequately subject to prevailing technologies, expectations, and definitions. Prevailing technologies (systems) make available certain subject positions, such that these seem normal and natural ways of thinking of oneself. The form of governance that results is both more subtle and extensive than mere naked power because historical conditions make possible the emergence of particular subject positions, to which good citizens in (at least) Western societies conform. The range of subject positions thus far treated in this way includes the psychological self (Rose, 1990), creative/innovative self (Osborne, 2004), neurochemical self (Vrecko, 2006), biosocial self (Dumit and Rabinow, 2003; Hedgecoe *et al.*, 2004), and calculable self (Miller and O'Leary, 1994; Rose, 1998). These subject positions are articulated and reaffirmed through discourses such that individuals come to think of themselves as, for example, calculable individuals—appropriately subject to assessment and evaluation for our productivity and creativity.

The Foucauldian meaning of governance (or governmentality) offers a less mechanical picture than the argument that organizational structures can bring about behavioural change. However, several points are noteworthy.

First, these Foucauldian approaches work at a level of generality that tends not to account for idiosyncratic or 'unmotivated' behaviour. Historical changes have shaped the kind of persons we are, but do we always consistently and authentically act and behave in accordance with that personness? The neo-Foucauldian schema can seem a little too general and smooth if it is assumed that every person and action is reducible to an assessment according to a single rationale (that is, can my household waste disposal activities all be addressed by the question do I adhere to a recycling mentality?). In this kind of schema the actors appear as ciphers, that is, as cultural dopes (Garfinkel, 1967) who respond automatically to defined subjectivities of the self; they seem to have little difficulty in knowing or corresponding to one's own self. There seems little room for irony, or for resistance, interpretation, recursion, or reflexivity.

One response by neo-Foucauldian scholars to critiques of the absence of resistance in analyses of governmentality has been to emphasize a particular understanding of resistance. The suggestion is made that resistance 'seldom takes the form of a heroic meta-subject', but instead involves a 'conflict of rival programs and strategies' (Rose *et al.*, 2006: 100).

> It is not, then, that studies of governmentality neglect resistance to programs of government, or to techniques for the shaping of conduct; what they do refuse is the idea of resistance derived from the analytical framework of agency versus structure that has haunted so much contemporary social theory. After all, if freedom is not to be defined as the absence of constraint, but as a rather diverse array of invented technologies of the self, such a binary is meaningless. But more than this, structure almost always implies limits to freedom and almost always implies some underlying logic or social force that has to be overcome in order that the structures be breached or transformed. Ironically, by focusing instead on how those who seek to govern imagine their world and seek to fashion it anew, governmentality escapes the cage of structure that itself limits and constrains so much of the sociological imagination. (Rose *et al.*, 2006: 100).

Governmentality then seeks to escape the 'cage of structure' that limits the historical and contemporary sociological imagination. But what replaces this structural cage appears narrowly focused. Governance is to be understood from the perspective of those 'who seek to govern' (and the implication is that this occurs in government). Freedom (or liberty) is to be understood as a series of mechanisms through which individuals respond to rationales of governance. And resistance is to be understood either as a mistaken focus on the 'heroic meta-subject' or as a conflict between 'programs and strategies' of governments. But what about ordinary, non-creative, not very motivated messiness? What about governance beyond notions of freedom and rationales? What about non-individualized subjects? Collectives that come together for moments, disperse frequently, or only account for some aspects of action (rather than souls)? In terms of our interest in waste management, what explains the multiple and messy responses to recycling initiatives? Is this the result of a failure of self-governance, even when householders themselves seem quite content that they are doing their bit? Perhaps the problem lies in recycling staff collection activities or in communication between local authorities and recyclers. But what, from a Foucauldian perspective, illuminates such issues?

Second, these Foucauldian approaches use the metaphor of technology to denote aspects of social (and political) arrangements, which are not, as commonly understood, 'technical' (Miller and O'Leary, 1994; Rose, 1996, 1999; Power, 1997).[6] An advantage of this is to draw attention to the systematic

---

[6] Clearly, the school system is not commonly thought of as 'technological' in the same way as, say, the assemblage of electronic components on the motherboard of a personal computer.

arrangements involved in social phenomena. Thus, to speak of 'the school system' or 'clinical examinations' or 'insurance' as technologies, is to suggest that these systems have been designed with specific intended purposes, that they operate according to preconceived means, and that they are anticipated to have particular effects. A further implication is that a full understanding of the rationale, operation, and effects of this 'technology' is restricted to a specific group or groups. In other words, the description of a social system as a technology is another way of saying that knowledge and power are socially distributed. Only certain people know about and are capable of changing the situation, and only they possess the skills and expertise to determine whether and to what extent the system is working effectively.

The disadvantage of this metaphorical use of technology for our analysis is that little attention is paid to the status and enactment of claims about technological capacity, such as disputes and ambivalence over what a technology can do. Indeed Rose suggests that although STS and governmentality have been drawn together in certain circumscribed ways (for example, in drawing on Latour's ideas in elaborating governance at a distance), there has not been an extensive, recognizably STS analysis of the nature, status, role, or identity of technologies undertaken in studies of governmentality. 'Governmentality studies do not explicitly take up Latour and Callon's call to consider the agency of things' (Rose *et al.*, 2006: 93).

Multiple, simultaneous, and competing claims and uncertainties regarding the capacities of (technologies of) governance are only admitted under certain conditions. For example, in response to accusations that governmentality does not deal with messiness, neo-Foucauldians talk of the ongoing work to establish, rework or modify rationalities:

> Rationalities are constantly undergoing modification in the face of some newly identified problem or solution, while retaining certain styles of thought and technological preferences. This is why it is useful to speak about social rationalities of government, without implying that these are all identical in origin or in detail: They form a broad family of ways of thinking about and seeking to enact government, conceiving of that which is to be governed as a society of interdependent citizens and interlinked social and economic processes that are amenable to knowledge and planning. (Rose *et al.*, 2006: 98).

What this admits is a limited form of messiness. Governance still fits within the terms of governmentality, but the latter is to be seen as an ongoing

---

Notwithstanding the advantages of exposing the 'technological' features of a relatively (perceivedly) 'soft' social system (such as insurance, the school system, hospitals), it arguably remains more difficult and challenging to expose the societal dimensions of a 'hard' technical system (the computer motherboard).

project. What this does not admit is a more thorough messiness, situatedness, or moment-to-moment accomplishment of the very nature of technologies of governance. It is presumed in neo-Foucauldian approaches that certain technologies of representation more or less straightforwardly provide the conditions of possibility within which conceptions of self are enacted. Consequently, these approaches tend to overlook the connection between the contingencies of technical capacity—competing claims about capacity and attempts to resolve questions about ambiguity and interpretive flexibility—and ensuing forms of governance and accountability. The alternative approach we need to develop is that ongoing claims, disputes, and temporary resolutions over what technologies can, should, and may do, operate as sites for the articulation of accountability relations and of attempts at governance.

Thus, we see that the term 'governance' has come to enjoy great popularity and declares a wide range of uses and interpretations. These range from the focus on organizational structures and processes to neo-Foucauldian conceptions of the governance of the self. The connection between these different uses is unclear, most notably that between corporate governance and self-policing governance. But they share a marked neglect of the ontological status of objects and technologies. Neo-Foucauldian approaches to governance use the term 'technology' metaphorically and thereby overlook most aspects of the indeterminancy of the technical.

Thus far, we have also seen little of the content of governance relations. Just what is the stuff of governance? How does it work? How are various people, things, processes drawn together or even constituted through governance relations? Our contention will be that investigating accountability relations forms one means to address these questions. Hence, in Section 2.2.3 we turn attention to the notion of accountability to explore the ways in which governance, politics, science, technology, and ontology can be drawn together.

2.2.3 Accountability

If governance is broadly about the process and practice of regulation and control, accountability can be understood as its primary constituent. It is through systems, practices, and relations of accountability that information is produced, circulated, disputed, and/or agreed upon in forms of governance. Accountability can also be assigned, assumed, taken, or resisted as part of the general process of governance. Here we examine some different ideas about accountability to determine how they might help us get to grips with key aspects of mundane governance. As a heuristic device, we divide our discussion into what we term 'mutual' and 'organizational' approaches to accountability.

Mutual accountability can be used as a term to refer initially to the circumstances, typically under conditions of constitutional government, whereby those who govern are accountable to at least a portion of those governed; and accountability is owed to the electorate by all persons in government. Accountability is enforced through measures such as elections, systems of promotion and discipline, fiscal accounting, recall, and referenda. Mutual accountability is thus part of a two-way process whereby the accountability of government officials to the citizenry makes possible citizens' responsibility for the acts of government. In an election, citizens have the opportunity to judge the performance of the elected official, and to re-elect them or dismiss him or her from office. 'The official has thus rendered his account and has been held accountable' (Britannica Online, 1996).

Discussions of democracy often hark back to ancient Greece when the society of fifth century BC Athens was based on mutual accountability. Efforts to promote accountability had their origins in fears about the abuse of kingly and dictatorial power. The Athenian solution was to pluralize power by involving more people in the structures of accountability. The idea that citizens should hold each other to account was the basis of the Socratic process: the promotion of open questioning of individuals' character, their life, associations, and past history (Euben, 1996).

While this makes accountability seem relatively straightforward, the dictionary definitions of 'accountable' reveal two slightly different meanings of the term:

> **accountable**: adj. 1. Subject to having to report, explain or justify; responsible, answerable. 2. That can be explained, explicable (*Random House Dictionary*, 1967).

and

> **accountable** (adjective). 1. **responsible**. Responsible to somebody else or to others, or responsible for something 2. **able to be explained**. Capable of being explained (*Encarta Dictionary*, 2006).

In each of these, a first sense connotes moral or ethical compulsion. A second sense connotes technical capability.[7] But what lies behind this language of capacity and compulsion? For whom, which groups and organizations define what is capable of being explained? And who says that something should be explained, to whom, when, and why? The clarity of the dictionary definitions belies the range and complexity of the various different audiences involved.

---

[7] We can perhaps say that the institutionalized enactment of accountability over the four decades between these definitions has had the effect of blurring the distinction between these two notions of accountable. That which **can** be explained and justified (the second sense) has now also become that which **should** be explained and justified (the first sense).

A more pervasive sense of mutual accountability, beyond the confines of political relations, is developed in ethnomethodology. For ethnomethodologists, what is accountable is a mundane, pervasive organizing orientation for social action. The claim here is that in making sense of the world each turn in a social interaction (a conversation) involves demonstrably making available (accountable) a turn (or account), while also holding to account the adequacy of the previous turn by demonstrating in a conversation that the previous turn has been understood in a particular way, thus rendering that understanding available for the scrutiny (accounting) of other interactors (see Garfinkel, 1967; Luff and Heath, 1993). The oft quoted *locus classicus* is (Garfinkel, 1967: 33, emphasis in original):

> Any setting organizes its activities to make its properties as an organized environment of practical activities detectable, countable, recordable, reportable, tell-a-story-about-able, analyzable—in short *accountable*.

In referring to his early study of jurors' deliberations Garfinkel (1974: 17) puts it like this:

> ...in some way the good sense of somebody's inquiries was for them observable and notable. It was available, somehow or other, for that peculiar way of looking that a member has. The peculiar way of searching, of scanning, of sensing, of seeing finally but not only seeing, but seeing-reporting. It is observable-reportable. It is available to observation and report. Now I need to run them together. If there was one word in the English language that would run them together, I would use it. There is not, so I have been using the term 'accounting' or 'accountable' or 'account'.[8]

In this sense, interaction is constantly focused on making accounts, accountably available. Garfinkel wanted to examine 'how various types of social activity are brought to adequate description and thus rendered "account-able"' (Heritage, 1984: 136). This does not rule out consideration of more formal mechanisms of accountability (for example, in workplace studies of air traffic control centres; Suchman, 1993). Instead the claim is made that even formal mechanisms of accountability are dependent on routine, moment to moment interaction through which sense is made of the system, and accountability accomplished (for example, Lynch, 1998).

Importantly, formal, professional mechanisms of accountability are given the same treatment as conversations. Hence, in the work of Heath and Luff (1999) we find that London Underground CCTV operatives produce

---

[8] Anne Rawls (2002: 10) provides a biographical insight into the origin of Garfinkel's use of 'accounting' terminology. A family decision that he should follow in his father's furniture business led Garfinkel to follow an unaccredited course in business and accounting. His later work on accounts owes much to a business course called 'the theory of accounts'.

accounts, in interactions with colleagues, with the interaction forging the focus of mutual accountability. These interactions are also technologically mediated. Heath and Luff argue that 'video technologies used in concert with other devices, like radio, form a critical resource for collaborating with colleagues and developing a coordinated response to an emerging incident' (1999: 3). Such social and technical co-ordination can help to produce a relatively coherent and seemingly complete response to an incident. This work fits closely with a broader ethnomethodological concern for questions of accountability involving issues of visibility and representation (see for example, Suchman, 1993; Goodwin and Goodwin, 1995, 1996; Jasanoff, 1998; Jordan and Lynch, 1998).

An alternative focus is what we will term *organizational accountability*—the processes whereby organizations, for example, are required to produce information on which they are held to account. By contrast, with the ethnomethodological focus on the production of accounts, organizational accountability is not necessarily mutual, is often considered asymmetric and is more closely tied to a clear articulation of governance.

One approach to organizational accountability is provided by neo-Foucauldian scholars whose work we have already discussed (Miller, 1992; Miller and O'Leary, 1994; Rose, 1996, 1999; Ericson *et al.*, 2003). The suggestion made by these scholars is that accountability relations are the means through which rationales of governance (or governmentality) are communicated. And it is through being held to account as part of the governance apparatus that individuals are directed to produce certain kinds of information about themselves, their role in an organization, their spending, expense claims, performance, value for money, and effectiveness. Hence, members of an organization or section of the population are made aware of their own subjectivity and reflect on their actions accordingly (Miller, 1992; Miller and O'Leary, 1994).[9] And auditing provides a particularly significant accounting rationale (see, for example, Power, 1997).

An alternative approach to organizational accountability focuses more explicitly on the technologies of accounting. For example, actor–network theorists have examined both the durability and fluidity of organizational accounts. In their study of anaemia diagnosis in Africa, Mol and Law (1994) highlight a range of fluidities. Law and Mol (1998) ask 'what can be held and what by contrast escapes the grasp. Our object is to distinguish between that which is (ac)countable and that which is fluid' (1998: 23). Hence, the organizational distinction to be made is between the accountable (which is to be understood as durable, easy to move, combine, and so on) and the fluid

---

[9] Similar Foucauldian ideas form the basis for Neu's (2006) work on accounting and public space and Jeacle and Walsh's (2002) work on accounting and the history of credit.

(which evades easy grasp). Law and Mol (1998) talk of this distinction as the outcome of 'a labour of division' (1998: 23) enabled through 'technologies of calculation' (1998: 27). Law (1996) further argues that this shift between the fluid and the (ac)countable requires 'an active process of blocking, summarizing, simplifying and deleting...[which decides] what is to count and what, therefore, becomes counted' (1996: 291).

Strathern's (1999, 2000, 2002) analysis of British academic research provides a further detailed exploration of this labour of accounting. According to Strathern (2002) quantification of research output into already-agreed-upon indicators, sets in motion the abstraction and decontextualization of research into assessable and accountable criteria. Indicators are a key mechanism, Strathern argues, for emphasizing a focus on outcome 'for it restricts the output (results) of observation to data suitable for constructing measures of it', and, 'indicators come in turn to have a life or efficacy of their own' (2002: 307). In this way, things are no longer measured by indicators, but rather indicators establish targets to aim toward.

Within organizational accountability, a neo-Foucauldian take on governmentality positions accountability as the means through which rationales for action might be communicated and assessed. Accountability thus shifts from being a matter of measurement, to a potential site for (organizational) change. By contrast, an actor–network theory (ANT) take on organizational forms of accountability focuses on the work done to make an organizational account durable, moveable, and combinable. It also involves work to keep the account distinct from fluid network entities, which evade easy grasp, and are not straightforward to mobilize or combine. The ontological status of fluids, this approach suggests, is continuously unsettled, while the status of accounts is durable.[10]

In sum, we see how different modes of accountability variously offer the opportunity to engage in great depth with the ongoing constitution of accountable sense, and insights into ways of understanding the work of producing accounts. As yet, however, we are still without a clear sense of where accountability comes from, what it is that accountability relations might do (to whom, by whom, with what outcome), and how accountability might be positioned at the heart of ontological governance.

---

[10] Two further varieties of accountability not discussed here might be termed 'demonstrative'—whereby members of an organization work to make it accountable (for example, Gray, 1992; Canning and O'Dwyer, 2001; Sikka, 2001; Drew, 2004) and 'participatory'—which focuses on opening up new forms of participation in organizations, decision-making, local and regional politics, and scientific and technological projects (for an overview see Irwin, 1995; Kleinman, 2000; Kitcher, 2001; Gregory, 2001).

2.2.4 The Effects of Governance and Accountability

Our opening chapter showed the extent of reactions to mundane governance. But how can we understand in more detail how governance and accountability are experienced? What are experienced as the impacts of governance and accountability? A case that helped us to think through these issues featured a woman who sued McDonalds for serving hot coffee. It was widely reported that she had successfully sued McDonalds for $2.7 million after she had spilled the coffee on her lap. The media portrayed the episode as a classic example of what happens in an over-litigious society whose members refuse to accept personal responsibility (Greenbaum, 2005). This refusal is both anchored in and feeds on a presumption of individual legal rights and on an associated system of legal redress. The apparent absurdity of the case stems from the common sense assumption that, after all, coffee is (surely) meant to be hot. If you opt to purchase a coffee (from McDonalds), you might expect it to be hot and so should take all normal precautions when handling hot coffee. As the responsibility thus (naturally) lies with you, the purchaser of the coffee, it is absurd to hold the vendor accountable.

But this version of affairs was contested, both by McDonalds and in legal commentary. Thus, Greenbaum (2005) claims that various facts were left out of the popular version by 'the talk show pundits and columnists' and offers the following alternative rendition of the episode:

> 79 year old Stella Liebeck suffered third degree burns on her groin and inner thighs while trying to add sugar to her coffee at a McDonalds drive through. Third degree burns are the most serious kind of burn. McDonalds knew it had a problem. There were at least 700 previous cases of scalding coffee incidents at McDonalds before Liebeck's case. McDonalds had settled many claims before but refused Liebeck's request for $20,000 compensation, forcing the case into court. Lawyers found that McDonalds makes its coffee 30–50 degrees hotter than other restaurants, about 190 degrees. Doctors testified that it only takes 2–7 seconds to cause a third degree burn at 190 degrees. McDonalds knew its coffee was exceptionally hot but testified that they had never consulted with burn specialists. The Shriner Burn Institute had previously warned McDonalds not to serve coffee above 130 degrees. And so the jury came back with a decision—$160,000 for compensatory damages. But because McDonalds was guilty of 'willful, reckless, malicious or wanton conduct' punitive damages were also applied. The jury set the award at $2.7 million. The judge then reduced the fine to less than half a million. Ms. Liebeck then settled with McDonalds for a sum reported to be much less than a half million dollars. McDonalds coffee is now sold at the same temperature as most other restaurants.

It would be possible here to draw in previously articulated theories of governance and accountability. For example, we could look at this as an example of corporate governance. Alternatively, it would be possible to draw in a neo-Foucauldian approach to analyse the rationales of governmentality connecting McDonalds, the legal system, and Stella Liebeck. From an ANT perspective, we could look at the assemblage of coffee and consumer and its moves through distinct network spaces (from Drive Thru, to the court of law). And we could use ethnomethodology to tease out the ongoing, mutually accountable relations of the trial. However, none of these approaches captures the key features of the incident that need to be brought to the fore.

Importantly, for our purposes, Greenbaum's account transforms the media story in all its essential features. The burn becomes the most serious kind of burn. This event, now described as a 'scalding coffee incident', is rendered as one in a long line of similar events. It is only by chance that this case comes to court at all, and there are now said to have been many previous claims and settlements out of court. Crucially, the coffee itself is subject to a key respecification in terms of its technical or objective attributes. It is no longer just hot, it is '30–50 degrees hotter than other restaurants', it is at a temperature that 'doctors testified... only takes 2–7 seconds to cause a third degree burn'. And, to make matters worse, in this version McDonalds 'knew its coffee was exceptionally hot', 'had never consulted burn specialists [sic]' and had been previously warned by the Shriner Burn Institute. Hence, the application of punitive damages—for 'wilful, reckless, malicious or wanton conduct'—in addition to the compensatory damages.

We thus see how the latter respecification of the ontology of the coffee re-inscribes the network of accountability relations at issue. The coffee is no longer merely hot, it is now recklessly, knowably, in-defiance-of-warnings-from-others-ably, as-just-one-of-a-history-of-similar-events-ably hot. The pool of actants who populated the original story is now enlarged and their characteristics are elaborated. In particular, a series of previous events, warnings, and knowledge are cited with the effect of making McDonalds' responsibility and culpability known. By contrast with the initial common sensical reaction—how on earth could someone really try and sue McDonalds for providing hot coffee—the subsequent version achieves the kind of hotness of coffee for which McDonalds becomes appropriately accountable. The revised ontology of the coffee performs new accountability relations.

In sum then, existing discussions of governance and accountability are notable for several key reasons. First, like governance, the term accountability is used in several quite different senses. Second, we saw how shifts in accountability could have significant consequences for identities. Whole new ontological entities—such as reckless coffee—are brought into being and sustained by the realignment of accountability relations. Yet, third, it is clear, especially from disputes such as the McDonalds case, that the ontological status of objects is highly consequential for shifts in accountability. It turns out that different versions of accountability correspond to differing underlying assumptions about the nature of the audiences that are implicated. In Section 2.3, we address the ways in which this ontological respecification allows us to engage with the mundane.

2.3 The Ontological Dynamics of Governance and Accountability

We see that in many discussions of governance and accountability, things such as objects and technologies are often omitted from consideration. In consequence, governance and accountability are largely treated as a condition pertaining exclusively between human subjects, or between groupings of humans in collectivities. It turns out this is not merely a problem of leaving out one class of entities[11] but, more significantly, neglects what we call the ontological dynamics of governance and accountability.

Our argument draws on and develops a particular dual sense of the 'mundane'. On the one hand, in common use, mundane denotes any of: ordinary, dull, routine, every day, unremarkable, commonplace, boring, unexciting, humdrum, dreary, monotonous, tedious, uninteresting, and, most certainly, non-exotic. Indeed the English language offers an extensive vocabulary of related descriptions: normal, usual, familiar, regular, run of the mill, average, banal, and, definitely, not extraordinary. All these uses suggest a sense of *pervasiveness*: objects and technologies are mundane in virtue of their being everywhere. On the other hand, and most importantly for our analysis, objects and technologies are also mundane in the sense that they are, literally and etymologically, *of the world*.

This second sense of mundane, meaning of the world, refers to our experience of the obvious, the taken for granted quality of the way the world is, its worldliness, the facts of the matter, the way things are, and so on. Pollner (1974) captures this well in his study of mundane reasoning. These are reasoning practices premised upon and reinforcing core assumptions about the way the world is. He argues that institutions such as traffic courts, for example, are in the business of reasserting certain mundane assumptions. Their organization of evidential practices and interrogation and questioning, their procedures for considering evidence, and of determining the facts, reaffirm and reassert, for example, the core mundaneity that a car is incapable of travelling at both 30 mph and 60 mph the same time.

---

[11] In particular, this is not merely a problem of neglecting 'the material'. As we argue in subsequent chapters, current emphases on materiality tend to bestow entities with a form of agency, which distracts from an investigation of how entities get to be material in the first place.

Our interest in the mundane is not to challenge this 'obvious' brutish fact, but rather to investigate how it is maintained, celebrated, enacted, and, in particular, how and what kinds of consequence for behaviour and activity are derived from it. We need to make the obvious unobvious. And to do this, we need to develop and maintain an analytically 'sceptical' stance with respect to such 'obvious' mundane features of the world, to highlight the mechanisms of regulation and control that are said appropriately to follow from it. Our point is not to throw doubt on the impossibility of travelling at both 30 mph and 60 mph at the same time but, to suspend, momentarily at least, our readiness to accept this as a passing matter of fact.

Mundane in this second sense is thus inextricably tied to ontology. For an entity to be 'of the world' it is mundane in just this second sense. For an entity to be what it is, to possess certain properties or characteristics, is for it to exist as it is, in the world. Objects are mundane in virtue of their ontological status. The question then becomes how it is that entities acquire and maintain this status, about their ontological constitution. Moreover, as we argue in detail in subsequent chapters, ontological constitution is recursive. That is, the processes of ontological constitution are repeatedly applied to themselves. In this way, the mundane object comes to seem what it is.

2.3.1 Objects and Technology in Science and Technology Studies

The recent literature in STS offers an important re-conceptualization of objects and technology. Some of this is captured by the idea of *interpretive flexibility*, but this term admits two related but significantly distinct senses. First, interpretive flexibility signals that the processes of inception, development, and construction of objects and technology are subject to 'non-technical' factors. Social, political, cultural, and organizational aspects are pertinent to the technical outcome. In other words, the nature and capacity of the technology is not extrapolated in a straightforward way from existing technical systems and solutions. They are instead the upshot of contingent circumstances. This anti-essentialist point supports the important constructivist dictum that the (objects and) technology could have been otherwise. In particular, there is an important sense in which social and political factors, among others, can be understood as *built into* the object or technology. This sense is summarized in the STS tradition by slogans such as 'technology is congealed social relations' and 'technology is politics by other means'.

The second sense of interpretive flexibility, less common in STS literature, is that the apprehension, use, and interpretation of technology is also subject to an in principle unknowability. The first sense of interpretive flexibility implies the emergence of consensus during technical development whereby agreement is reached about the nature and capacity of the technology, which has evolved. The second sense argues for a more open-ended approach. It suggests that the business of interpretation and use extends beyond any putative moment of consensus, and that we need to apprehend technology as being in a constant process of interpretation and understanding.

The difference between the two senses of interpretive flexibility is important for understanding the role of technology in governance. In the first sense, technology can be understood as having had certain social and political predilections 'built in'. However, the reading of structural form here is questionable. It is unclear, for example, whether and to what extent technologies have the effects that STS authors ascribe to them.[12] Rather, the very attribution of effect seems to be part and parcel of the determination of technological characteristics by the STS author. While this is very suggestive in unlocking and deconstructing the contention/assumption that technologies are neutral, and have fixed capacities, it merely shifts the weight of essentialist reasoning from the technical to the social/political. In other words, the presumption is that, whereas we cannot straightforwardly read-off the technical characteristics of the technology, we are somehow capable of reading off the (actual) social and/or political characteristics that apply.

The second sense of interpretive flexibility instead encourages the view that all interpretations and uses of technology, including understandings of their effect and impact, their origins, and their putatively inculcated politics, are inescapably contingent, at best construable in terms of the radically local circumstances of their apprehension. Or, to put it in slightly less trenchant terms, readings of the governance implications of technology are occasioned. This means that a primary focus for analysis is the ways in which objects and technologies are made to 'do' political work.[13]

Law (1996) comes close to articulating the connections between objects and technologies, ontology, and forms of accountability we seek to engage when he spells out a general requirement for an ontological, rather than a (merely) epistemological, approach to 'organizing accountabilities'. The work of representation, he says, is not merely about describing something that is already there. Rather, it is about making the knower and making what

---

[12] For example, Winner (1999) suggests Moses' bridges in New York contain an underlying racial bias (from the architect), which prevents certain parts of the community accessing local parks (also designed by Moses). It is not clear that this prevention has ever taken place.

[13] This argument could be developed by relating the conceptualization of technology as governance to three important related themes in STS namely the nature and extent to which technology development can be understood as involving the configuration of its users; a reappraisal of the nature of the rather static current models of the producer–consumer relationship (where in this case producers and consumers are respectively considered as the proponents and dependents on systems of governance); and a re-evaluation of the problems of affordances and post-essentialist approaches to the 'textuality' of technology (where 'affordance' can be understood as a feature of the technology text temporarily and reflexively accomplished in the light of germane accountability relations).

is known. In a manner directly reminiscent of Latour and Woolgar's (1979) splitting and inversion model of scientific discovery, Law suggests that the constitution of the knower and the known, the creation of the distinction between them, and the concealment of the (original) connection between the two, are all vital parts of the organization of accountability. Law indicates how a concern with the merely epistemological restricts us to questions about the quality of our knowledge, reliability of our accounts and adequacy of connections between the world and our representation of it. These kinds of questions depend on and reinforce the assumption that the world out there pre-exists our (more or less reliable) knowledge of it. Instead, Law argues, we need to know about the constitution of the world in the first place, in particular, about the ways in which there came into being a 'new organizational world or object. And a new kind of knowing subject or manager' (Law, 1996: 283).[14]

Although Law's (1996) work provides a useful conceptualization of accountability, his approach is not designed as an engagement with forms of governance or the mundane. For example, there is no clear sense in which the kinds of accountability Law refers to connects with the kinds of behaviour modification or regulation discussed in traditional treatments of governance. Similarly, we need to know how the very suggestive notion of 'material semiotics' (Mol, 2011) might help us understand the ontological politics involved in mundane governance.

2.3.2 Enrolling Latour to Recursive Ontology

Bruno Latour's work provides one of the few attempts to offer a specifically STS perspective on mundane objects, technology, and behaviour modification.[15] His early work (Latour, 1988, 1991, 1992) is especially germane to our purposes because the argument is illustrated with objects and technologies drawn from ordinary everyday experience: for example, a door closer, sleeping policemen, child car restraints, and hotel keys. In Latour's perspective, how are objects and technologies (artefacts) implicated in relations of governance and accountability? We have argued that determinations of ontological status are crucial, that we need to know about what we call the recursive dynamics of ontological practice. So in what ways and to what extent does Latour's argument take into account the ontological status of objects and technologies?[16] To answer this

---

[14] This kind of approach to constitution sits centrally in Mol's work on ontological intervention and material semiotics (Mol, 2011; and to a lesser extent, Mann *et al.*, 2011).

[15] Others include the work by writers such as Lefebvre (1947), Goffman (1959), De Certeau (1984), Shove (Chappels and Shove, 1999a,b; Shove and Southerton, 2000; Shove, 2003a,b; Shove *et al.*, 2012), and Michael (2006), some of which we return to in later empirical chapters.

[16] Latour tends to favour the nomenclature of artefacts, machines, and things, rather than objects and technologies, although he sometimes uses them interchangeably. There is perhaps some significance in this distinction because for the most part, the artefacts and machines in Latour's accounts are motivated, that is, they feature in his stories as part of an agonistic struggle.

question we need to look closely at the structure of Latour's account and at some of its key assumptions about the ontology of objects. Here we concentrate on the idea of delegation.

In speaking of the relation between the social and the technical, Latour says that the object does not (merely) reflect the social. It does more. 'It transcribes and displaces the contradictory interests of people and things' (1992: 226). In this way, an object can transform a major problem into a minor one. For example, the 'wall-hole dilemma' (how to open a space in a solid wall in order to get through and then restore the wall) is transformed into a minor problem (pushing the door open) by virtue of the use of a door hinge. To put it differently, the work of reversibly solving the wall-hole dilemma has been delegated (or translated or displaced or shifted down) to the hinge.

But because people still leave the hinged door open, an assemblage of non-humans (the hinges) plus a human (the porter) is needed to solve the wall-hole dilemma. But then again the work of disciplining the porter to do her job properly is very costly. The porter's behaviour is unreliable. Also this does not achieve the folding of time—that is, the continuation of action regardless of date or time of day—which can be done with a non-human. This can be achieved by delegating the task to an automatic door closer. A pneumatic mechanism acquires its energy in virtue of the human pushing the door open. It then gently closes the door again after the human has passed through.

Latour argues that delegation does not just occur in one direction. Non-human delegates impose behaviour back on to the human (Latour, 1992: 232). This is called 'prescription' (Akrich, 1992)—'the moral and ethical dimensions of mechanisms'. Humans have thus been able to delegate to nonhumans 'not only force as we have known it for centuries but also values, duties and ethics' (1992: 232). Our human ability to behave ethically is intimately tied to, and dependent on, the delegated ethics (value, duties, etc), which reside in non-humans, '...the stable sum of morality...increases enormously with the population of nonhumans'.

When discussing the range of ways in which human behaviour is controlled (regulated, governed), Latour speaks of a gradient along which more or less figurative delegations are ranged. In the case of attempts to control the speeding motorist, this gradient ranges from 'stubborn and efficient mechanisms' such as bumps across the road (the sleeping policeman) to signage ('the usual power of signs and symbols') and to the will power of well-behaved humans ('classical moral human beings endowed with self respect and able to speak and obey laws'; 1992: 244).

Roughly speaking, machines are devices artfully constructed to bring about particular outcomes; objects do not come with such motivations embedded in them.

Latour (1992: 248) insists that we understand engineers as those who 'constantly shift out characters in other spaces and other times, devise positions for human and non-human users, break down competences that they can redistribute to many different actors, and build complicated narrative programs and subprograms that are evaluated and judged by their ability to stave off antiprograms'.[17]

A major part, if not all, of the strength of the engineer's achievement is that he or she devises a programme of action that substitutes parts of its character to other material elements. Latour contrasts his failed attempts to control his son's behaviour (as a passenger in the back seat of his car) by shouting and admonition, with the success of the metal child car restraint. 'I could not tie Robinson to the order, but through a detour and a translation I now hold together my will and my son' (1992: 251).

Without doubt, this line of argument provided a significant contribution to breaking down the formulaic divide between the social and technical, to the disruption of this divide as an analytic given and to the need to bring materiality into the picture. What then are the salient features of the Latourian account upon which we wish to build?

A feature of the argument is key, namely his use of definitive depictions of the actual attributes and effects of various objects. Of the sleeping policemen, Latour says: 'It is impossible for us not to slow down or else we break our suspension' (1992: 244). The steel bar keeps his son at arm's length. In the face of a heavy weight attached to a hotel key, customers 'suddenly become only too happy to rid themselves of this annoying object which makes their pockets bulge and weighs down their handbags: they go to the front desk of their own accord to get rid of it' (1991: 104). However, this is not a determinist account. Latour is not saying these properties determine a particular action, '...nothing in a given scene can prevent the inscribed user or reader from behaving differently from what was expected... The reader in the flesh may totally ignore my definition of him or her. The user of the traffic light may well cross on the red' (1992: 237). Instead, the picture is one of a constant struggle between protagonists, trying to regulate and control behaviour by shifting, substituting, and delegating entities and properties. These entities and their properties are brought into association with each other, in assemblages. Against this, there is the constant, unpredictable, wayward behaviour of those who are the subject of regulation.

---

[17] An interesting feature of this description is its heroic depiction of the engineer (for a counter view see de Laet and Mol, 2000). This is not couched in terms of an empirical report of observations of engineers at work, the messiness of their practice, but rather seems to voice the engineers' aspirations to success.

What happens when things go wrong? When keys are not actually heavy enough to force the guests to leave them at the front desk? The analytic response is significant. We are told that the allies have deserted, or that the assemblage is not strong enough. Non-compliance is tantamount to the failure of the programme, and defeat by an antiprogramme.

Now what is not clear in all this is what is happening to the status of the weight of the keys? Is it the same weight throughout? Is it the same weight but differentially experienced by the actors involved? Or, as we suggest later, is the weight a kind of proto attribute, an attribute wished for, but not necessarily realized, by the programme's hero protagonist?

At certain points, Latour hints at the possibility that in the course of struggles between programmes and antiprogrammes the very ontological status of the object changes. For example, again in the case of the weighted keys:

> The program 'leave your key at the front desk', which is now scrupulously executed by the majority of the customers is simply not the one we started with. Its displacement has transformed it. Customers no longer leave their room keys: instead they get rid of an unwieldy object that deforms their pockets. If they conform to the sign it is not because they read the sign, nor because they are particularly well mannered. It is because they cannot do otherwise. They don't even think about it. The statement is no longer the same, *the key is no longer the same*—even the hotel is no longer quite the same (1992: 105, our emphasis).

This might mean that the same key-with-a-metal-lump-attached can be experienced as heavy or light, according to the state of the struggle between programmes and antiprogrammes. Indeed, that it doesn't make much sense to speak of it as the same key. This is in line with a general thrust of ANT that the property of any component is equivalent to (sometimes 'the upshot of') the network of actants that constitute it (or elsewhere, which hold it in place). On the other hand the (given? obvious? actual?) weight of the key seems crucial, in Latour's account, to the elaboration of the hotel proprietor's programme. We are told that guests behave because it **is** an unwieldy object that deforms their pockets, and they cannot do otherwise. The substitution of the steel bar **is** the cause of Robinson's compliance. The success of the programme is not guaranteed by any kind of delegation, but by delegation to material objects with specific properties.[18]

Part of the problem here might be, as hinted already, the conflation between two subtly different approaches to ontology: (i) the attributes of the key as envisaged by the hotel proprietor (he attaches a weight because he hopes this will have a particular effect on the guests), and (ii) the transcendental

---

[18] Of course, what is particularly delightful in interrogating this rather ancient example is that few hotel managers now care about the return of room keys. Room keys are now plastic cards with an electronic strip, easily and cheaply replaced and duplicated.

properties attributed to the key in the course of an account of the success or failure of the programme. Much of the time, this issue is hedged by use of the idea of assemblage or network. The object itself is said not to be the proper focus of attention, it is instead the network or assemblage that holds it in place (or in other versions, the upshot of which becomes the property in question).

A major difference between the two approaches is the extent to which they implicate audience. In the first perspective, the hotel proprietor, and his friend the innovator, believe in the attributes of a heavily weighted key whereas others do not. These two characters are examples of the familiar hero figures of Latourian stories (cf especially Pasteur). In the second perspective, it is not belief but actual properties that make the difference.

The difference is subtle but crucial. It involves a form of ontological gerrymandering (Woolgar and Pawluch, 1985) whereby certain kinds of entity and audience are brought under the analytic spotlight at certain points of the exposition, and others are not. Specifically, the attributes of some selected entities are highlighted as contingent, shifting, changing—whereas the attributes of other entities pass, are unremarked upon, taken for granted. The political metaphor is apposite and is intended here in exactly the same spirit that Latour elsewhere speaks admiringly of Machiavellian machinations (Latour, 1988b). To say that Latour is doing ontological gerrymandering is not, of course, to cast aspersions on his motives but, rather, to make a (technical!) point about the rhetorical organization of his account.

This particular kind of ontological gerrymandering involves the implicit differential performance of audience. We know that each time we lay claim to a realist (or objective or definitive) description or terminology we necessarily appeal to (or perhaps better, invoke, or circumscribe or perform) an implied or unspecified community/audience. Objective truth is everyone's truth. It is the view from everywhere. It is the god trick (Haraway, 1988). It is the stripping of propositions of their modalities as one way to lay claim to the universality of the proposition (Latour and Woolgar, 1979). To mobilize (or to imply the existence of) a silent universal consensus, one needs to represent technical attributes stripped of their modalities.

What we might call 'assemblage-based' accounts of course take us a long way beyond technical determinism, and far from the great divide between the technical and the social. The source of stability, the essence of the object itself is now displaced and distributed throughout what is to become, in the fully articulated version of the argument, an actor–network. This displacement thereby entails a slightly nuanced form of ontological gerrymandering. None of the individual elements of the assembly (or network) are responsible for its effect. So the specific ontological status of each element is immaterial to the cumulative effect of all the elements. At the same time, the description of each element contained in the assemblage recruits definitive accounts of its actual, that is, its modality independent properties. Notice, for example, how the following passage includes depictions of the definite properties of each element.

> The accumulation of elements—the will of the manager, the hardness of his words, the multiplicity of his signs, the weight of his keys—ends up trying the patience of some customers, who finally give up and agree to conspire with the manager, faithfully returning the keys (Latour, 1991: 108).

In this kind of account, none of the individual properties of each element is responsible for the overall effect. Instead, they work together in accumulation. None the less, the very depiction of each element's properties deploys a form of essentialism. The straight forward essentialist account—the weight of the keys forces customers to leave them at the desk—has been replaced by a form of distributed essentialism. It is now the properties of the network or assemblage as a whole that forces customers to leave the keys at the desk. Now Latour (1991: 129) quite rightly casts aspersion on the classical epistemological distinction between description and explanation. We know, especially in legal and policy settings, how apparently mere description can do explanation and vice versa. Yet it is hard to read this passage as other than claiming some kind of explanatory value—'the accumulation of elements…ends up trying the patience of some customers'. And it is hard not to recognize that the claim that the assemblage has had an effect, itself involves a definitive description of the actual (that is, ontologically uncontested) properties of its constituents. To see that this is the case, consider the marked weakening of the explanatory force of this passage, which results when we add (or reinsert?) modalities that point up ontological contingency.

> The accumulation of elements—what may or may not be considered the will of the manager, the possible hardness or softness of his words, the multiplicity or perhaps singularity of his signs, the keys that are experienced as light by some and as heavy by others—may or may not end up trying the patience of some customers…

This also points up the importance of stability. To bring off a satisfactory description of the (effects of the) network, we need to exorcize sources of uncertainty and instability. Or, to put it differently, successful depictions of the effects of objects (or their assemblages) require a degree of ontological certitude.[19]

---

[19] Latour's scheme applies particularly to situations of contestation (which are then resolved)—the father trying to compel his passenger son to comply and the wayward son resisting; the hotelier trying to force his unruly clients into submission vis à vis the key. Each of the parties involved seems actively engaged in pushing a programme or antiprogramme. But this leaves out the vast majority of situations where there is no overt struggle between the involved parties (cf

One of Latour's best known slogans is 'technology is society made durable' (Latour, 1991). Tweaked for our own purposes, the equivalent slogan we might adopt is something like 'objects (and technologies) are governance and accountability made durable'. But this section has shown that we need something more. We are suggesting, in effect, the need radically to unpack what counts as 'durable'. As we hope to show in subsequent chapters, the existence and properties of objects and technologies are only ever recursively available, occasionally to be extracted from a wholesale messiness of interpretation and use. Their aspiration to stability is rare indeed.

2.4 The Wrong Bin Bag

To begin to tackle these questions, we turn to a specific episode of contention about the status of an object, as reported in a British tabloid newspaper. Our analysis centres on the media coverage of an episode in which a woman is fined by her local council for (allegedly) using the 'wrong' kind of black plastic sack for her rubbish. It is customary to introduce such a specific example by providing an indication of its context. We are no exception to this custom—see the brief comment given here. However, and in line with our earlier remarks, we wish to resist the temptation simply to take this next description as a definitive statement of 'the context'. Descriptions construed as conveying the actual 'context' can all too quickly be regarded as sufficient explanation of what is happening. Rather, a corollary of our under-the-skin approach to ontological analysis is to appreciate how the invocation, construction, and constitution of 'the context' or 'the setting' is intimately implicated in the situated determination of what the object is. In other words, the construction and invocation of 'the context' turns out to be important for the achievement of the ontological character of the entities at stake. This does not mean that we should try to avoid specification of context. Even if that were possible, it would not be desirable. Instead, we pursue a reflexive perspective on the invocations of context that we (unavoidably) deploy.

Star, 1991; Helgesson and Kjellberg, 2005), where, we might say, objects just are. Or, where there is an ambivalence about the properties of the object (Singleton and Michael, 1993). Or, where there is a multiplicity of the object (Mol, 2002). Or, in particular, as Rappert's (2001) work shows, where protagonists exercise strategies of deferral vis à vis the ontological status of the object. Thus, in the case of the hotel keys, we might expect the matter of whether or not the weight attached to the key is heavy to be deferred, either for later determination or for determination by some other group or actants. Or, in the case of the sleeping policemen, whether or not the bumps really cause broken suspension is an indeterminate matter subject to deferral. In sum, the programme–antiprogramme schema neglects situations where there is no overt contestation, and yet where the objects and technologies may none the less be considered to be part of (social) ordering, regulation, and control.

The wrong bin bag episode took place at a time of highly charged public concern in the UK about the regulation and control of waste disposal. This included questions about excessive government interference, intrusion of the nanny state, and overzealous policing of matters thought to be better left within the autonomy of the private individual. At the same time, a vociferous pro-recycling lobby, while also critical of deficiencies in government policy, argued that not enough was being done, that local authorities should introduce tougher measures to make citizens more responsive, that the recycling initiatives were misguided because they directed attention away from the real culprits (for example, the manufacturers and suppliers of plastic packaging), and so on.

It would be easy to wrap up the whole 'wrong bin bag' story within various narratives about the continued persistent interference of government and councils, the nanny state, an increasing climate of government by coercion, the growing emphasis on the need for individuals to take more responsibility for their own actions, and so on. However, our interest here is to consider practices that enable the mutual constitution of the properties of the entities involved and the context in which they are situated.

How can we get at the processes of ontological enactment of the entities involved in this story? We draw here on the work of Dorothy Smith (1990, 2001) the feminist writer who argues that the organization of texts is isomorphic with the conceptual schema which is used to make sense of it. Smith speaks of the ways in which discursive organization makes possible 'the relations of ruling'. By analogy, we are interested in looking closely at this newspaper story for what its organization tells us about the relations of governance with respect to ordinary objects.

Smith's insight is that the organization of texts is isomorphic with the 'relations of ruling'. This not just a matter of spatial organization—where on the page do items, things or descriptions appear—although this does turn out to be of incidental importance. Rather, we take it that organization here refers primarily to the ways in which the text depicts the character of the entities mentioned and, crucially, of the ways in which they relate to each other. The organization of texts is thus to be inspected for the ways in which it makes available a cast of relevant characters, assigns attributes to each, and depicts the network of rights and responsibilities that characterize the situation at hand. In short, the organization of the text is to be understood as enacting a moral universe comprising all its constituent elements. In this case, the text tells us who and what is on the scene, who should do what, what might be expected to result, who is liable for what, who did what, and whether and how that is legitimate or otherwise.

At the heart of the story is the figure of the bin bag, the common or garden black plastic bag that features in the main photograph that accompanied the news article. In the story, it is rendered as an obviously ordinary object,

BOX 2.1 THE NEWSPAPER TEXT[a]

1. ANOTHER DAY, ANOTHER POTTY PENALTY
2. *Fined £50 for using* WRONG *bin bags*
   [Pictures of Lynette with caption:]
3. Stunned…Lynette with her own bag and daft penalty notice
4. *By LYNDSEY WEATHERALL*
5. **Barmy Council bosses have fined a woman £50 for putting her rubbish out in the WRONG KIND of bin bags.**
6. Lynette Vickers got into trouble after she ran out of council-issued sacks.
7. So she put her trash in her **OWN** black sacks instead and left them out the night
8. before collection day.
9. But they were spotted by two over-zealous wardens who ripped them open to find
10. out who they belonged to, then hammered on Lynette's door.
11. *The unmarried mum of four was stunned when told she was being fined £50 for*
12. *using the wrong bags and causing an obstruction.*
13. It is the latest in a catalogue of crazy penalties being introduced by the
14. Government and councils in recent months.
15. Lynette is refusing to pay the penalty and has been warned she faces a court fine
16. of up to £2,500.
17. Lynette, 36, of Crewe, Cheshire said last night: 'It's absolutely ridiculous.
18. 'I thought I was being stitched up when the wardens knocked on my door. I had
19. no option but to put the extra rubbish out in bags. There was no way they were
20. causing an obstruction.
21. 'I'm not paying the fine. They can take me to court if they want but it's stupid'.
22. The madness came about because of a delayed collection over the festive period.
23. Lynette had to wait ten days—between December 29 and January 8—for the
24. dustmen to do their rounds.
25. Like any normal family, she had a lot of extra garbage.
26. But a notice placed on her wheelie bin said extra bags **WOULD** be taken.
27. ***Dumping***
28. So Lynette put her rubbish in four of her own bags and tied them up.
29. Just before 7pm on January 7, she took them to the edge of the road for collection
30. at 8am the next day.
31. But within minutes a warden was on her doorstep.
32. Lynette added: 'She had opened all the bags to see if she could find where they
33. had come from. Then she was on my doorstep saying I was being fined. It was
34. crazy'.
35. The pre-printed penalty notice says the fine is for an 'offence of leaving litter'.
36. The warden had added that the fine is also for 'the dumping of rubbish on the
37. grassed area'
38. Lynette phoned wardens boss Keith Boughey who insisted the decision was right.
39. She said: 'He said I was being fined because I hadn't put the rubbish in council
40. bin bags. I said I hadn't been left any, so then he said it was because I had too
41. many bags and they were causing an obstruction'.
42. Lynette had to re-bag the rubbish and put it out next day. To add to the craziness,
43. the binmen were happy to take away **ALL** of Lynette's rubbish, plus her
44. Christmas tree.
45. *The angry mum added: 'I have kids to feed and clothe. Fifty pounds is a lot of*

46. *money to families like us. I'm all for the wardens stopping litterbugs—but I'm not*
47. *one of them'.*
48. Wardens for Crewe and Nantwich Borough Council have already been
49. condemned for fining a woman for littering when she was feeding birds.
50. Mr Boughey insists Lynette is in the wrong. He said: 'I am standing by the
51. decision. We don't collect bags in areas with wheelie bins, unless there has been a
52. missed collection and the rubbish is in a council bag'.
53. *The Sun Says—Page Eight*[b]

[a] ©Lyndsey Weatherall, News Syndication, 3 August 2007. The full article first appeared in *The Sun* newspaper (available at: http://www.thesun.co.uk/sol/homepage/news/143750/Rubbish-fine-madness. html). The layout here inevitably misses the full iconography of the text as it appeared in the newspaper. In this presentation, we have transposed the emphases, in bold and capitals, and the italics from the original.
[b] This last line links to the Editorial column of the newspaper: 'Fine Mess. Just when you thought the jobsworths couldn't get any barmier... Along come the rubbish wardens of Crewe and Nantwich Borough Council. With small minds and empty hearts, they fine a family £50 for putting their Christmas rubbish into the wrong kind of bags. What pettifogging, curmudgeonly, toe-curling stupidity. Angry Lynette Vickers is right to tell the council to go to hell. She should file the council's letters where they belong'.

around which a series of absurd council actions have taken place. This raises some interesting initial questions. Of all the things that can be contentious, that could be fought over, why this bag? (cf Diprose, 2010). Can a (mere) bag disrupt political relations? What, to coin a phrase, are the conditions of possibility whereby a bag can become an event (cf Lakoff, 2006)? Above all, and most starkly, how can a bin bag be 'wrong'?

A noticeable feature of the story is its organization in terms of an additive contrast structure between two main classes of entity. The central contrast here is between what Lee (1984) calls 'Evil Doers' and 'Innocent Victims', in this case between people such as the 'barmy' council bosses and normal individuals like the woman Lynette. This contrast is introduced early on: 'Barmy council bosses have fined a woman £50...' (5). This contrast is then restated and elaborated as the text unfolds. Indeed, in the way Smith suggests, this contrast acts as an important preliminary instruction to the reader for making sense of the text. It provides a contrast, which can be used to make sense of, that is, to categorize, the actions and entities mentioned in the subsequent text. The cast of characters associated with the 'barmies' turns out to include 'overzealous wardens' (9), 'the government and councils' (13/14), 'the wardens' (18), 'a warden' (31), 'the warden' (36), 'wardens [sic] boss Keith Boughey' (38), 'he' (39), 'the binmen' (43), 'Wardens for Crewe and Nantwich Borough Council' (48), and 'Mr Boughey' (50). The cast of characters associated with the 'normals' includes 'Lynette' (3, 10, 15, 23, 32, 38, 42, 50), 'a woman' (5), 'Lynette Vickers' (6), 'an unmarried mum of four' (11), and, curiously, 'a woman (fined) for littering when she was feeding birds' (49).

This key contrast between categories is reiterated and reinforced through-out. It is elaborated through the depiction of various activities and attributes that can be understood, by and large, to both be in keeping with, and to reaffirm, the dualistic typology being mooted.

So far so good. And so far, by and large, in keeping with Dorothy Smith's innovative analysis of the relations of ruling. Roughly speaking, the actions and attitudes of members of the class of 'barmies' are in a denigratory relation with those of the 'normals'. The contrast structure provides for the unfairness of the relation between the two classes. Thus, overzealous wardens enjoy a pre-eminent relation of ruling over people like an unmarried mum of four: 'Lynette Vickers got into trouble...' (6). However, an important extension to Smith's scheme is to notice how the relations between these elements are constituted in relation to the entities in the story. In particular, the contrast between barmies and normals is played out in relation to (what we take as) their contrasting dealings with the objects at the heart of the story. Moreover, the organization of the text makes possible the very sameness of the objects throughout. Different things are being done, said, assumed, assessed, and so on, in relation to *the very same thing*. That the object of barmies and normals is indeed a singular thing is critical in sustaining that contrast: the contradiction would have been considerably mitigated, and the political charge of the episode altered, if the text had encouraged an alternative 'ontological' reading, that is, if the organization of the text had provided for the possibility that both sides were referring to *different* bin bags.

Now comes the killer move. The contrast structure provides that barmies and normals perform completely different actions in relation to the same thing. But it additionally turns out that the thing's character is such that only the actions of the normals are appropriate towards it. It is, after all, just a black bin bag! Appropriate actions are those of normals who recognize the bag for what it actually is.[20] It is the very *ordinariness* of the bag that legitimates the actions of the normals towards it. That ordinariness achieves, in virtue of the contrast structure that divides the two great camps, the oddity, inappropriateness, and downright bizarre behaviour of the barmies.

Crucially, then, we see that this is not just a story weaved around acceptable and/or curious behaviours in relation to a given object. Instead, the very character of the object, the ontology of the bin bag, is constituted in and through its articulation, in this case through the organization of the text. In particular, we see that the mundaneity of the bin bag is not given; it is instead achieved in virtue of its articulation as part of the structure of the moral order

---

[20] In Smith's (1990) 'K is mentally ill', reliable witnesses are those who, by contrast with K herself, recognize the facts of the matter, that is, K's illness, as stated at the outset.

of which it is part. The mundaneity of the bin bag—what every reasonable (normal) person knows about the nature and purpose of bin bags—reinforces the moral contrast between barmies and normals. So what the thing is, what it's for, what should be in it, and what is (in)appropriate behaviour towards it, are all tied to (and exemplify) the structure of the moral order.

Notice here also how features of the story's organization achieve the formulation of 'its' context. For example, the story offers that the whole daft episode can be made sense of by placing it in the context of a series of similar episodes and actions. 'Another day, another potty penalty' (1) provides a preliminary instruction that the content of the report can be read as part of a collection of similar occurrences. The item is to be read, in other words, as the same kind of item as other members of an available collection. The available collection suggests that this same thing has happened on other occasions, and possibly so frequently as to be a daily occurrence! And it is indeed the same kind of episode (another potty penalty), or perhaps even an identical incident, or at least sufficiently similar to include them all in the same series of events, being just one incident in an un-enumerated series of similar incidents. And important to this is the extension of the contrast structure noted already. For 'potty penalty' can be read as an action, vested upon hapless innocents, which performs the pair parts of perpetrators and victims of the penalty. And this pair maps on to the contrast between barmies and normals. So the availability of the collection, together with its adequacy as a relevant collection of which the new episode is an appropriate member, provides for a reading of 'the context'.

In sum, the example suggests that understanding the politics involved requires us to take seriously the *accomplished* ontology of entities (objects, technologies, persons). In this view, entities are not given, but rather offer a reference point for temporary imputations of moral orders of accountability ('*it could be otherwise*'). This means that the normative significance of an ontological approach is much more than a matter of how to behave in relation to familiar, *given*, common objects. Instead, it requires that we treat entities as themselves a form of ontological enactment.

More than this, the importance of the ontological work is that it sustains the singularity of the object at the heart of the discussion. The proposition that barmies and normals hold contrasting views at all depends on establishing and maintaining that the entity at the heart of the discussion is just the thing that it is: the contrasting views are contrasting views of the same thing. This point resonates with Pollner's (1978) aforementioned ontologically inflected analysis of mundane reasoning in traffic courts, where witnesses are interrogated as to the speed of the car driven by the defendant. Pollner suggests that the whole proceedings are organized to maintain the key supposition that a car cannot be travelling at both 30 mph and 60 mph at the same time. This also echoes Garfinkel's (2002) much misunderstood promotion of the notion of quiddity. The proper target for social science inquiry, in his view, is to interrogate the whatness of things, to understand how entities come to seem what they are, not just to ironicize differences in perceptions (treatments, interpretations, etc) of those entities.

We can think of the whole wrong bin bag episode as a struggle over what after all is appropriate and inappropriate behaviour in relation to what the thing actually is, and who or what should act in what ways towards it. It is a story of politics in which the ontological status of the various entities is up for grabs. But it is also a story whereby politics depend on the achievement of ontological singularity. Whereas Mol (2002) shows how politics can be discerned in virtue of ontological multiplicity—the distinct enactment of separate entities is indicative of the operation of politics—the wrong bin bag suggests politics are possible in virtue of the achievement of ontological singularity.

Clearly, the kind of politics being suggested here has profound implications. It implies the need to problematize previously taken for granted statuses of humans, non-humans, objects, technologies, and matter. It implies that we reconsider the ways in which ideas like agency, ontology, materiality, and representation are interlinked. Moreover, changes in our ways of thinking about these things may necessitate a new approach to understanding the nature of the political subject/object, perhaps even a change in our thinking about the nature of politics. In the traditional view of politics advanced by political theory, the ontological status of the entities in question is largely given. The question addressed is the nature of the relationships between given, stable, figures—that is, between the given and (largely) known persons or things, humans or non-humans, and so on. The familiar political questions are: who holds power over whom? What kinds of political institution enable which kinds of involvement by whom in the distribution of resources? Increasingly, and especially since the emergence of ANT, these familiar questions have somewhat expanded to include non-humans. Who or what holds power over whom or what?

In the more insistent view that we develop here, the ontological status of the entities involved is a key accomplishment. That is, the status is not assumed as given, and is possibly in a state of continual flux. Note here that this is much more than merely saying that (fixed) non-humans deserve a voice alongside (fixed) humans. For one thing, it is by no means clear what distinguishes human from non-human in this sort of account. For example, the increasing materialization of human capacities in recent times means that the apparently non-human, material parts of the body—the brain, the muscles—as well as the technical devices to which the body is attached, are reckoned to be vital (in both senses of the term) for the production of humanness

(Rubio and Lezaun, 2011). In addition, the identity of all players (entities), their capacities, attributes, responsibilities, expectations, and so on is up for grabs. Determinations of these identities are achievements (Stengers, 2006). They are the (temporary) upshot of practices, interactions, and interventions. So the position we are advocating here goes beyond merely calling for the (re) enfranchisement of non-humans. It insists that the political constitution of humans and non-humans is in the very constitution of these entities in those terms (human and non-human). In short, the old STS slogan 'technology is politics by other means' (Latour, 1991) needs updating: entities are politics by other means.

2.5 Conclusion

This chapter has explored the potential of various analytic perspectives for beginning to understand mundane governance. Although 'governance' and 'accountability' have enjoyed considerable discussion in recent years, their analytic treatment exhibits a marked neglect of the mundane, and a disregard for the ontological status of objects and technologies. In their general expression, STS sensibilities offer some promising ways of getting under the skin of the mundane. Yet even some STS informed writing either treats governance and accountability as antecedent to ontology, or adopts uninterrogated assumptions about the definitive character of ordinary objects.

What then is the import for STS of attending to the ontological? Three main points arise. First, it is a professed move away from, and beyond, epistemology. The object of inquiry is the very existence or being of entities, not merely the modes of knowing pre-existing entities. Secondly, the ontological tendency in STS is empirical. In line with established traditions of STS inquiry, the emphasis is on showing how in practice, and in detail, particular ontologies are achieved. Thirdly, key terms in the accomplishment of ontologies are constitution and enactment. Our analysis of the 'wrong bin bag' illustrated and explored some of these key moves, outlining some advantages of an empirically oriented focus on ontological enactment.

We now build on the STS inclined re-conceptualizations of objects and technology outlined in this chapter, to develop an understanding of mundane governance in practice. We examine how ontological attributes are constituted, assigned, and distributed, and how governance and accountability relations are created, across three main empirical areas: waste management and recycling (Chapters 3 and 4), traffic management especially speeding regulation (Chapters 5 and 6), and passenger movement through airports (Chapters 7 and 8).

Chapter 3 takes a critical look at classification schemes as a form of ordering device, using waste management as the example. In Chapter 4, we consider the rationales for mundane governance, focusing in particular on the ways in which ontologies implicate morality and action in the constitution of evidence about recycling. Chapter 5 examines the constitution of structures of governance in the regulation of speed. Chapter 6 then discusses the idea of compliance, again with reference to speeding vehicles, as a way of considering the effectiveness of mundane governance. Chapter 7 looks at spaces of governance, with reference to the control of passengers in a London airport. This leads us, in Chapter 8, to investigate the phenomenon of mundane terror, the ways in which certain ordinary objects, especially in airports, are respecified as threatening. Chapter 9 tackles the topic of disruption and breakdown, to reveal what is taken for granted about mundane governance, with examples from all three of our empirical areas. Finally, our concluding chapter pulls together the threads of our argument to consider some of the main implications, outstanding issues, and future directions for mundane governance.

3

Classification as Governance: Typologies of Waste

3.1 Introduction

In Chapter 1, we noted a key feature of mundane governance: the consternation and moral outrage associated with changes in regulations about ordinary stuff. Chapter 2 then considered ways of understanding how the ontological constitution of stuff can give rise to assessments of appropriate behaviour. As one example, our analysis of the 'wrong bin bag' showed how the situated ontology of an entity (the bin bag) made possible its apprehension as a moral matter ('wrong'). Moral assessments of action and behaviour can be tied to ontological constitution. We saw how governance relations could bring into being people and things as governable entities.

We also saw how the constitution of people and things was intimately tied up with the respecification of the entities of governance: coffee was reclassified as hot, too hot, recklessly and irresponsibly hot; rubbish was respecified as subject to criminal action, tied to a particular household and a particular person. Through this segmentation, what we began to witness were not just distributions of people and things into categories, but also attendant distributions of accountabilities, responsibilities, rights, wrongs, and consequences. In this sense, to recognize the respecification of coffee from simply being coffee to being the kind of coffee served too hot and recklessly and irresponsibly hot, is to buy into a putative distribution of accountability, responsibility, rights, and wrongs. To recognize that coffee can be subject to such ontological segmentation is to recognize that constituting the nature of coffee constitutes its accountable character (that is, that it can take part in the distribution of relations of accountability). Segmentation is thus not limited to a simple or straightforward division, from one coffee to several types of coffee; instead it becomes a focal point for classification, governing people and things through their positioning in an order that simultaneously accomplishes the possibility of distributing accountability and responsibility for that order.

In some ways, this should not surprise us. We know that social relations are suffused with classification schemes (Bowker and Star, 2000). Foucault (1970) uses Borges' fable of 'a certain Chinese encyclopaedia'—in which animals are classified on a range from 'sucking pigs' to 'animals which from a long way off look like flies'—to reflect on the deep cultural embeddedness of typologies of classification. Ericson *et al.* (2003) demonstrate how systems of insurance incorporate their subjects into forms of governable classifications. These and many similar sources suggest that classification and governance are constitutively entangled: that doing governance involves doing (and re-doing, questioning and challenging) classification. But how do governance, classification, and accountability work together? How are they produced, managed, and renewed? This chapter addresses these questions by drawing on an ethnography of waste management. We begin by discussing the connection between forms of classification and relations of accountability. We develop the argument that central to any understanding of governance is the production and emergence of classificatory schemas that order the ontology of people and things, and that order is policed through distributions of accountability and ongoing accountability relations. Second, we describe the background to waste management, outlining why it entails a mode of governance that is at once mundane and important, ordinary and consequential, pervasive and significant. Third, we illustrate the complexities that arise in the entanglement of governance, classification, and accountability, using materials from our study of a local waste management centre and of an ever more elaborate series of recycling schemes developed by the local council. The chapter concludes with an analysis of the continual emergence of certainty and uncertainty, singularity and multiplicity in governance, classification, and accountability.

3.2 Governance through Classification and Accountability

If we approach governance as ongoing acts of ontological constitution, then we might be persuaded to treat classifications as the basis for distributing the nature of people and things into orders. We might even argue that classifications are integral to making entities available to be governed. However, the relationship between governance and classification requires further specification. In their study of classification, Bowker and Star suggest that: 'A classification is a spatial, temporal, or spatio-temporal segmentation of the world. A "classification system" is a set of boxes (metaphorical or literal) into which things can be put to then do some kind of work' (2000: 10). The particular kind of work we are interested in here is governance and ordering work. Ericson *et al.* (2003) treat insurance as a form of classificatory ordering work. They argue that insurance objectifies everything into a classification scheme based on the chance of harm, everything thus objectified is made calculable, each calculation is given a cost, the effects of chance are paid for (by the insured) and those paying are formed into a collective by the organization with an interest in ensuring chance events do not occur. This ordering is accomplished principally via classificatory schemes. Thus, when renewing our car insurance we are asked about our age, status (married or not, employed or not), driving history (accidents, penalties, having cars stolen), and so on. The classifications typify our risk to the collective of people with whom we are now as a group insured. However, for Ericson *et al.* the crucial feature of governance through classification is that we are made aware of and effectively subscribe ourselves into the classification scheme. We thus accomplish our own risk classification at the same time as being made aware of the kinds of activity that are considered risky. In this way: 'As a system of governance, insurance defines how people should act' (2003: 10).

The example of insurance provides some initial ideas on how classifications might do governance. However, what of accountability? Ericson *et al.* suggest that: 'Instead of social solidarity and moral binding of durable relationships, private insurance tends to fragment populations into selective risk-rated communities with a price tag' (2003: 13). The insured thereby become accountable, via insurance companies, to the rest of the community of the insured; hence, car insurance has a 'focus on individual drivers as the locus of responsibility and governance' (2003: 271). More generally private insurance companies, often together with state agencies, develop 'technologies that make individuals responsible for their own well-being and that of others in their immediate environment' (2003: 46).

This provides us with a starting point for analysing the relations between governance, accountability, and classification. The classification schemes of insurance firms do ordering by asking that we subscribe ourselves to pre-ordained categories of the classification system. We thereby accept the accountability to which we are subject and agree to enter into relations of governance designed for the good of the community of the insured (and the good of the revenue accruing to insurance companies).

If governance can be taken to mean the forms of management, co-ordination, and programmes of work involved in producing ontological classifications—orders that at once establish the nature and ranking of people and things—accountability relations can be understood as providing the means for co-ordinating, distributing, and assessing (in short policing) the moral, financial, and/or political distributions ensuing from such orders. However, what is accountability? If we want to make a claim for the centrality of accountability in enabling governance, then we first need to furnish the term with greater detail. As argued in Chapter 2, accountability is no single thing, fixed in time and place. Instead, accountability admits a range of inter-pretations in terms of the direction, intent, audience for, and distribution of responsibility. On this basis, we proposed a twofold typology of accountabil-ity. This comprised: *mutual* accountability, drawing on ethnomethodological studies to explore the ways in which accountability is a feature of ordinary and everyday sense-making in interactions; and *organizational* accountabil-ity, drawing both on neo-Foucauldian work that positions governance ration-ales as the means through which subjects of governance can be rendered accountably calculable and on actor–network theory (ANT), which examines the production of durable, movable, and combinable accounts.

We also noted several problems with these approaches to accountability. For example, we suggested that in their attempt to question the nature, ori-gins, and increasing prevalence of accountability, they tend to fall back on uninterrogated assumptions about 'real' values and prevailing truths. We also argued that shifts in accountability could have significant consequences for entities held to account, to such a degree that completely new ontological entities are brought into being and sustained by the realignment of accounta-bility relations. Some approaches tend entirely to overlook the role of objects, materials, and technology in accountability relations. And we suggested that different approaches to accountability correspond to differing underlying assumptions about the nature of the audiences that are implicated. In this chapter, we aim to address these problems by way of three main questions. First, how are classification systems produced in the first place? If forms of classification are integral to the classification of people and things as govern-able, then it is important to understand the genesis of classification. Second, with reference to the ethnomethodological sense of accountability, how do classification schemes actually work in practice? For example, how in detail does the reclassification of coffee produce its accountable order? We now draw upon our study of waste management to look at governance, account-ability, and classification in action.

3.3 A Background to Waste Management

Although waste could be said to have been subject to governance for several centuries, social science interest in waste is much more recent. Many studies provide helpful insights into disposal and waste management (see Wynne, 1989; Hawkins, 2000; Strasser, 2000; BRASS, 2006; Grossman, 2006; Saphores *et al.*, 2006), but tend not to look in detail at the ontological constitution of rubbish or the implications for accountability relations. Waste research has tended to focus on attitudes towards composting (Tucker, 1999) and the role of community waste projects in influencing household behaviour (Sharp, 2005). Research with more ontological sensitivity asks: what counts as rubbish (Thompson, 1979; Douglas, 1984); how has the history of disposal developed (Chappells and Shove, 1999); how do we come to terms with throwing things away (Hetherington, 2002; Gregson, 2005); and how do we understand reuse (Strathern, 1999)? Anthropology has a significant history of research on disposal from analyses of sacrificial death (Hubert and Mauss, 1964) and funeral rites (Hertz, 1960) to rubbish and its separation from everyday life (Douglas, 1984).

Hetherington (2002) suggests that these latter analyses deploy a very limited notion of ordering, whereby stuff moves between distinct realms through processes of separation. He argues for more emphasis on the uncertain and indeterminate nature of disposal: disposal is not a final state, but an uncertain and generative process. Drawing on Thompson (1979), Hetherington details the movement of things from 'valued' to 'rubbish' (and, on occasion, back again). These are fluid categories that depend on liminal or non-fixed in-between states for their own definition. So whereas the valued *can* be seen in straightforward contrast with the non-valued, it is important to consider all the in-between states of not-rubbish and not-value: what counts as valued, how does it get counted, through what times and spaces does it move to generate a shift from one state to another, and by which groups are these shifts recognized? In-between sites of possible value are important for establishing or even re-establishing value where value did not previously exist or had been long forgotten. These non-final sites lead Hetherington to emphasize that 'ordering is made as uncertain process' (2002: 5).

Munro (1998) similarly looks at how we are held accountable for disposal and how we attempt to translate things through placing activities. Placing is always dependent upon the possibility of otherness and uncertainty, with things leaking out of place and back into the very areas from which we have placed them. Also there are gaps (which Hetherington calls blank figures) that pose troubling questions about what should be placed where, and what the effects of such placing might be. As Strathern (1999) suggests 'those involved in the activity of waste disposal know that one cannot dispose of waste, only convert it into something else' (1999: 61).

This emphasis on ontological shifts and uncertainty stands in marked contrast to most policy discussions focused on waste management. For example, in the UK, successive government initiatives have strived for ever more certainty in the management of household waste. In place of social science insights into the multiplicity of what counts as waste, a matter of uncertainty or concern, blank figures, and liminal states, comes a series of regimented initiatives. Concerns about managing waste have emphasized the importance of evidence-based policy (see Chapter 4) and have led to a drive to persuade the UK population to recycle more. A popular mantra is 'Reduce, Reuse, Recycle'—the three desired components of waste management activities.[1] Several sources have given impetus to these initiatives, ranging from environmental campaign organizations such as Friends of the Earth, to European Parliament legislation[2] aimed at reducing levels of disposal in member states.

However, it would be a mistake to assume that there is one single mode of waste management governance in the UK. Instead, we came across a variety of sometimes distinct, sometimes overlapping, and sometimes disappearing waste management activities. In these, we could discern four main characteristics. First, governance was devolved through successive layers of government. The UK waste management system was established on a partially devolved political principle that, although national government would set policies and some broad rules, it would be down to local and regional authorities (such as city and county councils) to put in place particular schemes and initiatives, which fulfilled the obligations handed to them. For example, national government (Department for Environment, Food and Rural Affairs—DEFRA) attempted to collect data on the weight of waste collected and disposed of by each local authority in the UK. This involved a system whereby vehicles that collected waste had to be weighed by local authorities before emptying, the weight of the vehicle subtracted, and resulting weight recorded. The summation of figures from all vehicles provided a measure of weight of waste disposed by the local authority, compiled and presented annually. DEFRA similarly assessed the weight of 'non-waste' recycled by each local authority. The figures were then combined to establish recycling percentages (of weight recycled/weight disposed) for each local authority. DEFRA set targets for each local authority to increase its recycling percentage.[3]

Given the enthusiasm for market-based initiatives in UK government schemes,[4] DEFRA did not stop there. Each local authority was provided with a number of 'waste credits' up to its target limit for weight of waste. The idea was that the 'best' authorities would be encouraged to cut back their weight of waste dramatically, giving them spare credits to sell to the 'worst' authorities who could buy credits. One proposal was that the overall weight of waste disposed in the UK would still decline as the total credits available represented a reduction of waste weight. This had parallels with other environmental cap and trade schemes. A second proposal was that authorities

---

[1] See, for example, the green recycling guide website: http://www.reducereuserecycle.co.uk/

[2] Including the EU Waste Framework Directive and the EU Waste Catalogue (a complex classification device of its own).

[3] This was partly said to derive from EU waste directive and targets, see: http://ec.europa.eu/environment/waste/landfill_index.htm

[4] Similar schemes included the marketization of urban governance, education, and health.

would compete to be the 'best' and thus save money on waste management facilities and have credits to sell (a double 'win'). A third proposal was that authorities could bank credits for future years in case they foresaw problems. A fourth proposal was that authorities might borrow credits from future years if they foresaw dramatic reductions in landfilling in their area in future years. As with most market-based initiatives, a series of unintended consequences ensued: authorities had trouble establishing the price/value of credits; some authorities did not bother to recycle and waited to buy up cheap credits instead as a cost-cutting measure (credits turned out to be cheaper than a fully fledged recycling system perhaps because the only 'buyers' were those local authorities without much budget, looking to cut costs); local populations were sometimes uninterested in recycling; local authorities were sometimes unsure of the best means to encourage more recycling; some local authorities claimed there was a lack of clear guidance about what their recycling efforts should focus on—reducing land used for waste disposal, reducing waste, or saving the environment. These questions and uncertainties contrasted with DEFRA's weight-based certainty and aim to instil a 'recycling mentality' in the UK population.[5] As a form of governance, it appeared that waste and recycling were ontologically constituted through classifications into weight-based measures, and policed through a market-based system of accountability. This market-based scheme was due to end in 2013, with landfill taxation then reckoned to be a more effective means to pursue similar ends.[6]

Second, governance was pursued through recourse to the law. Waste management, as we noted in the case of the wrong bin bag (Chapter 2), was increasingly subject to forms of criminalization in the UK.[7] It became possible for individuals to be fined for putting out the wrong waste, in the wrong place, at the wrong time, and for putting the wrong items (or no items) in recycling containers.[8] Although in principle this meant drawing on a standard set of national laws at local level, standardization was not the clear result. We found an increase in reporting in some places; fining residents for not recycling, for putting out waste early, the wrong waste, in the wrong bags, and so on. But elsewhere residents were not fined, neither was waste disposal criminalized and so on.[9] In effect, a distributed geography of ontological constitution

---

[5] See *Daily Telegraph* article (2004) available here: http://www.telegraph.co.uk/news/uknews/1468984/Rubbish-tax-plan-to-boost-recycling.html

[6] See, for example, DEFRA's account of the end of market system: http://www.defra.gov.uk/environment/waste/local-authorities/landfill-scheme/

[7] Although this may change in the future, see: http://www.bbc.co.uk/news/uk-politics-13027352

[8] See BBC story (2004) available here: http://news.bbc.co.uk/1/hi/england/london/3571227.stm

[9] See, for example, This Is London (2006) article on different councils having options for introducing different schemes and considering different levels of fines: http://www.thisislondon.co.uk/news/article-23371719-200-charges-for-not-recycling.do

emerged: variations in classifications of waste and criminality were policed through accountability relations.

Third, education provided a focal point for developing governance and relations of accountability. Over the last ten years,[10] various educational initiatives have attempted to encourage the UK to become a nation of recyclers. By contrast, with the drive to criminalize waste wrongdoers, national TV, radio, and cinema advertising campaigns have used light humour and cartoons to provide a friendly face/voice to recycling. Popular comedians have been employed to provide voiceovers to commercials extolling the virtues of recycling. Schools organized events to encourage children to participate in recycling and local communities sponsored schemes to distribute information on the virtues of recycling.[11] Although they appeared to involve the articulation of relations of accountability, it is not clear to what extent these schemes were successful.

Fourth, local authority–household schemes provided a form of governance. These locally organized schemes were designed to provide householders with the means to recycle to increase the percentage weight of non-disposed/recycled waste achieved by the local authority. A typical scheme was operated in Oxford. Here a series of sites (waste management centres) were established where residents could take their waste/recycling and sort it into containers. Simultaneously every household was given a recycling box[12] (tens of thousands of boxes were distributed across Oxford) and a leaflet with instructions about what should be put in the box and when the box should be put out for collection. The City Council sent out collection vehicles every day to different areas of the city. Each area thus had a weekly kerbside collection, whereby collection crews on 'recycling rounds' emptied the boxes into a segmented recycling vehicle with clearly delineated (caged-off) sections for each type of material the household had been instructed to put in its box. Crews who found non-recyclable items (according to the terms of the leaflet) were instructed to leave such items in the recycling box and to inform households of their transgression.[13] A separate collection was offered for garden waste, with its own containers and vehicles.[14] These kinds of schemes encountered significant challenges. For example, the types of item that households were

---

[10] See for example national recycling adverts (available here: http://www.youtube.com/watch?v=xbQPtuh9hzs) and regional campaigns (such as Recycle for London campaign: http://www.recycleforlondon.com/starve/tv/weak.jsp)

[11] A typical regional example can be found here, run by Bath and Somerset local authorities: http://www.bathnes.gov.uk/BathNES/environmentandplanning/recyclingandwaste/Recycling/schools.htm

[12] These have recently been replaced by larger recycling wheelie bins.

[13] To return to the key exemplar of Chapter 2, the very existence of the recycling scheme can be said to further emphasize the wrongness of the bin bag.

[14] This is tied to EU targets on limiting biodegradable waste that enters landfill to pre-1996 levels (see Reno, 2011).

expected to put out for collection and the ways in which items were to be presented, both shifted in line with changes in contracts between local authorities and the private companies that purchased the recycling materials.[15] Many questions were asked about these schemes.[16] Given the environmental orientation of recycling, what was the carbon footprint of vehicles, boxes, lids, and leaflets? Why was there such an emphasis on garden waste?[17] Why was the UK's recycling rate one of the worst in the developed world and why did Oxford have one of the worst recycling rates in the UK[18] (implying that Oxford was one of the worst places for recycling in the world)? What would make these schemes work?[19]

In contrast to recent social science emphasis on shifting and uncertain ontologies in waste management (Strathern, 1999; Hetherington, 2002), these governance drives were based on conceptions of waste as a known and knowable certainty. In these schemes, waste is the subject of evidence to be collected to inform policy, waste is managed, waste is traded in markets, and waste becomes the subject of education initiatives. However, the diversity of these governance initiatives suggests instead that waste is not such a singular entity. It is a matter for criminalization and education, national and local policy, environmental science, and plastic boxes.

How can these waste management schemes help us understand relations of governance, accountability, and classification? It is possible to think of market-based schemes as systems of regulation. Local authorities are assessed by the weight of waste they achieve and are expected to report these weights annually. These reports distinguish between 'good' and 'bad' authorities, and this is underlined by rewards and sanctions brought into effect by the credit trading scheme. Local authorities were thus held accountable by means of measures, targets, credits, and implied costs of failure (having to buy/not having any credits to sell). In turn, local authorities attempted to displace

---

[15] For example, at one point households were expected to separate different colour glass so that the recycling company could more easily recycle that glass. However, a new contract with a new company that used glass in road foundations, placed no particular value on glass of separate colours and so households were then encouraged to present less segregated material. Some households expressed concern about the sudden and, for them, unexplained change.

[16] Questions have been raised about the benefits of recycling schemes as a whole. Here is a US example: http://www.griffex.com/Griff-gpec-and-tables.pdf In the UK, government discussion has focused at times on the environmental impact of recycling schemes: http://www.parliament.uk/documents/post/postpn252.pdf

[17] One environmental campaigner suggested to Dan that garden waste was collected because it was heavy, so increasing the weight of recyclable material percentages and helping meet EU targets.

[18] Data released just before the start of our research ranked Oxford City Council 246th in a national recycling league table: http://www.letsrecycle.com/councils/league-tables-1/2003-04

[19] Suggestions range from an absence of a market for recycling material (see, for example: http://www.parliament.uk/post/postpn252.pdf), to a lack of facilities for dealing with particular materials, such as plastic (see, for example: http://www.foodmanufacture.co.uk/Business-News/Coca-Cola-calls-for-better-recycling) to the need for more exporting of waste (see, for example: http://www.packagingnews.co.uk/news/export-markets-uk-recycling/).

this accountability by holding households to account for their waste disposal actions. Classifications of objects and people (as waste/recycling, correct/ incorrect items, good/bad households) were policed by accountability relations, for example, when recycling collectors assess items left out for recycling by householders and inform them of transgressions. Attempts to criminalize waste can also be understood as an entanglement of governance, accountability, and classification. Waste was governed by invoking legal sanctions such as on-the-spot fines or court prosecutions. Similarly, educational initiatives can be understood as based upon principles of accountability: viewers of adverts are implored to take responsibility for the future of the planet by placing things in recycling containers, and by conforming to the classification of objects (not waste, but recyclable) and people (as bad disposers or good recyclers).

All this reaffirms, in general terms, the interconnection between governance, accountability, and classification. But, to understand in more detail how governance accomplishes the ontology of waste we need to get closer to the action in waste management. How does ontological constitution work, how does it derive from classification, and how does this enact distributions of accountability relations? We need to understand the genesis of classifications of waste and the distinct modes of accountability at work. To do this we now turn to our ethnographic study of recycling and waste management in the UK.

3.4 Waste Management in Action

The range of waste management schemes in operation in the UK, the search for a recycling mentality and existing social science research all suggested that waste management would be a fertile area for investigating mundane governance. How then to set up a close study of waste management in action? How to gain entry and to where or what?

As mentioned, Oxford had a reputation for recycling little in comparison to the UK, which was said to recycle little in relation to the developed world. Oxford seemed an ideal place to carry out our research! We approached the Oxford County Council waste management representative responsible for operating a local waste management centre (where people in Oxford could bring items to recycle or dispose), and we contacted the Oxford City Council waste management team that had responsibility for distributing recycling boxes and leaflets and collecting recyclable material weekly. We now discuss each of these ethnographic sites in turn.

3.4.1 The Local Waste Management Centre

The local Waste Disposal Authority (WDA), Oxford County Council, handled an average of 324 kg of waste per person per year. Its waste management centre was open 362 days a year (not Christmas, Boxing, or New Year's Days), from 8 a.m. to 5 p.m., with late night opening on Thursdays in the summer. The website stating these details led us to believe that access for 'users' was relatively straightforward—they just needed to turn up with their items for recycling and (if necessary) waste when the centre was open. The only barriers to entry were the opening/closing times, the need for transport, and a preference for recycling rather than disposal. However, the response from Oxford County Council made us quickly realize that 'researchers' are a category quite different from ordinary, everyday users. Our request to video record the site prompted a lengthy discussion: video for what, made available to whom, and with what consequence? Satisfactory answers to these questions (it was a video to be made for an academic project, to be used by academics, to understand better the nature of the centre) prompted further concerns: who would carry out the health and safety assessment of making a video in the centre and how could the centre fulfil its health and safety obligations with academics on site? We offered that academics are not a special health and safety risk, they are much like normal users, albeit with cameras. But the centre manager remained troubled by the hybrid entity of quasi-user-academic-with-camera. He suggested we should be subject to the same health and safety routines as the staff who worked on site; would we be happy with that? Fearing a tedious bureaucratic process, but seeing no alternative, this was agreed. We[20] were asked to report to the site hut on arrival at the waste management centre and to show staff an e-mail from the WDA representative confirming our willingness to be healthy and safe.

We arrived at the site hut for our health and safety induction. This turned out to consist of being handed high visibility yellow vests, being told we had to wear them at all times, and being asked to agree not to climb into recycling containers 'because they are dangerous'. This was our first experience of governance and accountability on the ground. Any ontological uncertainty about our monstrous hybridity and the supposed risk to our own bodies and to the accountability of the waste management centre was resolved and redistributed through the donning of high visibility vests. Through our navigation of the health and safety induction, we had accomplished an entirely new and unique classification—neither users nor staff, neither recyclable material nor waste, but 'academics'. This ontological reconstitution also redistributed the accountability involved. Handing over vests and instructing us not to

---

[20] In this case Dan, Steve, and research student Ju Min.

Figure 3.1. Warnings on the gates to the recycling centre

climb into containers had fulfilled the centre's accountability requirements and shifted responsibility for our health and safety on to us.[21]

What struck us immediately upon entry—even in a high visibility health and safety vest—was the mechanistic chaos of the waste management centre. A series of large metal boxes, akin to open top shipping containers, were arranged along a curved circular roadway along which cars full of recycling/waste were moving. Inside the curve and away from the vehicles, large cranes swung into action, shifting full containers and dropping empty containers into place. Dirty looking waste trucks drove full containers out of the centre.[22] Staff shouted across long distances and above the noise, yelling instructions about containers nearly full or in need of attention, or just the latest daily joke. At busy times, visitors jostled with each other to get their car closest to the container they wanted to use, in open defiance of normal parking protocol. By contrast with parking behaviour in, say, a town centre, visitors to the waste management centre stopped their cars at will, blocked other users

---

[21] All we had to do was stay out of one type of container (for waste or recycling) and stay in another (the high visibility vest).

[22] Their final destination depended on the contents of the container and the contracts the County Council had in place at any time. For example, during the research much waste was taken to Milton Keynes, about 46 miles from Oxford, where a company had a contract with Oxford County Council for reprocessing recyclable material.

from moving away and blocked routes to other containers. Containers, recyclables, waste, and social etiquette were thrown around with equal abandon.

Also striking were the signs. At the entrance, signs warned of the presence of CCTV cameras; signs on the high metal fence surrounding the site warned about the fines for dumping waste outside the site (particularly, but not exclusively, outside of the hours of opening). Also at the entrance, a large billboard posted the latest centre's weight of waste recycling percentage. To the right was the circuit of containers. Here signs were abundant. Some of these signs appeared to be long standing, marked, and slightly weather beaten. These were fixed above the sites where metal containers were dropped, filled, and moved. These banner signs announced such matters as 'Garden Waste', 'Computers', 'Textiles', and 'Newspapers'. Closer to the containers and normally smaller in size, were more recent, less permanent looking signs. For example, under the banner sign 'Garden Waste' were laminated sheets of A4 paper, stuck to the railing next to the container, reminding users 'No plastic', 'Garden waste only', 'No bags', and 'Garden waste only' (again). Under the banner sign declaring 'Hardcore and topsoil only. No bags' two further signs attached to the container itself bore the messages 'Hardcore' and 'Hardcore and soil (no plastic bags)'. Staff in high visibility vests moved between containers and occasionally pointed out to users which items should go in what containers.

At first sight all this suggests a smooth and certain system of waste governance, involving a clear classification and distribution of accountability. The signs next to and attached to containers articulated the classificatory scheme and mutual accountability occurred through face-to-face interactions between staff and users. Accountability was further assured by the presence of CCTV cameras and the possibility of fines for those caught dumping waste illegally outside the centre. The appropriate disposal of waste was governed with certainty. The sign announcing the high percentage of recycled waste seemed to index that the local authority (Oxford County Council) was fulfilling its governance relations with national government (DEFRA). On closer inspection, however, it became apparent that governance relations were not so straightforward.

In three ways the messy ontologies of waste intermingled with this more stark and straightforward scheme of classification and accountability.

First, it became apparent that positioning of the containers around the circuit was not accidental. Containers at the early part of the circuit were labelled with some certainty: 'Computers', 'Newspapers', 'Cardboard', and 'Garden Waste'. As users moved around the circuit, the categories became less clear cut: 'Bric a brac', 'Bulky items', and 'Household waste'. This latter typology appeared to be predicated on the recyclability of items. 'Bulky items', for example, were removed from the container by staff who then decided which other categories they should be assigned to. 'Household waste' was designed as a final miscellaneous container of items to be disposed (in landfill) and not recycled. This container had no banner sign above it, reducing its visibility from the rest of the centre and its users and containers. The 'Household waste' sign was only visible when users got very close to it, having already passed all the other containers. More signs affixed to the railings next to this container tried to dissuade users from placing items in it: 'No plastic, cardboard, newspaper' and 'Please use the recycling containers'. The position of the landfill container at the end of the circuit, absence of a banner sign, and last desperate plea to 'Please use the recycling containers' suggest this container acted as a messy miscellaneous end point (landfill) required to preserve the integrity of other (recycling) containers. Its positioning denoted its identity as an unfortunate and reluctant necessity. Ontologically speaking, the landfill container acted as the recycling centre's etcetera clause (Garfinkel, 1967).

Secondly, staff were frequently called upon to carry out repairs to violations of the classificatory system. For example, when one of us was standing next to the container bearing the sign 'Hardcore and topsoil only. No bags', an estate car drove up and its occupants started to throw plastic bags full of hardcore rubble into the container. Emboldened by his high visibility vest, Steve took it upon himself to point out the sign saying 'No bags'. The offenders apologized profusely (to what they perhaps imagined was an authority figure) but made no move to remove the heavy plastic bags now resting at the bottom of a deep container. After they drove away, centre staff had to climb into the container, empty the contents of bags into the containers, and remove the plastic bags to an adjacent wheelie-bin. The integrity of the classification system was accomplished, but only through repair. These kinds of repairs were entirely routine and a taken for granted feature of the centre. Just a little way from 'Hardcore and topsoil' another member of staff had climbed into 'Garden waste only' and was busy removing plastic plant pots. The classification system in action clearly depended on continual repair for its integrity and for its role in accomplishing the governance of waste/recycling items.

Thirdly, the role of accountability was also less certain than it first appeared. It was not straightforwardly the case that accountability relations policed the constitution of ontological classification. For example, while staff sometimes directed and held users to account, most of the time no staff were in evidence. Indeed there were far more containers than staff members. Although the signs could be said to constitute a typology of classification, they did not accomplish accountability. They did not appear to act as Foucauldian rationales, which users internalized in considering themselves accountable to, for example, the greater good of the environment. Rather, the signs were there to be read, overlooked, or ignored while throwing items into containers. The CCTV cameras seemed to be oriented to policing the perimeter of the centre, rather than making users accountable for their classificatory transgressions within the centre. And even when staff were positioned by containers, either transgressors were politely directed toward the correct action or, more frequently, their transgressions were repaired by staff after the act. Apart from Steve's efforts to discipline users of the 'Hardcore and topsoil' container, no users were seen holding other users to account. Hence one might speculate that the kind of accountability that occurred in the recycling centre was oblique, perhaps occasionally mutual between staff and users, but mostly unnoticeable beyond the actions of putting stuff in containers that accomplished and maintained the classification scheme.

In sum, the recycling centre is characterized by a messy form of classification in action. It is classification that requires miscellany and continuous repair. Furthermore, accountability is at particular moments uncertain and unclear. Even if one were to focus on the weight of waste recycled sign as representative of a form of accountability between local authority (Oxford County Council) and national government (DEFRA), this seems to be something of an imposition of clarity. Weight of waste/recycling percentages were sent annually and electronically to DEFRA, so it was not clear for whom this sign was representative of accountability. At most it might be seen as a general encouragement to users that their continual efforts were contributing to recycling. What was more certain in the recycling centre was that the governance system of classifying, sorting, weighing, and then moving recyclable goods produced a system for the constitution of ontologies. Those ontologies were on occasions uncertain, required the protection of miscellanies and repair work by centre staff, but none the less items were contained and assessed on the adequacy of the presentation of their containment. This begins to suggest that governance and accountability are intermingled in a broad number of ways. However, we are left with questions of accountability (by whom, for whom, in what way?) and classification (where do systems of classification come from, through what means?). In order to address these questions, we now consider Oxford's kerbside recycling scheme.

3.4.2 Kerbside Recycling

In response to an initial e-mail requesting access to research Oxford City Council's[23] kerbside recycling scheme, Dan was invited to a meeting with the waste management team. The team comprised three people: Sheila, Trevor, and Harry (in ascending order of seniority), who enthusiastically welcomed

---

[23] The City Council is the local Waste Collection Authority (WCA). They differ from the County Council who are the Waste Disposal Authority (WDA) who manage the waste management centre.

the ethnographer into the waste management depot.[24] Sheila presented herself as something of an environmental campaigner. She did her job in waste management to try to encourage recycling. She was particularly keen on the mode of governance through education described earlier in this chapter. She hoped to run her own initiatives tied into the government's national TV advertising campaign. Sheila introduced Dan to some of the details of the recycling scheme. Every household was given a box and a leaflet on how to use it, the boxes were collected weekly by collection crews, the crews sorted recyclable items into separate containers at the kerbside, and recyclable material collected on each round was weighed.

Dan encouraged Sheila to talk about the leaflets given to households (she had one on her desk). She set out the basic distinction to be communicated to householders, between what could be recycled and should be placed in the container and what could not be recycled and should be placed in ordinary household waste. The top half of the leaflet was entitled 'Yes we can collect...' and the bottom half entitled 'No we cannot collect...'. Sheila explained that this simple binary division was designed to keep things straightforward for the household. Each heading described a list of corresponding items (paper, tin cans, etc) that could or could not be placed in the recycling box. Sheila explained that there was no natural limit to these categories; many things on the 'No we cannot collect...' list were potentially recyclable, but each recycling collection vehicle only had a limited number of segregated containers and the council only had contracts with companies who wanted to recycle certain goods. The full classification scheme of the leaflet was as follows:

Yes, we can collect

> Glass bottles and jars
>
> Food tins and drink cans
>
> Paper
>
> Clothing

No, we cannot collect

> Other types of glass
>
> Other metals
>
> Other types of paper
>
> Other textiles
>
> Other materials

---

[24] The reason for their enthusiasm became clear later on when it transpired they were interested in having some research done for which they did not have sufficient resources (see Chapter 4).

Each of the subheadings provided instructions for dealing with the material. For example, under the subheading 'Glass bottles and jars' readers were told 'These should be rinsed clean; Please remove lids and stoppers; Labels and metal collars can be left on; Glass can be green, brown, blue or clear'. Green ticks were appended to each entry below the subheading, affirming the environmentally friendly status and thus morally approved nature of each action/object. Under the 'No, we cannot collect' heading, lilac crosses were positioned next to negative instructions. For example, under 'Other types of glass' households were warned about objects that could not be collected, the moral counterpoint to environmentally welcome glass: 'Broken glass (for safety reasons); Window panes and flat glass; Pyrex and other glass cookware; Drinking glasses and tableware; Spectacles and lenses; Lightbulbs and fluorescent tubes'. One could note how some entries in these lists were accountable; that is, they were able demonstrably to account for their nature, their morality and thus their inclusion in the positive or negative part of the list. In this way, 'Broken glass' was positioned on the 'No, we cannot collect' list, its presence made demonstrably accountable through its apparently hazardous nature '(for safety reasons)'.

Without prompting Sheila began to talk about the recycling boxes themselves. These were green to signify their environmental credentials and made from 100 per cent recycled plastic. Sheila said the City Council had decided not to give out box lids to households to cut down on 'resource use'. She said that if households wanted to keep the boxes outside they could apply for a lid, which collection crews would deliver. Households also occasionally applied for new or extra recycling boxes, which were delivered in the same way. The boxes came with a set of instructions printed on the outside of the box. If households put the wrong things in the box, collection crews would put paper notes through household letterboxes offering instructions on the correct procedure.

Again, on the face of it, this appears a somewhat comprehensive system for classifying items of recycling/waste. The binary organization seemed clear in Sheila's description. Stuff was either one thing or another, and this should be evident to households. The City Council sought to fulfil its accountability to national government (DEFRA) by introducing a two-part classification system. The recycling box and its household owners were the key components of the system. Units of accountability were not quite individual—households could have multiple occupants—but were discussed as if they were the smallest possible unit of accountability/responsibility. As Sheila put it, the City Council produced the leaflet (the classification system) and it was up to households to recycle (and hence comply with the classification).

Given the apparent unity and smoothness of this scheme, Dan asked Sheila to talk about the collection of waste and recycling material. Maybe it was here that difficulties in governance would be revealed. Sheila explained that collection crews would walk the rounds on particular days, collecting and emptying recycling boxes, and depositing items into the segmented sections on the collection vehicles. She presented this as a quick and efficient means to accomplish a detailed classification—paper went into one section, glass into another, tin cans into another. Sheila argued that it was appropriate to do this at kerbside otherwise households would have to take on this further (perhaps too complex?) responsibility—sorting materials themselves into subcategories. It seemed to Dan that the collection crews acted as a kind of check on the classificatory work done by the household. The problem, as far as Sheila was concerned, was that despite these logistics Oxford remained poor at recycling.

Partly as a result of their concern to address the problem of their poor recycling record, the City Council waste management team agreed that Dan and Ju Min could accompany the collection crews and study kerbside recycling.[25] Dan and Steve also started to spend time visiting the houses of Oxford residents.[26] Typically, these visits involved sitting and talking with residents about their recycling habits, and being shown typical efforts at recycling. We also took photos of boxes and their households. Although Sheila had seemed to suggest that kerbside recycling worked smoothly, these excursions beyond the waste management team's office revealed several other important features of household recycling.

First, of the small sample[27] of households participating in this research, none had a recycling leaflet. None could recall ever having received a recycling leaflet. None had ever noticed the instructions on the side of the recycling box (until pointed out by the researchers). In Sheila's description, the classification scheme clearly distinguished between recyclable and non-recyclable items. In practice, the distinctions were very much less clear. When householders discussed the leaflet with Dan they raised many questions about the typology. Why did shoes appear both in the 'Yes we can . . .' and the 'No we cannot . . .' lists? Why does it say dry paper or damp paper can be recycled but not wet or soggy paper—what is the difference? What is waxed paper and plain paper and why can only plain paper be recycled? It says tin cans must be cleaned—why and how clean do they need to be? In each conversation with a member of a household more new questions emerged. Dan found himself in the position of trying to defend the classification system. Why did it suddenly seem

---

[25] This was not an entirely free ride—it turned out the City Council were interested in recruiting researchers to a survey of recycling in Oxford, see Chapter 4.

[26] The rounds were completed early in the morning and time spent with households was in the afternoon and evenings.

[27] We spent time with ten households. In Chapter 4, we look at the recycling boxes of 10,000 households.

so unclear? What was the reason for the subtle degrees of difference (damp or soggy) that had to be navigated? In his conversations with householders, Steve noticed how interpretations of the unfolding moral order exhibited considerable ambivalence and uncertainty. Varying views about the correct operation of the system were offered: you can't leave the box out overnight; it's got to be right near the kerb; they won't take cardboard; they don't do plastic, but they are going to soon; you don't want everyone to see all your wine bottles!; well, it all ends up in the same skip anyway. Householders thus explained their own and very varied theories of what might not, could not, should be, and often was left in the recycling box to be collected. A strong sense of the importance of correct and incorrect behaviour permeated these attempts to describe how the system worked. Although when questioned most households recognized they might be throwing things away that otherwise might be recycled, most felt they were contributing to recycling by putting in the box those items (particularly newspapers) that they routinely remembered. One household refused to participate because recycling was an imposition by a left wing/liberalist government. One household wished they could recycle more and put aside items they could not leave in their recycling box to take on their weekly trip to the waste management centre. We see that far from being ontologically pristine, the classification system in the hands of householders exhibited considerable ontological uncertainty.

Secondly, in addition to these uncertainties in ontological classification, it was striking to realize that the properties of the recycling box themselves seemed to shift.[28] Boxes were mostly kept at the back of the house (frequently in the kitchen) or in the back garden or yard. They sat there during the week gradually being filled with various household items. On the same day that the household put out bags of waste to be collected and landfilled, the box was taken out and placed outside the front of the house ready to be collected. In this movement things shifted. The City Council waste management team made it clear that once outside the house, the items were theirs (this was important for their collection and surveying activities, see Chapter 4). So the movement from back to front of the house was a shift in legal ownership. It was also a shift in accountability relations. In the house, the box was at the centre of household members' mutual accountability. Family members, for example, would monitor each other's use of the box and assess the extent to which items placed in the box fitted their weekly recycling routine. Moving the box to the front of the house was also a matter of internal household accountability, often with the same household member expected (and held to account) to perform the task. Once outside the front of the house, the box

---

[28] Thanks to Ju Min Wong for this observation.

was then the focus of accountability relations involving governance of the household as an aggregate entity, governed by the local authority and relations of governance between the local authority and national government (DEFRA). The move from the back of the house to the front was, then, a shift in legal ownership, internal accountability, and external governance. That is, except for the householder who refused to recycle, the absence of his box being intended as a protest against the left wing/liberalist government. As the box moved, its ontological constitution also shifted; from a member of the household to a demonstration of the household's ability to recycle; from a container to be filled to a container to be emptied; from a container integrated into household routines to a container for inspection by the survey team.

In sum, questions about the nature of an item (whether or not it was recyclable) became the basis for assessing the appropriateness of its containment (in recycling boxes or bin bags). This could be understood as a response to the City Council's leaflet and its binary division of waste (Yes we can collect, No we cannot collect). It could be said that the position and presentation of containment operated within sets of accountability relations inside and outside the household. But the classification scheme in the leaflet did not determine the ontology of items, the adequacy of their presentation or their attendant accountability relations. As we said, none of the households in this research could recall ever having the leaflet. Instead, households tended to generate their own local classification schemes. They constituted items as (most probably) recyclable and hence to be placed in the recycling box and (most likely) waste and hence to be placed in a bin bag. The movement of the recycling box from (frequently) the back of the house to the pavement, shifted the nature and ownership of the box, translated its contents and accountability relations, from things to be recycled to things to be taken as accountably demonstrative (or not) of the household's ability to recycle adequately.

3.5 Analysis: Governance, Accountability, and Classification

What to make of our experiences and observations from the waste management centre and from the kerbside recycling scheme, to understand the interconnection between governance, accountability, and classification? Our ethnography of waste management brings together some of the ideas about ordering, classification, and accountability with which we began the chapter. For example, local and regional authorities in the UK can be seen to be held to account by national government (in the form of DEFRA). This accountability provides the basis for policing the ontological constitution and classification of waste and recycling, weights, and percentages. Educational initiatives aimed at boosting the percentage of recycled waste, can be seen to include further relations of accountability, in which classification provides a basis for bringing into governable being specific groups and authorities and their concomitant accountability relations. Those who recycle little become a target to persuade them to change; school age children become a target to get them to hold their parents to account—or embarrass them—for their (lack of) recycling behaviour. These local educational initiatives resonate with national TV advertising campaigns, which perform their own kinds of accountability and classification (constituting who should pay attention, why recycling might be considered good, and the terms of accountability). Alongside these initiatives, local authorities accomplish a range of accountability relations, publicizing information on recycling successes, on opportunities for recycling and making less available opportunities for waste disposal through landfill. Local authority websites thus demonstratively bring into existence their own account-able order as successful-in-encouraging-recycling and against-landfill-waste-disposal.

The constitution of ordered, governable, and accountable entities occurs by way of several forms of classification. Key to this is the classification of the materials themselves: what can and cannot be recycled and the means by which items can be recycled. These classifications are morally and, on occasions, legally consequential: what can and cannot be recycled appears inseparable from what should and should not be recycled (see also Chapter 4). For example, the waste recycling leaflet constitutes the nature and moral order of objects and actions of recyclables and recyclers, and at the same time spells out the accountability relations that will police this order. So, in terms of the questions with which we started the chapter, we can understand the classification system for household waste and recycling as emerging through the binary division enshrined in the city council leaflet. We can also note how this ordering is policed through distinct modes of accountability (leaflets provided a basis for accountability between council and household, between members of households and between recycling boxes and collection crews). From the perspective of the city council waste management team, the leaflet, classification, and accountability relations were what made governance.

However, we also saw the operation of these waste management systems, ontologies, classifications, and modes of accountability were far from smooth. Both the waste management centre and kerbside recycling system experienced problems, challenges, and changes in direction. In the recycling centre, a seemingly desperate amalgam of signs and containers, staff, and CCTV cameras attempted to establish classification and accountability. In kerbside recycling, attempts were made to get leaflets to do classification work, through households and via green boxes, to get households to accept some responsibility for being accountable for their waste, with kerbside collection crews issuing reminders and notices of transgression in an effort to maintain classification and accountability. In both systems, we found messiness, confusion, classificatory slippage, and lengthy discussions about whether there was too little or too much accountability. Hence, in the waste management centre, miscellaneous containers were enrolled to try to maintain the integrity of the classification scheme, and staff were constantly working to repair failures of classification. The operation of accountability (by, for example, staff and CCTV cameras) seemed selective, uneven or, at times, non-existent. In kerbside recycling we found that none of the participating households had leaflets setting out the City Council's classification scheme. So we cannot treat the leaflet as a straightforward determinant of classification. Rather it seems a form of classification in practice emerged as households established their own local routines for dealing with stuff. We saw that recycling boxes mutate as they moved through houses and through forms of ownership and accountability, and that householders responded to recycling in a wide variety of ways (as begrudgingly accepting the necessity of sorting waste, as keen recyclers or as political protest).

We also found that the ontologies of very ordinary materials in these two waste management systems were multiple. For example, paper was variously constituted through: type classifications (plain paper, waxy or shiny paper, newspaper, telephone directories) and condition classifications (soggy, damp, wet, dry); forms of ownership and responsibility (household or City Council); local and national policy (through percentage of weight of waste recycled figures); notions of private (something taken from the intimate confines of the household) and public (to be sorted by waste collection crews); anticipation of familiar practice (the kind of paper that household members most often more or less knew could be recycled); and confusion (paper that might be wrong), among many other things. And that was just paper. Similar multiplicities were apparent for the ontologies of tin cans, bottles, and other matters of waste/recycling.

None the less, in the midst of this overbearing multiplicity, certain specific relations seemed to remain steady. For example, the box and its household constituted a key ontological pairing at the centre of governance relations. Most governance relations in kerbside recycling were organized around this relatively stable pairing. But what is its origin? The household emerged as the unit of accountability because of the City Council's pursuit of a scheme to distribute boxes to households, rather than to smaller units such as individuals or to larger units such as a street. Having undertaken the ethnographic study, spending a lot of time with all parties involved, it seems strange to question the obviousness of the pairing: it is so entrenched in practice and seems so 'natural'. However, members of the City Council waste management team did occasionally ask themselves whether it might be advantageous to place containers on street corners, to which people could carry their waste. (This would require fewer collection vehicles and staff.) So the house-hold was not the inevitable or 'natural' centre of classification, responsibility, and accountability. Rather, it was chosen as a way of disseminating classifica-tion (via the leaflet), encouraging responsibility (the theory being that street corner bins would be too easy to ignore), and assigning accountability (notes could be put through the door of deviant recyclers and/or information col-lected for follow-up educational visits to houses; see Chapter 4). This achieve-ment of the ontological ordering of people and things, through classification and accountability, held at its centre the governance pair of the recycling box and its owner. That ontological governance may not have been accom-plished smoothly—with leaflets lost or ignored or never possessed, responsi-bility only taken on occasionally and to a limited extent and accountability shifting between and perhaps falling between parties—did not diminish the centrality of the governance pairing. The pairing remained obdurate while classification and accountability shifted.

3.6 Conclusion

In this chapter, we have used the example of waste management to detail the ways in which governance brings people and things into ontological being through classification, and the ways in which the ordering of people and things is policed through various forms of accountability. However, we also noted that classifications, accountabilities, and ontologies are subject to criti-cism and revision, and are noted as problematic, multiple, or, on occasion, rendered uncertain.

Recycling in Britain in recent years has been based on the mobilization of a complex problem—that too many things are being classified as rubbish (where rubbish connotes, for example, things buried in the ground, out of sight) and that many of these items could be productively converted (trans-lated, shifted from one category to another) through recycling schemes. The definition of this problem has involved the construction and imposition of a central ordering, namely, that things should be separated out, not just into categories of recyclable and non-recyclable, but also into types of recycla-ble material (and contracts established between local authorities who collect the items and private companies who do the recycling). This also entailed the establishment of a national system, operated by DEFRA, to collect and compare and set targets for, and establish a market for, percentages of weight of waste recycled. The responsibility for increasing the weight of waste recy-cled was delegated to local authorities. In Oxford this resulted in the County and City Council effecting a further distribution of accountability whereby householders were configured as 'responsible' (where responsible recycling equated to a range of different actions including cleaning certain things so they can be put in boxes, putting certain things in certain boxes, travelling to certain locations to find correct containers, and so on). The whole process involved the use of a range of mundane technologies (green recycling boxes, recycling lorries, recycling centres, containers, signs), attempts at configuring via mundane technologies (instructions for households on how to fill the boxes, signs in recycling centres about the appropriate use of containers), and accountability relations (reprimands when recycling boxes are incorrectly filled, people and cameras to monitor activity in recycling centres, the publication of achieved percentages of recycled waste).

On the face of it, this is a formidable governance system.[29] However, on closer inspection messiness and multiplicity abound. There are multiple classification systems, accountability relations in theory and sometimes in practice, questions of responsibility delegated, deferred, or ignored and a system of governance that seems only just to hang together. Within this, though, one particular governance pairing remains relatively constant; in this case, boxes and their households. It is through this pairing that a form of governance, accountability, and classification is accomplished. It is also because of this pairing that ontologies are established (as waste or not, as responsible or not, as correct or incorrect actions). In subsequent chapters, we trace out these governance pairings (and other configurations of governance) and map out their stability or multiplicity, their endurance or fluidity. More immediately, however, we need to consider a feature of mundane governance thus far missing from our discussion. Although we have noted connections between, for example, national government policy, local authority work, and the governance pairing of the box and its household, we have not looked in detail at the moral basis for accountability relations. We have argued that entities are brought into being for governance through classification schemes that in turn establish the moral, sometimes financial, and sometimes political order of people and things. We have further suggested that ordering is policed in virtue of accountability relations. But we have not yet considered the very basis of mundane governance. Why should waste and recycling activities be governed? What is the basic rationale for mundane governance? Why govern in the first place? We turn to these questions in Chapter 4.

---

[29] The extent to which a better environment emerges as a result of the forms of mundane governance discussed here remains unclear. How effective is mundane governance? We return to this issue in Chapter 6.

4

Why Govern?—Is, Ought, and Actionability in Mundane Governance

4.1 Introduction

In the last chapter, we discussed the role of classification schemes in mundane governance. We showed how the constitution of ontologies through classification can provide the basis for accountability relations, and thence for assessments of appropriate and inappropriate behaviour. We also noted, however, at least as indicated by our observations of the recycling centre and kerbside recycling, that classification in action is very far from a straightforward determinant of action. It is instead characterized by messiness and indeterminancy.

In this chapter we interrogate the connection between ontological constitution and moral order in another way. We ask how mundane governance is justified in the first place. We ask how mundane governance is justified in the first place. Drawing again on the example of waste management activities, we ask what is the rationale for governing the disposal of stuff. Why do we need recycling? In recent years, the need for recycling has become an established feature of contemporary moral discourse of (at least) advanced Western societies. Many people share the sense that being a good citizen means contributing to the recycling cause. In school, children in many Western countries learn that recycling is good for the environment. While it is beyond the scope of our investigation to consider how this situation came about, to detail the socio-historical construction of recycling as a valued contemporary activity (Hawkins, 2006), it is important for understanding mundane governance that we examine extant rationales for recycling. What is the rationale for the collection and disposal of different kinds of stuff? What is it about the current state of waste disposal that necessitates particular courses of action? How do certain kinds of waste come to require one sort of treatment rather than another? In short, we examine the evidential and moral work involved in governing the mundane: how is a particular state of affairs, or set of attributes, established and how these are made to implicate certain courses of preferred action?

The collection and use of 'evidence' was clearly central to the activities and operations of the local council waste management team we studied: from council inspections and surveys of household recycling containers to the use of CCTV cameras at the waste management centre. Evidence was used to provide a basis for establishing the nature, appropriateness, and accountability of governance in relation to recycling. But how does evidence work? How is it produced? To what degree does evidence move in a stable, immutably mobile manner (Latour, 1990)? How are the nature, morality, and accountability of evidence established and maintained?

To address these questions we begin by considering recent social science research on evidence. We then discuss this in relation to a longstanding philosophical problem—the centuries old question of how to move from matters of 'is' to matters of 'ought'. By closely examining how this kind of move is managed by our local council recycling team, we propose a respecification of the relation between what is the case and what ought to be done about it.

4.2 Evidence, Is and Ought

How then to understand the nature and consequences of the ways in which assertions of 'mere' facts of the matter turn out to have an inbuilt moral imperative? What resources can we draw upon to address this question?[1]

Evidence-based research is a major feature of much recent social science. The focus of attention is the importance of evidence for establishing the basis for better policy making (Young *et al.*, 2002), decision making (Brownson *et al.*, 1999), or redirecting existing policy initiatives. Studies of evidence-based medicine (Dobrow *et al.*, 2003) have been especially prominent. These studies are associated with a more general enthusiasm for evidence-based policy and decision making. For example, the UK government has launched successive evidence-based initiatives[2] and has more generally emphasized the importance of evidence for policy choices.[3] The importance attached to evidence-based policy affects the priorities set by social science research funding councils, requiring that social scientists seeking research funding must demonstrate how the evidence (data) they produce will be of utility beyond

---

[1] What existing social science arguments *should* we recycle?

[2] See, for example, the spokesperson from the Prime Minister's strategy office discussing evidence-based policy in education: http://www.nationalschool.gov.uk/policyhub/downloads/JerryLeeLecture1202041.pdf

[3] For a typical example, see the evidence base, which is presented to back up the government small business policy: http://www.berr.gov.uk/files/file39768.pdf

mere social science audiences (Rappert, 1997) or will be made available to others who might make something of the evidence.[4] In all this, the faith in evidence as objective, scientific, and able to inform policy is paramount. It is claimed, for example, that evidence-based decision making involves 'moving professional decisions away from personal preference and unsystematic experience toward those based on best available scientific evidence' (Rousseau, 2005: 256). The challenge, as far as Rousseau and other advocates of evidence-based procedures are concerned, is to make professionals more accountable for producing good evidence, by ensuring they use specified procedures designed to minimize subjective influence, and by assessing how well they use these procedures. The contemporary drive for evidence bases can thus be understood as a technocratic flavoured search for improved guidance or justification for action.

By contrast, much other social science interest in evidence has focused on the way it is generated and used, largely without the aim of producing good or better evidence. The focus is on the generation and production of evidence rather than on identifying and securing evidence for policy purposes. This work is exemplified by studies of, for example, fingerprinting (Cole, 2002), DNA (Lynch and McNally, 1995) and expert testimony (Jasanoff, 1998). These studies treat evidence as an accomplishment rather than a matter of fact. They draw on the traditions of Science and Technology Studies (STS)—with its longstanding interest in the construction of laboratory scientific facts (for example, Latour and Woolgar, 1986)—and on ethnomethodology—with its concern for the ways in which members accomplish an everyday sense of the world (for example, Pollner, 1974). The ethnomethodological approach investigates the use of members' methods in the production of evidence, drawing on early work by Garfinkel (1967), particularly on coroners, and Sacks (1972) on police officers. In this approach, the production and use of evidence is not interrogated for the adequacy of its reference to some matter available out there in the world. Instead, evidence is understood as an active, directed, accountable, and occasioned accomplishment. In this sense, evidence does not straightforwardly stand in for some other matter, but neither does evidence speak for itself (Daemmrich, 1998). Through complex and co-ordinated interactions, evidence is accountably, demonstrably accepted as evidence for all practical purposes of the matter at hand. In our investigations of governance, this suggests treating the evidence of governance as an accountable accomplishment.

Whereas the former approach to evidence corresponds to a largely epistemological interest in evidence—how best to apprehend (and act upon) the

---

[4] See, for example, Economic and Social Research Council for criteria for outreach in research, available from: http://www.esrc.ac.uk

state of the world 'out there'—the latter approach hints at a more ontological concern—how is the world enacted or brought into being in the first place. This way of expressing the distinction perhaps starts to explain why the former approach can seem more conducive to policy relevance than the latter approach. Confidence in capturing (evidence of) the world seems to make recommendations and action more possible than does the sceptical stance characteristic of STS and ethnomethodology. This way of thinking about the problem depends on the idea that reliable evidence is the necessary precondition for action. Yet this proposition itself has a somewhat chequered history. For philosophers this is a debate focused on matters of 'is' and 'ought.' David Hume wrote in 1739:

> In every system of morality, which I have hitherto met with, I have always remark'd, that the author proceeds for some time in the ordinary ways of reasoning, and establishes the being of a God, or makes observations concerning human affairs; when of a sudden I am surpriz'd to find, that instead of the usual copulations of propositions, is, and is not, I meet with no proposition that is not connected with an ought, or an ought not. This change is imperceptible; but is however, of the last consequence. For as this ought, or ought not, expresses some new relation or affirmation, 'tis necessary that it shou'd be observ'd and explain'd; and at the same time that a reason should be given; for what seems altogether inconceivable, how this new relation can be a deduction from others, which are entirely different from it. (Section 3.1.1, page 27)

The distinction between 'is' and 'ought' became known as Hume's guillotine (Black, 1964). The cut is one of logical reasoning. Hume argues that statements about what something 'is' do not provide the grounds for saying what 'ought' to be. This led to a back and forth debate about the value of the guillotine.[5] Shurz (1997), for example, dismisses counter-examples of logical statements where 'ought' appears to follow from 'is' on grounds of relevance. This follows Searle's (1964) attempts to derive an 'ought' from an 'is'. The problem of moving between 'is' and 'ought' has also been taken up in trying to analyse the logic of connections between ethics and economics (Cassidy, 1995), objectivity and objectivism (O'Neil, 1983), and even tea drinking and Englishness (Prior, 1960). However, Singer (1973) argues that the whole is–ought debate is trivial and far from central to questions of moral philosophy.

Hume argues that although derivations of 'ought' from 'is' are often presented as sequential and additive (the 'ought' is enabled by the 'is'), the 'is' in fact provides no logical basis for the 'ought'. Of course, we are more interested in the practices of waste management and recycling than in contributing to debates about logic. So how does this work in discussions of recycling?

---

[5] Even including bad jokes about an obsession with oughtism, see: http://veritasnoctis.blogspot.com/

Consider, for example, this excerpt from the BBC radio interview that opened Chapter 1, in which the Chair of the UK Local Government Association's Environment Board (Paul Bessant) articulates the following rationale for recycling:

> [We've previously had] the luxury of taking everything away and simply dumping it in a hole in the ground and those holes in the ground are not going to be there in the future because we have filled them all up.

An obvious summary interpretation: it is a lack of landfill that makes recycling necessary. But look more closely at how this is done. It is not that the (un)availability of landfill sites (holes in the ground) straightforwardly suggests particular courses of action. Rather, the linkage is accomplished by way of a whole series of morally weighted descriptions and enactments. Previous actions are said to have been a luxury. So already we know this was something we should not have taken for granted. Those actions are described as 'simply dumping'. Some rather less simple and more responsible actions are thereby presaged. The hole in the ground was just there, and we took advantage of it, but the holes are disappearing, or will disappear, so in this rendition 'simply dumping' becomes a somewhat short-sighted form of advantage taking. And, throughout, culpability for this state of affairs is assigned to a generalized collective ('we'). It is the actions of the 'we' that now need to be redressed. In line with our Dorothy Smith inspired understanding of the wrong bin bag in Chapter 2 we see, even in this short extract, how the world of holes and dumping is richly invested with moral order. For immediate purposes the key point is that this is much more than mere facts of the matter straightforwardly requiring a particular form of action. Instead, those 'facts' are inextricably entangled with a set of preferred activities, which they recommend.

Or consider the following example (taken from http://recycling-guide.org.uk/). Information about the benefits of recycling is provided under the heading: 'Recycling facts and figures'. The text begins: 'UK households produced 30.5 million tonnes of waste in 2003/04, of which 17% was collected for recycling (source: defra.gov.uk). This figure is still quite low compared to some of our neighbouring EU countries, some recycling over 50% of their waste'. The webpage states that 'Recycling is an excellent way of saving energy and conserving the environment' and readers are asked:

> Did you know that:
> 1 recycled tin can would save enough energy to power a television for 3 hours.
> 1 recycled glass bottle would save enough energy to power a computer for 25 minutes.
> 1 recycled plastic bottle would save enough energy to power a 60-watt light bulb for 3 hours.

A further paragraph is entitled 'Some Interesting Facts' and comprises a series of bullet points such as 'Up to 60% of the rubbish that ends up in the dustbin could be recycled; The unreleased energy contained in the average dustbin each year could power a television for 5,000 hours; The largest lake in the [sic] Britain could be filled with rubbish from the UK in 8 months; Up to 80% of a vehicle can be recycled', and so on.

Once again a simple summary message can be discerned: the array of 'facts and figures' *makes clear* the benefits of recycling. The statement of facts includes, in particular, a selection of familiar energy consuming activities (television, computer, light bulb, paper) each tied to an item of recycling. The list is organized so as to link each recycling item to a calculated measure of energy saving. The value of recycling is thereby articulated. And in articulating the value, the implicit good of the activity is asserted. So, just as in the first example, we start to see how the values are decidedly not innocent. They are expressed in virtue of a constituted moral order richly populated with 'ordinary' activities, dispreferred behaviours, unappealing actions, generalized actors ('you', 'people'), things that could be done (composting, recycling), and unfulfilled desires (people who would recycle if it were made easier).

All this is in line with the way we have presented previous examples. We have seen that coffee is not just coffee, it can instead be recklessly and irresponsibly hot. We saw that the bin bag was not just a bag, it can be 'wrong'. We shall see that the 'presentation' of one's recycling container can be 'incorrect'. So we could quite happily conclude that the moral 'ought' associated with an entity is not sequentially derived from an 'is', but is instead already contained within the constitution of what that entity 'is'. In other words, the 'ought' already inhabits the ontological classification of stuff.

Fair enough. But a reflexive observation suggests a subtle further development of this. We are saying there is no logical problem of moving from an 'is' to an 'ought' because the 'ought' is already part of the 'is' (and vice versa). Of course, this statement makes an ontological claim (that ought *is* already part of is) from which we derive a particular preferred course of action (that we should pursue a different problem from Hume). On the one hand this re-emphasizes the deep entanglement of 'ought' and 'is': it reinforces the idea that descriptions of a situation are always bound up with considerations of what can or should be done in response to the situation. By the same token, this suggests that work is always necessary to accomplish the 'is' and the 'ought' and the relation between them. So instead of just concluding that the 'ought' already inhabits the ontological classification of stuff, we would be better saying that whether or not the 'ought' inhabits ontological classification is the upshot of the work done in rendering ontology. In other words, we need in every case to figure out what is the constitutive work being done to make it seem as if the 'ought' is separate from the 'is'; to represent statements as the objective basis for making decisions about what to do; or to make the possibility of action separate from the (mere) description of the state of affairs. So our problem is very different from Hume's. We want to understand how evidence is produced for all the ways it implies something other than, or different from, straightforward descriptions of the way things are. Importantly, as we say here, this includes not just what ought to be done but also what can be done.

To pursue this we ask two questions of our empirical material. The first question begins from the ethnomethodological and STS tradition described earlier: in matters of mundane governance, how in practice is evidence constituted? The second question addresses a largely overlooked aspect of evidence-based policy discussions. Namely, in what ways and to what extent does the practical constitution of evidence also imply what can and/ or should be done? Note that this extends the remit beyond the is–ought question. We need in addition to explore in detail how the constitution of evidence brings or fails to bring into being further action, on whose terms, assessed by what means and with what consequences? In other words, we need to explore the constitution of action-able[6] evidence.

If we allow that 'ought' is entangled with 'is', there is no reason to suppose that what-can-be-done is not also entangled. So we need to understand how all three of what is, what ought to be done, and what can be done are in principle constituted both in the gathering of evidence and in its representation. And where there is a cut (guillotine) between any of these three elements, we need to understand how that cut is accomplished and sustained.

In place of a philosophical question about logic and derivation, then, we are faced with a practical question of mundane governance. How does the constitution of evidence bring further governance activity into being? The connection between the constitution of evidence and subsequent action often appears strained, challenging and unclear to those involved in governance. How, for example, does a detailed picture of the recycling activities of a city population and how that city ought to act constitute the basis for more of that action?

---

[6] The term action-able draws on ethnomethodology's use of the hyphenated version of account-able; denoting, for example, a turn in a conversation that demonstrably and accountably carries its ability to be an account.

4.3 Constituting Evidence as 'Is', 'Ought', and Actionable[7]

Over a number of years national UK government initiatives[8] have put increasing pressure on local authorities to recycle more. This has generated a wide range of activities whereby waste can be measured, assessed, traded, shipped out, or recycled. In line with these pressures and hopes to attain higher rates of recycling, the waste management activities of Oxford City Council abound with candidates for treatment as matters of 'is' (mostly focused on questions of what it is that householders do with their waste and recycling and on discussions of techniques for amassing evidence of this activity). However, each of these activities can also be seen to involve putative 'oughts' (what should be done in response to this situation) and putative further actions (what means can be used to encourage householders to recycle more). Hence it would be too simple to say that waste management activities fell neatly into a singular dichotomy of 'is' and 'ought'. Here are three illustrative examples of the ways in which attempts to constitute the nature of what a matter 'is' always and already involve constituting matters of 'ought'.

First, the City Council devoted a great deal of time and effort to establish the most appropriate means of representing what recycling householders in Oxford were doing. Dan participated in a series of meetings with the Oxford City Council waste management team (whose members Sheila, Trevor, and Harry we first met in Chapter 3), which discussed at length the best way of producing evidence of recycling in Oxford. Different methods appeared to move in and out of favour at each meeting according to available budgets, theories about what residents were like, availability of staff to carry out the work, and so on. The managers did not always agree which was the best method for capturing what householders did with their recycling nor how they might best encourage or reaffirm the moral virtues of recycling. Over several months, Dan, Sheila, Trevor, and Harry discussed more or less equally argued but incompatible methods:[9]

---

[7] The materials for this chapter are drawn from an ethnography of Oxford City Council waste management, also discussed in Chapter 3.

[8] Although recycling was said to be a prominent local business activity up until 1950, successive local government acts placed the formal policy emphasis on landfill. Although California among other places was noted as introducing kerbside recycling in 1973, it took until 1990 for the UK government to pass the Environmental Protection Act, which placed an emphasis on local authority recycling. This Act was followed by a series of further pieces of legislation discussed in Chapter 3, for a history of these Acts, see: http://www.greatgreenlist.com/Recycling-History-222.html

[9] The indented sections of this chapter are based on Dan's field notes. Round brackets indicate comments noted at the time in the diaries as asides. Square brackets indicate comments added later for clarification.

Door to door surveys These were initially pushed by Trevor on grounds of scale—that many households across the city could be included [a more comprehensive 'is']—and as an opportunity for distributing leaflets to householders on how they could recycle more [a potentially effective 'ought']. However, Harry eventually decided—after several meetings in which door to door surveys came into and out of prominence in discussions—that these were too expensive. While the 'budget move' in these meetings seemed to provide Harry with a decisive hand in shaping decisions (he was recognized as the person in control of budgets), Harry also seemed to work to assuage Trevor who had been championing this way of doing things. Harry suggested that perhaps door to door surveys could be reconsidered and might be more effective once further data on householders' activity had been collected. This was a successful deferral, despite appearing [to Dan] to be devoid of a clear rationale.[10] Harry vaguely suggested that other data could perhaps be used to target surveys at specific householders more effectively.

Focus groups Sheila suggested it would be a good idea to run focus groups in schools or community centres on the basis of wanting to both collect ['is'] and give ['ought'] people information on her proposed scheme to reward recycling. The scheme appeared to involve having a number of residents (perhaps only one) in each street sign up to be local 'champions of recycling'. It would then be their job to encourage others to recycle. They would receive a fridge magnet as a reward for being a champion [the relevance of this token was not clear to Dan, although he somehow felt obliged to nod enthusiastically when this suggestion came up]. Once again, these focus groups were deemed a more appropriate later activity, mostly this time by Trevor. The deferral in this instance was predicated on the need to find out more about residents first, prior to carrying out focus groups. Trevor also raised questions about the objectivity of a focus group as part of which a pro-recycling scheme was launched. Harry concurred, confirmed the deferral, and suggested focus groups could be carried out on a smaller scale after the more general collection of data on householder activities (without specifying what the more general collection might involve).

Waste audits These were discussed at two meetings. Sheila had picked up the term at a national recycling meeting. However, it turned out that no-one knew what exactly the term meant. Between them, Sheila and Dan decided that it probably involved collecting black bin bags that had been left by households for collection, taking them back to waste management headquarters, opening them up, and separating and weighing the landfill and the materials which could have been recycled. Harry said this might contravene the Data Protection Act, although he was certain that it was the council's rubbish, not the householders (on the grounds that once waste was put out for collection it legally belonged to the council). Waste audits were never definitively shelved, they just seemed to slip

---

[10] It was frustrating that matters of apparent concern just seemed to slip into and out of view in these meetings. But perhaps the frustration in trying to identify a rationale for the team's decision making arose because the ethnographer mistakenly assumed that there must be such a rationale.

from conversation in line with a distinct lack of enthusiasm (and volunteers) for going through household waste.

Participation surveys These were pushed by Sheila on the basis that the City Council had used them on a previous occasion. The method involved sending out survey teams to score households' recycling boxes [each household is given a green recycling box and instructions on how to use it (see Chapter 3) and so the rationale goes that each box could be scored on how successfully the household has followed the instructions on use]. Harry expressed some reluctance as the previous survey had been carried out and the results ignored or discarded. Sheila thought this was because previous surveys had been relatively crude and did not return entirely useful information. At this point Sheila suggested that Dan (the social science researcher) could help make the surveys more scientific. Harry and Trevor eventually agreed to surveys on the basis that they had been done before (even though they suggested that these had been unsuccessful), and they could be carried out by available staff (that is, injured binmen restricted to 'light duties', and the seemingly keen ethnographer) and so would not impinge on the budget. Sheila agreed to redesign the surveys, and to add more categories and 'science'.

After several meetings, then, participation surveys became the principal candidate for constituting recycling evidence.[11] So we see that the decision to adopt surveys was the upshot of various meetings, discussions, claims and counter claims, and incorporated ongoing discontent among members of the waste management team (which re-emerged later, discussed further). Whereas Humean concerns centre on the logical challenge of getting from an 'is' to an 'ought', the concerns of the waste management team centred on how even to begin the process of getting an 'is'.

Second, constitution of evidence always and already contained both matters of 'is' and 'ought'. For example, focus groups were designed both to figure out why residents were currently recycling little and to encourage more recycling. Similarly, door to door surveys constituted both 'is' and 'ought', finding out more about households while also encouraging more recycling. It took nearly three months to reach the decision that participation surveys were the appropriate way forward. Tied into these discussions were various assumptions about what would follow these participation surveys. That is, potential, putative 'oughts' that were already on the table as candidate methods (focus groups, door to door surveys) were deferred. Hence each of the alternative methods for constituting householders' recycling activities—as matters of 'is'—was already 'contaminated' with a possible future 'ought'.

Furthermore, these potential means for constituting evidence were already being discussed in terms of future, more specific, more targeted activities, which would aim to use data to target areas that did not recycle much, but

---

[11] Even though Harry and, to some extent, Trevor remained concerned that the surveys might just repeat the disappointing results of previous occasions.

in the view of the waste management team could recycle more. As part of these discussions, the recycling managers voiced their various assumptions about particular areas of Oxford that they expected the surveys to confirm or support. Sheila said 'we all know North Oxford...' with no further explanation. She suggested that people in Blackbird Leys (a council estate to the east of Oxford) don't recycle much. Harry began to talk about the 'Marston problem'—Marston being another area in Oxford—although the nature of the 'problem' did not become clear to Dan until a later meeting, discussed further. So in deciding that participation surveys were the preferred instrument for constituting evidence, the managers brought to bear a form of folk sociology about the kinds of people and their likely recycling behaviour. They anticipated that surveys would confirm their expectations about the recycling characteristics of north Oxford, Blackbird Leys, and Marston.

Third, having settled on participation surveys as a means to constitute evidence of recycling in Oxford, discussions continued on the most appropriate means to carry out a survey. It seemed that a survey team would be sent out with recycling crews to give a score to household recycling boxes. But there was a question of resourcing the survey: who would do the surveying? Dan agreed to act as a surveyor along with two students Ju Min and Hamden. Further, although participation surveys had raised the least opposition among the recycling managers, Sheila thought that previous surveys had been limited in the range of things they scored. The following is from a meeting between Shelia, Dan, Ju Min, and Hamden:

> Sheila sets out the logistics of the survey. There are between 1400 and 2000 houses on each [waste collection] round and 43,000 houses in total. She wants to get 100 per cent of houses [incorporated into the survey]...There are five rounds per day and she wants one [surveying] person working twenty minutes ahead of each collection crew round. This is difficult because if the [surveying] person gets there too early, the recycling may not have been put out [by households], too late and the van will have already collected it. Hamden asks what if people rush out with boxes when they see the van? Sheila suggests no survey is 100 per cent. [This seems to contradict her earlier aim for 100 per cent].

The surveys would hence involve five survey members who would attempt to give a score to each household's recycling box by walking twenty minutes ahead on the round that recycling collection crews followed. For Dan, Ju Min, and Hamden this left a question mark about the scoring. What were they supposed to use to score householders' recycling boxes? Sheila left the room for some time at this point, when she returned:

> Sheila comes in with coffee [just for her] and a range of folders and files. She reveals these to contain lists of streets taken from 'GIS' data with house numbers and street names. Each set of streets is prefaced by a map showing the day and

round (such as Monday round one) which includes a picture of streets. The GIS data has been 'scored' using a four part number system to record '1 box out' '2 contaminated' '3 box collected' '4 box not out.'

It turned out that Sheila was giving us the results of the previous 'failed' participation survey. The survey team on that occasion had scored the boxes on the rounds they had covered using a four-part system. This had then been lightly collated to present areas scoring a high number of 1s, 2s, and so on. Ju Min asked what counted as box contamination:

> Sheila said that 'contaminated' can mean cardboard and plastic [which Oxford City Council did not recycle at this time] being left in the box. Sheila suggests she knows that there will be no other contaminates. [However, in this survey 'box contaminated'] can also mean the box was not in the right place. Not in the right place is different from box not out. Sheila informs us that the box must be within a metre of the kerb.

Sheila seemed to suggest that having an extra score for 'box not in the right place' will repair the deficiencies of the previous survey. Dan was surprised that survey results would be overlooked just on the basis of a missing category. Ju Min and Hamden were confused. Why did the survey need a score for 'box not out' and 'box not in the right place'. Rather than offer a reassuring answer, Sheila seemed to agree with the potential confusion and added more weight to the difficulty of scoring recycling boxes:

> Sheila points out that there are several circumstances under which boxes cannot be placed within a metre of the kerb and these are still recorded [she suggests some pavements are too narrow and in some places parents would not be able to get past with pushchairs/prams so boxes must be left further back from the kerb]. These boxes must be left in sight, although sometimes this is still OK if it is behind a gate. Sheila wants to add a new and separate category in the new survey '5 box not at kerbside'.

Meeting participants deferred to Sheila's greater expertise in surveys, given that she had completed the previous study. Although 'box not out' and 'box not at kerbside' seemed indistinguishable, the members of the meeting settled on the following scoring system for recycling boxes. The score sheet was different for each round and each day of each round. The left-hand column contained the road name and house numbers based on what Sheila called 'GIS data'. Then there were columns to the right of this with week 1, 2, 3, and 4. In the columns under each week we were expected to place a score next to the house number of 1–box out and ready to be collected, 2–box contaminated by incorrect material, weather, etc, 3–box already collected, 4–box not out, or 5–box not by kerbside, within a metre of kerb. The surveys would operate for four weeks and collect data on the same 10,000 recycling boxes each week.

The survey scoring system was designed to be a compilable, comparative tool. The results would be drawn together by weeks, by streets, by individual houses if necessary and could be further compiled into areas of Oxford (by drawing out data from streets in each area and adding these together). This might appear to have formed a comprehensive means for constituting evidence of the recycling activities of residents of Oxford. However, in the same meeting, surveys were already being drawn into future occasions for constituting further evidence both of matters of 'is' and what 'ought' to take place in Oxford household recycling:

> Sheila says the only things that can be recycled are paper, glass, cans and textiles [although paper must also be dry or damp, not wet or soggy; see Chapter 3]. She is interested in how much other stuff such as cardboard and plastic is left out. She is also interested in drawing this data house by house into follow up questionnaires so people can be educated into putting correct things in the boxes and to tell people where they can take things like cardboard and plastic.

These follow-up activities were already being drawn up by Sheila at this point in the form of surveys or her (hoped for) focus groups (to further this she had looked into the availability and cost of fridge magnets). Yet, simultaneous to consideration of potential future activities, the participation surveys at particular moments still seemed uncertain. On several occasions during the meeting Sheila turned to Dan, who seemed to have acquired a position of expertise in all matters of research, for reassurance that the scoring system, survey aims, and techniques were reasonable. On the day before the surveys were due to start, Sheila phoned Dan to discuss problems:

> Sheila phones and is worried about the survey selections she is making. She doesn't think that we can each cover an entire round so she is trying to look at the order of the round and decide which streets should be covered in what order. She says she is calling to find out if there is a scientific way of doing this. I suggest that if she works out a rationale for why certain streets have been selected, this is sufficiently scientific. I suggest that she constructs a sample of streets which map onto a geographical spread of each round. Is this scientific she asks? I suggest that samples are somewhere between what is practically possible and what you might want to do (she has previously suggested she wants 100 per cent coverage). She says she is 'relieved'. I am worried about being placed in the position of expert and the responsibility this role involves, but I do not say so.

Dan began to realize that he and the students were in no way neutral observers of waste management. They were closely and intimately entangled in the constitution of evidence, both in establishing what actions characterized recycling, and in constituting the moral character of governance pairs such as recycling boxes and their households (building on activities witnessed in Chapter 3). This felt uncomfortable: Dan began to feel responsible for whatever outcomes might follow the results of the survey work. But this sense of active involvement was not about to diminish. The survey team headed out on to the streets of Oxford to constitute evidence of households' recycling.

4.4 Evidence in Action

For Dan, it seemed very strange turning up at the bleak waste management yard early in the morning, during the wettest part of the year, and far removed from the comfortable environs of the University.

> We have to meet at 6.30 a.m. at the Cowley Marsh depot in order to receive our instructions from Sheila. I bump into Hamden outside who is wondering how to get into the building. When we get in, Ju Min is already inside helping Sheila to photocopy and colour in highlighter pen the routes of each round. In the reception area, crews are getting ready to go out. 'Light workers' [that is, those with back injuries who have never been called by their official title before today, but have been referred to as 'the lame and lazy', 'the walking wounded', etc] are joining the survey team to make the number up to five.
>
> There are some jokes amongst the crews about how 'light workers' will be dropped off, picked up and then taken home to bed as if they are a very delicate commodity . . . Sheila hands out the photo-copied maps that Ju Min has finished, A-Z maps of Oxford and clipboards (both of which she has purchased from WHSmith specially for this job), yellow jackets and pens (if we don't have one). Ju Min is working in Cowley so I drop her off before heading for Blackbird Leys.
>
> [On arrival] I look at my map and the route I am to survey for the first time and get lost while still in the car. Blackbird Leys has hundreds of tiny streets with similar looking houses. [I only work out later that it is divided up into themed regions—birds, flowers, spices, etc]. The first road I am supposed to survey appears to be totally wrong. The street is nothing like the photo-copied/highlighted map, houses don't match up to the . . . score-sheet I have been given. I do what I can and then I get back in the car as the recycling crew are already in the street and are looking to collect the [materials in the] boxes.

Constituting survey evidence of household recycling had begun to seem uncomfortably challenging. The streets, maps, routes, and directions seemed to have both an uncompromising systemic character (they had to be followed, otherwise, for example, recycling crews would catch up with the survey team and want to empty the recycling boxes before they had been surveyed) and a strange but instant messiness (the map looked nothing like the street, but the survey had to be completed quickly). Messiness rapidly extended into the survey scoring system:

> The scoring system is also confusing. Although only five numbers there is just about infinite variety in what each number can be made to do. If a box is out,

it should get a 1. But if it is just behind a gate, is this a 1 or a 5 (not by kerb-side)? Sheila said in some places pavements are too narrow to put boxes out so they get a 1 from me, but do they get the same from [all the survey] crews? And if a box is halfway back down a drive, is this a 1 or 5? Also if a box has paper on top, and is out, it should get a 1. However, what if there are things hidden beneath such as cardboard or plastic? Should it then be a 2 (box con-taminated)? Do I have time to check each box? As decisions have to be made really quickly to stay ahead of the collection crew I try and apply my scoring relatively consistently, but this is very tricky. Not all pavements are the same width so in some streets I think residents should have made more of an effort in putting the boxes out [closer to the kerb] and so I give them a 5. Is this fair? Also it turns out some people stack cardboard next to their box—do they expect this to be collected and so should I give them a 2 [box contaminated]? Or is it rubbish [coincidentally left next to the recycling box] and should I just focus on the green box and give them a 1? This is very confusing this early in the morning.

The [recycling collection] crew is very close behind me after three streets and they eventually catch up with me as I am finishing a street. They 'direct' me to where I am supposed to be going next, but their directions are completely wrong and after a few minutes I have to turn round and walk back past them again to go the correct way. The collection crew find this humorous. They want to overtake me, but they've been asked not to, but they don't want a longer working day because I am holding them up. This is not a very tense situation, but they make jokes such as 'if you've got a pen, you've got an easy job' and 'you'll have to run if you want to stay ahead of us'.

By day three of the survey, scoring methods were being placed under further scrutiny:

I have to work out if each box is just a 1 or a 2 (contaminated) or even a 5 (out, but not close to the kerb). Trying to work out what is contaminated or not can be very slow (going through each box and working out how wet the paper[12] is or if the wrong things are in the box) or very quick (a quick glance to see if things are more or less, or at least visibly apparently OK).

Here then are some of the problems of constituting evidence in action. The household recycling box, its content, and position all have to be translated into a single score. But what about the boxes and their contents? Questions such as 'Does this box contain the correct contents?' and 'Is the box 1 metre from the kerb?' prove to be much more difficult than they appear. Does the box look like it has the right kind of contents, are the contents correct enough, is the box close enough to the kerb? The survey has no space for recording problems and uncertainty. Instead, fixed numbers have to be recorded at

---

[12] As in the classification system of Chapter 3, dry and damp paper can be collected for recycling, but not wet or soggy paper.

speed. Following concerns raised by the survey team, Sheila called a meeting to establish if scoring was being done consistently.[13]

In addition to the basic challenge of scoring household boxes at speed, four main difficulties played into our attempts to constitute evidence. First, the difficulties of scoring were exacerbated by seemingly continuous mismatches between the number of houses in a street as stated on the survey sheets, and the number of houses in the streets themselves. Second, bank holidays proved problematic. The normal schedule of recycling rounds was disrupted when a bank holiday fell on a Friday or Monday (or on both days at Easter) because recycling collectors were entitled to a day off. This meant that householders should put out their waste and recycling in line with the disrupted schedule, crews should collect on different days and the survey team should follow. As Sheila explained on day four:

> Tuesday's round will be Friday because of the holiday and that Wednesday will be Monday, Thursday will be Tuesday (etc). Hamden is confused and looks like he wants to give up. Sheila seems quite relaxed about the confusion.

Members of the survey team wondered if survey results might be adversely affected by these changes in shifts: perhaps households would find they had missed their recycling collection day. Third, the scoring process began to speed up. One reason was the weather: the survey team just wanted to get out of the rain as quickly as possible:

> Today's round is relatively quick as the weather spurs me on to not look into potentially contaminated boxes too closely: if the paper looks wet, it is contaminated, otherwise boxes are fine.

But in any case, and irrespective of the weather, the survey team found their scoring was getting faster. Dan recalls that by day twelve, his scoring of surveys had become 'incredibly quick':

> I am getting very quick at assessing boxes now. In a quick glance I can quite reliably constitute the correct score for the box (a couple of times I test myself by giving the box a quick score and then looking through it more thoroughly. Each time I score it the same by both methods). This quick glance scoring system, I think, is based on my expectations of the area and an approximate view of the street and what kind of street it might be, what I can see on the top of the box, where I think the box is and how much effort I think the people have put into placing the box where it is. Under this system to score a 1 is easier on some streets than others. If it is a low participation area and the box is not that close to the kerb it might still

---

[13] Although Dan and Ju Min dutifully turned up, no one else did. Consistency remained a mystery.

get a 1 (not a 5), but I score more harshly in high participation areas where the box must be closer to the kerb to get a 1. I have no idea what my justification is for this system.

We see how the increase in speed of scoring speaks to a particular combination of 'is' and 'ought'. Faster scoring was possible in part because of emerging ideas about how much recycling one might expect of a particular street, and how much recycling effort appeared to have been made. The survey team began to develop a sense of the kind of score that certain boxes in certain parts of the city ought to receive. This is not to say that the survey team no longer cared about the data they were collecting. Just as the rain spurred the survey team on to score recycling boxes quickly, by the latter stages of the research, team members were also deeply concerned that the rain might damage the paper survey. For example, on day fourteen:

> It is raining heavily today. I have the plastic sheet over the scores again. I really can't face the idea of weeks of work being washed away by the rain even if the survey and my technique are not very reliable.

Fourth, the survey team worried that changes in the recycling collectors' routine could also threaten the integrity of the scoring system. When the collectors changed the order in which they collected boxes, it often meant they got to the boxes and emptied them before the survey team could give the boxes a score. From day eight:

> Towards the end of the round the recycling crew drove past me in their van going the opposite way. I then discovered that [the boxes in] two out of my last three roads had already been collected. These were the first 3s [box already collected] that I had to score. They were a disappointment as in the . . . system they can only count as a failure [of the survey team]. If you are there in time, you should be able to see the box. I can only put this down to a change in route by the crew and make some comment on the score-sheet to that effect. I do not like being on the receiving end of my own . . . system.

Note here that by this stage the ethnographer is starting to assume ownership of the scoring system ('my own . . . system'). At about the same time, the survey team took it upon themselves to try to 'outwit' the collectors:[14]

> I change the order of the route today and do the roads that I had to score 3 (already collected) last week first. I then rush through the following streets in order to stay ahead of the crew. This requires me to run between some streets.

---

[14] This is of course based on the assumption (unquestioned by the ethnographer at the time) that the collection crew were indeed trying to outwit the survey team. This may not have been the case from the perspective of the collection crew.

I finish the round quite satisfied that I have successfully outwitted the crew who changed the route without letting me know.

All these features of evidence in action, experienced as difficulties by the survey team, can be understood as part and parcel of the resulting data generated by the survey exercise. Yet, over and above these particular problems, there emerged a further basic set of difficulties and uncertainties in apprehending the constituent elements of recycling. This set of difficulties, it turned out, was shared by the survey team and the collection crews (and, we surmise, by the householders themselves). The difficulties turned on such foundational matters as: what is in the box, what should be in the box, what should happen to the content of boxes, how should a box be 'presented',[15] who should be held accountable for the filling, positioning, and emptying of the box, and even what (actually) counts as a box?[16] Thus, for example, both surveyors and collection crews would come across black plastic bags piled up next to recycling boxes. The bags were intended for waste. The routine was that they were to be collected by the waste collection crews (who travelled the same round, the same day, but sometimes slightly later than the recycling crews), whereas the recycling boxes were to be collected and emptied by the recycling crews. However, when bags left next to recycling boxes were open and could be seen to contain recyclable material (such as newspapers), did they count as waste or recycling? Who should decide? How to figure out the intentions of the householders apparently responsible for such heinous category violation? Who should take responsibility for deciding the nature, correctness, and intent behind plastic bags?

Recycling crews made decisions based mostly on the time of day. They aimed to finish their rounds as early as possible to either go home or to get to their afternoon jobs. Often the recycling crews left items placed outside boxes for the waste crew to collect, thereby speeding up their own round. On occasions waste collection crews also left these bags to recycling collection crews (so as to speed up their rounds) meaning bags were not collected at all. An imminent lunch break sometimes provided the means to short-cut complex questions of ontology, morality, and intentionality.

This was just the start of difficulties for the recycling collection crews. Alongside decisions regarding who should collect bags of paper were decisions relating to the content of boxes. How wet was soggy? If the top few sheets of paper on a pile left in a recycling box were soaking wet, should all

---

[15] The term 'presentation' was used by the council in notices left for errant householders when chastising them for incorrectly placing their recycling containers (typically, too far from the kerb): 'We were unable to make a collection today because your wheelie bin was not correctly presented'.

[16] Collection might be refused, for example, if recycling paper was left out in a cardboard box, or in an unofficial plastic container.

the paper in the box be assumed to be the same? What if there was waxed paper in among plain paper; should all paper be sifted through at the kerbside? Tins should be clean. But how clean is clean? Should all tins be inspected at the kerbside before being taken? What about unofficial boxes left next to City Council issued boxes, should they be collected or left? And what about the system whereby households should be informed that they were recycling wrongly? All these actions took time and made rounds longer. Recycling collection crews often did not sift through boxes, checking levels of wetness or waxiness of paper or cleanliness of tin cans. Unofficial boxes were often just ignored. Notes were not written for households. Boxes that the City Council waste management team would describe as 'contaminated' (containing the wrong kinds of items) were either left or collected in their entirety depending on the amount of time crews felt they had available and how close it was to lunchtime. Figure 4.1 combines many of these uncertainties: a City Council recycling box not quite at the kerb; a box containing an apparent contaminant (a plastic bag); an unofficial extra box with more material in it. It seems 'wrong' in many ways and yet may be collected.

In sum, constituting evidence of recycling posed a number of challenges. Some effort was required to make the streets match the maps, the scores had to be made to match boxes, 'days changed' as public holidays disrupted the routine, the surveys had to be completed at speed, weather always appeared likely to intervene, and collection crews unexpectedly changed the order of their routes. In this sense, the actions of surveying and the objects and subjects of

Figure 4.1. Official and unofficial recycling boxes

surveys reconstituted the survey tool itself. For collection crews, questions were raised and not resolved over bags left by boxes and who should take responsibility for these; uncertainty remained as to whether the contents of boxes really needed checking that closely to maintain the integrity of the recycling system; and very few collectors maintained the accountability system, which required that they put notices through the doors of 'bad' recyclers. Although for philosophers such as Hume, the challenge lies in shifting from 'is' to 'ought', our survey experience leads us to propose that 'is' and 'ought' are both constituent features of the production of evidence. Scores were given on the basis of both visibility (for example, what we as members of the survey team thought we could see in boxes) and morality (for example, how much effort we felt had been made by householders and the score we felt they deserved). Evidence was thus morally imbued. In Section 4.5 we look at ways in which the content of boxes was treated as a moral depiction of the nature of households in attempts to constitute action-able evidence. As noted, we use the hyphenated term action-able here in a similar manner to ethnomethodologists hyphenated use of the term account-able; that is, accounts that are able demonstrably to prove their ability to be held to account.

4.5 Actionable Evidence

The work of constituting the survey materials in such a way that they provided a basis for further action involved the invocation of a variety of tensions, which occasionally dissipated or were held in abeyance. This was not a straightforward move from 'is' to 'ought', the moral was always and already contained in attempts to constitute the nature of people and things. Instead it was a shift from one focal point of ontologically moral constitution to another. How was evidence constituted as evidentially morally action-able? We will explore the idea that 'moral warrants' can be treated as discursive accomplishments (in this chapter in meetings between the ethnographer and the waste management team), which constitute the action-ability of evidence. We will look at the ways in which moral warrants might have sanctioned, brought into being, and ontologically constituted the action-ability of evidence (that evidence provided an evidential and moral basis for governance action). This builds on the work of Sacks (1972: 281) who suggests: 'We expect that there are specialized methods for producing from the appearances persons present such inferences as to moral character as can warrant the propriety of particular treatments of the persons observed'. What we propose is an extension of the subjects of moral character from people to people and things (to include recycling boxes, evidence, and survey tools).

4.5.1 Morally Actionable Evidence

In the recycling ethnography, the first set of questions raised subsequent to the surveying involved attempts to work the surveys into further action that would contain further combinations of 'is' and 'ought'. At this point Sheila had left work due to a non-specific stress complaint (never to return during the time of our study); this left the ethnographer playing the role of both describing the methodology and the results. The following is a field note excerpt from the first meeting after the survey with recycling managers Harry and Trevor:

> Harry then asks what the council wanted from this research. This surprises me. He seems to have little idea what Sheila's interests were.
>
> I explain that as far as I know, Sheila wanted to commission this participation survey as part of a recycling promotion drive to get more people recycling. The participation survey would give the council a starting point on what people were currently doing and this could feed into a range of activities such as a door to door survey (which could have [drawn on the participation survey for] accurate information on what people normally do), local events (like school promotions), localized posters (saying how much an area currently recycles), local personal recruitment (for example getting area agents to encourage neighbours to recycle) and so on. I also suggested that Sheila wanted to use the door-to-door questionnaire/survey and some focus groups to gather more information on what local people thought of [and to promote] recycling. [Looking back afterwards, this is perhaps the clearest expression of what the surveys were for.]

In this moment it seemed that the ethnographer was the central focus for constituting the surveys as morally action-able; this seemed to go so far that if the ethnographer failed to constitute a morally action-able path forward, the surveys would have been overlooked once again (this was the same fate that had met the previous incarnation of the survey). These interactions positioned the ethnographer as holding a tentative moral warrant—a warrant to be accomplished (or not) through further discussion with the waste management team. By moral warrant here, we refer to a discursively accomplished position whereby an interactor is situated as holding the kind of warrants to enable evidence to demonstrate its action-able moral nature (that is, the ethnographer is in a position to declare that the nature of the evidence is such that it itself is able to be put into action as a resolution to a particular governance challenge, such as the 'Marston problem', discussed further).

Initially this positioning and holding of tentative moral warrants was doubly surprising for the ethnographer. First, surely this was the City Council's own research? Although the ethnographer had helped with the research, why did he now hold the warrants that appeared to decide the fate of the evidence? Second, Harry was now asking questions as if he had never attended any of the previous meetings where different options were discussed for producing evidence of Oxford. Although a few months had passed since the surveys were first discussed and presumably Harry had other matters to attend to, this did seem bizarre. More was to follow. Even though the idea of recruiting recycling 'agents' and rewarding them with fridge magnets had seemed amusingly absurd to the ethnographer when introduced by Sheila, he now found himself in the position of promoting (or at least defending) this as the way forward from the survey in Sheila's absence. Harry seemed uninterested in fridge magnets and Trevor raised concerns about the integrity of the survey evidence itself. This excerpt is from the same meeting:

> Trevor then initiated a discussion of the problems with the participation surveys. These included: The start of the survey where we had no idea what the routes were or how to score accurately. The suggestion was made that in future, maps would be given out earlier and all surveyors would be taken on a test run of the scoring system; The problems with ambiguous scores. It was not always clear what score should be given to recycling boxes—particularly 'box contaminated' and 'box not at kerbside'. I said that we had to have a meeting early on to make sure we were all scoring this consistently. Trevor then tried to test me by asking if I would score a dirty can as contaminated. I said yes [I think this was correct]; The problem of whether or not to go through boxes. I said given the time constraints of being caught up by the collection crews, it was not always possible to go through the boxes in detail and see what was there, whether or not it was contaminated and so on. Trevor suggested that surveyors could go out earlier, but then the problem was whether or not people put their boxes out the night before or whether [household members] rushed out when they could see or hear collection crews and how this would affect early surveys.

These questions appeared to be inspired by Trevor's recent evening class diploma on social science research methods. It seemed that Trevor had a mild concern provoked by a desire to have run the surveys himself (perhaps this was a job he felt he should have been given rather than Sheila as he now had a diploma).

Even post-survey, the questions of what might form an appropriate method for constituting evidence continued. There was no particular resolution of these questions. The ethnographer attempted to defend what Sheila had been trying to do, Harry seemed to be losing interest, and Trevor seemed to want to discuss research methods. The only sign of resolution was that questions regarding the detailed completion of the surveys ceased for a time. As the ethnographer had apparently successfully defended the integrity of the surveys, the recycling managers' concerns turned to what to do with the surveys.

4.5.2 Evidence in Action?

Dan and Ju Min were invited back to the City Council to discuss the cost and utility of various follow-up activities, which could use the participation surveys as a basis to promote recycling. Ju Min suggested that door to door surveys might be too expensive with little reward and the ethnographer suggested focus groups might be smaller scale, quicker, cheaper, and produce more rewards than knocking on lots of doors that householders might not answer:

> Harry agreed that the large-scale survey would probably be out of the question. He also agreed that the focus groups could be a useful way forward. He then mentioned something worrying about scaling the focus groups up to cover 800 people. I was not sure what this meant. He was keen to get my availability known as soon as possible. He was worried that I was about to disappear on another research project for 6 months. I explained that this project was one of three I was working on and that my time was shared between them.

In this excerpt, the ethnographer appears once again to be positioned discursively as the holder of a tentative moral warrant, allowing him to talk on behalf of and propose bringing into being a course of action. Three weeks later we re-convened (it initially seemed) to discuss the development of focus groups. However:

> Harry announces that the purpose of the meeting is to set up and produce actions for the door-to-door questionnaire/survey. This is a surprise to me as I thought we were going to discuss the focus groups and I thought door-to-door stuff was on the back burner. It is also a surprise to Trevor who has come prepared to talk about the participation surveys and has prepared a report on this and a set of questions to ask me [concerns regarding the surveys it turned out had only been deferred not resolved].
>
> Harry says it is all very well to keep discussing things, but we need to turn the participation data into something useful and the way to do that is to use it for door-to-door questionnaires. Trevor says 'well actually there are some good reasons to talk about the data.' This is part of Trevor and Harry's on-going tension [more on the tension to follow]. Harry does not really spell out how the door-to-door questionnaires will make the previous survey useful, but it seems to be something like 'if we know what people actually do in their recycling, then we can look at what they tell us they do on their doorstep.' I am not sure why this is useful. Harry says the important thing is to talk about the practicalities.
>
> This begins a thirty minute discussion on what size of door-to-door survey is appropriate, what sorts of questions are appropriate, what sorts of answers should be collected (data protection is raised as a problem again) and whether or not this is an objective means of collecting data or a chance to promote recycling—Harry says it is both. This really annoys Trevor who declares that he has no interest in promoting recycling 'just for the sake of it and if people don't want recycling,

fair enough, they should be allowed to say so and the council could save some money.' Harry suggests the quick wins [that is, quick increases in overall recycling to waste percentage which is part of national government targets; see Chapter 3] can be gained in those relatively affluent areas that don't recycle much at present. Harry suggests this is the 'Marston problem'. Harry outlines that less wealthy areas are not interested in recycling [following the line of argument that less wealthy households have other more important things to consider like surviving, getting a job, etc] and wealthy areas like North Oxford already recycle quite a bit. The 'Marston problem' is that it is a relatively wealthy area that recycles little. It must, in Harry's logic, be targeted.

In these excerpts we see how the City Council waste management team and in particular its most senior member, Harry, were constituting the survey as evidence of the problems they had initially articulated before the survey. In this sense the moral order of the survey was pre-figured through the waste manager's understanding of the nature of those areas that were not recycling enough. However, the ethnographer's moral warrant appears to have been rescinded in this excerpt. It may no longer be the ethnographer who articulates the future course of action. What remained clear was that the nature of the evidence was moral throughout. There was no question of a Humean guillotine in trying to move from 'is' to 'ought'. Yet, this does not quite explain the upshot of all these efforts to constitute actionable evidence. To bring the story to a (temporary) end, a different kind of guillotine came into play.

4.5.3 A New Guillotine?

Although Harry's articulation of the 'Marston problem' neatly encapsulated the simultaneous constitution of 'is' and 'ought', evidence from the surveys did not accomplish stability in their discursive movements between participants in these ongoing meetings. The survey evidence did not move immutably (Latour, 1990), nor did the survey data 'performate' (Cochoy, 1998) Oxford recycling. Instead the evidence was subject to ceaseless and tireless further constitution and reconstitution, each act combining and re-combining is, ought, and action-ability in slightly new and distinct ways. Certainly, the evidence did not generate a definitive and final moral warrant for a new action-able mode of governance. This ongoing work was manifested in five main ways.

First, following his articulation of the 'Marston problem', Harry left for another meeting. Trevor then broadened the discussion and was keen to question whether or not recycling itself 'ought' to happen:

We then discuss Trevor's ambivalence to recycling. He says that he is against having to pay the council [through council tax] money to recycle stuff like junk mail that he never wanted. He says other people are probably against the idea of recycling more generally, that it's not like rubbish that you really are happy to pay to get rid of. If people don't want recycling, they shouldn't have to pay for it. On the subject of charging, he then says that if the council start charging for rubbish collection, that will be a mess—there is no way of knowing if bins definitely belong to single specific houses and, as with skips, people will start dumping what they can get away with in other people's bins so you will need bin security.

For Trevor it seemed unclear as to whether the surveys provided the kind of warrant he sought (a form of political support for recycling) to action a response.

Secondly, after Sheila's departure, the recycling initiatives seemed to lose momentum. It also apparently left the City Council with little idea of what it was they had been doing and it was down to the ethnographer to inform them of their own recycling survey activities. Although the ethnographer was positioned in these discussions as holding a tentative moral warrant through which he might demonstrably accomplish the action-ability of the evidence, he was slow to realize this position and was reluctant to play the warrant. By the time the ethnographer realized that in the absence of his warrant playing, nothing would happen with the surveys, discursive positions had moved on and the warrant to render the evidence action-able had slipped away.

Thirdly, tensions remained between Harry and Trevor. Although the source of the tension never became clear, Trevor's dislike of recycling seemed at odds with his position in waste management and contrasted markedly with Sheila's stance as an environmental campaigner. His dislike of recycling seemed only to emerge at moments where he was also saying something negative about Harry. Trevor was reluctant to use the surveys to constitute an action-able response in line with his negative views of recycling, but these negative views were not easily separable from his ongoing tension with Harry. The longer this tension continued and the more prominent it became in meetings, the more the tentative moral warrant held by the ethnographer slipped away from discussions. Although initially the ethnographer had been positioned in these discussions as an authoritative figure of research, he now found himself positioned as a figure called upon to witness (although not necessarily judge) the tension between members of the waste management team.

Fourthly, Trevor had recently completed an evening class diploma in social science research methods and appeared keen to be the person who decided on questions of how the local population should be researched. Having Sheila organize and run the surveys and then go off work did not leave the surveys in a strong position. Trevor's newly acquired expertise further shifted the moral warrant for rendering the evidence action-able away from the ethnographer; he no longer held an exclusive position as someone assumed to know something about research (although, of course, the extent of his knowledge of large-scale surveys was always open to question as far as he was concerned).

Fifthly, during the course of the meetings with Oxford City Council waste managers, Sheila had mentioned previous failed attempts to bring in external sources of funding for recycling initiatives. She had been in the process of attempting to get internal City Council funding for the fridge magnet initiative when she took sick leave. It seemed that City Council funding was highly sought after and without Sheila there was insufficient momentum to continue applying for funds for recycling. Harry even looked to the ethnographer as a potential resource. The continued absence of Sheila and of applications for further resources seemed to mean that the survey was left as evidence (10,000 household recycling boxes across the city, recorded each week for four weeks) for which no action-able response was likely to emerge. In this sense, there was no momentum to playing a moral warrant to render the evidence action-able as there was little funding for any action or drive to secure funding.

The cumulative result of three months of meetings building up to the surveys, a month of surveying and a further two months of reconstitution of the evidence as embodying various moral and political values and limitations was that nothing happened. Sheila remained off work, Trevor remained disgruntled with Harry, the council had no funding for their recycling initiatives, and the ethnography ended. A guillotine-in-action emerged, cutting the constitution of evidence from further moves to render that evidence action-able.

4.6 Conclusion

In this chapter we have explored the ways in which evidence is central to acts of ontological constitution. We have argued that the constitution of evidence involves bringing into being both 'is' and 'ought', always and already at the same time. This shifted our focus away from Hume's guillotine and the notion that a question of what some matter 'is' cannot provide a logical sequential relationship to questions of what some matter 'ought' to be.

We have also noted an important sense in which this constitutive work never settles. Our study of Oxford City Council's attempt to govern household recycling, featured three months of negotiation work, which went into building a tool of ontological evidential constitution—the household participation survey. This emerged through various invocations of alternate tools for bringing household recycling into being and constituting the rights and wrongs of such recycling (including other kinds of surveys, reward schemes, and focus groups). The production of a tool, however, did not lead to a settling of the matter of recycling. Instead weeks of work followed, focused on fine tuning and putting the survey tool to work. This survey involved eviden-tial and moral work. Navigating the city streets and attempting to fit streets to maps, dealing with the weather, waste collectors, the need to score recy-cling boxes at speed, accomplishing the nature of boxes, their households, and streets filtered into the evidence produced. Nor did the tool and the sur-vey work together finally establish a settled ontology of Oxford household recycling. Further work involved ongoing efforts to summarize, present, and analyse the survey data. Matters of 'is' and 'ought' were more or less skil-fully articulated in accounts of, for example, the 'Marston problem'. And yet more constitutive work was to follow. This involved work to reconstitute the evidence as action-able (constituting the evidence as promoting the action that the evidence itself could be presented as justifying). In place of any final settling of the nature of the moral order of Oxford recycling, a further guil-lotine emerged. This new guillotine cut the survey evidence from further action-able ontological constitution work, through the main proponent of recycling being off work, local tension emerging among the waste manage-ment team and the continued absence of a City Council budget for promot-ing recycling.

For studies of evidence-based policy that featured in the opening sections of this chapter, our analysis suggests we move away from assumptions that evi-dence needs to be objective and scientific (and that this can be achieved by following certain steps), and that challenges lie in policy decisions, to recog-nizing that the very nature of policy matters is predicated upon the nature of (practices, claims, ways of structuring) evidence in matters of governance. In the deep sense of ontological governance being pursued in this book, it seems that both 'evidence' and 'policy' require rigorous interrogation. Our initial analytic sensibilities (Chapter 1) remind us that it can always be otherwise, so that appar-ently very ordinary things (from survey scores to recycling boxes) can be use-fully confronted with what they have become. A detailed moral evidential order can be found in the very nature of the columns and figures compiled on sheets of survey paper listing scores for recycling boxes and their Oxford addresses.

Evidential work is thus continual (for example, each time a possible settling of matters of 'is' and matters of 'ought' emerges, it is subject to further ques-tions) and recursive (for example, each question of governance falls back into questions of evidence, accountability, classification, or alternative modes of governance). We can understand that this work to constitute the ontology of recycling boxes and their households through recourse to evidence both accomplishes and is accomplished through modes of accountability. In this sense, the City Council seeks to fulfil its accountability relations to national government (DEFRA) through bringing into being evidence that can simulta-neously represent and create more recycling in Oxford. This evidential consti-tution through surveys augments existing accountability relations between the local authority and pairings of governance (in this case the recycling box and its household). The constitution of such evidence acts as a further means to render people and things governable, while simultaneously providing a focal point for continuous articulations of the need for more evidence, accountability, and recycling. The moral order of evidence is hence both produced through accountability relations and open to continual reconstitution through accountability relations.

Chapter 5 now builds on the analysis presented thus far in Chapters 3 and 4 by turning attention to a hitherto neglected set of governance relationships. In Chapters 3 and 4 we mentioned the connections between governing authorities (for example, between DEFRA and local authorities) but did not explore these relationships. In Chapter 5, we begin to disaggregate these apparently monolithic entities: structures, institutions, and relations of governance. Drawing on our research into traffic management, we explore governance relations between national, local, and regional government. We explore how these governance structures come together, hold together, but also at times prove fragile.

5

Structures of Governance

5.1 Introduction

Barbara tries to manoeuvre the transparent film slide into a position where she can read it. She has been staring at the screen of the microfiche-style reader all day. Day after day. Her eyes are taking the strain. And her hands. And what about her back? She wonders if Health and Safety has any provision for eye-strain. But she has work to do. A seemingly endless stream of strips of film have to be read and identified, written about and sent off. Barbara peers again at the number plate on the image. The car looks like a black Nissan Primera. She had already scribbled that down on her notebook with the blue biro she was given. But the flash of the camera doesn't seem to have captured the black numbers and letters on the yellow background of the rear number plate as clearly as she would like.

Her job is all about being clear, coherent and intelligible; seeing the image, writing down the letters and numbers, verifying the identity of the vehicle. The Safety Camera Partnership can only issue a Notice of Intended Prosecution (NIP) if Barbara can read the number plate clearly. Her growing pile of 'unidentifieds' contains all the images for which clarity remains just out of reach. Too much glare, poorly rendered photographs, number plates modified to avoid detection, even mud strategically placed to conceal the number plate—now an offence in its own right.

Perhaps this one will not join her pile of 'unidentifieds' just yet. Barbara flicks the switch to turn the image from positive to negative. Black becomes white, white becomes black. The letters and numbers seem a little clearer. Less glare when you go positive-negative. She scribbles down a set of letters and numbers in her notebook. She looks up at the image again. Is it good enough? She has a whole pile of further images to get through. Barbara checks on the Police National Computer (PNC) and finds a black Nissan Primera with the very same letters and numbers on its number plate. This is clear enough. The image can be shuffled forward with the rest of her day's work, the images which will lead to Notices, fines for drivers and income for the Safety Camera Partnership which will keep her in her job.

Barbara's work at one of two microfiche-style readers in the office is central to the system of governing speed. In particular, and in line with our earlier discussions of waste management, we can see the importance of her work in constituting[1] the key ontologies that populate a different system of governance, in this instance the regulation and control of speeding traffic. In this case, ontological constitution includes bringing into being number plates, cars, and potential offences; operating classifications of speed, enacting responsibility pairings (in this case cars and their drivers), simultaneously accomplishing 'is', 'ought', and 'action' (a particular car is found to be driving too fast and its driver can and should be punished), establishing the identity of the driver (using the PNC to discover the owner of the car, and subsequently issuing a NIP to ask who was driving) and asserting various accountability relations (for example, by means of the NIP stating the legal responsibility of the owner to supply information about the driver). However, in this chapter we extend our portrayal of ontological constitution by considering the 'contexts' of mundane governance.

To what extent and in what ways does the context in which Barbara works bear upon the work of ontological constitution, and hence the operation of mundane governance? This way of expressing the question draws upon a familiar social science vocabulary. 'Context' is one of a set of allied terms—circumstances, prevailing conditions, situation, setting, climate, environment, surroundings, and so on—commonly invoked to make sense of interactions and activities. The uses of structure and organization are particular examples derived from this general collection. One or more of these explanatory staples are typically invoked in claiming to illuminate activities and practices that occur 'within' the context in question. The key assumptions in this usage are: scalar (that context is a wider, bigger, more encompassing entity than the activities being described); explanatory (that context explains, illuminates, or makes sense of these activities[2]); and, most important for our purposes, ontological (that context is a fixed, given entity that appears relatively stable by comparison with the activities and practices that

---

[1] Constituting is one of many similar terms, which have been used in recent years to critique the idea that entities, structures, etc pre-exist participants' active apprehension of those entities and structures. Related terms include shaping, aggregating, constructing, apprehending, performing, accomplishing, constituting, and enacting. This list represents (that is, constitutes) a continuum along which each term has a slightly different connotation to the extent that its usage differentially acquiesces with the presumption of a pre-existing external world. Thus, 'social shaping of knowledge' has much less critical edge than 'enactment of knowledge'. In this chapter, we favour constituting but sometimes use this interchangeably with other terms situated towards the right-hand end of the continuum (see also Chapter 10).

[2] Similar formulations of the explanatory relation include the injunction to understand practice 'in the light of' the context, or by 'taking into account' the context.

take place 'within'. In this chapter, we interrogate the notion of context in relation to the mundane governance of speeding traffic.[3]

Questioning the notion of context is particularly important for interrogating two key features of current understandings of governance. First, as noted in Chapter 2, a substantial literature on corporate governance gives priority to the nature and influence of organizational structure. Organizational structures are assessed for their ability to encourage or prevent the kind of organizational activities that lead to corporate scandals[4] (McLean and Elkind, 2003; Beaty and Gwynne, 2004); new organizational forms are said to promise better governance and this in turn means greater efficiency and productivity; corporate governance is said to increase responsiveness to relevant 'stakeholders', thereby reducing the distance between shareholders making investments in companies, and company boards, directors, and employees who are responsible for making something from those investments (Blowfield and Murray, 2008). In the UK a succession of reports and codes [the Cadbury Code (1992); Greenbury Report (1995); Hampel Report (1998); Combined Code (1998); Turnbull Report (1999); Higgs Report (2003); Smith Report (2003); Revised Combined Code (2003); each reported in Blowfield and Murray, 2008] have attempted to define the most appropriate means of structuring corporate governance. The central feature of all this is the uninterrogated assumption that changes in organizational structure or legislation determine changes in behaviour. But in what sense can governance be simply 'read off' organizational structure?

Second, as also noted in Chapter 2, neo-Foucauldian analyses of governmentality emphasize the work done to produce the truth of any particular topic of government; the work involved in producing the immoral as outside normative rationales from which ideal subjects can be assessed; efforts involved in the 'regularisation of liberty' (Osborne and Rose, 1999: 744) through which adherence to a rationale can be assessed; and the dependence on technologies of government to carry out assessment and generate liberty (for more detail, see Chapter 2 and Rose and Miller, 1992; Rose, 1996; Osborne and Rose, 1999; Ferguson and Gupta, 2002). But to what extent are rationales straightforwardly produced and communicated through technologies of government? Are these rationales analytically equivalent to another form of 'structure' within which subject positions act?

---

[3] This chapter draws on empirical materials from our ethnography of UK speed cameras. Dan spent time over a six-month period with ten safety camera partnerships (described further), observing their activities, collecting printed materials, and carrying out a series of interviews within each partnership. The interviews lasted for several hours each and were semi-structured. They involved key figures such as partnership managers, communication team members, and statisticians, along with police officers and management consultants. The materials have been anonymized in recognition of ethical sensitivities involved in road safety issues.

[4] For example, Enron, BCCI, and Robert Maxwell.

Our interrogation of the notion of structure looks first at the ways in which Barbara's work, reading number plates and issuing NIPs, contributes to the constitution of the speeding driver. Second, we look more generally at how structures of mundane governance are constituted and maintained. How do participants invoke notions of the 'context' in which they are working? In particular, what is the role of mundane entities such as speed limits and speed cameras in constituting structure? Third, we examine how the classification and positioning of the subjects of mundane governance (in this case drivers)—in particular through communication activities—contributes to ensure the endurance of governance structures.

5.2 Constituting the Speeding Driver

Barbara does not work alone. She sits at the centre of a large open-plan office, separated by moveable screens from various other people, representing other organizational functions. The office is part of the regional headquarters of the police force that forms part of the regional safety camera partnership (see below for more about partnerships). The office colour scheme is predominantly beige, in keeping with its dull atmosphere, the carpets a little worn, and the technology not quite cutting edge. It is an unspectacular setting. Barbara speaks of herself as sitting within an organizational structure. She talks about her line manager, Harold, who manages the safety camera partnership. She talks about the speed camera teams who remove the film from the cameras. She delivers her number plate identifications to the penalty notice team who in turn send out the NIPs (which require that drivers declare their responsibility for an offence) and penalty notices (which order drivers to pay their fines). Her description of these immediate others situates herself in an organizational chain for the production of evidence of speeding drivers.

Harold similarly portrays Barbara's role as somewhere in the middle of the process of producing speed camera evidence. Speed camera teams go out to collect films from a series of locations where the partnership have fixed cameras. The partnership has seventy-six fixed cameras, rather more than most other partnerships, and fifty-eight sites for mobile enforcement. Harold said the fixed cameras are the main means of reducing speeding.[5] When the speed camera teams return to the office with the film, the team's activities, when

---

[5] Mobile sites were operated by teams in vans who drove out to the location and recorded the speed of passing cars.

they went out, when they returned, what film they collected, who carried it, to whom they passed it in the partnership, are all recorded. These records make up what Lynch (1998) would call chains of custody for evidence, the integrity of which can be subject to dispute and detailed interrogation in court.

The production of an evidential chain of custody may sound straightforward. But it was subject to several contingencies. Harold explains that as the partnership operated under annual budget constraints (see Section 5.3), it can only employ a certain number of team members to collect and read film, and issue NIPs and penalty notices. The partnership had to decide how often to put in film, in which camera, how soon the film would be used up (that is, how many drivers would drive too fast past the camera and be photographed), how quickly film had to be collected to issue NIPs within legal stipulations (drivers had to receive the notice within fourteen days of their (alleged) offence) and whether or not certain cameras had sufficient deterrent effect through their presence that they did not need to be loaded with film. The partnership—comprising representatives of local authorities, the police, fire service, and NHS trust—would meet sometimes as frequently as once a month, sitting around the large round table outside Harold's office. They would articulate the evidential chain and set priorities for the enforcement of cameras, trying to strike a balance between budget, costs, road safety, and enforcement. The round table was the place for discussing chains of evidence: cameras, films, teams, collections, and possible occasions of future accountability. But evidential chains did not start and stop around the table. Once the wet film had been collected, the activities of the team recorded and stored, the film handed over and its hand-over recorded and stored, Barbara could then get on with reading the images. As we have seen, it was Barbara's task to come up with a viable, justifiable number plate, make and model of car, and address of the owner of the vehicle to pass on to the penalty notice team.

What is in the notice that subsequently hits the doormat of the (allegedly) offending driver? Any of this information about the number of cameras, budgets, road safety priorities, partnership meetings, the round table, Barbara's complaints about her eyes, back, hands, the PNC, the photograph of the driver or the car or the number plate? No. Harold gives the ethnographer a quizzical look. Surely, nobody could think this information would be made available to the driver? Harold showed Dan the partnership's filing system. Here row upon row and year upon year of paper records of offences are stored, evidential chains available in case the provenance of the case (which team had collected the film and when, who had taken custody of the image, the image itself, the record from the PNC, a copy of the NIP and penalty notice, the timing, identity, and address of the notice) should be challenged. Apart from the NIP and penalty notice, none of this was sent to the (alleged) driver.

The NIP merely informs the car owner that the car was caught on camera, driving above the speed limit, on a certain date, and at a certain time. The car owner is asked to confirm he or she was driving at the time of the offence or declare, instead, who was driving the vehicle. The subsequent penalty notice, addressed to the driver, states the availability of photographic evidence: 'This allegation WILL be supported by photographic evidence at any subsequent court hearing'. Otherwise words such as 'dispute' and 'appeal' are made less prominent. The notice is largely devoted to giving instructions on easy ways to pay (over the phone, in person, by cash, cheque, or card) and warning of the problems that would ensue should the driver fail to pay (a court appearance, a criminal record, a higher fine, recourse to a bailiff company entitled to seize possessions up to the value of the fine and to cover their own costs and make these available for public auction). The partnership wanted to encourage the driver to pay without disputing the penalty. If at any point, a driver chose to dispute a penalty notice, the case would go to court and any income produced would go to the court, not the partnership.

Once a NIP had been issued, a variety of responses can ensue. The registered owner of the vehicle can agree that they had been caught speeding and pay the fine. Or it can turn out that the vehicle ownership details are wrong. For example, it could have a different owner, have been stolen, be registered to an incorrect address, or have 'cloned plates'. Although each of these problems with the ownership details can lead to further prosecution, this depends on an assessment of how easy it would be to generate further evidence. Police officers from the relevant partnership force decide on the likelihood of tracking down the owner, the correct vehicle, correct address, and so on. The extent to which partnerships and police forces pursue these offences varies across the UK, according to differing priorities established for what counted as a worthwhile use of resources. For example, partnership managers described their success in getting penalty notices paid without dispute as the 'flash to cash rate'.

We have an 88 per cent success rate from flash to cash. There is a drop off. Drivers going 20 mph over the speed limit are dangerous drivers and we don't get the £60. [...] It will always be the case that we will get pictures you can't use, but technology is not a panacea. (David, 7/2/2005)

We're very active in pursuing non-payers. Up to 82 per cent now pay their fines. We have police officers now knocking on doors getting payments. If we can't find a car we'll use whatever we can to find that vehicle. We also use mobile vans and video to catch up with criminals. It's a good source of intelligence. (Christine, 18/2/2005)

Or vehicle owners choose to appeal against a penalty by going to court. Owners claim they were not driving the vehicle; fleet operators say they do not know who was driving the vehicle at the time; my aunt borrowed the car when she was visiting from the USA. Partnership managers again reflected on these issues:

> More people are going to court because of websites and literature on how to get off. Mobile cameras are not always as accepted as fixed. (Lucy, 8/2/2005)
>
> We have small non-payment problems. We'll pursue every offender. From a policing perspective people avoiding fines might have one or two other things to hide. More people are not responding, registering vehicles elsewhere, getting the wife to take the blame—we're trying to stay ahead of that game the public are trying to stay ahead of us. (Brian, 9/12/2004)

So we see that considerable work went into constructing a NIP and penalty notice, constituting evidence for the notice, and establishing a provenance in case of dispute. This follows themes we encountered in waste management (Chapters 3 and 4). The mundane governance of speeding traffic involves constituting evidence, constituting the ontology of people and things—in this case the governance pairing of vehicle and its driver—these ontologies are constituted as evidential, moral, and actionable throughout. Thus, drivers are positioned as accountably, demonstrably in the wrong and hence both deserving of and liable to punishment. At the same time, Barbara and her colleagues have helped us move a little further. We begin to see how structures of governance emerge as a result of the combination of partnerships, teams, staff, films, tables, microfiche readers, and meetings through which evidence was made to make sense, held steady, and backed up by further evidence should it be needed. The work of constituting the speeding driver can be understood as simultaneously constituting the structure of governance 'within which' speeding drivers are brought into existence.

The chain of activities goes toward constituting and maintaining a structure of governance, one notable effect of which is the structure protects itself from questions of accountability that subjects of governance might ask. Thus, penalty notices were designed to limit questions that could be asked about the evidence. The existence of photographic evidence was stated but none would be provided unless the driver chose to take the case to court. When on occasion (through disputes and in court cases) the evidence was challenged, the structure of governance was not itself called into question. Questions of accountability concerned matters such as 'Is that my car?' or 'Is it me driving?' rather than 'What right does the Partnership have to issue a Notice?'.

Furthermore, attempts were made to secure income for the ongoing constitution of structures of governance by positioning a dispute or appeal within a penalty notice as a difficult or risky option.

But why? Why did the governance structure work like this? Harold crumpled into a look of exasperation: the structure would take a while to explain.

5.3 Constituting Structures of Governance

Barbara's location in a set of regional police offices was not untypical. Hers was one of a national system of 38 safety camera partnerships. Almost all were based in local council offices[6] or in police buildings. This is perhaps unsurprising in that the two organizations were central to what partnerships did, drawing together local political management and legal enforcement. A notable exception was the UK's smallest partnership, with its office nestling anonymously in a row of more or less identical residential houses. So anonymous was this partnership headquarters that the ethnographer drove up and down the street, searching for it in vain. On advice and directions from passers-by, and nervously ringing on what appeared to be the front door of a private residence, Dan was ushered into a fairly typical British dining room. The partnership communication officer explained that this was the meeting room. The kitchen was the place for a cup of tea; the living room a place for relaxing on breaks; and Barbara and Harold's equivalents were at work in what would ordinarily be the bedrooms. Except they were not quite equivalent; while Barbara worked with wet film and microfiche readers, the staff in the 'bedrooms' were working with digital footage from mobile enforcement teams, using a system called Star Track.

The difference in this set-up raises questions about the uniformity of governance structures involved in traffic management. To what extent and in what ways do partnerships differ? More importantly, what are the consequences of differences between them, in terms of the constitution and pursuit of speeding drivers? It turned out that two distinct discursive registers were at play. On the one hand the invocation of a standard governance structure portrayed people, things, and practices as adhering to and in the process constituting a governance structure repeated across the UK. On the other, the invocation of a non-standard governance structure drew attention to the ways in which people, things, geographies, and rules differed (especially) in certain regional partnerships. What is the origin of this dual repertoire of

---

[6] Local and regional councils are political bodies in the UK with responsibilities for road and traffic management, alongside waste management, the maintenance of local facilities and utilities, and so on.

structures of governance? We decided to visit the management consultancy charged with setting up safety camera partnerships.

5.3.1 Invoking a Standard Governance Structure

In stark contrast both to the safety camera partnership operating from a private residence, and to Barbara's relatively modern, non-descript open-plan office, the ethnographer entered the plush offices of Grabitt and Scarper (G&S). He was offered a seat, at a glass table, in a meeting room, looking out over a glass atrium containing exotic palms, in a huge glass office building close to one of central London's transport hubs. Before the door was closed on the hectic goings-on of the office building, Dan was offered a mineral water. Still or sparkling?

Opposite Dan sat a management consultant in an expensive looking suit. He did not wish to be named, or recorded, or quoted, or see his company named in any publication.[7] He was happy, though, to talk about the ways in which the safety camera partnership national network was set up, and the role his consultancy had played. It was in this very office building that the national structure of safety camera partnerships, the assemblage of speed cameras, national guidelines, the handbook, the national safety camera board, vehicle drivers, and penalty notice payers was first brought into being. Dan was about to hear the invocation of a standard governance structure.

In 2000, in response to mounting criticism that speed cameras were unregulated and primarily designed to raise revenue, the Department for Transport, Home Office, the Treasury, and G&S introduced a pilot system for the formation of regional safety camera partnerships to be managed by a national safety camera board. Partnerships could include local police, highways agencies, unitary authorities[8] and other local political groups, NHS trusts, partnership managers, road safety engineers, communication staff, and so on. Over five years, the eight pilot partnerships were expanded to thirty-eight, encompassing 4500 fixed speed cameras and 1000 mobile cameras. The first Safety Camera Handbook established that partnerships were required to produce an annual operational case and a communications case, to be submitted to the board for assessment. The handbook specified that the operational case should state the number of cameras to be installed in the forthcoming year,

---

[7] Grabitt and Scarper is a pseudonym.

[8] Unitary authorities are single tier regional structures present in parts of the UK for the unified management of, for example, some larger towns. There are fifty-five unitary authorities in England.

justifications for these sites, costs of putting in new and maintaining existing sites, and overall costs and projected income for the partnership.

'Income' equated to the predicted level of speeding offences that would be committed and paid in the forthcoming twelve months. Subsequent to the first year of operation, such a figure should take into account previous years' figures, expectations that cameras would slow people down (hence reducing income), the possibility that some drivers would go to court,[9] and the possibility that some fines would never be paid. Partnerships were not allowed to make a 'loss' and should aim to spend a maximum of 95 per cent of predicted 'income'. All penalties would be paid into the Treasury and hypothecated back to the partnerships in response to their operational cases. The Treasury would retain the surplus. In 2005 this surplus was £21 million. The consultant leant forward for effect: this was the first such hypothecation system since the thirteenth century.

Here then is an invocation of a national governance structure, specifying rules, accountability relations, and the place and function of various bodies. The consultant depicted the national board as the overseeing regulatory body to which the regional safety camera partnerships were accountable. What then was in the handbook?

The handbook set out the grounds for justifying a fixed site speed camera, mobile camera site, and combination red-light and speed camera[10] site. The term 'safety camera' was coined to reflect the fact that not all cameras focused solely on speed. The handbook specified that a partnership could install a new fixed camera site if four people had been killed or seriously injured (KSI) within 1 km of road in the course of three preceding years and 20 per cent of drivers in that same 1 km distance broke the speed limit when surveyed. A mobile site could be justified on the same speed criteria, plus two KSIs. A combination site (speed and red-light camera) also required two KSIs. Exceptionally, sites that did not fit these criteria could be established in areas of concern (raised by members of the partnership or members of the local community, particularly in response to child KSIs). However, these exceptional sites should not account for more than 15 per cent of enforcement time.[11]

---

[9] If a driver went to court (even if found guilty) they would pay the court and not the partnership and hence the partnership would not receive the money.

[10] A camera that both monitored speed and whether or not drivers had jumped a red traffic signal.

[11] A complex formula based on how many hours a partnerships' cameras were in operation, based on how often new film would be placed in fixed cameras, how long it took for that film to be used up, then emptied, then replaced, added to how many hours of how many mobile enforcement vans would be put into operation. A percentage of enforcement time was thus a notional figure based on best-guess estimates of how many drivers would break the speed limit and use up wet film.

The placing of cameras should also adhere to handbook rules on conspicuity. Signs warning of a camera's presence should be placed 1 km before the site and the camera should be painted yellow (paint colour: no. 363 Bold Yellow BSC381C). The partnerships, to take part in the cost recovery hypothecation system, also had to commit to producing an annual survey of local public opinion, consider all other engineering possibilities before choosing a camera, review existing camera sites, and ensure all equipment had been approved by the Home Office Police Scientific Development Branch and was in accurate working order (with an up to date calibration certificate). The handbook had been updated year on year since its inception with further detail on what could be paid for by each partnership (in terms of types of communication and types of equipment, see below). Although partnerships were expected to demonstrate adherence to the handbook, such adherence was not legalized. That is, not adhering to the handbook did not form grounds for drivers to appeal against a speeding penalty (although such things as calibration certificates did come under scrutiny during legal challenges).

During his recitation of the standard governance structure, the management consultant from time to time paused and leaned back in his chair. Each occasion appeared to signal the opportunity for asking a question. But the ethnographer's questions were not a great success, perhaps because they seemed only vaguely relevant to the consultant's articulation of governance structures. During one pause Dan asked how the Home Office became involved in the scheme. The consultant moved into his engaged, leaning forward position, and made direct eye-contact with the ethnographer. Let me explain to you how politics works.

In 2000 while designing the operational features of the national safety camera system, G&S designed themselves into the governance mechanism. There needed to be a national oversight body. The partnerships could not be left to run themselves. Someone had to manage the implementation and operationalization of the first handbooks. The system could not be left unaccountable. Who could do this? Was there a government office set up and ready to take on this governance and accountability function? No. Yet the invocation of a national standard safety camera system depended on this scalar link, from national to regional and back again. G&S established themselves as the first national board, undertaking to provide safety camera governance and hold regional partnerships to account for the first three years of the operation of the system (by which time the government, in particular the Department for Transport, would be able to set up their own governance operation).

In 2004, the national board was transferred to the Department for Transport and became the national safety camera programme office. In mid-2005, the Department for Transport announced a freeze on the programme: no new cameras would be installed, all camera sites would be subject to review, the hypothecation system would be reconsidered and attempts would be made to reassure drivers that speed/safety cameras were primarily about road safety, not revenue raising. The safety camera programme was in limbo awaiting decisions about its future. The anti-speed camera lobby[12] heralded the freeze as a sign of victory, road safety groups expressed concern that the freeze might place future limits on the number and use of speed cameras, and government opposition suggested the freeze was a prelude to moves by the Treasury to retain a greater percentage of the fine revenue. Eventually at the end of 2005 the Department for Transport announced that the programme was working but would also be changed. A new handbook would be issued for 2006–7 and in 2007–8 the hypothecation system would be replaced. Instead of partnerships predicting their fine 'income' and projected costs for assessment, partnerships would present an annual plan setting out their road safety needs, taking into account actual incurred costs for each preceding year, to be assessed by the Department for Transport and linked to local-regional road safety budgets. All fines would stay with the Treasury and the budget available for partnerships would be announced ahead of each new financial year. Partnerships would also be allowed to spend money on more than just new speed/safety cameras.

The ethnographer glanced at his notes, looked through the glass table to the floor, noted the garish colours of the carpet, and then decided to ask the difficult question. Given that the consultancy was now designed out of the national safety camera programme, was this a less than successful outcome? The consultant lent forward once again. G&S's involvement in establishing the programme was a necessary success. The programme was an inevitable and valuable form of governance that enabled regional partnerships to fund important road safety initiatives while also providing sufficient links between partnerships and national government to keep such spending accountable and transparent.

The consultant's narrative invoked a hierarchy of regional partnerships reporting to the national board. The function of each organization could be read off the corporate structure. It began to seem like the corporate governance literature was correct after all. The standard structure included the national programme, handbook, financial arrangements, and possible penalties. Partnerships were obliged at least to break even financially, and were prevented from including anything in their operational cases that did not fit the handbook. In this way, the partnerships were rendered auditable, accountable, and hence governable.

---

[12] The anti-speed camera lobby includes the Association of British Drivers (ABD) and Motorists Against Detection (MAD). Some anti-camera protestors had gone as far as blowing up speed cameras with small explosive devices.

So, Barbara and Harold were not only busy constituting evidence and linking cameras to penalty notices. They also had to think about their operational case. They had to consider next year's budget: how many drivers could be identified and how many would pay their speeding fine next year? They might be able to make a case for more speed cameras next year. Harold pondered aloud how their communications strategy might need to change in line with the new handbook. Invoking a national standard structure for speed/safety cameras also provided one means to articulate why the evidential chain of custody worked in the way it did. The partnership had to fit spending to an agreed annual budget, had to issue notices and receive payment up to the level of its predicted income, and had to get drivers to pay without disputing the evidence. The partnership held back on releasing details of the evidential chain to drivers, in case this would encourage drivers to dispute the charge.

We see how the workaday business of producing evidence was intertwined with the standard national governance structure. But to what extent and in what ways did Barbara, Harold, their colleagues, and their equivalents in thirty-seven other safety camera partnerships invoke this standard structure? Were they aware of the scalar connections between national and regional so clearly articulated by the management consultancy? How much did they try to match their actions with the dictates of the handbook? Did the standard national structure enable them to manage accountability and self-governance? Did they feel they were under the gaze of the national board or the programme office? In short, how far did the hierarchical format of the standard structure find expression in the practical business of governance in action?

5.3.2 Invoking Non-Standard Structures of Governance

It became apparent that those working in and managing safety camera partnerships frequently invoked what we can call non-standard structures of governance. In contrast to the standard structure these versions stressed variability and difference. People, things, rules, and terms of compliance varied between partnerships and were subject to ongoing changes in activity, between times of year, between members of staff, types of driver, available equipment, decisions made at monthly meetings, the availability of staff, and budget.

Harold discussed at length the challenges of figuring out an appropriate response to the handbook. While occasionally invoking the standard governance structure, for example, in describing how his partnership reported compliance to the national board, Harold also talked of needing to secure an apparent compliance that might sit slightly outside the rules. This kind of non-standard compliance only made sense in relation to the standard structure (for example, non-standard actions were articulated as something different that his partnership needed to do locally). At the same time, Harold and his equivalents in other partnerships were not always sure of the extent to which a particular non-standard governance action would in fact be recognized as non-standard by the national board.

> With the handbook it's not clear you either seek advice or try and see what you can get away with. On some things there's room for negotiation. If your 4th KSI is 1.1 km, there's no room for manoeuvre. There's a lot of politics you can't explain. All we wanted was some money back and now we've got this grand regimented system where we're not trusted to do the job we've always done and now the threat is that things won't be covered. At one point we got in trouble because we didn't get the cameras in on time and said can we have £0.5 million for next year, they said yes, then we spent the money from this year's budget that we didn't spend on cameras on comm[unication]s and took another £0.5 million from them for the cameras the following year. We got a rap on the knuckles. (Harold, 10/12/2004)

Harold thus invokes a governance structure as the basis for figuring out what he could 'get away with'. Harold knowingly, willingly, more or less accountably, pushed the terms of the standard governance structure, thereby revealing its limitations. At the same time, Harold notes some features of a standard invocation of the handbook from which he could not deviate without punishment (for example, four KSIs in 1 km of road). However, possible punishment is not the sole determinant of action. When he failed to get new speed cameras installed in time to cover their costs, Harold authorized expenditure on a road-safety communication programme and drew money for the cameras from the following year's budget. Harold did this in full awareness of the proscription of this course of action in the standard structure account, but seemed to want to find out what the punishment might entail. The ensuing 'rap on the knuckles' was due acknowledgement that they had strayed, but also revealed that operating outside the standard governance structure was unlikely to be severely punished.

Partnership managers frequently met to discuss what they understood as the standard structure 'within which' they were expected to work. This was not treated as a static or rigid set of arrangements. Here, one of Harold's counterparts, a manager of a smaller partnership, describes attempts to force change to what they understood as the standard structure:

> Most of the partnerships have the same issues when they meet with the DfT [Department for Transport] they gang up on them and air all their complaints. It's easy ganging up on the centre (Lucy, 8/2/2005)

Frequently, partnership managers spoke of the tensions involved in trying to understand and explain particular features of the standard structure:

it's difficult when we meet the public and there is a lag before cameras are approved. The public—say a mum whose fifteen-year old daughter has just been killed, we try and talk to them, but it's difficult to explain [the Handbook]. (John, 10/2/2005)

We're struggling to find sites now [which can be justified under the Handbook]. We've exhausted what's out there, but we haven't seen area wide reductions. We want everyone to obey the speed limit everywhere. My view is that the [Handbook] rules won't enable us to get there. [....] Mobile will be the key to success and covert activity. They should relax the rules to allow mobile with a touch of covert. We know casualties exist, but speed isn't there. We can't meet the speed, [but] we've got the KSIs. (Brian, 9/12/2004)

The Treasury are too concerned about the scheme. We would like to broaden out what we can spend money on. Can we pay for signs at sites? Can we put signs on non-core camera sites? We'd like to be pro-active and prevent deaths, not respond to deaths. Why the big fight with the Treasury? Why can't we have signs without cameras? I want to be able to fund more under the scheme than just cameras. A bit more flexibility would be welcomed, both in what money can be spent on and justification of cameras, in speed and KSIs. Why is money not guaranteed for road safety? Why does surplus just disappear into Treasury? We might get the business case wrong next year, so we have to err on the side of caution and make a surplus because if we don't, then what happens? And if we do, we get it in the neck from the public. (David, 7/2/2005)

We were told any excess would go into road safety, but there isn't. It should be ring-fenced nationally for road safety, but not to the partnerships who might be accused of revenue raising. [Another partnership] had £2 million excess last year. Where's that gone? (Lucy, 8/2/2005)

The concern for us is that the Handbook is getting tighter. This is no longer a road safety scheme, it is Treasury led. I hope it's not because they want to increase their coffers. (Harold, 10/12/2004)

These responses show that managers found the nationally standardized, structured governance account too limiting. It provides only one means for understanding the activities of safety camera partnerships. In addition, Harold and his counterparts in other safety camera partnerships invoke non-standard relations of governance as ways of making sense of what they understand to be pressing matters of local concern (a particular accident, a particular death, a particular complaint, a budget constraint, and so on). Managers attempt to get the Department for Transport to change the handbook, try to see if they could 'get away with' some action falling outside the handbook, or air their frustrations with the ways in which the standard structure restricted the range of their activities and thence their ability to improve 'road safety'.

Back in the London offices of G&S, the ethnographer put down his mineral water and asked about these tensions. Leaning back in his chair with an air of resignation, the consultant said they were aware of partnerships trying to 'bend' the rules. He moved his hands back and forth across the table. The ethnographer needed to understand that this was a back and forth game between the board and the partnerships. New rules are introduced to close down areas where partnerships try to push their luck and civil servants suggest changes. The picture was not static.

All this suggests that understanding governance in practice is much more than reading off governance functions from an organizational structure. While advocates of corporate governance might be tempted to seek more and better ways to ensure compliance (and to a large extent the consultancy seemed to be trying to do just this), the standard structure appears to offer only a narrow means of understanding how governance works. It risks treating governance structures as nationally standardized, more or less monolithic entities that require little further scrutiny. Non-standard responses, invoking an apparent standard while also trying 'to get away with it', antagonism towards the standard, and attempts to get a standard changed all coexisted with the standard structural account. This also makes it difficult to characterize the operation of the governance structure in neo-Foucauldian terms. There is little evidence that partnerships were straightforwardly adopting subject positions, internalizing the handbooks as rationales for how they ought to act and behave. Instead, antagonism, criticism, and rule bending all suggest a messier entanglement between partnerships, the board, and the handbook. As far as the partnerships were concerned accountability was accomplished through complicated and contingent ongoing relations of governance.

Drivers, speed limits, and cameras were just three of the many entities that were key to the ongoing constitution of governance. As far as drivers are concerned, we have already seen how Barbara and her colleagues were busy trying to constitute the speeding driver by generating stable chains of evidence. We also saw how this evidential work was entangled with the invocation of standard and non-standard governance structures. How are relations between partnerships and drivers entangled with the handbook and national board as a structure of governance? Before carrying out the ethnography, relations between partnerships and drivers appeared to be straightforward: a driver broke the speed limit and was photographed and within two weeks was issued an NIP and penalty notice, which they were legally expected to pay. Across the country Barbara and her counterparts in other partnerships worked at producing evidence of the offence. The handbook also set out numerous rules on cameras, speed limits, photographing drivers, issuing penalties, and communicating road safety messages to drivers. However, the constitution of evidence, standardized and non-standardized governance structures, and moment-to-moment decision making by partnerships were entangled in numerous and complex ways. In the next sections we explore these entanglements by focusing on setting speed limits on cameras and on the installation of cameras.

5.3.3 Setting Camera Speed Limits

Roads in the UK are subject to national standards for speed limits according to the type of road. However, variations in time and road conditions can result in several speed limits operating on the same road. The same road can carry a 60 mph limit in a rural area then enter an urban area with an initial 40 mph limit, a subsequent city centre 30 mph limit, and even a residential 20 mph limit. The appropriate limit is a road safety decision taken at a local-regional level. These decisions change over time, in response to accidents and/or other speed problems and both limits and changes to limits need to be signalled clearly to drivers. If a particular stretch of road met the safety camera programme handbook criteria for KSIs and speed, a fixed camera or mobile enforcement set-up could be introduced. However, further decisions were then necessary. At what speed should speed cameras be set to photograph drivers? The handbook specified that the minimum threshold setting for a camera was 35 mph on a 30 mph road (to allow for inaccuracies in vehicle speedometers and to reduce the likelihood of dispute). But the handbook made no mention of higher speeds. So partnerships were left to decide any speed setting greater than 35 mph.

Speed became a focal point for partnerships in figuring out the different ways in which they could constitute evidence and comply with the national standard governance structure. Harold's partnership would set the speed limit well above the 35 mph minimum: 'Some thresholds are very high–45 mph on a 30'. For Harold this enabled them to manage a particular kind of entanglement of evidence and governance structure. The partnership could present evidence through which only those driving recklessly fast would be prosecuted; only those whose offences were indisputable would be fined. So Harold simultaneously constituted evidence as indisputably factual and moral; drivers would only be photographed well above the limit, which would both rule out any marginal disputes and help position the driver as reckless. At the same time, this made it possible to conform to the rule that NIPs had to be issued within fourteen days because, at 45 mph, this generated a workload that Barbara and her colleagues could manage. A lower setting would result in issuing so many penalties, require so much loading and unloading of film, and generate so many images needing identification that the costs would exceed their budget. The figure judged to generate the appropriate number of indisputable penalties was 45 mph, which the partnership could afford to issue and process and would allow them to collect just about the right level of income (in line with the predictions of their operational case), without having to return too much surplus to the Treasury.

A similar entanglement of drivers, speed, evidence, and governance structure characterized the governance decisions made by other partnerships. Indeed some partnership managers were openly critical of partnerships that set their cameras too close to the minimum speed thresholds:

> I could not do this job in [other region] because they work so close to tolerance thresholds. (David, 7/2/2005)

David suggests that the practice of issuing penalties to marginal speeders is likely to lead to numerous complaints and to high staffing levels in partnerships as they issue large numbers of penalties to cover their staff costs. However, other managers took the entanglement of evidence constitution and governance structure to suggest a quite different strategy. Thus, one partnership set their cameras below threshold as a way of warning drivers:

> 1mph under threshold we do send out warning letters about risks, likely death. This got a lot of feedback. If we have that sort of targeted education it may be better. (Christine, 18/2/2005)

In this partnership, drivers received a warning letter stating that they had come close to receiving a notice. This meant the constitution of evidence had to encompass all speeding drivers from marginal to excessive speed, managed 'within' a governance structure of large budgets, large staff numbers, and large numbers of penalties to fund both. Harold's approach was more circumspect but his partnership also adopted other approaches. For example, Harold installed cameras with dummy flashes in between enforcement periods when cameras did not contain film. In this way, he sought to warn drivers without having to constitute evidence and issue penalties, although he speculated that such warnings might fall outside the national standard governance guidelines:

> On the engineering, only one in six cameras has an active housing in it. If you went through six only one would get you so in the others we've put dummies with just a flash and a radar. We think they're brilliant because we can set the threshold lower we set it at 35 mph. Real cameras are set higher,

we don't need to enforce at 35 mph. If we did we'd need five times as many staff. The Treasury have now banned dummy flashes. Why? Their argument is someone gets flashed, they worry for a couple of weeks and then think they've got away with it. I say well if they are worried about it it's better than if they drive at high speed past a camera and there's no intervention. People phone up and say I've been flashed was it a dummy and if I know I *might* tell them. Because the threshold is lower more people get flashed by dummy cameras. If you ask me which cameras next week are dummies, I won't tell you. If you ask last Saturday was such and such a camera a dummy I *might* tell you... People might try to work out patterns and ratios for dummy cameras. It's not in the public interest and the data commissioner agrees. The Treasury won't save money. We've got enough dummy cameras already to carry on anyway and we aren't getting no new fixed sites next year. Their rules don't apply retrospectively. I wrote my operational case for next year on the guidelines. I guess their intention is if a dummy unit breaks down I won't replace it, but we'll see. (Harold, 10/12/2004)

While Harold talked of enforcement at high speeds, dummy flashes at lower speeds, and issuing penalties within budgets and battles with the Treasury, other partnerships found themselves responding to the handbook by way of ever greater and more systematic enforcement, so they could build an operational case that would satisfy the national programme office.

Each camera has a different level of enforcement—red, yellow and green—which is how often the camera operates according to highest KSIs. Mobiles could be every week, once a month, once every eight weeks. Seven days or fourteen days for fixed sites, but we don't publicize when. It costs a lot to keep every housing with a live camera. It is a risk. New cameras would take at least nine months to pay back revenue and they have to be paid for within twelve months. We used to enforce one in six now it's one in two or three. A fixed is live for seven days because drivers have to be told within fourteen days. (Brian, 9/12/2004)

The entanglement of evidence and governance structures was continuous and yet, as we have seen, subject to great differences between partnerships. It was also subject to continuous change as partnerships set and entangled new priorities.

5.3.4 Installing Cameras

These kinds of entanglement did not focus solely on speed settings. Partnerships also managed the installation of cameras. On the face of it, the handbook offered straightforward guidance about the choice of camera and camera installation. Partnerships could install fixed cameras, mobile enforcement, combination red-light and speed cameras and, although no partnerships could afford them, average speed or speed over distance systems. In the case of a fixed camera, partnerships could choose between: Gatso[13] cameras (which used radar to measure speed and a camera to photograph the rear of vehicles); Gatso cameras backed up by front-facing cameras (to try to capture the driver's face); cameras that used sensors embedded in the road instead of radar; wet film cameras (which took high-quality pictures, but needed to be emptied and re-filled); or digital cameras (which were lower in quality, but could be operated by sending images down a remote line to the partnership).

The handbook criteria for installing new cameras seemed equally clear. A camera should only be installed if it was in a location where it could be maintained, if it could be rendered conspicuous and if all other road safety engineering options were unavailable. However, this turned out to be more complicated than it first seemed because the handbook also specified criteria relating to speed and to numbers of KSIs.

The speed criterion was that a specific percentage of vehicles had to be shown to be breaking the speed limit over a specified length of road. For example, it needed 20 per cent of vehicles to exceed the speed limit over a 1 km stretch of road to justify a camera. Partnerships were free to choose the time of day to carry out a speed survey. So Harold sought to run the surveys on days and at times he considered would offer the greatest likelihood of generating speed data that fitted the handbook criteria, and so entitle him to install a new camera. The data constituted by the survey would be those moments where most people drove at greatest speed above the speed limit. Once the speed justification had been established with the national board, the cameras would then operate at times of the partnership's choosing, not just at those times when speed surveys were taken. So, although initially justified by survey data collected at a particular time, partnerships were free to decide when to put film in, the speed at which to set the camera, and so on.

Harold and his counterparts in other partnerships acknowledged that only the speed-related KSIs should be included in justifications for speed cameras.[14] But what counted as a speed-related KSI?[15] How could historical records be used clearly to depict a speeding-related event? Harold suggested that current systems for recording and categorizing accidents did not reflect

---

[13] Named after speed measuring devices first invented by Dutch rally driver Maurice Gatsonides.

[14] Four KSIs had to be recorded on a 1 km stretch of road within three years of the account to justify a fixed speed camera.

[15] Further problems with definitions of KSIs include what counted as 'killed' and what counted as 'serious injury' and minor injury. An initial definition suggested that if a person had died within thirty days of an accident (and the accident was speed related) then they counted as 'killed'. To die after thirty-one days would merely be a serious injury. Combining killed with serious injury into KSI overcame some of this problem. A serious injury was defined as an injury that required hospital treatment, whereas a 'minor injury' did not.

the complexity of a motor vehicle accident. The partnerships had limited means to reproduce the detail of an accident that had happened at some point in the three preceding years. They had little information other than the road traffic accident (RTA) statistics recorded locally. Often RTAs recorded a single type of accident cause. This could sometimes mention speed directly (such as 'excessive speed'). These kinds of RTA reports could feature speed in the portrayal of a dangerous stretch of road, as part of the annual operational case sent to the national board. At other times the RTA report might only hint at speed (when, for example, focusing on dangerous driving). To constitute a successful operational case, partnership data analysts would produce KSI maps for particular sections of local roads. If the historical data appeared inconclusive (that is, an accident leading to a KSI may or may not have been speed related) the partnership manager would have to decide whether or not to include an accident when portraying a particular stretch of road as dangerous. Several partnerships said they had no clear way of knowing if all the KSIs they had incorporated into their justifications were definitively speed related.

> There is no data collection in [this area] specifically on speeding stats. Just general RTA [Road Traffic Accident] category. The stats reporting procedure means accidents are sometimes not recorded by police as 'speed' related but could be that the driver 'lost control' but that could still be due to speed. To go back through the years and check these sort of statistics manually we don't have the staff. The Partnership hasn't led to an improvement in stats. There have been attempts to look into it. (John, 10/2/2005)
>
> I've been a road safety engineer since 1984, but I'm conscious that not all KSIs are affected by speeding, maybe just inappropriate speed. Speed is not the universal answer to every accident. We have to take out KSIs not speed related, then apply criteria. Under FOI [Freedom Of Information] Act, partnerships are high risk and we want to be in a better position to defend camera sites. (Brian, 9/12/2004)

In relation to the handbook rule that that cameras could only be justified if all other available road safety engineering solutions had been considered, partnership managers spent some time focused on what was meant by 'available.' As Harold suggests, 'availability' might relate simply to finances:

> We would look at any potential site through public complaint or by plotting casualties on a map. It's a very subjective art to look and see if there's anything we can engineer. We look and if there's six crashes in three years, a roundabout costs £250k, two crashes a year at £100k, that would only save us £200k a year then that might not be a viable scheme, you may just walk away from it. Or you find a cheaper solution. That's how the priority rating system works—the greatest

number of crash savings for the cheapest solution, that's a community saving. A camera costs £35k, traffic lights £150k. Every year the DfT release a cost per accident. Every crash has a value. (Harold, 10/12/2004)

Ideally I want to eliminate all speeding but pragmatically I want to focus on excessive speed. I would put a camera everywhere I can that fits the criteria. But a camera is a last resort—can you engineer out a problem, can you afford to engineer? It probably is easier to fund a camera than a speed bump, except the timescale is so slow for cameras. (David, 7/2/2005)

The camera is the only option for us—we have to show there are no engineering measures and need to get the local authority to sign off on this. (Christine, 18/2/2005)

We want the freedom to use cameras where we have problems. Local authorities might have sites on traffic calming lists to put in something else or we can't always put a camera in. You have to say there's no engineering solution available—it might not be available because of money. You might put a camera in until you can afford [an alternative]. (Margaret, 16/12/2004)

So to make a case for camera installation, partnership managers had to: give evidence of a speed survey showing 20 per cent of drivers breaking the speed limit, provide a map of a 1 km stretch of road showing four speed-related KSIs, and establish that other road safety engineering solutions had been considered and ruled out. To do this, partnerships had to constitute, hold in place, and demonstrate a particular entanglement of evidence and governance structure: the dangerous road that justified a speed camera. Typically, this involved decisions about when to carry out a survey, how to draw up the map (and what to include as 'speed related') and ways to report their assessment of alternative road safety solutions. Once again we see that governance does not happen solely because of rules (such as the handbook) determining organizational action. Governance happens in virtue of organizations (both the partnership and the national board) working to constitute, hold steady, demonstrate, and read evidence in particular ways.

5.4 Reconstituting Structures of Governance through Communication

The handbook is the touchstone for partnership activities in the constitution of speeding drivers, in the setting of speed camera limits, and in installing new cameras. But it also stipulates that partnerships must produce both an operational case and an annual communication strategy to be assessed by the board. This means that partnerships must enter into further relations with their main subjects of governance, the drivers. How did partnerships manage to draw drivers into the ongoing constitution of structures of governance while managing their own identity as governed entities?

Sitting at the table used for regular partnership meetings, Harold described how they had attempted to classify drivers into different types, and attach varying degrees of danger to each type. For example, the partnership had recently classified motorcyclists as dangerous.

> Motorbikes are 2–3 per cent of the traffic and 20 per cent of the casualties. They say it's cos of cars, sometimes they're going too fast or doing a stupid overtake. (Harold, 10/12/2004)

The partnership then looked at how the category of motorcyclist could be incorporated into their annual communication strategy. Harold had looked at a variety of national campaigns that were running at the time and had decided to buy into (and thus help fund) one aimed at motorcyclists.

> We've bought into the 'handle it or lose it' campaign. Our budget is £250k. We bought into the website so there's [our] stuff on it. Riders give their stories of good rides and this alerts the highways to problems. (Harold, 10/12/2004)

However, when the communication strategy was sent to the board for assessment, the response was that 'Handle It or Lose It', although a national government campaign, was more about road safety in general than about safety and speed cameras.

> [Handle It or Lose It]'s not strictly cameras and it's now a big no no. As I say it was probably a bit iffy to begin with, now they've said no way. [Harold shrugs his shoulders as if to say: what can I do?] (Harold, 10/12/2004)

Other partnership managers were sceptical about national campaigns (partly because of similar experiences to Harold) and so attempted to keep their communications local. They used their own communications staff, occasionally in combination with PR agencies, to decide which kinds of local people were likely to speed, the kinds of messages to be given to these groups, and what was the most 'appropriate' medium available within budget.

> We have been focusing on adults so far. Young males, the troublemakers, they have too much testosterone. Seventeen to twenty-five-year old males are a problem for speeding. Fifty year olds are also problematic, but it's too late for them. Fifty plus drivers have upmarket cars and experience and confidence and speed. (John, 10/2/2005)
>
> We use busbacks, bus shelters, pub toilets, radio, we're doing TV as a region. We look at the data to see what people we should be targeting. (Brian, 9/12/2004)

Once again we see that classification constitutes entities as simultaneously evidential ('we look at the data'), moral ('fifty year olds are also problematic') and actionable ('people we should be targeting'). These entities are constituted in such a way as to build a case that accountably demonstrates the partnership's fulfilment of the handbook in terms of the annual communication strategy, and in concert with attempts to constitute the nature of the governance structure itself (that is, working out what counts as 'iffy'). In constituting different categories of dangerous drivers, partnerships sometimes reconstituted the boundaries of governance structures according to the characteristics they attributed to particular drivers:

> We target young drivers and bikers and obviously they're completely different audiences and we talk to the target audience beforehand to see what they expect and some people might say that's [pointing to a card given to the ethnographer] a shock tactic because that's a valentine's card. [Referring to a campaign launched on Valentine's Day]. Lot of the younger drivers were shocked. We've got the Irish TV adverts on DVD and they're too gruesome to show. These shock tactics will hit home to the right target audience. If it's not aimed at you, you might not understand it. Bikers they're attitude is 'wa-hey I'm a lad'. The gentle, gentle approach with them, they're not listening. The advertising company have talked to people caught speeding and they said the images are not shocking enough so now we're getting a hearse for the county show and saying 'this is the last thing you'll slow down for.' It gets people talking. It doesn't always get the message across. We have pictures of you know sexy models draped over bikes, but when you look closely one's got a leg missing, one's got an arm missing, one's got an eye sewn up, but the DfT [Department for Transport] wouldn't run them. Our latest slogan is 'people are dying for you to slow down.' And we have children's faces on the posters. (Harold, 10/12/2004)

Harold thus constituted particular types of road user (for example, bikers) who listen to particular things (shock tactics) in particular ways, while ignoring other things (gentle, gentle approach). It was not just that a certain age group or type of vehicle user was invoked, but that their identity, preferences, and ways of paying attention, were all brought into being. At the same time the ontological constitution of driver entities was entangled with the partnership's efforts to make sense of the governance structure 'within which' they operated and the strength of the accountability relations that they understood as policing the governance structure. The category of 'bikers', what they would listen to, and what they would ignore, was closely tied to assessments of what the Department for Transport might allow in the communication strategy and hence in next year's spend. Drivers, vehicles, communication, governance structure, and accountability relations were simultaneously constituted in such a way that the nature of each could stand as providing an appropriate account for each of the others. Other partnership managers similarly described their ongoing struggles in launching communication campaigns that could render the most dangerous drivers its subject, draw them into governance structures, while at the same time trying to anticipate the reactions of the national board, and figure out the effects of budget constraints:

The thirty-five to fifty-four-year old age group, professional high mileage drivers are highest offenders and least supportive of speed cameras. We know low mileage female drivers are very supportive. We know who is seeing these adverts and thirty-five to fifty-four-year old males aren't getting this message so we're not working totally blind. [...] There are conflicting views on what's most hard-hitting and effective. Some research shows using children has no impact at all, other research suggests it's most hard hitting. [...] The hardest people to talk to are high mileage drivers who don't think road safety relates to me. They want to drive at the speed they want to drive at because they think they're safe to do it. (Lucy, 8/2/2005)

Thirty-five to fifty-five is highest offender category. It's very difficult to talk to them they think they're the best drivers. We need to think a lot about who we're targeting, what they read—then you have problems of non-residents. How do I talk to them? We need a regional and national campaign. (Christine, 18/2/2005) We run several campaigns a year. We have no TV—it's too expensive. We do radio and press bits. The [Regional] News is very good, but other local papers are wannabe Daily Mails. They are difficult. (John, 10/2/2005)

Drink driving is generally unacceptable but still done by some people and you can change people's attitudes through PR but you can only change their behaviour by enforcement. Some people will only stop speeding if they lose their licence. You've got to tell them how it is through blood and gore and tell them they're vulnerable. (Margaret, 16/12/2004)

We saw earlier (Section 5.2) the importance of the detailed practical work of manipulating and interpreting images in constituting the speeding driver as the subject of a system of identification and punishment. In this section, we have seen the work of constituting drivers as the subjects of communication campaigns. For the partnerships, communication was one way to try to constitute the subjects of governance—in particular, vehicles and their drivers—as simultaneously evidential, moral, and actionable. Constituting work also contributed to ongoing attempts to produce, navigate, reproduce, challenge, and redirect structures of governance. Thus, the invocation of categories of road users, their likes and dislikes, what they might pay attention to, was entangled with available budgets, the annual communication strategy, and what the national board might permit. The annual communication strategy featured prominently in the handbook, and so was implicated in relations of governance between partnerships and the national board, and partnerships and drivers. Yet partnership managers were sanguine about the likely effectiveness of a communication strategy. It was not clear how far communication could resolve tensions and uncertainties between partnerships and the board or turn drivers into compliant subjects of governance. Notably, however, drivers became a category with little or no opportunity to talk back,[16] let alone to comment on the structures of governance that communication channels operated.

Disaggregating this aspect of governance relations (between board, partnership, and drivers) has enabled us to explore the variety of distinct attempts to classify and attribute moral character to cars and their drivers, the means through which such governance pairs are articulated with particular responses to governance rationales (such as the handbook) but also, the ways in which bodies such as partnerships are involved in the very constitution of the structures of governance of which the handbook is a part.

5.5 Conclusion

In this chapter we have seen that mundane governance features acts of ontological constitution (of people and things, vehicles and their drivers, films and cameras, strategies and communication), tied to the production of evidential, moral, and actionable entities (speeding drivers, reckless drivers, fifty-year old drivers who won't listen, and unsafe bikers) and ordered through classification (who is dangerous, sorting budgets into accounts to manage road safety). We have also argued that functions cannot simply be read off structures of governance, as some corporate governance studies imply. We have argued instead that governance involves the constitution of multiple, ongoing acts of governance, sometimes invoked as complying with and hence reproducing a standard structure, sometimes noted as beyond and hence challenging a standard structure, or sometimes involved in developing the very nature of what counts as a standard governance structure. This can at times appear quite fragile; for example, with partnerships testing how far they can bend or go beyond their understanding of the rules. However, at other times governance structures appear set to endure. The production and issue of penalties, the retention of governance disputes within relationships between partnerships and board, and the unidirectional nature of communication relationships with drivers, ensures a(n at least) temporary stability. Governance structures are continually

---

[16] Although some of the partnerships with larger budgets paid companies to carry out market research on drivers.

constituted and reconstituted, and mostly exempt from questioning by their subjects of governance.

The (temporary) endurance of governance structures does not support arguments about the benefits of corporate governance. This chapter has shown that 'reading off' functions from governance structures is only one way of understanding the work that characterizes governance focused organizations. This chapter also suggests that certain aspects of neo-Foucauldian governmentality require further specification: it is not so much that rules, instructions, or rationales are internalized by governed subjects, and then assessed through governance structures; instead, the constitution of structures of governance is ongoing, relational, subject to dispute, negotiation, partial, and temporary resolution, and then further change. Rules and instructions are the upshot of ontological constitution rather than existing as a rationale to take on, internalize, and be assessed. Structures of governance are often brought into being, sustained, and continually subject to change. In place of the internalization of rationales, authorities involved in doing and being held to account through structures of governance, are also continually involved in the simultaneous constitution, questioning, endurance, and transformation both of rationales and structures of governance. Hence, in disaggregating governance structures, we have challenged the idea that these structures exist before relations of governance, and we have criticized perspectives that suggest that structures provide a context 'within which' acts of governance take place. We have further argued that governance structures are neither monolithic nor agential entities that do governance. Instead, 'structures' are continuously invoked, made, re-made, questioned, and redeveloped through actions of mundane governance. Structures that seem to endure in a more or less stable manner (at least for a time) appear to be maintained by the careful management of accountability relations such that the direction and extent of questions that can be asked of governance structures are minimized.[17]

Our advocacy of this perspective on the structures of mundane governance has a general resonance with some longstanding theories of organization. For example, Giddens (1984) famously coined the term structuration to propose a compromise that suggests aspects of structure and action are intertwined. Management scholars such as Weick (1995) have drawn upon ethnomethodological insights to portray organizations as sense making entities, which are much more process oriented than structure oriented. Sociologists such as Selznick (1948) have argued that the normative idealizations wrapped up in the notion of formal organization and structure need constant adaptation

---

[17] Here, perhaps, we glimpse a possible sociological explanation for the frustrations experienced by the grumpy old men we met in Chapter 1.

and continual interpretation to be effective. Ethnomethodologists such as Bittner (1965) have argued that as formal structures are ideal types of action that are practically unattainable, we need to focus on understanding common sense uses of terms such as organization. And, perhaps closest to our perspective, Wieder's (1974) analysis of organizational rules establishes that the practical activity of following a rule entails the active formulation of that rule in the course of that activity. All these approaches support the general point that structure cannot be treated as pre-existing its constitution in the course of practice. Our contribution in this chapter is to show how this applies in the case of mundane governance, especially focusing on governance, accountability, and ontology. In the same way that the wrong bin bag was brought into being through ongoing, co-ordinated actions and relationships, this chapter has argued that the conditions, structures, and institutions, which are often represented as merely external or prior to any collection of evidence, are also constituted through ongoing, co-ordinated actions and relationships. But, additionally, we have shown that in mundane governance the invocation of structure crucially involves the active ontological constitution of entities under conditions of accountability.

We have shown that mundane governance entails classifications policed by accountability relations (Chapter 3), the constitution of is–ought–actionable entities (Chapter 4), and the active enactment of structures 'within which' governance takes place (this chapter). This leaves a key question: does mundane governance work? In Chapter 6 we tackle this question, again with reference to traffic management. By drawing on the experiences of drivers we ask what it means to say whether or not governance works, on whose terms, using what means of assessment, and to what ends.

6

Compliance: Does Mundane Governance Work?

6.1 Introduction

Thus far we have established the ontological bases of mundane governance (Chapters 1 and 2); showed how these were constituted in classificatory systems and policed through accountability relations (Chapter 3); argued that ontological constitution enacts entities, which are at once evidential–moral–actionable (Chapter 4); and demonstrated how the 'contexts' of mundane governance are continuously and actively invoked, challenged, and tested (Chapter 5). But given all we have said about the importance of ontology and accountability in the regulation of behaviour, what does this depiction of mundane governance tell us about the effectiveness of the various schemes we have described? We have yet to address a key question: does mundane governance work? In this chapter we start to tackle this question, again drawing on materials from our study of traffic management.

It is important to recognize from the outset that what counts as 'working' and/or 'effective' can be interpreted in many ways. We might say, for example, that the very establishment of a local council waste management initiative might in one way count as mundane governance working; or the fact that a system of speed cameras is in place indicates the workingness of traffic regulation. Other criteria of working might, for example, include whether or not the installation of speed cameras in a particular local authority occurred on time and within budget. These examples give us a first clue that terms such as 'working' and 'effective' are multifaceted. What counts as working is not straightforward: we need to ask 'working' on whose terms, according to whose definition, assessed by what means, in what circumstances, when, for how long and to what ends? In this chapter we focus on 'compliance' as one aspect of whether or not mundane governance can be said to work.

Compliance occupies a largely untroubled position in theories of governance. For example, in studies of corporate governance (see Chapters 2 and 5) a form of regulation or a structural model of organizational governance is assumed to provide a description of what will subsequently occur in organizations. Compliance is treated as a straightforward matter to be read-off from, for example, the regulations and checked by compliance officers responsible for ensuring consistency of compliance over time and across organizations. Compliance in these approaches is akin to *acquiescence* in the sense that the actions of members of an organization, or even of organizations themselves, are presented as the outcome of the structures of governance through which they are regulated. In neo-Foucauldian approaches (see Chapters 2 and 5), governance rationales provide the basis upon which individuals will internalize (or at least make sense of) particular desired modes of action. Compliance is thus the upshot of the extent to which individuals take on board, demonstrate, and are assessed as demonstrating the rationale made available through systems of governance. Hence, in these approaches, questions of compliance centre largely on notions of *assessment*. For example, audit is used to assess the extent to which members of an organization have adopted a particular governance rationale and put it into practice.

By contrast with these accounts of governance, we have argued that mundane governance involves the ontological constitution of the objects and subjects of governance. It follows that just as we need to ask how and what constitutes the 'hotness' of coffee, the 'wrongness' of bin bags, the nature of recycling, the speed at which a vehicle can be driven, or the speed at which a camera should be set, so too should we ask about the situated constitution of the various ontologies involved in compliance. We have seen that bin bags are not always wrong, coffee is not always recklessly hot, and speed is not always excessive. So it is reasonable to assume that drivers (even those caught speeding) do not speed all the time, that irresponsible recyclers sometimes put the right things in their recycling boxes, and fast-food coffee only rarely gets served at recklessly hot temperatures or leads to litigation. Indeed it is often the apparently exceptional nature of these cases that becomes the central feature of interest. This suggests we need to look closely at how compliance is normally done, or avoided, in practice. We need to ask what is the ontological constitution of people and objects in the practice of compliance. In the case of compliance, how is the situated moral order of the objects and subjects of governance constituted? And, what accountability relations are wrapped up in this? We also need to ask how and to what extent compliance endures. Do the same objects and people respond in the same way to the dictates of governance? Do they do so consistently over time, in distinct locations, and between different individuals and organizations? In short, we need to ask what, when, and how is compliance constituted? On whose terms? Assessed through what means? For how long? To what ends?

This chapter begins with a brief overview of some features of compliance in theoretical treatments of the topic, and specifically in recent initiatives in UK traffic management. We then look at some examples of compliance in action, looking at driving in practice, and drawing on drivers' own accounts as they attend to the possibilities of compliance and non-compliance in the course of their driving. Subsequently, we turn attention to the treatment of drivers who have transgressed the dictates of governance and who undertake a form of driver re-education, drawing on our ethnographic experience as a participant in a speed awareness course.

6.2 Compliance in Theory

The nature of compliance has been the subject of debate, challenge, and counter-challenge in many different fields. For example, in social psychology, compliance has famously been the subject of the experiments by Milgram (1974) and Asch (1951). Of particular pertinence for this study is the work of Festinger (1959) on cognitive dissonance. In experiments measuring compliance, Festinger found that the extent to which people were happy to produce statements or actions counter to their underlying beliefs (without modifying those beliefs to fit the action or statement) varied according to the size of punishment or reward in prospect. The bigger the reward or threat of punishment the easier experimental subjects found it to say or act (comply) in line with what the experimenter asked without changing their underlying beliefs. In situations where the reward or punishment was less clear, more subjects changed their underlying belief to match the statement or action to which they were asked to comply. Festinger suggests that the larger the punishment or reward at stake, the easier individuals found it to manage cognitive dissonance (doing or saying something against their beliefs). This might suggest that encouraging compliance with governance through punishment or reward might induce similar results—a change in words or actions, without a change in belief.[1] Taking this approach, rewarding or punishing drivers who comply with road safety measures might only encourage drivers to become more able at managing cognitive dissonance—complying through actions or words without changing their attitudes to road safety.[2]

---

[1] Although this does imply it is easy straightforwardly to determine individuals' beliefs, separate from their words and actions.

[2] Compliance is not the sole preserve of social psychologists. In medicine, for example, an enduring problem is to persuade patients to comply with treatments (Wright, 1993). Despite

These studies suggest that compliance is neither a single nor a simple process, but instead involves various degrees, sources, and explanations of compliance. In this chapter we develop this multiplicity in compliance. We argue for treating compliance as an accomplishment, where what constitutes compliance, how the degree of compliance can be assessed, and what consequences follow (non)compliance are the result of ongoing work. For our attempt to understand mundane governance, we need to figure out how compliance is done, where it emerges in different modes of governance, who does and does not comply, and with what consequence.

In recent UK road safety initiatives, compliance has come to the fore with the introduction of successive initiatives to try to ensure, improve, alter, or better manage road safety. For example, in 2008 the Department for Transport launched an external consultation that sought views on which road safety issues (speeding, drink driving, seatbelt (non)wearing, drug driving, careless driving) might be best tackled by what means (fines, awareness/education, license endorsements, and/or technology).[3] The consultation document proposed changing the degree of punishment individual motorists would receive for committing offences, combined with education and information to help encourage compliance.

On fixed penalties for driving offences, the Department for Transport consultation suggested:

> Extreme speeders are more likely to be involved in an accident and the consequences will be more severe when they are ... *We therefore propose to introduce a graduated fixed penalty of 6 penalty points for drivers who exceed the speed limit by a very large margin–20 mph in most speed limits.* (DfT, November, 2008, emphasis in original)

Here the importance of compliance is underscored by linking a specified evidential–moral–actionable occurrence with a proposed penalty. A feature of the consultation is that compliance is currently inadequate or absent. Hence, the need for greater penalties can be read as a need for greater (or any) compliance among those particularly dangerous drivers, positioned here as the non-compliant culprits. We note that the penalties are to be 'graduated' in line with the margins of speeding infraction. Thus, not all non-compliance is the same, not all non-compliance will receive the same penalty, and not

---

numerous theories, models, arguments, approaches, supposed improvements, and advancements, it remains the case that most studies of compliance find one-third of patients obediently complying, one-third complying to some or most of the treatment, and one-third not getting close to compliance. Elsewhere, discussions about compliance are also found in environmental initiatives and road safety schemes (see below), and is a growing area of employment (even warranting its own subsection in UK Job Centres).

[3] See Road safety compliance consultation: http://collections.europarchive.org/tna/20081223120624/http:/dft.gov.uk/consultations/open/compliance/

all types of potential offence will be targeted in the same way. However, the consultation does not only propose an increase in fines. On new offences, the consultation says:

> We are proposing to make careless driving a fixed penalty offence, which will enable the police to enforce with a minimum of bureaucracy against careless drivers who admit their fault. This would reduce the costs of enforcement, as well as being simpler for drivers, and could free up police resources, allowing more police time to be spent on the road. (DfT, November, 2008)

This excerpt justifies the proposed change through a combination of: reducing bureaucracy for the police issuing penalties, making it easier for drivers to be penalized and understand their penalty, and allowing the police to enforce other non-compliant activities. Compliance and non-compliance are here constituted simultaneously as a matter of bureaucracy, simplification, fault, carelessness, the need to redistribute police activity, and as a cost. It appears to be a problem of compliance that is difficult to argue against; targeting the careless and expensively non-compliant. Reference to the cost of governance also suggests a possible change in the register of accountability relations at play: the basis for governance and compliance is not just about danger or safety, but also about wasting money, and the need for minimal government. So compliance cannot be understood simply as a matter of acquiescence to a mode of governance or even as a matter of demonstrating adherence to a preferred order of action in a moment of assessment. Instead, compliance is caught up with the need for local authorities to meet nationally imposed restrictions on budgets, demonstrations of cost-effectiveness, and responsiveness to local concerns. The compliance of drivers and the compliance of distinct political units of organization are inseparable. But compliance does not end with concerns over increased and new penalties. On the matter of compliance, technology, and education, the consultation says:

> We are helping compliant drivers to understand the effects of speed, and to make compliance easier through technology. (DfT, November, 2008)

The consultation includes reference to one particular technology for enhancing compliance: Intelligent Speed Adaptation (ISA). ISA is said to help drivers voluntarily comply with road safety measures. For example, a digital display installed in cars will highlight the speed limit each time a driver exceeds it, thereby encouraging drivers to slow down. Yet these are not just any drivers. These are drivers willing to have the equipment installed in their vehicles. So in one sense these drivers are already 'compliant', and it seems unlikely that such drivers would need an ISA device. Perhaps then the 'compliant' driver is a driver who is open to being compliant (in contrast to 'extreme speeders' who require punishment). This begins to suggest a more complex picture of compliance; not all drivers can be constituted as requiring the same forms of governance, not all drivers are brought into being as likely to respond to governance in the same way, different drivers are identified as likely to become entangled in different forms of compliance, operated by different agencies, and with different types of outcome. In matters of compliance at least, the driver is a complex, contingent, and variable category.

The consultation draws together assumptions and profiles of driver types, the kinds of stimulus to which drivers might respond, and alternative means of governing compliance. The consultation begins with an evidential–moral–actionable account of why dangerous non-compliance occurs. Although theories of governance tend to suggest combinations of acquiescence and assessment in compliance, our reading of the consultation document begins substantially to broaden the nature and number of entities incorporated into compliance: who is doing compliance, who is likely (or not) to comply, how compliance might be encouraged, how much compliance costs, what might be effective, how straightforward or complex a system for managing compliance might be, what are appropriate technologies of compliance, what is an appropriate message for educational campaigns, and how big or small should be the punishment or reward. Compliance is thus broader than acquiescence and assessment alone would allow. The moral order of compliance is constituted through a broader number of entities than we initially considered.

Similar considerations are apparent in attempts to constitute evidence of driver compliance. For example, in 2011 the Department for Transport proposed the introduction of a set of 'league tables' for speed cameras in the UK.[4] The league tables were advocated as a means of presenting 'the best and worst performing cameras' in the UK. We again see how objects (technologies)—this time speed cameras rather than bin bags—are imbued with moral qualities as part of the texture of accountability relations.[5] For our immediate purposes, the league tables portray the relative success of the cameras in effecting compliance with speed limits, based on a comparison of the numbers of casualties before and after the camera's installation. The tables draw together data previously made available region-by-region through safety camera partnerships. Road Safety MP Mike Penning is reported as saying: 'This will expose where cameras are and are not doing their job'. However, in the same way that the 2008 consultation document began by focusing on compliance and then broadened the range of entities involved, speed camera league tables rapidly become the focus for a broader range

---

[4] See: http://www.dailymail.co.uk/news/article-2008340/Cash-cow-speed-cameras-named-time-transparency-drive.html

[5] The league tables included the explicit instruction that the recorded (poor) performance of a speed camera could not be used as the basis for a complaint against a speeding conviction.

of governance concerns. For example, Mike Penning continued: 'We want to stop motorists being used as cash cows. For too long information about speed cameras has been hidden in the shadows. This data will end that by clearly showing whether a camera is saving lives or just making money'. It is further reported that at least 28,000 accidents have been caused by speed cameras in the UK, that drivers drive 'erratically' as a result of speed cameras and that councils have been 'reluctant' to make information available on speed cameras. Peter Roberts of the Drivers' Alliance is quoted as saying: 'Speed cameras don't improve safety'. So the extent to which a governance technology 'works' by producing compliant drivers and vehicles becomes mired in issues of cost, excessive state regulation, the danger posed by the very same technologies of governance, unjustifiable governance, and the 'income' extracted from cash cow drivers.

Whereas the theoretical treatment of compliance can begin with a narrow conception of the key entities involved, namely cameras and drivers, we see that even a cursory discussion of the operation of compliance rapidly proliferates the population of relevant entities involved. Does this carry over into practice? Is the apprehension of compliance in the course of driving similarly characterized by the multiplication of governance entities? To examine compliance activities in practice we draw on two kinds of empirical materials. In Section 6.3 we examine driving in action. In Section 6.4 we consider the experience of drivers attending a speed awareness course.

6.3 Managing Compliance in Practice

We accompanied six drivers on short trips (ranging from 11 to 33 minutes) in and around Oxford, and made video recordings of the (driver's) view out of the front windscreen of the car.[6] We asked drivers to provide a commentary on their driving experience as they navigated their way through traffic, in particular, to articulate what features of the roads and traffic they attended to as they were driving. We then reviewed the videos of the drivers, as a result of which we identified three main kinds of compliance (and non-compliance) in practice.

6.3.1 Three Varieties of Compliance

Firstly, drivers attempted to articulate the extent to which, in the course of driving, they paid attention to various road safety devices, their car, the

---

[6] We took inspiration here from the small but interesting corpus of studies featuring drivers doing driving (see, for example, Dant, 2004; Laurier, 2004), which do not however explore governance and accountability.

141

surroundings, other road users, cyclists, pedestrians, the weather, and any-thing that stood out from normal proceedings (including the video-taping itself). Their descriptions of these various aspects of the scene were usually not very detailed. Instead drivers seemed to offer just enough to articulate their corresponding driving actions. For example, in this excerpt, Fabian remarks on an upcoming pedestrian crossing:

[DRIVING ALONG]

FABIAN: OK so driving down this road there's not much to pay attention to apart from that [zebra] crossing.

DAN: Do you stop for that?

FABIAN: Well there's this person stood sort of near the crossing.

DAN: But you're not going to stop.

FABIAN: Mmmm you sort of need to make a judgement: are they crossing or just standing around.

Although drivers in the UK are expected to be familiar with the Highway Code (which constitutes a formal compliance with regard to pedestrian cross-ings), Fabian articulates a version of compliance, which is a kind of practi-cal orientation to the official version of compliance. In the Highway Code, pedestrian crossings without traffic lights are known as zebra crossings (due to the black and white stripes painted on the road), and the rule is as follows:

Rule 195
Zebra crossings. As you approach a zebra crossing look out for pedestrians waiting to cross and be ready to slow down or stop to let them cross

For Fabian, compliance with this rule is about figuring out whether the person wants to cross or is doing some other kind of standing still. The kind of stand-ing still that the pedestrian is doing is not that close to the crossing, he is not facing the crossing, but his standing still is not the kind that might be seen at bus stops, he is not standing talking, he is not in any clear sense stopping for a rest (he is not putting down heavy shopping bags, for example). In the second or two it takes Fabian to approach and then drive across the pedestrian cross-ing without stopping, a variety of entities of compliance (pedestrian, location, position, direction faced, things that are not happening) come into considera-tion. Denise provides a similar example when approaching a yellow box junc-tion. The 'official' version of compliance in the Highway Code is as follows:

Rule 174
Box junctions. These have criss-cross yellow lines painted on the road (see 'Road markings'). You MUST NOT enter the box until your exit road or lane is clear. However, you may enter the box and wait when you want to turn right, and are only stopped from doing so by oncoming traffic, or by other vehicles waiting to

turn right. At signalled roundabouts you MUST NOT enter the box unless you can cross over it completely without stopping.

For Denise, the orientation is rather less formal and more practical:

[MOVING THROUGH A BOX JUNCTION]

DAN: Do you pay much attention to these yellow lines?

DENISE: Um no [...] I think the yellow lines are um common sensical places er where you shouldn't stop too long.

Zebra crossings and yellow box junctions pose a question of compliance for drivers. How can a driver constitute the nature of the object as permitting their actions to be compliant? Crossings and junctions are visible as a mechanism of road safety engineering, they are a product that has clearly been designed to generate a response from road users and yet instructions for their use remain somewhat abstruse. The material object does not itself convey the precise nature of what the road safety engineering object is, how a driver ought to respond to it, nor what the consequences of an inappropriate response might be. One upshot of this is that drivers doing driving figure out a kind of compliance for all practical purposes, a compliance that seems to work in the moment of driving over, through, or past the instrument of governance. Do other forms of road safety governance—such as speed cameras—appear to communicate their mode of operation and enforcement more clearly? On occasions, yes, drivers imbued material objects of road safety such as speed cameras with characteristics of governance, which were clear and circumscribed. Hence some drivers talked of the need to slow down for speed cameras to specific miles per hour and thought this slowing down was necessary to avoid penalty points on their driving licence. But other drivers were not so sure about the nature of speed cameras and, as a result, what compliance might mean. In this next excerpt, Renugan attempts to account for what would count as an appropriate way to drive past a speed camera. The articulation of compliance here draws together ideas about the direction of cameras, what cameras might do, other locations, previous actions, and local practices:

[DRIVING ALONG]

RENUGAN: There's a speed camera coming up.

DAN: Right.

RENUGAN: Which is always worth slowing down for it seems to be on quite a lot but it operates the other way. Most speed cameras just operate one way don't they?

DAN: Is that what you think?

RENUGAN: Well there is one on the way to Cambridge which is pointing in the reverse way of travel but takes pictures of cars going the other way too.

DAN: Mmm there are front facing cameras.

RENUGAN: Front facing. Is that what they're called?

DAN: Yes they're round in the middle instead of square. I shouldn't be telling you that should I. What makes you say that the other one is frequently active?

RENUGAN: I've seen it flash and there's a local practice before if you're going down the way you would be going to get caught cars coming the other way will flash to alert you the camera's on. I've seen it flash and I think I was caught there some time back.

For Renugan, the few seconds approaching and then passing the speed camera involve an articulation of times, places, actions, and the practices of others, which might enable constitution of the nature of the technology and of this particular act of driving as compliant. Compliance appears to go beyond acquiescence or assessment. It involves an active drawing together of various material aspects of doing driving, which are used to account for and accomplish a particular way of doing driving as compliant. For these drivers compliance seems to involve producing an account of the grounds for compliance at the same time as producing driving actions, which accomplish something that can be noted as similar to or fitting in to the verbal account offered. However, compliance in the driving videos did not start and end with attempts to do this kind of accountable accomplishment.

Secondly, some drivers gave up on the possibility of adequately accounting for or accomplishing compliance and instead drove either extremely cautiously (on the grounds that this would avoid any questions of the extent to which their driving was compliant) or recklessly (on the grounds that at some point some other authority would surely intervene if they overstepped the mark too greatly). Both caution and recklessness were articulated by the drivers themselves. In the following excerpts Denise and Farzana advocate caution:

[DRIVING ALONG]

DENISE: In fact driving is a generally worrying experience. I worry about this little yellow car trying to pull out. I worry about this cyclist. I worry about this white car parked in the middle of the road. No I think I can go.

DAN: Do you worry about that speed camera?

DENISE: Mmm no because I'm going too slow to be honest.

DAN: Do you think about the fact it's on the other side of the road?

DENISE: No and here's another one [on our side of the road] but I am usually going too slow to worry. I usually think the lines on the road [the speed camera distance markers] must be something to do with cameras but I'm too slow.

[DRIVING TWO MINUTES LATER]

DAN: Did you pay attention to that speed camera?

DENISE: Yes well no. I assume that's a dummy and I'm usually slowing down here because I turn off.

DAN: But you assume it's a dummy because it's never actually

DENISE: Caught me? Well I guess actually I don't care that much in that I assume that um I'm driving too slowly at that point anyway that the speed camera won't affect me. And I guess in many ways the familiarity of the speed camera I know it more than um other speed cameras and so in many ways maybe I've filtered the camera into my brain so I don't notice it.

[DRIVING ALONG]

FARZANA: Oh argh. Speed camera on the right.

DAN: Yes.

FARZANA: But you know you get paranoid. Can that camera catch me even though it's on the other side of the road, even if there are no [speed camera distance] markings it might flash so I should drive really slowly so I don't get caught and sent to prison.

DAN: How do you relate to those cameras on the other side of the road?

FARZANA: Fear [...] You know people assure me there are no markings but it's there watching and what if you trigger something?

The kind of compliance being accomplished in these two excerpts appears to be distinct from the kind of articulation of material features we noted previously. In these excerpts drivers do compliance through exemption. Instead of articulating the basis for compliance, these drivers exercised immense caution. It was as if this would enable them to avoid or exempt themselves from considerations of compliance. By contrast, other drivers adopted an entirely opposite tack. For example, in this next excerpt Marta suggests compliance can be accomplished not through detailed articulation or extreme caution, but instead just by driving and seeing what happens.

MARTA: So when I'm driving along here I'm normally thinking about the traffic lights [CAR GOES OVER SPEED BUMP FAST, DAN NEARLY DROPS CAMERA]

DAN: Woah

MARTA: Even though I should be thinking about the speed bumps

DAN: You don't think about the speed bumps?

MARTA: Er I think it's because I'm used to driving along here

[GOING THROUGH LIGHTS INTO YELLOW BOX JUNCTION]

MARTA: Now will I get caught where I'm not supposed to stop? Yes

DAN: So there you've decided to go across even though there might not be enough space

MARTA: But being as I was the second car I thought I might have enough space.

In this excerpt Marta espouses a kind of compliance by exemption. In place of articulation of and following the means to achieve compliance and in place of extreme caution comes a kind of recklessness whereby the degree of compliance is left as an upshot of the ways in which other road users (presumably also including law enforcement officers) might react to Marta's actions. Her driving and its relative degree of non-compliance are accomplished without any clear articulation of, or acquiescence to, an authorized notion of compliance, and without any particular concern to demonstrate compliance to an assessor (human or technological). Marta will see how fast she can drive over speed bumps and will enter box junctions in the hope that her exit becomes clear in time. The result is a kind of hoped-for compliance if everything falls into place. She exempts herself from detailed articulations of compliance on the grounds that if things work out compliance will be accomplished.

Thirdly, other drivers took distinct approaches to compliance. In place of actively accounting for the grounds for compliance or exempting themselves from compliance on the grounds of caution or recklessness, some drivers talked of the regular routine aspects of driving. Compliance for these drivers derived from just doing the same thing, on the same roads, with similar looking road users at all times. This was not caution as such, it did not require a detailed articulation of the grounds for compliance, nor was it clearly articulated as recklessness. The routines were recognizable to these drivers as the kinds of things they did every day without encountering any problems with compliance. For example, Sara tells how she routinely drives past a speed camera:

[DRIVING ALONG]

SARA: There's a speed camera coming up um in about half a mile and it does work.
DAN: Right.
SARA: So I've been told.
DAN: Right, right. So that's from being told by other people.
SARA: Absolutely yes. It's very hard to stick to 30 down here for some reason.
DAN: What would you put that down to do you reckon?
SARA: Well it's so wide and you can see everything. The speed camera doesn't seem to make any sense.
[…]
DAN: So it's a speed camera you're quite familiar with?
SARA: Yes.

Sara talks of being familiar with a particular camera and this is combined with discussing familiarity with this particular road, which is discussed in combination with the kinds of things other people have told her. Routines stand in for an explicit articulation of the grounds and means for compliance. Indeed, several drivers found it hard to articulate what it might mean to notice and demonstrate adherence to a road safety measure (such as a speed camera, traffic light, or roundabout). This was not to say that these drivers were unfamiliar with such objects, but rather that they suggested their routine ways of driving past these objects were just too mundane to discuss.

These excerpts demonstrate that drivers doing driving accomplished compliance in several ways. Drivers described how their driving practice took into account various material objects that populated the driving experience. Drivers also exempted themselves from detailed discussion of compliance either by driving with extreme caution or with a kind of recklessness that they hoped would accomplish a kind of compliance if everything fell into place at any particular moment (and with little regard for the consequences if it did not). Drivers also found their regular driving extremely routine, dull, and hardly worthy of consideration. Compliance thus became the upshot of routine: drivers just assumed there would have been some kind of intervention at some point if the routine was in some way inadequately compliant. Drivers thereby accomplished a moral order of their own driving, others' driving, the technologies of driving, and the technologies of governance. To provide an account of crossing a yellow box junction was simultaneously to manifest the ontology of the lines painted on the road, the driver driving, other vehicles and their drivers, the means of governance that could at some point intervene in driving, the moral appropriateness of their own and others' actions, and the reasonableness (or otherwise) of technologies of governance.

6.3.2 Consistency of Compliance

To what extent can these accomplishments of compliance be considered consistent between drivers and between different locations? We have asked what is being complied with, how does one know how to comply, on whose terms might compliance be judged, how might compliance be constituted in relation to objects of governance, and how are ontologies of governance brought into being in moments of compliance/non-compliance? But how and in what ways and according to whom might compliance and non-compliance be termed consistent? Do all drivers, for example, bring compliance into being in the same way, are all drivers judged on the same terms, do drivers maintain the same kind of driving activities, and do objects of governance attain a steady ontology through various moments of governance? These are all questions of consistency, but how does consistency operate, on whose terms, with what consequence, invoking what kinds of associations between people, objects, times, and places? Our suggestion in the rest of this section is that consistency is accomplished as a matter of equivalence. That is, one moment of, for example, compliant driving, is constituted as equivalent to other moments of driving, as equivalent to the driving of other drivers, or, in varying ways, as non-equivalent.[7]

Throughout the driving videos a persistent and ordinary feature of talking about driving proved to be constituting equivalence between the particular moment of driving in which the driver was engaged with other moments of driving. This included talk of driving being routine and ordinary. The following excerpt nicely captures many of the central features of this kind of talk:

> MARTA: Right there's a speed camera coming up. I know I can go at least 33mph so I try and drive at that speed.
>
> DAN: Is this a speed camera you're familiar with?
>
> MARTA: I know that speed camera so I go 30, but others I don't always know and I slow right down and then it turns out to be 50. I hate that

Marta starts by constituting an equivalence between the kind of driving she is doing in this moment with other occasions of driving. Consistency is accomplished via this invoked equivalence. Thus, Marta knows there is a speed camera coming up, knows the speed at which to drive, knows this camera in distinction with other cameras with which she is not familiar, and drives accordingly. None of this equivalence is available as a straightforward set of facts, independent of the moment of articulation. The talk invokes these ontologies of what the camera is, what it will do, her driving, her speed, and so on. Consistency ('I know that speed camera') and compliance ('so I go 30') derive from the invoked equivalence.

Much of the work done by drivers to accomplish consistency specifically focuses on the objects of road safety governance. Marta (as we have seen) focuses on a familiar speed camera and Sara, in this next excerpt, talks of speed bumps. The pluralization of the bump is important here. The constitution of consistency being accomplished in this next excerpt is between speed bumps as equivalent ontological entities.

> [DRIVING ALONG SLOWLY]
>
> SARA: Speed humps I take a lot of notice of. Wear and tear on my vehicle. They do my head in.
>
> DAN: Would you prefer some sort of other measure in place there other than speed humps?
>
> SARA: Um so I suppose speed humps are better than chicanes because that definitely stops the line of traffic. I mean there's all kinds of measures tried aren't there.

---

[7] Recent years have seen a marked interest in equivalence in STS research. For example, Espeland and Sauder (2007) discuss metrics for commensuration, an argument similar to MacKenzie's (2009) discussion of calculable devices for making things the same. Instead of focusing on formal metrics or measures, we argue for the importance of understanding how equivalence is discursively accomplished.

In this excerpt the nature of what particular speed bump/hump is being encountered in the video is invoked through equivalence with bump/humps more generally. Speed bump/humps are to be understood through their common nature. They are something to look out for and to slow down for. Equivalence, consistency, and compliance work together. However, this is not a tale reducible to road safety. The equivalence between the aggregate, pluralized bumps/humps is used to articulate a view about vehicle damage. Sara wants to slow down to protect her own car rather than any other road users. In Latourian terms, the hump/bump is part of a translation in relations of governance between road safety (drive safely for the good of others) and a materially instantiated warning (watch out for this bump/hump). Although Sara invokes a consistent ontology of humps/bumps, one can note that in terms of compliance the driver's view (avoiding 'wear and tear') is somewhat distinct from an official version (road safety) of what ought to count as compliance with bumps/humps. Hence, this driver's view of what the nature of a bump/hump is retains consistency while also being at odds with an 'official' ontology of the bump/hump.

Drivers did not just focus on the consistency of objects of road safety. Drivers also frequently invoked times of driving as moments for doing and not doing consistency. Drivers thus articulated their consistent (or not) compliance with what they understood to be road safety imperatives at the same time as articulating how their driving practices had altered (or not), how road safety measures had changed (or not), and how the objects and mechanisms of road safety engineering had shifted (or not). One moment of driving was thus rendered equivalent (or not) to other moments. These temporal equivalences enabled invocations of distinct ontologies of governance objects while also opening up spaces for the discussion of drivers' approaches to road safety. In the following excerpt, Fabian discusses speed and governance at different times.

[DRIVING ALONG]

DAN: So when the roads are wider do you drive differently?

FABIAN: I think I'm probably paying less attention to my driving to my speed. Until I just noticed that speed camera. Now I'm thinking I should probably slow down to demonstrate that I am a law abiding citizen. And there's a police car up ahead.

DAN: Yes

FABIAN: So that's a double combination of um forcing me to pay attention to what I'm doing and now we've all got to slow down because of the police car—that's a pain. I think one of the good things about speed cameras is that you get less police out on the road trying to get people to slow down.

DAN: How would you know for sure?

FABIAN: Oh I'm sure that's the case. Um I think that means most often you can drive a bit faster or with a bit of a relaxed manner and just look out for the odd speed camera here and there rather than having to worry about police cars.

In this excerpt the nature of what speed enforcement is (mostly 'cameras') is made non-equivalent to what it was (mostly 'police cars'). Fabian talks of such non-equivalence in terms of a move to what might now constitute compliance ('just look out for the odd speed camera here and there rather than having to worry about police cars'). This occasion in the driving video is marked by a kind of novelty—noting the police car and speed camera together—and initially this is seen as an inconvenience ('a pain'), but it also provides the opportunity to do this invocation work. It is the novel moment through which the past and present, notions of consistency and inconsistency can be invoked.

Drivers in the videos frequently articulated the distinctiveness or otherwise of driving in different locales, what compliance might mean between those locales and the extent to which their driving was modified in association with their articulation of distinct places of driving. In the following excerpt, Farzana articulates consistency between driving places.

[DRIVING ALONG]

FARZANA: The thing that I always take into account wherever I am driving in the world is that I hate other drivers swearing at me. I mean I don't want to be the cause of any misery on the road. So yeah I take into account other road users. I take into account the situation at hand, but you know being human it depends on your mood.

DAN: Yeah.

Farzana here invokes a standard of consistency between places borne out of her declared wish to avoid misery, swearing, and the wrath of other road users. For Farzana, consistency is a product of concern for other road users, rather than the means of road safety governance. Potential equivalents are considered broadly here (anywhere in the world) and the nature of what should count as appropriate driving is apparently fixed (avoiding any of the negatives listed).

Up to this point we have noted consistency in drivers' actions, in drawing equivalence between objects, times, and places. However, this might place too great an emphasis on consistency. Alongside and intermingled with these articulations of doing driving through consistent associations were multiple occasions, working outs, and doings of inconsistency. Indeed at times in the videos it appeared that inconsistency was the default position and consistency the exception. In Section 6.3.1 we found Farzana articulating her view of the world of driving, including that she did not wish to upset anyone and would like to take other road users into account. Immediately following that excerpt, Farzana talked through the following driving action.

FARZANA: You know sometimes you want to be able to er er you know you want to be considerate and everything but sometimes you just have to go and you hope other people will understand.

[GOING THROUGH TRAFFIC LIGHTS]

DAN: Well that was an amber light. That was on the edge.

FARZANA: But that changed as I went across. That's not fair. [APPROACHING A CYCLIST]. Argh I hate cyclists.

DAN: Hate them because?

FARZANA: Look at what she's doing?

DAN: Slowing you down you mean?

FARZANA: Not just slowing me down but sometimes they don't seem to know what they are doing. They veer off course sometimes they cycle two abreast. Um they I mean we are lucky here because we have these cycle paths but er in other places there aren't and sometimes cyclists are in the way.

Farzana thus immediately follows her concern for other road users and the desire to avoid upsetting others with an outburst about cyclists, 'sometimes you just have to go and hope others understand', and driving through a traffic signal very close to red. What might outwardly appear to be inconsistent is dealt with unproblematically by Farzana. Her account expresses little inclination to discuss or offer an explanation for this apparent inconsistency. One means to invoke such an explanation would be to suggest that the previous excerpt focuses on being held to account and the subsequent excerpt on holding to account—the switch in direction of accountability relations providing the grounds to absolve any need for further explanation. For Denise in the following excerpt, a different kind of inconsistency emerged. This focused on her distinct identities as a driver (in the video) and a cyclist (at other times).

[DRIVING ALONG]

DENISE: So here I am looking out for cyclists. In the morning I am a cyclist and actually I prefer it if cars just drive straight past I don't like looking over my shoulder.

DAN: So when you're driving do you normally drive straight past [cyclists]?

DENISE: Er no actually I tend to give them space. Um no because I swerve sometimes.

DAN: On your bike you mean?

DENISE: Mmmm so you need to give them quite a lot of allowance.

[STOPPED AT TRAFFIC LIGHTS]

Denise prefers motorists just to drive past when she is a cyclist so that she does not have to look over her shoulder to see what car drivers are doing.

Yet while driving she does not drive straight past cyclists in case they swerve. Instead she hangs back behind the cyclist and gives them plenty of room. Once again what might be considered inconsistent in the driver's account is treated as an ordinary matter of road use. It does not seem to trouble Denise greatly that she does not follow her own preferred instructions for drivers moving past cyclists. In the following excerpt Marta again appears to follow a troublingly[8] inconsistent course of action when faced with a traffic jam and an empty bus lane.

[STUCK IN TRAFFIC]

MARTA: Right this bit's always busy with traffic so I could pull into the bus lane or I could stay where I'm supposed to stay.

DAN: What happens when you go down the bus lane?

MARTA: Um then I need to pull in before I get to the traffic lights which can either be easy or quite difficult.

DAN: And do you think that's gonna annoy everyone else if you do that?

MARTA: No not really. It doesn't seem to annoy anyone. It annoys me if someone else does it. But no-one's ever beeped at me so I don't think I've upset anyone.

DAN: Yeah [CAR NOW MOVING FORWARD].

MARTA: And now people are pulling in front of me [FROM THE BUS LANE] which is what I would normally do. That really annoys me.

In this excerpt Marta is stuck in a traffic jam and finds the allure of the empty bus lane quite difficult to resist. She considers driving down the bus lane to get ahead of the traffic jam and wonders if she might be able to pull back into the traffic further down the road. Although she seems to think this course of action is morally justified ('it doesn't seem to annoy anyone') she chooses to remain in the traffic jam, is then witness to other road users trying to follow her usual course of action and finds their actions morally questionable ('that really annoys me'). The apparent inconsistency (in this case between others not being annoyed with her and her annoyance with others) appears unproblematic and is not remarked upon by the driver.

For all the claims regarding invocations of consistency and the connection between consistency and compliance, the frequency of apparent inconsistency suggests that drivers doing driving do not each comply in the same way while driving, in any great consistency, even when confronted with the 'same' road users, conditions, or objects of road safety governance.

---

[8] The 'trouble' here is most notably for the analyst struggling to figure out what the driver is doing and how she is accounting for her actions. The analyst is also sat in the car carrying out video-taping and starts to wonder to what extent he might be held partly responsible by other road users for the actions of the vehicle in which he is sat as a passenger.

Consistency can thus be understood as a matter of constituting equivalence between objects, actions, times, and places. Inconsistency can be understood as a matter of producing non-equivalents. However, in the videos, 'inconsistency' seems to be of much greater relevance to the analyst than the driver. Drivers make sense of their driving by way of frequent and unproblematic ontological shifts (between road users being a matter of concern and a pain, between cyclists being something to ignore and something to worry about, and between bus lanes as a rightful domain for overtaking slow traffic and a location for immoral overtaking by other drivers) and switches in the direction of accountability relations (particularly between holding to account and being held to account; the lack of mutual accountability somewhat mediated by the materiality of the car). Driving is a matter of such ontological multiplicity (with matters continually shifting) that such apparent inconsistency (to the analyst) does not appear troubling to the driver. Ontological multiplicity, it seems, is frequently the normal condition for driving.

6.4 Re-educating the Speeding Driver

Of course, it is difficult to know whether the nature and extent of drivers' noticings (and their articulation) were due to the fact that a researcher was sitting filming and asking questions as they drove along. Were drivers articulating these particular compliance narratives because of these circumstances? Would other occasions of driving compliance invoke similar issues? In order to assess the extent to which the bases for compliant driving differ between situations, we now turn our attention to a particular setting where compliance is rehearsed: the driver retraining speed awareness course.

As is already evident, the figure of the driver (motorist) is a key accomplishment in doing compliance with road safety. In the contemporary moral order of traffic governance, the driver is the primary entity deemed responsible for compliance or non-compliance, particularly in relation to speed. A series of objects and technologies—most notably speed cameras—are brought into play to reinforce this moral order and to make the driver accountable. Speed awareness courses are one means by which drivers are drawn into accountability work.[9] We imagined that the speed awareness course could provide

---

[9] These are relatively widespread in countries such as the USA. They were introduced in the UK in October 2003. By April 2005, only two police authorities in the UK were operating the scheme. A total of 10,000 drivers caught speeding in the first eighteen months after the scheme was introduced in October 2003 opted to go on courses to learn about the dangers of driving too fast (*Oxford Times*, 2005: 11). Those caught doing 36 mph in a 30 mph zone were

insights into many of the concerns already mentioned in this chapter, most notably the ways in which compliance might involve the many varied entities involved in the governance of traffic. But how to get access to a speed awareness course?

Over and above the call of ethnographic duty and in line with our happenstance methodological sensibility (see Chapter 10), Steve was caught speeding during the course of this study. Here the culprit tells his story:

> On a Tuesday night, returning from a College dinner, along the Woodstock Road, I noticed the flash of the camera. The sequence of notices which subsequently reached me by mail included an invitation to attend a speed awareness course. I was offered a place on a three hour interactive course, costing £71. This seemed an excellent opportunity to experience contemporary efforts to re-educate the speeding driver. There ensued a minor moral dilemma over whether or not to charge the cost of the course to the research budget of our funding agency, ESRC.

We anticipated that the experience of attending the speed awareness course could work as a highly focused ethnographic encounter, which would provide a sort of Geertzian 'thick description' (1973). The working hunch was that this would provide insights into the moral order of speeding, the moral universe of members of the tribe, as played through, enacted, and reaffirmed in the course of detailed ritual interactions. We were particularly interested in how attributions of accountability and responsibility were played out in this arena. How were the various entities of this moral order invoked, described, assigned, and brought into compliant relation with each other? How were the ontologies of these different entities managed?

It was clear from the very first point of contact with the course that individual participants were being positioned vis-à-vis their culpability, their relationship to those in authority, and, crucially for our purposes, to a non-compliant relation with the nature and purpose of speed cameras. The initial letter—'Notice of Intended Prosecution'—came from Regional Police Force[10] and was addressed to the culprit. 'It is intended to take proceedings against the driver of motor vehicle [number plate] for the alleged offence of (Speed 36mph) Exceeding 30mph on restricted road at 23:41 on 26/11/04 at (place) A4144 Woodstock Road Oxford'. 'You are recorded

---

offered a place on a three hour interactive course; the course cost £71 and no penalty points accrued to the licence. This was instead of the normal fine of £60 plus three penalty points. Those caught doing 59 mph in a 50 mph zone (or 96 mph in a 70 mph zone) were offered a place on a five hour interactive course, including two hours on the road with a trainer; this course cost £91 and three penalty points. This was instead of the normal six penalty points and a fine between £1000 and £2000.

[10] A pseudonym, of course.

as the Owner/Keeper/Hirer of the above vehicle at the time of the alleged offence'. The first crucial step was thus to tie the driver to the speeding car.[11]

The next letter, also from regional police was headed 'Offer of Speed Awareness Scheme Workshop'. It explained that the offence carried a 'maximum penalty of £1000 and 3–6 penalty points' and that normally offenders were given the opportunity to 'accept a £60 fixed penalty and 3 penalty points on your driving licence...'

> However, Regional Police seeks to educate and not prosecute and irrespective of the number of penalty points you may currently have, I am of the opinion that your attendance at a Speed Awareness Scheme Workshop would be beneficial and am prepared to offer this as an alternative to the fixed penalty on this occasion. On satisfactory completion of the Speed Workshop the Notice of Intended Prosecution will be withdrawn (Regional Police Force, 15 December 2004).

The culprit's acceptance of the place on the course was followed by a letter from Drive Tech (5 January 2005), the 'chosen provider of Regional Police speed awareness workshops', with instructions on how to pay for and arrange a date to participate in a workshop. The letter spelled out a lengthy set of conditions for taking the course. Among the conditions for satisfactorily completing the course was the requirement to 'show improvement in terms of attitude'. The letter itself, bearing the logos of the Drive Tech company rather than those of the regional police, denoted a transition of purview of accountability between these agencies of regulation. It also began to set out the grounds for compliance, a basic idea of why compliance might be a good thing (a reduced penalty and an increase in road safety awareness) and some consequences of compliance (better future attitude to driving).

Here the culprit reflects on his initial entry into the assembly of bad/ non-compliant drivers:

> When I arrive at the main entrance to what looks like a former army barracks in north Oxfordshire, there are barriers across the entrance and an entry guard on duty. He greets me with: 'Hello sunshine what can I do for you?' I reckon he knows what I am there for. His greeting sounds chummy/vernacular/patronizing. He gives me instructions to get to a somewhat distant car park.

---

[11] A common attempt to resist prosecution turned on the disruption of this attempt to tie driver to car, for example by the owner replying that he or she did not know (or could not remember) who was driving the car at the time of the offence. This form of resistance apparently met with some success because the costs of the extra administrative effort in following this up were thought prohibitive. See Chapter 5 for a discussion of the costs of this form of accountability.

It is difficult to get into the rather sombre looking building...When we eventually get into the building we are ushered with some others down the end of a corridor and into what seems to be a reception area. Twenty or so people, mostly men are sitting silently in chairs placed around the perimeter of the room. The general mood of the participants seems sullen and resentful. It is not clear what the transition from police to Drive Tech actually entails. Participants are uncertain what is going to happen to them or what, if any, are the sanctions which might apply in the event of a less than satisfactory performance on the course. Their identities are being individually checked by two men. Both men wear pristinely ironed white shirts, highly polished black shoes and name tags: Terry and Paul.

Terry and Paul use terms of greeting such as 'my friend', 'buddy' and 'gents', all of which feel patronizing and vaguely threatening, as did 'hello sunshine' at the front gate. I feel these are terms characteristic of police vocabulary. The room's occupants hand over their documents meekly.

The instruction room has posters and Regional Police signs on the walls. The posters are fairly graphic depictions of the dangers of speeding, specifically going faster than 30 mph. One says: 'Driver in a Hurry. Child in a Coma'. Another has the legend: 'At 5mph over the speed limit, how much further does it take to stop? Not here. Not here. Here.' (Body of child in street.)

Speed awareness courses are purportedly 'designed to challenge, change and improve an individual driver's attitude and behaviour when driving...Speed Awareness engages the participant from the beginning by focusing on their driving mind-set. The course never criticises a driver's attitude but takes them on a journey of discovery... Speed Awareness does not employ shock tactics; it causes the participant to reflect and reassess their own views on speed and speeding' (Drive Tech, 2004). The central assumption then is psychological, that the driver's attitude and behaviour are responsible for speeding. And the corollary assumption is that the necessary change in mind-set can be brought about through the driver's reflection and reassessment. Crucially, then, the responsibility for speeding lies with the individual driver and his or her mind-set. The driver is responsible for changing the mind-set. They can choose whether or not to change their mind, to be compliant or not.

These assumptions lie behind the interactive style of the course. Speeding drivers are encouraged to come to the realization that they (their minds) need to change. The discussion is open and informal. The candidate for re-education records his experiences:

Once in the instruction room, Terry starts things off by declaring: 'As you can see we are not ourselves police'. It is not clear how or why this should be evident. The tone throughout seems meant to be reassuring, but I'm not sure that it is. It is especially not so in light of the threatening rules and conditions spelled out as the basis for attending the workshop. And the idea that we are each individuals is reinforced by the initial computer based task.[12]

'Professor Frank Mckenna, the leading psychologist in this country, is doing a three year study. We are a captive audience. To get off the three points, you give this information. Some of the questions are a bit obscure but they are set by psychologists, we all know how their brains work! The thing is to try not to think too much about the questions. Professor Frank McKenna then has a profile for you.'

There then follow a series of five interactive computer exercises which take about 75 minutes to complete. Exercise 1 has approximately fifty multiple choice questions which ask about the individual. 'How would you assess your personality?' I feel I am being forced into preconceived and inappropriate responses. 'Would you describe yourself as aggressive, not very aggressive, calm?' Well, I probably wouldn't describe myself as any of these things. If I had to choose, it would depend very much on the situation I was in, who I was talking to and what I thought might be done with the answer. I have the sense that just about any response could be used against me, as a negative attribute.

The 'profiles' are print outs which summarize each individual's performance on the computer exercises. Each task is graded on a scale. For example, the 'Video Speed Test Feedback' is graded on a seven point scale between 'Very much slower than average' through 'Average' to 'Very much faster than average'. My own printout has a large X printed in the 'Average' box. Underneath is the comment:

While your speed responses were generally in the normal range, when interpreting your scores you must remember that 1) your speed choice is one of the best predictors of your likely involvement in an accident—those with high scores are more likely to be involved in speed related accidents 2) Even those who receive an average score are frequently breaking the speed limit.

Steve's feedback on the 'Close Following Test' similarly scores him as 'Average' on a seven-point scale between 'Very much further away than average' and 'Very much closer than average'. The accompanying comment reads:

While your following distance is generally in the average range, you should note that when riders are observed on the road the average driver is generally following too close to the vehicle in front, so being close to average is not something to feel comfortable about. Driving too close to the vehicle in front is one of the most common driving errors. By adding as little as 1 second to your following distance you can give yourself a better view of events ahead. You also give yourself more time to react to events and provide a smoother more professional drive.

---

[12] The individualization of the driver entity goes hand in hand with the psychologization of that entity. Thus, from time to time we noticed how different categories of personality were earmarked as deserving treatment. For example, in 2004 a newspaper article reported the claim by a 'sleep expert' that fat and overweight drivers may actually be more dangerous than drunk drivers (*Daily Mail*, 2004); or the BBC report that the UK government was to spend £1.3 million to provide driving lessons specially targeted to 'white van man'—the stereotypical aggressive driver—to 'make them more considerate behind the wheel' (BBC, 2006e).

    I am left feeling unsure whether or not to be pleased with my result. The suspicion arises that however one's 'profile' turns out, it will be accompanied by admonishing remarks. Average is still potentially dangerous. That is, individuals revealed as average on the test should not be allowed to think they are exempt from configuration.

A crucial, omnipresent feature of the speed awareness course is the reassertion throughout of the relations of accountability and responsibility that pertain in matters of vehicle speed. This includes not just the individuation of the driver entity and his or her psychological responsibility for speeding, but the specification of sources of authority about a wide range of issues, including the statistics for road deaths and injuries, driver reaction times, the effectiveness of car braking systems, whether or not parents should be responsible for their children, and so on. Compliance, then, involves a far broader remit than might initially be considered in road safety matters. In a similar manner to the examples we used to open this chapter, matters of compliance appear continually to multiply. It is not just about the speed at which one drives, it is about one's treatment of other road users, the extent to which one can successfully navigate the individual psychologization offered by speed awareness courses, the ability to move through different relations of accountability, and the recognition that responsible driving also involves statistics, death, children, distances, and so on.

    Up until this point on the course, compliance still seems a relatively straightforward matter of turning up, getting in, demonstrating one's identity, and navigating a test (the results of which one might never be able to perfect). However, other features of the course drew compliance into different kinds of questions of accountability.

    Terry goes round the room asking each person in turn why they were speeding when they were caught. The responses include:

> Lack of concentration
> No reason, really
> Just unlucky
> It was a newly installed camera!
> I got done twice that same day!
> Just not concentrating
> I was late
> Late
> I was trying to see how soon you had to reduce speed when you come out of a 50 mph zone
> Arguing with my passenger!
> Late for an appointment
> Don't know really.

Several others are unable to offer a reason for speeding. The discussion moves on but subsequently, later in the class, when Terry is discussing a particular video in which we are shown an accident:

TERRY: That car was doing 39mph. And what do you think the toughest job was for the police? It was to tell the boy's parents. And the parents asked: why was the driver speeding. Now I want you to think back to your earlier answers as to why you were speeding.
Lack of concentration
No reason, really
Just unlucky
…

Here then is a striking redirection of accountability relations. In a clever rhetorical move, our earlier answers are now seen to have been relatively inconsequential confessions, presumed to be only for the ears of fellow participants in the re-education class. There may even have been a slight bravado, a jokiness associated with the earlier responses. We are all in it together, the import of what we say is for others in the room, or perhaps for mates, friends, and acquaintances with which we joke about having been caught speeding. Terry now asks us to imagine how those same excuses will sound when conveyed to the parents of the boy killed in the accident.

Lack of concentration
No reason, really
Just unlucky
….

Terry thereby reasserts what we are asked to accept as the proper moral order of accountability. In stark contrast with the casual jokiness of our initial answers, we are instructed that we are accountable for our actions and excuses to the parents of dead children. Drivers are responsible through their actions not just for the occurrence of accidents but for a whole series of consequences that follow, in this case the distress of a child's parents.

The assertion of this aspect of driver accountability also found expression in a series of anecdotes told by Terry. He had been a member of a traffic police unit charged with the task of 'clearing up' after motorway accidents. This generated several gruesome stories about the severe consequences of accidents. For example:

TERRY: What is the number one cause of accidents? Driver error. And what do you know about humans?
They are unpredictable.

TERRY: Spot on. Some persons are living in the land of the fairies. Driver fatigue. There was this truck driver, he'd driven all the way from Portugal without stopping. And you know what happens next. Six people were killed. And the driver didn't give a monkeys. Twelve months ban and a £600 fine. One woman was in a wheelchair for the next five years. She attempted suicide. Her marriage broke up. A tragedy. The truck driver has psychological damage. I was second on the scene for that one. And my sergeant he comes up to me and says Terry, I can't find the head.

These and similar anecdotes attempt a form of responsibilization by fear. Drivers are told of the dreadful consequences of accidents and asked to accept that these are caused by driver error and/or driver fatigue. They are thereby asked to comply with the distribution of accountability relations, which is being asserted between the key enacted entities.

A similar assertion of the moral order of driver accountability centred on the relationship between the driver and his or her vehicle. Terry initiates consideration of this topic by asking 'What about the vehicle'? This elicits several suggestions from the class, all of which seem to centre on the driver's actions and responsibilities in relation to the vehicle:

Misjudging an overtaking manoeuvre
Overestimating your ability
Performance perception

(Suddenly, there is an intervention from the back of the class.)

But you get in a car and it's going 100 mph before you know it, with some cars.
TERRY: But who makes the car go at that speed?
Yeah but with some cars it's so easy.
TERRY: But who's driving?
But these just are fast cars some of them.
TERRY: But it's *your* decision.
But no really some cars just have to be driven fast, I mean some of these high spec cars.....
(Some consternation in the rest of the class. This person is being reckless, foolhardy, maybe even courting sanction from the trainers. And we want to get out of here soon, please...)

The disruption is instructive. This participant is challenging a basic feature of the moral order: that drivers are always responsible for the actions of their vehicle, regardless of any special features the car might possess. The reaction from the rest of the class is especially telling. It is as if everyone else *knows* the correct answer. Whether or not some cars 'have to be driven fast', everyone else seems to realize that the appropriate behaviour as a member of the class is to comply with the moral order being declaimed by the instructor.

A surprising feature of this particular class was the nature and extent of interventions that seemed to challenge or disrupt the moral order being unfolded by the instructor.

TERRY: What aspect of driving isn't so good?
Speed cameras!
(Laughter, somewhat embarrassed laughter. Is it really okay to joke about this?)

TERRY: Now, what do you think is the toughest job that any policeman has to do?
[Participants make several guesses, clearing up after a crash, picking up the pieces, the paperwork. But apparently nobody gets it right]
TERRY: To inform the family after an accident. What do you think it's like to have to go and inform my wife that I won't be coming home anymore?
(Pause. No answer is forthcoming)
TERRY: How do you think she'd feel?
She might be quite pleased!!
(Laughter)
TERRY: Ah, but not if it was one of my grandchildren.
(Silence)

TERRY: Why do you think they put that camera there?
Easy money!
(Laughter)
They should put more repeaters [40mph signs] up to remind people.
TERRY: But who's going to pay for this, for more repeaters?
The cash from all the fines!!
(Laughter)

We are shown a video of a road safety ad. A little girl is walking along a pavement. She then steps out into the road. I think this is the one I've seen on TV, which asks: Where does the car stop when it is travelling at 30 mph? Here? Here? No, here (impact with little girl).

Where is the mother that's what I want to know!
(Muted laughter)
TERRY: Are you a father?
No.
TERRY: No.

Another video clip. This time a car is driving along, rounds a corner and sees too late a group of young boys in the road. The driver breaks, skids, and hits at least one of the boys.

TERRY: Whose fault is it? The driver or the boys?
The boys!
(Muted laughter)

The laughter is accompanied by some consternation among the group.

> I find myself getting increasingly annoyed with this one person—'that plonker' in my notes—who keeps making these interruptions. He must realize that his constant interruptions are simply going to delay how long we have to stay here. The interventions all seem obvious, but highly inappropriate. He's probably 'right', but only in some context outside of and beyond this little cocoon of re-education.

The interventions are surprising in the sense that they could be heard as contestations of the moral order and hence as a form of resistance or defiance. But their expression through a form of jokiness, together with the somewhat embarrassed laughter from other participants suggests something different. It is as if these interventions are a comment on the proceedings themselves, rather than a challenge to the moral order with which we are being asked to comply. The jokes seemed to direct attention to the obviousness of everything the instructor is claiming: they work as an ironic comment on the catechism in which we participants are forced to participate.

The speed awareness course illustrates the labour of compliance required in mundane governance, and the kinds of accountability relations through which compliance is to be measured, discussed, and accomplished. The course is monotonous in its repetition of similar messages (by Terry, the road safety posters, messages on video clips, and the preferred answers to the interactive computer tests), so that what count as appropriate responses becomes obvious and predictable as the course progresses, the ontology of what constitutes good/compliant driving is made clear and consistent again and again. And the monotony conveys consistent messages of accountability. Yet there is also a dynamic of jokes and ironic commentary that reinforces the obviousness of what participants recognize counts as compliance in this context. Compliance is clearly much more complicated than straightforward acquiescence and assessment. In this relatively formal setting at least, compliance involves the reassertion of a moral order comprising the key ontologies and the distribution of accountability and responsibility between them.

Is this mechanism for reasserting the moral order of driving effective? Does the speed awareness course work? Terry claims that only one in twelve people who have taken the course reoffend, whereas the figure was one in four before the courses started. It is not clear what is the basis for this claim, especially given that our ethnographer was again caught speeding a mere two weeks after the end of the course. But the more important point is that the very enunciation of this statistic reinforces the ontological basis of compliance. The individual driver is enacted as an entity, which is adjudged to offend (or not). And this individual is deemed capable of carrying with him or her the propensity not to reoffend after having participated in the course, having internalized the moral order that it reasserts. The capacity of drivers to give lip service to a catechism of driver accountabilities, while at the same time keeping a sense of irony, is not part of what counts as compliance.

6.5 Conclusion

Does mundane governance work? In this chapter we focused on one aspect of effectiveness and 'working', namely the phenomenon of compliance. In relation to traffic management this turns out to be much more than just a question of straightforward acquiescence and assessment.

In our videos we found drivers doing different kinds of compliance and non-compliance, in distinct kinds of accountability relationships, with different articulations of responsibility. Whereas the speed awareness course placed much emphasis on drivers needing to take individual responsibility for their actions, our video drivers actively assigned and distributed responsibility through, for example, figuring out what other road users (including pedestrians) were doing, attending to material features of the road, drawing on accounts they had been given by others, referencing driving routines with which they were familiar, claiming that extreme caution exempted them from having to take other matters into account, and invoking a very wide variety of other factors (from the time of day to the weather to the fact that their driving actions were being recorded). At the same time, some drivers did none of this. There were drivers who just drove and hoped things would work out. For objects of governance such as the yellow box junction, ontologies of governance seemed to shift between obviousness and mystery. Drivers noted that objects of governance did not carry their own instructions for use, so it was not clear how drivers might acquiesce, by whom they might be assessed, nor what might count as an act of compliance. The box junction was apprehended as both formal and at the same time practice oriented, uncertain, and fluid. As a consequence, the box junction was variously the focus for invoking caution, common sense, and recklessness.

Our mini-ethnography of the speed awareness course revealed further means by which compliance—in this case in formal settings—might be enacted, assessed, or resisted. The course provided a forum for the reassertion of the moral order of accountability vis à vis speeding. A forum where, if you will, the 'correct' forms of accountability relation were demonstrably and consensually rehearsed. The proceedings were strikingly ritualistic. This perhaps accounts for the curious feature of the 're-education', the pervasive sense throughout that almost all participants already 'knew' the right answers to the trainers' questions. They were all fairly proficient in articulating the correct moral order of accountability, they knew what was the appropriate distribution of ontologies for this purpose. From time to time, as we saw, there was some minor haggling over the facts of the matter. But in an important sense these did not matter. Participants knew that to participate acceptably (and hence comply) they should hear the numbers, advice, stopping distances, and grading awarded by the interactive computer exercise as mere examples of the central agenda, that is, the reassertion of a particular distribution of moral authority and accountability. At almost no point was there obvious puzzlement or misunderstanding. The interjections and comic remarks seemed to reinforce rather than undermine the moral order that was being performed. It seemed that everyone knew, for example, that it was ludicrous to challenge the basis for the moral order that was being sketched out. So when participants were shown a video clip where a small child slipped her mother's hand and ran into the path of a speeding car, the cry from the back of the room—'I blame the mother'—could be heard as a parody of the moral order with which everyone was familiar, rather than a serious disagreement with the message of the film.[13]

An aim of the speed awareness course was to change drivers' attitudes and driving. This set up the expectation that, upon leaving the course, drivers might continue to drive within the moral, accountable, and responsible set of relations which they had just performed. In other words, the course provides expectations of consistency (that drivers would take on, adhere to, and retain certain driving standards). As we noted in the chapter, consistency involved constituting equivalence between drivers, objects, times, places, or was not considered relevant at all. In many of the videos, apparent inconsistencies were more troubling for the analyst than the driver. At the same time, most assessments of the effectiveness of governance depend upon a measure of the consistency of compliance achieved by the means of governance.

Compliance and non-compliance then appear to involve materials, relations, accountabilities, and responsibilities. The ontologies of compliance are multiple. What counts as a governance artefact, how drivers might be assessed, as individuals or in aggregation, what their responsibilities are, can all shift swiftly and seemingly without effort from moment to moment when driving, or they can retain a stubbornness in action and orientation or provide the focus of ironic comment when presented as tokens of re-education.

---

[13] We wished to discuss our research interpretations with Drive Tech but, despite the course trainers' professed willingness to help, the company failed to reply either to letters or phone messages.

So driving is sometimes accomplished through the invocation of ordered, consistent, compliant ontologies of people, things, modes of governance, and road conditions. However, just as often, driving is accomplished without considering what it means to comply with an object of road safety governance. Drivers were freely able to admit to not seeing signs, to not noticing bumps and other ordering devices, and to continue speeding. Our examination of compliance demonstrates that attempts to account for governance actions immediately produce a multiplication of entities of governance.

But in one sense, objects such as signs were not there to be seen or read. Drivers new to the area, who slow down 'excessively' or stop to read signs, are liable to get hooted at by cars behind them. Added layers of ordering devices (signs, instructions, lights, road markings) do not necessarily make courses of compliant action any clearer to the driver. As we noted in the recycling centre (Chapter 3), the ever increasing number of signs did not decrease the number of occasions on which staff had to repair category transgressions by visitors to the centre. What then are the road markings for if they are not doing moral ordering? One possible answer is that they are doing ordering in relation to categories of actor other than drivers. The state of the road at any time can be understood as the momentary manifestation of an archaeology of previous discussions, disputes, representations, and past and anticipated future developments. In Chapter 7 we take on these archaeologies by investigating a location (an airport terminal) where histories of material governance are played out.

7

Spaces of Governance

7.1 Introduction

In a busy international airport just outside London, through which upwards of 20 million passengers pass each year,[1] the terminal manager[2] turns away from his colleague and toward the ethnographer. He sighs: 'another one has turned up airside'.[3] This, it turns out, is a regular occurrence. 'Members of the public' without tickets, sometimes without passports, hoping to meet arriving passengers, misunderstand the 'wayfinding technologies'[4] and wander through passport control, airport security, and 'somehow' end up in the departure lounge. At which point they have to be gathered up and escorted back to arrivals. The terminal manager shakes his head in mild exasperation. With a broad sweeping movement of his arm he points out all the numerous signs, barriers, information kiosks, TV screens, furniture layouts, and floor coverings that the latest errant 'member of the public' must have had to walk past and ignore.

In many ways, the busy airport is a natural laboratory for social science. Here are gathered in a geographically specific locale a huge variety of people from different nationalities and backgrounds, intent on travelling to innumerable destinations, or meeting or seeing off others who are travelling, individuals and families and groups, mostly accompanied by possessions, holding different forms of certification of identity, all with more or less familiarity with the opportunities and obligations entailed in being a passenger.

---

[1] We were asked to keep the identity of the airport confidential.

[2] In this chapter 'managers' and 'airport managers' are used to refer to aggregate groups of managers. When specific individual managers are focused upon, their individual titles are used.

[3] It was explained to us that UK airports are split between 'landside' (generally open areas for check-in, meeting arriving passengers, and so on) and 'airside' (the space beyond security and passport control, where passengers await departure).

[4] Airport staff used the term 'wayfinding technologies' to refer to the signs, announcements, screens, furniture layouts, floor colouring, and so on, which are designed to direct passenger movement.

And this is to say nothing of the thousands of staff, airline agents, aircrew, ground staff, baggage handlers, managers, shop assistants, service personnel, security staff, and on and on. Especially in the busiest airports, how does all this hold together? While those responsible for the operation of airports tend to refer to one of their key problems as that of *passenger* management,[5] for our purposes we prefer to deploy a more expansive definition. From our ontologically inflected perspective, the airport comprises a massive seething throng of *entities*—including, notably, a wide range of objects and their people—passing through a relatively limited space in a definite period of time.

The airport can thus be considered as a space of governance. It is a space within which signs are erected, barriers put in place, means to survey the population of objects and their owners/users are established, and attempts made to manage errant people/objects. In what ways does it help to understand these governance activities spatially?[6] This chapter explores the utility of treating particular locales as spaces of governance. First, we review some existing approaches to space as a form of governance. Second, we draw on observations in a London airport to investigate in what ways and to what extent terminal[7] space accomplishes governance. Third, we focus on the experiences of the key governed entities, namely the passengers, as they attempt to navigate their way through governed space. Finally, we conclude with an analysis of the ways in which spatial governance is accomplished through ontological constitution.

7.2 Governance and Space

Foucauldian approaches to governance and governmentality frequently use spatial formations as the starting point for understanding notions and relations of ordering. For example, in the *Order of Things* (1966), Foucault suggests ordering things is distinct from ordering people:

> The history of madness would be the history of the other—of that which, for a given culture, is at once interior and foreign, therefore to be excluded (so as to exorcise the interior danger) but by being shut away (in order to reduce its otherness); whereas the history of the order imposed on things would be the history

[5] For example, in conferences (we attended) entitled 'Optimizing Passenger Processes Through Manpower, Technology and Process Innovation' as part of the Global Passenger Operations Summit (26–27 April 2007, London), the passenger was constituted as the key accountable entity, in a way parallel to the constitution of the responsible driver in Chapters 5 and 6.

[6] At the end of Chapter 6, we mentioned that the layout of roads and the 'furniture' that populates them could be understood as ossified histories of traffic governance; and that these histories are variously invoked on occasion or ignored at other times.

[7] In this chapter the 'terminal' refers to the specific building whereas the 'airport' refers to the broader set of buildings, car parks, etc.

of the same—of that which, for a given culture, is both dispersed and related, therefore to be distinguished by kinds and to be collected together into identities. (Foucault, 1966: xxvi).

In developing his genealogy of orders, in *Madness and Civilisation* (1967) Foucault refers to epistemes as particular periods of time characterized by specific practices of knowing order. Each of these epistemes focuses on a different object, machine, or architecture. Medieval forms of knowing order involved shipping out the disorderly, insane, or morally corrupt in, for example, ships of fools. The great confinement that subsequently followed and signalled a shift in episteme, included new architectural apparatus, for example, prisons. A further shift in episteme to rehabilitation had a corresponding and individualizing architecture of its own. Foucault presents John Howard's[8] view of confinement as a main motive for shifting toward rehabilitation; Howard 'was outraged by the fact that the same walls could contain those condemned by common law, young men who disturbed their families' peace or who squandered their goods, people without profession, and the insane' (1967: 41). Confinement 'had become the abusive amalgam of heterogeneous elements' (1967: 41). Rehabilitation became a way of knowing order, focused on the individual subject and directed toward making them aware of their own actions, responsibility, (potential) otherness, and need to be orderly. Madness was thus 'finally chained to the humiliation of being its own object' (1967: 251) and 'everything was organised so that the madman would recognise himself in a world of judgement that enveloped him on all sides; he must know that he is watched, judged and condemned' (1967: 253).

From shipping out, to containing within, to rehabilitation are key shifts in architectural technologies of knowing order. For Foucault, the French political–historical apparatus from the revolution onwards was motivated by a particular kind of ordering. 'It was the dream of a transparent society, visible and legible in each of its own parts, the dream of there no longer existing any zones of darkness, zones established by the privilege of royal power or the prerogative of some corporation. It was the dream that each individual, whatever position he occupied, might be able to see the whole of society' (1980: 152). These themes of visibility, transparency, and order pervade Foucault's work, particularly evident in his concerns with architectures as disciplining mechanisms imbued by the professional gaze. Thus, the panopticon was characterized by 'an inspecting gaze, a gaze which each individual under its weight will end by *interiorising* to the point that he is his own overseer, each individual thus experiencing this surveillance over

---

[8] John Howard was an eighteenth century English prison reformer, philanthropist, and occasional hospital inspector. The Howard League for penal reform was named after him and still promotes prison reform: http://www.howardleague.org/

and against himself. A superb formula: power exercised continuously and for what turned out to be a minimal cost' (1980: 158, emphasis added). Orderliness in Foucault's work has a clear focus on the classification of people and things into neat and separate spatial containers (in a similar manner to the recycling and waste management we noted in Chapter 3) along with the means to prevent contamination between such containers, combined with a range of diverse features: the gaze through which classification might operate; the cost of ordering; the professionalization of vision; and discipline in governance. In this approach, interiorizing is key to explaining how and why governance operates. The individualized subjects of governance become responsibilized through taking on—interiorizing—appropriate rationales of governance, and through developing an awareness of the architecture, in relation to which the extent and appropriateness of interiorizing is measured, judged, and becomes consequential.

Although Foucault introduces a rich litany of ideas about history, people and things, relations of governing, rationales of government, and the possibility of interiorizing, the precise nature or role of architecture is left unclear.[9] How exactly does architecture do ordering, governance, and governmentality? Some elements of Foucault's work, read from the Science and Technology Studies (STS) perspective we are developing here, appear taken as given, and unproblematized. That is, what the architecture is and what it does appear settled, and it operates straightforwardly to achieve the intended goals of the architect. For example, the ship of fools features as a designated space of ordering that transported madness away from society. Madness was literally 'othered' through its transportation from here (orderly society) to there (just about anywhere else). In this account, the architecture, spaces, and links between them appear unquestioned. Yet, at other moments, Foucault portrays architecture as the focus for disciplinary relations, through which power is organized, providing the conditions of possibility through which interiorizing and hence governance is achieved. The panopticon, for example, can be considered as the outcome of relations between people, things, modes of ordering (such as the collection, compilation, and ordering of information), and ways of acting. This appears less focused on ontological singularity (the space does not simply and singularly create governance).

Recent analyses of Foucault's work on themes of space and security provide further insights into how these forms of spatial governance could be said to operate. For example, Cadman (2010) and Elden (2007) suggest Foucault's later writing on security and territory draws together concepts of space, calculation, and notions of the secured in historical developments traced from

---

[9] This continues our argument in Chapter 2 that the material properties of technologies of order remain on occasions somewhat unspecified in approaches to governmentality.

forms of calculation to international treaties. Within this line of argument, Elden suggests that Foucault focuses on a shift in the kind of guarantee offered by the state, from one of territory (within these borders you will be free) to one of population. The latter 'guarantee is from uncertainty, accident, damage, risk, illness, lack of work, tidal wave, and anti-social behaviour' (Elden, 2007: 563). Elden draws on Foucault's analysis of town planning, food shortages, and vaccination campaigns to highlight key traits of the apparatus of security. In particular, Elden suggests that Foucault argues that the management of spaces such as towns has shifted from a focus on disciplinary mechanisms (involving segmentation and closure of space for sorting and monitoring of the population) to one of security. This focus on security involves opening up passages and forms of movement, a minimization of regulation, and a wider distribution of security mechanisms than witnessed in disciplinary architectures. This 'opening up' expands the scope of security risk to which we might all be subject, but is also central to economic and market expansion. The change in spatial relations, it is argued, leads to new forms of governmentality; establishing security focused relationships between people, things, and calculative mechanisms. Hence we can understand the fabrication of liberty (see Chapter 2) as a particular kind of security, dependent on a redrawing of relationships, allowing passage for economic gain.

Although these arguments appear to move away from the effects of an ontologically singular architecture, a precise role for the architecture remains unclear. Just how, in what way, and through what means does, for example, a panoptic prison, or form of town planning, accomplish a kind of architectural governance (for example, how is architecture involved in the interiorization of order)? Is space to be understood as one of several related elements involved in governance, or can it be understood in more precise terms? Does space provide a singular condition of possibility for order and who would come to know these conditions, through what means? What, in other words, are the ontologies of spatial/architectural governance, how are these accomplished, and through what actions? What would be the consequences of treating governance space as ontologically multiple?

One means for getting closer to the detail of how spaces and order are accomplished is provided by ethnomethodology. Ethnomethodology's concern with members' methods for making sense of the world has a spatial focus in studies of walking. For example, ethnomethodological studies of streets focus on the ways in which space is made through the walking of that street. Hence Ryave and Schenkein (1974) refer to the doing of walking. 'We use the verb "doing" to underscore a conception of walking as the concerted accomplishment of members of the community involved as a matter of course in its production and recognition' (1974: 265). The emphasis on the doing of walking opens up walking for analysis as an action, but also opens up the ontology of the spaces accomplished through the doing. Spaces of doing walking also feature in Livingston's (1987) study of people crossing roads towards each other. Livingston detailed the ways in which crossers are tied into a constant mutual accomplishment. They are involved in accomplishing the possibility of crossing the road and of crossing the road in an ordered way, allowing for the possibility of many people crossing the road toward each other without colliding. We could say the orderly production of the space is an ontological accomplishment of the members taking part in its production.

Space as a mutual accomplishment places an emphasis on matters of practical, ongoing constitution work. As Crabtree suggests, 'space is not a worldly abstraction then, but embodied in, and integral to, the accomplishment of the activities that we do' (2000: 2). Hester and Francis term these accomplishments the 'visually available mundane order' (2003: 36). These approaches differ significantly from Foucault. In place of the latter's concern with broad historical sweeps through which individual examples (such as the ship of fools) operate as exemplars, we have numerous practical, mundane incidents that are shaped into a description of the accomplishment of space as ordered. Instead of space pre-existing and helping to shape action, ordered, mundane spaces are an outcome of action. Rather than focus on the nature of space as given, we are directed toward the active accomplishment of ordered space. Hence the two approaches contain distinct forms of directionality. The Foucauldian approach to space suggests that spaces form an important basis through which governance relations and governance subjects are determined. The more ethnomethodological approach suggests, by contrast, that space is an ordered outcome of work done to make sense of and account for spaces in ordinary, pervasive, and ongoing interactions (such as walking). Our approach in this chapter will be more closely attuned to the ethnomethodological approach, in that space will be treated as accomplished through ongoing constitution work. However, the Foucauldian approach is none the less useful for sensitizing us to the consequences of space for order. In this sense, our treatment of spaces as accomplished in ongoing constitution work will also need to pay attention to what follows on from work that accomplishes (an albeit temporary, sometimes unstable) spatial order. Following from this, constitutions of the nature of airport space (for example, dividing departure areas from check-in areas) producing a classificatory order, can also be treated as producing an aggregate basis for constituting a consequential nature for people within those spaces (security checked and unchecked passengers). Constitution work is thus not to be treated as singular; it is ongoing. But constitution work can also treated as consequential by key members of settings (such as airport security clerks).

These considerations open up challenging questions for understanding the role of spaces in relations of governance. How are spaces (such as airports) accomplished through members' methods for making sense? To what extent is it useful to understand these accomplishments as ordered modes of governance? How might a focus on the mundane and the spatial aid our understanding of governance? Can we retain Foucualt's focus on, for example, the passage as a means to enhance economic gain while also treating space as an orderly, everyday accomplishment?

7.3 A London Airport[10]

The terminal manager and terminal technology development manager move at pace through various parts of the terminal building. Dan tries to keep up. The managers talk to him, to each other, and to other members of staff (both face to face and over a radio) as they navigate various obstacles, point out things of possible interest to their visitor, and discuss their future and current problems. For example, as they pass through security into departures, the terminal manager points towards a row of seats. He says these are positioned so as to make passengers walk around the seats and towards the shops. He says the distinct carpet colour scheme is also meant to encourage passengers to head towards the shops and away from the seats.

Amid a whirlwind of movement of people, places, objects, and registers of conversation, the managers outline their three principal interests: security, retail, and efficient passenger movement. While sweeping rapidly through the check-in area and towards security, the terminal manager says his airport prides itself on its security record. The passengers travelling from this airport are known around the world (mostly by other airport managers, but also by government departments) to have been checked to the most stringent standards. He refers to passengers who have been security checked as 'clean' and newly arrived passengers as 'dirty'. The ability of the airport's security system successfully and appropriately to divide, categorize, and assess passengers is important for the airport's reputation and a marker of how well the managers are doing their job.

At the same time, says the terminal manager, now speeding through the retail sections of the departure lounge, the airport's business model is

---

[10] Our first approach to the airport manager to 'do some research' was met with an immediate and enthusiastic response. Dan was invited to tour the airport with the managers (this tour features in the first part of this chapter). Subsequently, Dan was invited to study the check-in area, security check, and departure area of the airport. This research was augmented by a series of airport ethnographies presented later in the chapter.

enormously dependent on retail income. The airport generates more income from shops than from planes taking off and landing. The managers are keen to figure out how they can enhance efficient passenger movement to maintain security levels, while reducing time 'wasted' by passengers—in queues, removing their coats and shoes for security checks, and so on, and increasing the time passengers can spend in retail outlets. While other airport managers in other airports are interested in claims about the integrity of their security, the airport's board of directors are the audience for assessing retail income.[11] The airport operates a formula for calculating the number of seconds each passenger spends in the departure lounge shopping area—the 'retail dwell time'—and the annual income this should yield. So a central focus of the accountability relations with the board was the managers' ability to encourage passengers to move quickly through security but slowly through the shops. We start to see how the furniture of the airport is implicated in its governance. The seats do not simply and straightforwardly face away from passengers as they enter departures; rather, the seats face away to direct passengers toward shops, accomplish the airport business model, and satisfy the airport board and shareholders.

The airport managers' three main interests (security, retail income, and efficient passenger movement) and the accountability relations in which they were embroiled, were all closely interwoven in their enactments of the capacity of features of the airport subtly to reshuffle the contours of airport governance. These features included the airport architecture, wayfinding technologies, and possibilities presented by new technological developments.

7.3.1 Architecture

The airport has a novel design, which includes a large single level arrivals and departure area, supported on concrete columns above the airport train station, and incorporated under a cantilever glass and steel roof. It has won architectural awards. But the airport managers expressed an ongoing frustration with the constraints that this apparently imposed.[12] The airport managers constantly sought ways to enhance efficient passenger movement through the space, but were under strict guidelines (from the airport board and legal planning regulations) not to alter or initiate any changes that might detract from the architecture. They looked to increase the size of signs, improve the clarity of announcements, identify locations where TV screens could be read

---

[11] The airport is a privately owned business, subject to government regulation, but also shareholder interest.

[12] For an account of the ways in which architectural controversies provide a means to engage with the hybrid productions of space, see Yaneva (2012).

more easily, expand the space occupied by retailers, and squeeze the space of non-profit airport activities (such as the space occupied by customs and excise officers). Their efforts to augment the governance capacity of the architecture thus combined concerns about planning, the capacity of signs, TV screens, and announcements to direct passengers, and the possibility that some occupied spaces were diminishing income.

Considerations of airport signs, flight information TV screens, and announcements were intended to enhance the governability of passengers and ensure the airport, managers, technologies, passengers, governance, and accountability relations held together. However, each of these constituent elements proved complex. For example, engineers brought in by the airport owners had recently proclaimed that suspending new signs from the cantilever roof to improve wayfinding was inadvisable and may be structurally unsafe, while the airport board worried that this would detract from the award-winning architecture. The airport managers had contemplated building the signs on large podiums rising from the airport floor. But the same engineers said this would require extra support from underneath, in an area currently occupied by trains, tracks, platforms, and passengers. As a result, the managers were left unsure as to how they could make a convincing business case for this development to the board.

The managers were having similar problems with TV screens, which were almost invisible in sunlight. The screens were also part of an ongoing custody battle between the managers and the airlines, both of whom were able to control the message display. Airport managers tried to display messages such as 'Go to Departures' and 'Wait in Lounge' for as long as possible to encourage passengers to remain in shopping areas; airlines tried to change the message to 'Go to Gate X' and 'Boarding' to get passengers out of the shops and into departure gates, lest they risk a late take-off fine or delays from 'missing their slot'. There were problems with announcements, which issued from loud speakers suspended from the award-winning roof and which echoed to the point of inaudibility. There were also problems with the positioning of retail outlets. For example, a coffee shop had recently been built around a set of flight information TV screens, thereby rendering the screens even less visible to passengers. The airport managers presented these attributions of technological capacity as a feature of relations between various groups with distinct interests, including the architects, the board, the managers themselves, engineers, and retailers. These groups were attributed various positions within forms of governance. In the course of the initial tour, the managers treated Dan to a rich tapestry of the capacities, interests, actions, and likely responses of people and things. Governance and accountability relations were central to the ongoing constitution of the ontologies of airport space.

7.3.2 Wayfinding Technologies

How to govern passengers in such a way as to maintain security, enhance retail income, and get the people on and off planes? And how to do this while attending to the accountability relations which prevail? Improvements in passenger management had to be weighed up against costs and against the risk of impacting on the architecture, and considered as a possible future business case to be presented to the board. The managers had identified problems with each of the wayfinding technologies in the airport: signs, TV screens, and announcements, but did not think any of the proposals for new wayfinding technologies (new signs on podiums, different types of or locations for TV screens) would make a compelling business case. Accepting the difficulties of replacing these systems, the managers sought to work with what they had. They looked to alter rather than re-site or replace existing wayfinding technologies.

The managers initially considered replacing some of the large advertising billboards in the terminal with directional signs. Perhaps the small current signs were limiting the capacity of the airport to make passengers pass through the terminal in an orderly and efficient manner. But the board might think the removal of billboards would decrease advertising income. The terminal manager shelved the plan. The managers then looked to change the colour, angle, and typeface of the signs. Perhaps it was something in the nature of the signs (not bright enough, didn't stand out enough) that prevented the space of the airport from accomplishing governed passengers (who should ideally move quickly through check-in and security and slowly through the shops). But the airport operated a standardized set of colours and typefaces for its signs. The terminal manager also asked (no one in particular, but perhaps Dan) if passengers could recognize the colour and typeface already in use, and whether alternatives might cause confusion. The plans were shelved.

The managers looked to reposition announcement loudspeakers to cut down on what they perceived as a confused combination of different messages about departure, arrival, and retail, echoing inaudibly throughout the single level building. Perhaps clearer announcements would better constitute the governed passenger. They struggled to identify new locations, seeing themselves as accountable both to architects, who might challenge the appropriateness of suspending larger speakers from the roof, and to engineers, who might, once again, start generating diagrams of stresses and loads in relation to the roof.[13] They were unable to find suitable places where flight information TV screens would be less affected by the sun's glare. This outcome was linked to several

---

[13] The managers did claim to have improved the clarity of each announcement, but this was disputed by the passengers to whom we spoke. They reported either being lost and not able to understand the announcements or claimed to know where they were going, but still could not understand the announcements.

distinct sets of accountability relations. The TV screens had been positioned in front of the main entry points to the terminal building to satisfy what the airport Passenger Services Group argued were the interests of passengers first arriving in the terminal. So moving the TV screens would be to risk the wrath of this group. The managers had hoped to be able to alter the glass roof of the external structure of the building to reduce the glare on the TV screens. But they anticipated this move would be contested on cost grounds by the airport board and on design grounds by unspecified architects. So these plans were shelved. Instead, the managers fitted each TV screen with a hood to cut down glare when the sun was at a particular angle for a few hours of each day (if it was sunny). This was a cheap and quick solution, which would more or less satisfy most of the audiences to whom the managers were accountable.

In the same way that new wayfinding developments were considered (and abandoned or shelved), attempts to alter existing wayfinding technologies also involved managers' assessments of their accountability to others. The extent to which passenger governance would be enhanced, security maintained, retail income increased, without excessive cost, and without threat to the architectural integrity of the terminal, were a prominent feature of managers' accounts of what they needed to do on a day to day basis.

Their anticipation of likely future accountability provided the airport managers with a basis for assessing their possible actions in changing the subtle contours of spatial governance in the airport. Responses by those who might hold a business case to account were imagined and utilized as a reason to shelve a series of plans for altering governance objects and their relations with passengers. Following this line of argument, it might be said that it was airport managers (rather than passengers) who most closely adhered to a Foucauldian scheme of governance (involving an interiorization of the likely future outcomes of action as a means to direct the feasibility and appropriateness of current activities). However, it is perhaps too straightforward to draw a direct connection from the suggestion that airport managers engaged in interiorizing considerations of governance, to an argument that suggests the architecture either straightforwardly brought into being this particular set of relations or was considered to be of sufficient stability to provide the conditions of possibility for this set of relations. Instead the ontology of the airport terminal appears to be multiple and accomplished. It was in and through accountability relations, expectations of accountability, talk of the airport architecture and wayfinding, and walking an ethnographer through the airport, that the space of the terminal as a locale for governance was articulated and accomplished. Claims regarding the ontology of each of the wayfinding technologies were oriented toward considerations of cost, architecture, the extent to which passenger governance would be or might be enhanced and the range of accountability relations through which such claims would be assessed.

7.3.3 Radio-Frequency Identification and Biometrics

Given the impasse in developing new and existing wayfinding technologies, caught in what the managers presented as a series of complex accountability relations, the managers looked to alternative possibilities. The UK government had recently announced (and disputed, threatened to abandon, or rapidly impose) changes to the design and information recorded in passports, incorporating biometric information. The airport managers were keen to explore how they might use these changes in identity governance as a possible way out of their own accountability impasse.

The technology development manager was particularly keen on the promise of biometric identification systems. Could biometrics translate terminal architecture into an efficient machinery of governance? The terminal technology development manager suggested that perhaps in future biometric data could be exported from passports at check-in and stored on a radio-frequency identification (RFID) chip (for example in a 'smart' boarding card). He envisaged a future in which identity information could be broadcast over short distances to scanners, which could decode the biometrics and use them as keys to access population information databases. The technology development manager was particularly keen on facial scans. He said that each second saved in security represented an extra second shopping, thereby increasing airport profitability. He was also interested in utilizing RFID chips to know passenger identity (according to the chip), where passengers were in the airport and where they should be (by reading chips and knowing who was checked on to which flight). Perhaps RFIDs could be used to locate passengers who had checked-in, but not made their way to the plane on time. He thought this would help security by preventing passengers straying into prohibited areas. He was also keen to see if signs could read chips and offer a personal response. Perhaps electronic signs could be adapted to target passengers wandering towards gates too early, to inform them that they 'still had x minutes shopping time' before their flight.

Ideas about new technologies entail changes to the contours of the airport space. They project a shift in governance from particular locales (security checks, questions at check-in, passport checks), to a more pervasive form of information broadcasting and assessment throughout the terminal, which in turn might change the somewhat linear architectural experience of some passengers moving from check-in to security and to the departure gates. These changes also hold out the possibility of changes in temporality (how long each passenger should spend in each space) and responsibility (with the airport staff in a better position to intervene when passengers ended up in the wrong place at the wrong time). However, each of these changes depends on the technology coming into being, working, and working in very particular ways.

The promise of RFID and biometrics provided the possibility of fulfilling the managers' three principal interests (security, retail, efficient passenger movement) and satisfying their accountability audiences (such as the airport board, government agencies, and other airport managers). However, to realize this possible future, the technology development manager had to make a persuasive case about the technical capacity of RFID and biometrics. In contrast, the terminal manager was sceptical. He portrayed biometrics as speeding up arrivals rather than departures. He also reckoned it would generate a mass of incorrect or mistaken identities, which would make governance impossible, and he was concerned this would jeopardize the airports' coveted security record. He was also concerned that to maintain security levels, passengers would have to move more slowly through security if, for example, an initial biometric identity check failed, threatening to reduce retail income.

We see then that attributions of the technical capacity of biometrics and RFID were intertwined with the architectural space of the airport terminal, and closely tied to managers' views about their ability to fulfil accountability expectations and maintain a system of governance. We thus understand that managers constitute airport space as an ordered locale in which passengers might be encouraged to move, stop, shop, and display identity. This ordered space is replete with considerations of accountability. At the same time as passengers might be accounted for in terms of who they are, where they are, at what time, doing what kind of activity, in which space of the airport, the airport managers are taking account of their accountability to the airport board, an imagined group of architects, engineers, and the Passenger Services Group. Simultaneously, the airport board invokes accountability to investors, shareholders and those interested in taking over the airport. And so on. The space of governance is busy with invocations of accountability, technological capacity, audience expectation, movement and non-movement and a variety of possible futures (either to be avoided or yet to be achieved). From this we can surmise that spatial governance is not a matter of single ontological constitution in which what-the-airport-is is brought into being and endures. Instead, our guided tour reveals a continuous recasting of space, order, disorder, accountability, governance, wayfinding, futures, and multiple ontologies. In this, managers' accounts of airport space resonate with several Foucauldian themes, especially the meshing of passage, bodies, governance, and economic relations. However, their accounts also differ significantly, in not construing space as providing a single condition of possibility for action nor as a rationale for interiorization of governance and accountability relations. Their understanding goes against a human-centric account of airport space by stressing the complexity and prominence of objects and technology; the multiplicity of their accounts of the space goes against the idea that there is only one rationale for governance; and they seem to oppose the assumption that the individual is the only or most appropriate unit of analysis, by drawing attention to the various aggregates with which they have to deal. In short, airport managers encourage us to resist the assumption that space is a settled ontology that (more or less) enacts governance.

All this suggests we need further to develop our treatment of space as an ontological accomplishment, achieved through governance, rather than as a singular ontology that does governance. One way to do this is to look in more detail at the experiences of those positioned in airport managers' accounts as subjects of governance—the airport passengers. Thus far, in contrast to the subjects of governance in previous chapters, passengers have largely appeared as aggregate entities, rather than as individualized, responsible-ized, or paired governance forms (such as recycling boxes and their households, or vehicles and their drivers). Section 7.4 turns attention to passengers, the ways in which they are accounted, and their accounts of airport space.

7.4 Airport Passengers

7.4.1 Airport Managers' Accounts of Passengers

The airport managers spoke about who passengers were, what they did, how they moved through the airport space, and what special measures were needed to deal with certain categories of exceptional passenger who required further scrutiny. First, as already mentioned, managers spoke of the importance of maintaining a separation between 'clean' passengers (who had been security checked) and 'dirty' passengers (who had newly arrived at the airport). This reflected their accountability to the UK Home Office, who would send plain-clothed operatives into the airport to attempt to breach spatial boundaries between 'clean' and 'dirty' passengers. The managers were keen to emphasize their strong record in preventing such breaches (although the results are not made public).

Second, the managers told us of what they regarded as 'non malicious' breaches of the 'clean'/'dirty' boundary. As with the opening example in our introduction, people coming to meet arriving passengers would often, or so the managers asserted, find their way through to airport departures. These non-malicious breachers often presented themselves as lost or confused and would be returned to the appropriate side of the boundary with a gentle reprimand. No further action was taken, perhaps on the grounds that formally to constitute their existence in the 'wrong' space, would entail formally accepting a failure of governance.

Third, the managers expressed the importance of monitoring the movement of passengers' things. They told us that bags, objects, mobile phones, etc could often be discovered having transgressed the 'clean'/'dirty' boundary.

The managers regularly reviewed locations where such transfers could or might occur and decided on ways either to monitor (for example, through security cameras) or prevent such movement (for example, by building bigger walls). Objects were especially the focus of scrutiny when separated from people. Passengers were constantly reminded not to leave their bags unattended. Packages without their persons could be designated as 'suspicious' (especially following the London bombings of July 2005), and things were separated from other things when they were regarded as requiring closer scrutiny (if, for example, a bag was searched and a knife found). Objects and their people constituted an important governance pairing, the co-ordinated movement of which, together with any necessary repairs to breakdown or disruption of the pairing, was central to ensuring an ordered space.[14]

Fourth, 'clean' passengers acting in unusual ways might require further scrutiny. This category included passengers who had checked in but not made it to their flight, passengers who had become ill in the departure area and passengers who had drunk too much in the airport bars to be admitted to a flight. The spatially oriented typology of 'clean' and 'dirty' (passengers became 'clean' when they had passed through the security check procedures and were in the airside departure areas) occasionally needed repair in much the same way as the recycling centre (Chapter 3) employed staff occasionally to climb into containers and remove matter out of place.

This begins to reveal the complexity of the category of passenger and ways in which passengers and airport spaces were governed into being. As yet, however, we have said little about passengers' own experiences and sense-making activities. In Section 7.4.2 we investigate the ways in which passengers accomplished the airport space.

7.4.2 Passengers' Accounts

As part of his visits to the airport terminal, Dan took the opportunity to discuss the airport space with passengers as they moved through check-in, security, and departures. Passengers noted the importance of TV screens, announcements, signs, and airport staff in finding their ways through the airport.[15] They used different varied aspects of the wayfinding technologies to navigate their way through the terminal. Some passengers looked to information on TV screens (when the sun's glare was not too bad) to work out where

---

[14] See Chapter 8 for more on terror objects, and Chapter 9 for an analysis of an inadvertent breach.

[15] In the light of staff cutbacks, managers discounted the possibility of employing more staff to help passengers navigate their way through the airport.

they should go, when, and for what purpose. Others sought out airport staff as the only sensible recourse in figuring out where to go and when. These passengers mostly ignored technological alternatives and looked for uniforms matching the airline with which they were flying; failing that, any uniform; or, failing that, any social scientists carrying out airport research (who by this point had become quite good at telling people where to go, if they agreed to talk about their experience of the airport). Other passengers looked to, and complained about, airport signage. The size of signs, their location (most complaints were directed toward signs under or next to large billboards) and the clarity of the information they contained each came in for criticism. But none of their complaints explicitly mentioned anything about the airport architecture. Announcements also came in for criticism, typically taking the form 'the airport really should do something about their announcements'.

'The airport' thus became an aggregate target of complaints by passengers. However, such complaints varied according to the ways in which passengers identified themselves. Often those presenting themselves to the ethnographer as frequent flyers viewed the announcements as a quirky characteristic of the airport and found it amusing that less frequent flyers were bemused by the inaudible echo. For frequent flyers, announcements were just part of the background noise. Thus, passengers constituted their actions and those of other passengers in terms of how easily they could navigate their way through the airport, and the importance they attached to the apparent limitations of the airport technologies. This variously translated into accounts of the airport as routine (and thereby usual, normal, unexceptional, and easy to move through) or complex (and thereby confusing, strangely laid out, and in need of improvement). So the extent to which questions needed to be asked about the airport and what constituted appropriate passenger movement through the airport related directly to considerations of whether or not the terminal and terminal technologies were seen as routine. The passengers only infrequently spoke of the importance of boundaries to airport managers, giving little consideration to their 'cleanliness' or 'dirtiness'.[16]

Passengers' accounts of the ordering capacities of signs, TV screens, and announcements were not consistent, but varied according to how passengers identified themselves and the current activity they were involved in (trying to find a check-in desk, trying to get to a gate, trying to purchase duty-free items). Furthermore, passengers were not simply focused on the attributes of wayfinding technologies. Many passengers were looking for comfortable

---

[16] The exception to this occurred when Dan asked the airport managers if, as a social scientist studying the airport, he was 'clean' or 'dirty'. This was resolved by Dan being given his own security guard in departures to monitor any possible boundary breaching.

seats, a decent cup of coffee or 'my husband who's probably in the pub'. Although the airport managers were keen to get passengers to focus on way-finding and security, passengers themselves did not solely orient toward the same categories. Finding their way through the airport had as much to do with finding coffee, seats, and their husband as it did check-in desks and flight departure gates. However, when invocations of the capacity of a broad array of wayfinding technologies were in focus, it was notable that passengers' problems and concerns with such wayfinding technologies closely matched those predicted by the airport managers (signs were too small, announcements inaudible, and TV screens subject to glare).

7.4.3 Passenger Ethnographies

In general, it was only possible to capture brief conversations with passengers as they passed through the terminal. To get more detailed accounts, we signed up seven volunteer 'passenger ethnographers' to write up their experiences in passing through various UK airports.[17] The passenger ethnographers were mostly Masters and Doctoral students who had followed Steve's courses in Advanced Qualitative Methods and in STS. Perhaps as a result, they were attuned to features of the airport environment from a largely onto-sceptic ethnographic perspective. In line with the teaching on these courses, they were asked to 'make strange' the environment as they experienced it. In this section, we present the outcomes of this initiative.[18]

A. JOINING QUEUES

Joining a queue was both the most frequent feature of the seven passenger ethnographies and the one taking up most space in their accounts. How are queues joined in airports and how do the queues accomplish the governed space?[19] In the following extract, the ethnographer attempts to navigate a way through the airport and figure out which queue might be for them.

---

[17] This kind of team ethnography, where researchers produce multiple reports of the 'same' action and then draw those reports together in analysis, is becoming more prevalent in social science research (see Neyland, 2008).

[18] The following analysis was drawn together by coding the ethnographies into an initial loose set of categories. The material drawn together under these categories was then reviewed and the categories refined. The final set of categories (presented in subheadings here) is based on the features of moving through an airport most frequently focused upon in the ethnographers' accounts. The following analysis is based on using one or two examples from the ethnographies to illustrate the pertinent features of each category.

[19] This analysis takes inspiration from ethnomethodological analyses of queues (see Garfinkel and Livingston, 2003).

JENNY: Departures; A, B, C, D; Toilets; Arrivals; British Airways; ropes; queues; customers; staff; bags; trolleys; stores; 2 for 1; magazine covers; advertisements. Signs yelled information at me from all angles; some messages useful but most redundant. I tried to create an order of precedence to these signs but could not find which came first. I ignored the colourful signs for the stores and yellow signs were informative. Larger signs that yelled 'Departures' lost relevance as soon as I knew I was at the right [level] and became annoying background noise as soon as they were read. I assumed I needed to join a queue, but on which queue should I stand? All flights indicated British Airways but I was flying Qantas.

I lifted my bag and moved through the signs until I discovered three televisions with flight numbers and check-in counters. My first station in my process of check-in was small, hidden and not visible from where I entered the hall. Check in Counter 'D.' In front of me was a queue that said 'D' but the screens above the check-in-people indicated that it was a British Airways flight for 'One World' passengers. I was neither a BA nor a One World passenger. I walked to the end of the queue, the shape of which was confined by a royal-red rope. I showed my ticket to a lady in a BA uniform and she confirmed I was on the correct line.

For the ethnographer in this excerpt, the space is not a straightforward, pre-given, or linear track along which she must pass. Instead, she moves very little, looking around and trying to make sense of the scene. She thinks she ought to join a queue, but which one? The signs, TV screens, and shops offer information of a kind, but not the kind she is seeking. It turns out that the plethora of directional signs is redundant; there is no sign that says Qantas passengers should also join this queue. Eventually she gets a member of staff to help her accomplish the space she is in. The staff member is needed to order this space for the passenger and to repair the apparent deficiency in the signs (in particular, the absence of 'Qantas'). The queue is joined and order is, at least temporarily, accomplished.

B. ELECTRONIC CHECK-IN

Joining queues was a routine expectation among the passenger ethnographers. So strong is this expectation that an airport manager we met at a passenger management conference even suggested the use of screens to make queues invisible to passengers in departures. This was on the basis that passengers' strong propensity to join any queue they see has a detrimental effect on retail income and hence on the airport's business model. In the following excerpt the ethnographer cannot resist the lure of the short queue.

ROBIN: The queue in front of the desks is small, with several metres of empty path space marked by barriers before it starts. I do what I've done before in such cases, namely duck the barriers to get to the end of the queue quickly (and not look like a fool following a winded pre-set course). Then I notice the signs around me. They say:

'2 easy steps to check-in. Step 1: check-in using the self-check machines
step 2: take your luggage to the economy bag drop check'

I did notice those self-check machines in front, but I ignored them, thinking that they wouldn't work without a printed ticket anyway (I have an electronic ticket consisting of only a code, booked on the internet). But now I think I should have used them... At the counter I cheerfully say 'sorry, I only just discovered these signs and I realize I may have skipped a step. Can you still check me in?' The clerk says no. I have to go back to the front of the BMI check-in zones and use the machines. I say I only have an e-ticket and will the machines cater for that. He says 'my colleague back there will help you' and tells me that I can come straight back to his desk after completion of step 1, without having to queue again. I run off, leaving my suitcase on the weight scales. He calls me back: I have to take it with me.

I go to the front and look at a machine. It says 'insert ticket or customer card'. I have neither. These self-check machines still do not seem to apply to me. But I've been sent back to use them, so I ask a BMI employee, who tells me to insert a bankcard. I don't like that idea, because I've already paid for my ticket. He says it is necessary 'for ID'. The first card I try brings up the following message on the screen: 'no ticket reserved under that name'. I start to get worried. The BMI employee suggests I try another card, which fortunately I have. This one works, my name is confirmed. The BMI employee asks for my destination and types it in (he seems to think that I am slow to understand how all of this works, or not very computer literate). Then I have to answer three security questions about my bags and press a button to confirm my flight. The BMI employee wanders off. The next step for me is to request airmiles, which proves another challenge: my airmiles card is not recognized as belonging to the same person who's just checked in, and is therefore rejected by the machine. I try again and take my time. A warning appears on the screen that if I don't react in 30 seconds the whole check-in procedure will be voided. A different BMI employee comes over to 'rescue' me; he quickly presses a series of buttons to complete the procedure and says I can get airmiles registered at baggage drop (step 2). He guides me through the seat selection process and finally a boarding card comes out of the machine. The same person then accompanies me past the self-check machines, opening a soft barrier to let me join the queue again. I protest, saying I already queued and that his colleague told me to go straight back to his desk via the left-hand side. He says 'but there aren't many people in the queue anyway'. I don't give in. He says 'if you think they'll let you through, then go ahead'. Which is what I do.

I now have to duck another barrier on the left-hand side and attract the attention of the clerk, which is not easy because he is looking to the right, to the front of the queue. I can only do it by waving my hands and shouting 'hello, hello, I'm back!' When he sees me he refers the next passenger in the queue to a colleague and gestures that I may approach his desk. He checks my passport, weighs my luggage and credits airmiles to my card. He asks the same security questions again.

It seems that accomplishing adequate membership of the queue is not straight-forward. The passenger attempts to navigate the airport space via experience; she has joined queues before, here is a short queue, she even thinks to duck under the barrier rather than walk the entire length of the roped off queue. But her reliance on previous experience of this kind of space proves inad-equate. Not only is she in the wrong place, and in the wrong sequence, she also then needs the help of several members of staff to keep her navigation of the airport on track through the self-service check-in machine, the use of two different cards, and her problems with airmiles. Even then, the failure adequately to accomplish order is not over; she has been told she can return to the front of the queue. She treats this as an organizational challenge (how to get to the right place and get the clerk's attention) rather than a challenge of potentially breaking everyday social/moral order by jumping the queue. Despite mild encouragement to rejoin the back of the queue ('there aren't many people in the queue anyway'), the ethnographer intrepidly pushes to the front. Accomplishing adequate membership of the group of airport passengers and accomplishing an ordered, governed airport space is closely intertwined. In accomplishing airport space, the passenger has a role to play alongside the signs, staff, and technologies.

C. MAKING ROUTINE MISTAKES

For six of the seven ethnographers, making mistakes was a significant feature of their movement through the airport. This is highlighted by the following excerpt in which the ethnographer determinedly attempts to make sense of the terminal information.

> WAYNE: I look up and see pictures of cars, airplanes, landscapes and logos. Among them, in blue, I notice two adjacent flat screen panels with 16 horizontal lines and a headline. The screens are [also] divided into vertical rows; one shows a point in time (in yellow), another a city name (in white), a third a code (flight—in yellow) and 'remarks' (blue). My eyes search for my destination, Geneva, and I locate it on the list. However, timewise, the information does not match the itinerary slip I have in my pocket—I get a little nervous—is it cancelled? Am I in the wrong airport? Is it the wrong date? I take an extra look at my travel plan and, again, juxtapose it with the information on the screen—it does not match. However, a feeling of relief occurs when I discover that I am not looking at the right place; the headline on the screen is 'Arrivals'.
>
> After walking around for a bit, trying to find the departure information by looking up, I decide to focus on people rather than screens—where do other people go? This turns out to be a fruitful strategy; immediately I notice a crowd standing in front of a similar blue screen, this time with the correct headline, 'Departures'.

Here we see the ethnographer attempting to become one of the orderly, efficient, and correct body of passengers. The first attempt, however, proves erroneous. It turns out that the screen with which he wishes to match his flight contains details of the wrong kind of flight. He is suddenly aware of his mistake; he is in the wrong place, looking at the wrong screen, matching his flight to the wrong flight on the screen, represented by the wrong time and wrong flight number. He then notices a group of passengers who seem to know what they are doing. The airport managers would not be surprised that passengers experience the airport as both tightly ordered and deeply disordered. Their objective to constitute orderly passengers always appeared just out of reach—the perfect wayfinding technology was always one step away, or too costly, or an engineering problem, something that would be disputed by the airport board or even by the Passenger Services Group. Nor should it be assumed that problems were only due to the wayfinding technologies and their misinterpretation. As the following excerpt suggests, following other passengers can prove equally problematic.

> JENNY: I entered a lift and chatted to a businessman about luggage while we were lifted to the higher level. I followed him out the door and mimicked his confident right-turn, only to discover I was in 'Arrivals.' I stood in the middle of a clearing and spied a tiny 'Departures' sign on the floor above. I took my bags up the lift to the higher level. The lift transported me to a doorway where I stood blocking the doors while I looked for a cue for what to do next.

Making mistakes and trying to repair them was a routine feature of passengers' experience. Against any expectation of an ordered and orderly space, comes a litany of examples of signs that are misread, passengers who look like they know what they are doing but turn out to be doing something else, TV screens that turn out to not display the kind of information initially thought, technologies that cannot be used in ways initially believed, promising looking routes that turn out to be dead-ends, circuitous links to places they had just left, or one-way passages that whisk passengers off into parts of the airport they did not wish to visit. At the same time, disorder, messiness, and mistakes were both routine and repairable. In terms of understanding airports as spaces of governance, this messiness further supports the idea that the nature/ontology of things, including the airport itself, is multiply accomplished. For the ethnographers there was little sense that a self-evident pre-existing terminal straightforwardly determined their transit.

D. OBJECTS AND THEIR PEOPLE

In addition to spending their time getting lost, making mistakes, and jumping queues, five of the seven ethnographers reflected in detail on the material tokens of transit. Ethnographers talked of their passports as forms of organizational classification, described luggage tags as mysterious and difficult to decode symbols of guided movement, and read the pictorial symbols on airport signs as condensed amalgams of theories of order. In the following excerpt, the ethnographer draws together several of these themes in considering his boarding pass.

> PAUL: This boarding pass encoded all types of information like, for instance, my seat number, whether the seat is in the smoking or non-smoking compartment, the flight number, the airport I was flying to, and the so called 'gate number'. Moreover, this boarding pass seemed to get gradually shorter the nearer I came to my actual seat on the aircraft itself, until I was eventually left with a perforated stamp which I could take to my seat and which only encoded the relevant information for the personnel upon the aircraft. In fact, the only relevant document, along with my passport, for this journey was the boarding card. Indeed, all my holiday planning, the money which I spent on the ticket, were encoded in the figures and letters represented on the card. This card provided the key to reaching the different stages of the travelling process.

Here Paul suggests that these material tokens of travel play an important part in accomplishing the ordered space of the airport. Although it is difficult to argue that the boarding card could travel without a passenger, it is equally difficult for a passenger to travel without the boarding card. In mundane governance, object and person (as noted in Chapters 3 and 4) are intimately tied together as a governance pair. Accomplishing an ordered movement through space requires various acts to match object with their person. The staff look to the object first, and then check the passport, and finally the person to match. The object must match the flight, seat number, and passport. The person must also eventually fit into this scheme. Not then a panoptic ordering whereby passengers are encouraged to interiorize a particular rationale of governance provided by the card. Instead, the passenger is repeatedly instructed to present the card and the card is judged for its correctness. The ontology of the 'passenger' (clean, dirty, suspect, or not) is assessed through inspection of the boarding card and passport. The segmentation of airport space is the accomplished upshot of these assessments. Passengers pass or do not, are filtered off into other areas or are allowed to shop, enter planes or do not, according to the adjudged status of their governable pairing (the card/passport and its person).

E. SHOPPING FIRST, THEN FLYING

Not all our ethnographers focused on accomplishing orderly transit. Many also wanted to shop. For the airport's business model the slow shopper was vital (indeed the airport managers removed, reduced, or repositioned some of the features of orderly governance to encourage shopping[20]). Several of the ethnographers took shopping as a priority activity for moving through the airport space.

> ROBIN: I find a set of monitors with flight information. A sign near the monitors says that flight information will be displayed approximately 30–40 minutes before departure. I wander around some shops, looking whether those skin care products I like are included in the Christmas offers (they are not). At 1.55 my flight is announced. I have ten minutes to get to the gate. I realize I am hungry and decide I can spare a few minutes to get a sandwich. I walk to a sandwich shop that I saw upon entering the departures [lounge]. I select a ciabatta from a self-service display, then queue to have it toasted and to pay. But this queue moves very slowly and I realize that toasting the ciabatta is going to take even more time. And the gate closes at 2.05. I put the sandwich back and walk towards my gate. On the way, I see another sandwich shop with no queue, where I buy a cold sandwich. I pass a lot more shops—all nice brands with early Christmas sales! Too bad there's no time to have a look.

Here we see the passenger encounter and negotiate many different airport activities, including queues, judging the length of queues, estimating how long things might take, noticing advertising, assessing the products on offer, dealing with a sense of urgency, and finally accepting the need to catch a plane despite it being nearly Christmas. The passenger seems to manage an orderly movement through the airport space, thereby accomplishing the managers' aims to have an ordered terminal, but we should not assume that the way in which passenger judgements bring the space into being is governed by a single logic of order. Judgements of time and space in relation to getting to a plane (how far is it, what time is it) are interwoven with other kinds of judgement (what is on sale, at what price, can I find that product I like, is it on sale, should I do some Christmas shopping, I'm quite hungry, what kind of sandwich should I get, hot or cold, do I have time for this?). The passenger accomplishes spatial orderliness through these judgements and by navigating and making judgements of the various ways in which they might be subject to governance. This theme of passengers figuring out and testing and making judgements about governance continues as they move on to planes.

F. BOARDING THE PLANE

In the following excerpt, the ethnographer considers her final steps on to the plane. These steps reveal a further series of decisions that contribute to constituting the airport and the actions of transit.

---

[20] For example, by placing a coffee shop around flight departure TV screens, so that muffins could be noticed in as much detail as gate numbers. Or by positioning of seats to encourage passengers to walk through the departure lounge shops. Or by retaining large billboard adverts for the shops instead of producing larger directional signs.

KATRINA: There were a lot of seats, a few TVs, public phones, and further glass walls with one glass door through to the passageway connecting that area to the aircraft. These glass doors were already opened and the lounge was relatively empty. An announcement was heard in that room that thanks the passengers for waiting and asked 'all remaining passengers to board the aircraft now. Please have your boarding slip with you'. The glass door opened into a long, narrow corridor. About a third of the way along the corridor there was a fork. There were two signs at the fork that said 'A' and 'B'. There was no indication who should go where but prior experiences, not the physical surroundings... made me follow the line that said 'B', which I assumed was for economy class. Also, there was a longer line of passengers going along corridor 'B', which I also assumed was for the economy class. The line didn't take long and we filtered onto the aircraft. At the entrance, there were two air stewardesses who then filtered the passengers into the more convenient aisle after looking at the remaining slip of the boarding card.

This excerpt suggests that even passengers' final movements through the airport depend on their constituting a sense of the airport space. Which direction to move in, is the difference between A and B significant, perhaps B refers to economy class passengers, what kind of passenger am I? These questions are all as pertinent to the ontological constitution of the passenger as to the constitution of the orderly space of the airport. The excerpt reveals that the passenger is again at the heart of doing orderly space. Just as previous ethnographers had to figure out which queue to join, had to navigate times and spaces, had to make sense of signs and TV screens and new and unfamiliar technology, so this passenger has to accomplish a sense of the distinction between A and B. That she is ushered through by the stewardesses is taken as evidence of her success in appropriately navigating the space and herself into its proper ontological classification.

This excerpt might suggest that every ethnographer experienced the airport as messy in some way and accomplished order through an active process of making sense of the space. However, as the next section demonstrates, accomplishing a sense of the airport, who takes most responsibility and is held accountable for that sense, can be a matter of further ontological classification.

G. TRAVELLING ELITE

One of our seven ethnographers travelled first (upper) class. His report offers a distinct take on accomplishing the orderliness of space. Whereas the others experienced the airport as messy and accomplished order through an active process of making sense of the space, his experience is that much of the orderliness is done for him. So during transit he is neither responsible nor accountable for accomplishing his ontological classification and segmentation of the space; others are paid to do this for him.

> MICHAEL: As part of the Upper Class Virgin ticket, the 'limo' picks me up from my home…The driver asks if I have done this (i.e. Upper Class limo pick up) before (no) and, as we set off, he explains the routine. He has an electronic pod thingy in the front of the car, on which he consults the details of my booking. 'Yes, you're there, seat 6K, is that alright?'
>
> Nearing the terminal at Heathrow, the driver takes a turn down an alleyway entrance in amongst the multilevel car parks, which I have never seen before. Forty yards down the road we come upon a sign illuminating a kiosk 'Virgin Upper Class Drive Through Check In'. The car stops and a uniformed Virgin clerk approaches the car…She looks at my passport and hands it back. Over her shoulder another uniformed person is (cursorily) incanting a series of questions about whether I have packed my bag myself, are there sharp objects etc. I give the right responses and the car drives me round to the main entrance to the Terminal…
>
> The other side of Fast Track [security] presents…[a] confluence with the lower classes. Before actually entering the departure 'lounge' I am forced into a queue which turns out to be a second check on passports. Some of my companions from Fast Track evince visible irritation at this development. I don't imagine they are in a hurry; are they upset at losing time? Or, perhaps, are they upset at the unexpected and enforced congregation with those from whom they have been promised segregation…
>
> The lift up to the lounge on the second floor has a padded bench seat in it…The (Upper) lounge is organized semiotically to speak for a curious combination of luxury, privilege, and convenience for the busy executive. Luxury and privilege: free glass of champagne on entrance, free drinks in general, free snacks, free (and impressively classy) food from restaurant menu and/or sushi bar. Convenience for the busy executive: hair dressing salon, shower facilities, shoe shine, free internet (fax and phone) access. All against a background of (typically Virgin) musak, i.e. upbeat rock of the genre with which baby boomers might identify. And a multitude of serving staff, waitresses, barmen… There are no (or few) announcements in this space. Instead, staff individually approach passengers and remind them when the time comes for their departure.

The challenges of time, space, order, and transit are literally cushioned for the upper class. Others take on the tasks of ordering, tracking time, working out locations, and moving the passenger at appropriate moments through particular spaces. The upper class buy their way out of messiness, confusion, mistakes, decisions, negotiations, a great many movements, and a degree of uncertainty. Their spatial sense-making obligations are instead focused on how to behave appropriately in the spaces of the lounge. Exclusivity is accomplished through luxury, convenience, and exclusion from the masses.

This ethnographer experiences the occasional mixing of upper and lower spaces as inconvenient and unwelcome, but which contrast perhaps serves to remind the uppers of their exclusive spatial status.

7.5 Conclusion

In this chapter we have taken an airport terminal as the focus of our examination of the spatial in mundane governance. We started by suggesting that some Foucauldian accounts of governance spaces were predicated upon assumptions about ontological status that detracted from an appreciation of how space is accomplished in governance. As one way of tracing the accomplishment of the contours of spatial governance, we introduced an ethnomethodological sensibility to understanding the mutual accomplishment of ordered spaces by members party to those spaces. We drew on the views of airport managers and experiences of passenger ethnographers to assess the utility of the idea of spatial governance as a form of ontological enactment.

The airport proved to be a particularly complex and messy, and only occasionally definitely ordered, organizational space. In this space the managers revealed a sense of their ordering of the terminal in which they worked. As a locale of governance, the airport is replete with accountability relations—between the managers and the board; between engineers, managers, and board; between architects, their peers, the airport managers, and board; between managers, objects and passengers; between airlines, passengers, and managers; and so on. The permutations of accountability are almost endless. And at the same time, they are a routine part of airport life. Every day, airport managers draw these relations together, navigate their way through them, and attempt to produce outcomes that will keep everyone happy.

The architecture of the airport was differentially enacted. For the airport board and owners it was an award-winning gem; for the managers it was a space in need of new arrangements of people and things; for the engineers it was a set of constraints around weights, pressures, costs, and stresses. For the managers, wayfinding was the focus for accomplishing the nature of the airport space and held out the possibility of accomplishing an ordered space.

What role does the space of the terminal play in this? We have seen that the airport terminal is variously invoked as a constraint (when managers negotiate with engineers over the size, weight, cost, and presentability of signage), as an attraction (an award-winning architectural achievement that can be used to market the airport), as a secure location (particularly in relations between airport managers, other managers, and government agencies), as a space for managing people and things (through security, passport control, customs and excise) and as a retail centre (upon which the airport business model depends), not to mention as a place where planes must take off and land. Unlike the ship of fools, airport space does not determine a singular governance outcome. Unlike the panopticon the airport space does not operate to communicate a singular condition of possibility. Instead, the airport is accomplished through its governance. The acts by various people and things of producing, maintaining, and holding various people and things to account, accomplishes what the airport is in its multiple instantiations.

Our passenger ethnographers offered a distinct view of airport space. While managers focused on security, retail, and efficient passenger movement, our ethnographers reported joining queues, negotiating new technologies, making mistakes, understanding objects, figuring out shopping, getting on a plane, and behaving like an elite passenger. No single rationale or condition of possibility directed passenger governance, nor did any single rationale provide a standard against which passengers assessed and oriented their transit. Instead, space was the subject of ongoing ontological constitution as luxurious, infuriating, confusing, panic inducing, consumption oriented, messy, over loaded, and so on. Spaces of governance were experienced as multiple, fluid, open to contestation, messy, and an ongoing accomplishment. And yet, despite the infinite possible enactments of airport space, all our passenger ethnographers successfully boarded their planes. We could be tempted into thinking that this is the ultimate bottom line measure of effective governance. Can we conclude that mundane governance in the airport works because passengers get on their planes? No! This is but one of many outcomes of mundane governance. In any case 'getting on the plane' is a singular formulation that conceals a multitude of eventualities: we could ask did they get on the plane on time, were there delays, did they get on but wish they had bought more duty free, and so on. And quite apart from 'getting on the plane' we know that mundane governance can apply to a whole series of events and experiences in the airport.

The radical indeterminacy of participants' claims about technological capacity and spatial ordering leads to a mess of discontinuous, partial and fragmentary forms of governance, and accountability. This is perhaps especially the case in settings such as airports that are characterized by a large number of competing invocations of technological, spatial, governance, and accountability capacity. The governance of airport passengers—ensuring passengers walk to the right places at the right time, queue in an orderly fashion, proceed through security protocols correctly, shop in the airport retail outlets, and get on the right plane—are vital to the airport. Accomplishing ordered, mundane, governed passengers, accomplishes the airport.

To reach this conclusion we have especially focused on the management of passengers, but have as yet said comparatively little (apart from briefly mentioning passports, boarding cards, and security technologies) about objects that move through airport space. We have also emphasized the (temporarily) stable outcome of both managers' and passengers' enactments of the ontologies that populate the airport. So we still need to look more closely at objects and at cases of ontological instability and uncertainty. Chapter 8 addresses these topics by looking at what happens to people, things, routines, and organizations in moments of ontological insecurity and mundane terror.

8

Mundane Terror

8.1 Introduction

In Chapter 7, an airport terminal provided the focus for our questions about the complexity of governance and space. That space is populated by many different kinds of objects: luggage and its contents, passports, clothing, carpets, signs, retail goods, cars and other vehicles, desks, uniforms, coffee cups, and water bottles, to name but a few. But we did not give these objects much voice in our discussion. To what extent and through what means do actions, processes, and documents constitute the ontology of these objects? And how does the ontological constitution of bodies—clean and dirty—relate to the ontology of objects? We have suggested throughout that ontological constitution is situated, which allows for the multiplicity of objects and means that any particular configuration of entities is temporary. This means that in general the status of any one entity is uncertain, in the sense that it is potentially amenable to change through the very next processes of constitution and configuration. Or, more exactly, the status of any entity can switch between certainty and uncertainty.

There is, however, an interesting class of entities whose uncertain status is itself an achievement of ontological constitution. This is the class of entities that are (or might turn out to be) other than they seem. They look like one thing but might turn out to be something very different. For example, as we shall discuss in more detail, an ordinary looking key that turns out to conceal a penknife; a letter that turns out to be a bomb; an innocent looking bottle of water that actually contains explosive liquids. We are especially interested in the contrast between the apparent ordinariness of these ordinary objects and the terrifying capacities they can turn out to manifest. The contrast is marked. These are quintessentially mundane objects: ordinary, everyday, and unexceptional, which are revealed to possess, or which are said to possess, anything but ordinary capacities. The contrast is the basis for what we call mundane terror. This chapter explores the constitution of radically uncertain ontologies as a central feature of mundane terror.

Furthermore, although preceding chapters have placed an emphasis on ontological multiplicity, each of the multiple accounts of people and objects have been treated as attaining a certainty in their own right. Where does this leave the governance of people and objects, which could be said to be characterized by ongoing uncertainty? This chapter explores the suggestion that attempts to govern objects in spaces such as airports can lead to radical ontological uncertainty or even ontological insecurity. In this situation, how is the very nature of things (and bodies) called into question? How does not knowing what things are become the basis for a kind of mundane terror, such that we are confronted with a deep insecurity about the nature of our ordinary everyday objects. It will be suggested that the phenomenon of mundane terror arises from problems of ontological certainty and raises questions about how insecure things might be governed.

To explore this argument, we start with a brief consideration of ontology and security. We then consider three examples of ontological insecurity in action: water bottles, letter bombs, and biometric ID cards. The chapter concludes with an analysis of the ways in which ontological insecurity pervades governance and the means introduced to manage it.

8.2 Ontology and Security

Even radical Science and Technology Studies (STS) approaches such as actor–network theory sometimes seem to deploy uninterrogated assumptions about ontological certainty (see also Chapter 2). For example, Latour's (1992) analysis of the child car restraint suggests that programmes of behaviour modification can be delegated or inscribed into the restraint. The key claim is that, once in place, the restraint does its job of restraining: a form of ontological certainty about what the restraint is and what it can do. Similarly, Callon's (1986) study of the electric car in France suggests that ontology of the component parts of the network is fairly straightforward and knowable. Hence, the collapse of the network is attributed to the failure of the batteries to perform the role delegated to them. Once again, the heart of the story depends on an ontological certainty, that the battery could not hold the charge.

By contrast, as also noted in Chapters 1 and 2, other STS perspectives find less comfort in ontological certainty. For example, Woolgar and Pawluch's (1985) notion of ontological gerrymandering draws attention to the work involved in questioning the ontological status of some entities while taking for granted the status of others. Thompson (2004) describes the intricacies of what she calls ontological choreography in IVF treatments. Most notably, perhaps, Mol (2002) explicitly opens the possibility that entities can possess more than one ontology. Mol is clear that this is not an argument about plurality—the same thing seen from different viewpoints—but multiplicity—simultaneously existing, ontologically multiple things. As also noted previously, this raises challenging questions for understanding ontological constitution in mundane governance, for example, does multiplicity imply that each ontology is in itself more or less coherent? Bruun Jensen (2010) has looked at ways in which ontological coherence is accomplished. But what about the possibility of radical uncertainty with respect to ontological status? In the sense that radically not knowing can be said to engender a sense of insecurity, we wish to explore the connection between this sense of (ontological) insecurity and the sense of insecurity associated with safety and protection from terrorism.

Recent work on (in)security opens up a broad range of questions regarding the nature of entities involved in security governance. Democratic political spaces such as the Washington Mall (Benton-Short, 2006), the 'fortress' city (Klauser, 2010), offshore border security (Amoore and Hall, 2009; Vaughan-Williams, 2010), and the spaces of the biometric body (Adey, 2009) provide some initial thoughts on how the security of particular spaces, for example, can become a question rather than an assertion. Where the border is located can become less clear. And 'democratic spaces' can be filled by distinct types of protest. However, this literature also appears to underplay ontological questions. To what extent are the very nature of spaces, people, and things at stake in these forms of (in)security governance? To what extent are the nature of spaces, people, and things rendered (in)secure? And how are processes, actions, documents, and relations of governance adapted to engage ontologically (in)secure people and things? We will suggest that moments of mundane terror are particularly useful for addressing these kinds of questions.

The following three examples address ontological insecurity under conditions of mundane terror. The examples are based on materials from our study of the London airport, which we first met in Chapter 7; instructions issued by a government department for dealing with terror incidents; and Dan's participation in a national biometric trial for the ill-fated UK identity card.

8.3 Objects and their Passengers

How did the airport managers and security staff at our London airport manage the threat posed by the redesignation of passengers' objects as threats of mundane terror? In Chapter 7, we noted that, for airport managers, three principal interests (of security, retail sales, and efficient passenger movement) and the relations of accountability into which they entered (with government departments focused on security, their board of directors focused on business models, and the Passenger Services Group) were closely intertwined with their concern to produce 'security ready' passengers. The managers were keen to reduce time 'wasted' by passengers turning up at security but not ready to go straight through the checks. They wanted passengers to have already taken off their coats and got their bags ready to go through x-ray machines. They wanted passengers to arrive at the security check without any 'sharps' (for example, scissors or knives) and, from August 2006, without liquid containers larger than 100 ml.

To produce security ready passengers who were not carrying 'sharps', airport managers pursued a three-part scheme of ontological constitution. First, the managers classified departing passengers as possible carriers of 'sharps'. Second, the managers separated objects from their people and reclassified them as 'sharps'. This entailed reclassifying ordinary things (such as knitting needles, for knitting) as potentially extraordinary (potential weapons, for acts of terror). Third, the managers invoked new sets of accountability relations as a way of justifying both the reclassification of passengers and objects, and their actions. In particular, departing passengers were called upon to recognize the terror threat posed by their 'sharps' and to remove these from their hand luggage. As we saw previously, governance pairings between objects and their humans are key. Whereas in other domains efforts were made to establish links between recycling boxes and their households (Chapters 3 and 4), or between vehicles and their drivers (Chapters 5 and 6), as a matter of accountability, here objects are similarly inspected and managed for what they might reflect about the character, intention, or motives of the person. But mundane terror is organized around the need to *dissociate* the offending object from its human pair. Thus, security ready passengers are those adequately separated from their 'sharp' things. The evidential–moral–actionable are once again inseparable, and the work of ontological constitution and accountability, slow shopping, and quick movement through security, is once again intertwined with achieving the airport's business model.

A first form of ontological respecification of objects preceded the August 2006 security alert focused on liquid containers. Notice boards were placed at the entry to airport security points, announcing that passengers should not carry 'sharps' in their hand luggage and encouraging them, for example, to take their coats off before they passed through the x-ray machine. The notices provided instructions on how passengers should make themselves 'security ready' but, as far as the managers could tell, they had little impact. Many still presented themselves in a 'security unready' state; there was no noticeable increase in passenger through-put times in the security area and hence no discernible increase in retail income. The managers commented that maybe passengers had better things to occupy their time such as talking about their forthcoming holidays. By way of reaffirming the ontological category of 'sharps', airport security positioned large 'knife buckets' just next to the security check, wherein any sharp items that passengers attempted to carry through security could be deposited by a security clerk. The physical separation of 'sharps' from security unready passengers was a slow process, with passengers not assuming responsibility for their objects as readily as managers wished and persisting in remaining puzzled by the new ontology of (for example) scissors, which was presented to them.[1]

A second attempt to enforce ontological respecification involved the use of plasma screens suspended above passengers in security queues. These screens displayed a looped animation sequence, showing passengers how they should prepare for the security check while waiting in line. The managers didn't think this had any discernible impact either. The managers had hoped to see an increase in throughput (number of passengers passing through security per hour), a decrease in the time taken to check passengers and an increase in retail dwell time (Chapter 7).[2] When pushed for a more detailed explanation, the managers suggested that perhaps passengers 'don't look up' in queues and so didn't see the new plasma screens.

A third form of ontological respecification occurred because of a security scare in August 2006, which generated concern about liquid containers.[3] All passengers were banned from taking liquid containers over 100 ml in their hand luggage (with partial exemptions for medications and baby milk, although passengers were on occasions called upon to demonstrate the non-explosive nature of these products). Liquids in containers less than 100 ml included in hand luggage had to be displayed to security staff in clear plastic bags.[4] Faced with the prospect of even slower security checks, less retail dwell time, and a greater number of ordinary objects to be considered threats (not just 'sharps' now but also liquid containers over 100 ml[5]), a new resource

---

[1] Also of note here is the apparently informal assessment of the success/failure of notice boards. The 'failure of the notice boards' was not based on questioning passengers. Instead, throughput times were taken as an adequate proxy for explaining passenger actions.

[2] Once again, this numerical evidence was taken as adequate basis for explaining passenger actions.

[3] It was suggested during this crisis that the Metropolitan Police, in association with UK and US intelligence agencies, had reliable information that terrorists were planning to use liquid containers to blow up planes in flight. It was said that up to ten flights leaving the UK for North America were being targeted. Twenty-five suspects were arrested in London and High Wycombe and accused of having links with Al Quaeda groups in Pakistan. Of the twenty-five, eight were later charged with conspiracy to murder (see: http://news.bbc.co.uk/1/hi/uk/8242238.stm).

[4] This has led some airports to expand their business model into the selling of plastic bags, although they remained free in many airports.

[5] The 100 ml limit became a matter of some discussion. Some suggested that combining several small containers of less than 100 ml each would still enable a plane to be blown up.

for ontological respecification was brought into play: leaflets were placed in the hands of departing passengers as they checked-in at the airport.

The leaflets set out the new ontological classification of items now associated with mundane terror, and specified which items were to be separated, how they were to be presented, and what security checks would ensue. The leaflets effectively tried to render the passengers newly responsible and accountable for managing the water bottle terror threats; they were asked to acknowledge and accept the new ontological specification of items. As a material instantiation of the desired respecification, did the leaflets work? Did the leaflets work where the boards and plasma screens had failed? The managers' view was that security chaos ensued. Initial attempts to mess with the prevailing ontological order, to transform the ontology of liquid containers from, for example, bottles of water to terrorist threats was, just like the other two forms of ontological respecification, messy and inconclusive on introduction. So many passengers arrived at security with water bottles and other liquid containers larger than 100 ml, airport security staff complained (to Dan) that the situation had turned them into waste management staff. They suddenly faced the new task of organizing the deposit of large numbers of liquid bottles in wheelie bins and found themselves arguing about whose turn it was to collect and empty the bins. Just as passengers carrying 'sharps' persisted in presenting themselves in a security unready manner, obliging security staff to establish a screening mechanism to separate the 'sharps' from their unreadies and reassert the newly re-inscribed ontology of things by placing 'sharps' in bins, the same occurred with liquid containers. We can note, however, that the redesignation of liquid containers as potential explosives was highly localized. In the leaflets, water bottles remained a terrorist threat. But in their actual passage through security most passengers understood their ordinary and mundane liquid containers as non-terrifying. Somewhat surprisingly, security staff screened and separated the potential terrifying liquid containers, and then placed them together in huge wheelie bins. At no point were these wheelie bins, now containing hundreds of potentially explosive liquid bottles, treated as anything other than wheelie bins full of ordinary water bottles. The security staff complained, not that they were being asked to handle large concentrations of potentially explosive material, but that removing the bins was not a proper job for security personnel.[6]

In sum, the respecification of objects from ordinary to extraordinary involved the reclassification of those objects as matters of concern (sharps,

---

[6] The handling of potentially explosive 'water' 'bottles' varies by airports. For some airports, the material is treated as hazardous, for others it is separated into different containers to be recycled and in other airports, it is placed in the same waste containers as other materials to be landfilled. In some airports outside Europe there is no liquids rule. For a summary, see: http://www.forbes. com/sites/andrewbender/2012/07/11/what-happens-to-liquids-surrendered-at-airport-security/

water bottles), the responsibilization of the departing passengers, the policing of a key governance pairing and, where necessary, separation of objects from their people. However, just as with sharps, it proved difficult to persuade passengers to pay attention to the new ontology and to re-orient their actions accordingly. Queues in security initially remained much longer than the managers wanted. Although bottles of water were the focal point for building a set of governance relations held together by ideas of terror threat, forms of responsibility and accountability—and these relations were focused on establishing a new ontological identity for bottles of water—this transformation was far from straightforward. The number of ways in which passengers did and did not re-orient their actions around bottles of water and the numbers of ways in which water was and was not a matter of concern led to confusion and delays. This prompted worries about deleterious effects on retail dwell time, about whether disgruntled shareholders might sell their stakes in the airport operator, and whether this would threaten the jobs of the airport managers.[7] And this all involved redistributions of accountability and responsibility. For example, the airport managers were to be held to account by government agencies and the airport security staff were held to account by their managers. The apparent ongoing failure of ontological respecification also meant that security staff had to work harder to screen passengers, separate out objects (as the passengers had not done so), and reaffirm the new ontology of terrifying things.

8.4 Letter Bombs

Our second example is the rise of concern about letter bombs, drawing in particular on information and advice provided by the UK's intelligence service MI5.[8] In place of its earlier wartime function of providing intelligence for the defence of the nation, MI5 latterly operates under similar bureaucratic constraints to many government departments. It has to demonstrate

---

[7] In the end, all of this happened.

[8] Britain's intelligence service has led a varied life, established in 1909 as the Home Section of the Secret Service Bureau. At the outbreak of the First World War in 1914 Britain established various military operation sections. Section 5 of Military Operations was dedicated to intelligence and gained the name MO5 (Military Operations section 5). In 1916, these operations went through a change of terminology to decrease confusion over what each section actually did in practice. This led to a re-branding of the section as Military Intelligence, section 5 or MI5. Although the re-branding was designed to reduce confusion, MI5 was a meaningless title in the sense that although there had been an MO1, 2, 3, 4, and 5, there was not an MI1, 2, 3, or 4. Following the war, the military designations were dropped. MI5 became the Defence Security Service in 1929 and then the Security Service in 1931. However, the name MI5 persists as a routine naming convention for the activities of the intelligence services in the UK (and indeed its website address retains the name: www.mi5.gov.uk).

its transparency (making certain types of information available), value for money (under annual assessments of returns on spending), and its value as a government department. In this last connection, MI5 presents itself as a useful information resource about terror threats facing Britain, and on the likely source and objects of terror. It positions itself as a provider of training on how to manage terror threats. In much the same way that airport managers are key in constituting the ontologies of passengers and objects, MI5 has become a focal point in constituting the ontologies associated with the activities of businesses in processing information and handling objects.

The MI5 website makes available an online video entitled 'Safe in the Knowledge' aimed at 'small and medium sized enterprises' (SMEs). The video conveys many of the central themes of MI5's perspective on mundane objects of potential terror. In the video a presenter acting as a 'rogue', seeks to infiltrate his way into a 'typical' British firm. Many ordinary objects—umbrellas, number plates, plastic cards, bags, briefcases, a mail trolley, a cleaner's mop and bucket, and a pad and pencil—are portrayed as potentially insecure items that might allow a firm (your firm) to become the target of a terror threat. Hence in the film the 'rogue' is seen recording the number plates of vehicles used by a firm, collects a discarded ID card to gain entry to a building, commandeers a mail trolley as a prop to convince others of his legitimate presence in the building and then collects company mail, and so on. The message is: secure your objects to secure your firm.

In recent years MI5 has especially highlighted letter bombs as a significant domestic terror threat. The 'threat' section of the MI5 website spells out who ought to be concerned about letters, emphasizes the threat posed by letters, and encourages those who should be concerned to follow certain courses of action. In other words, the website information classifies who is responsible, respecifies the ontological status of (apparently) ordinary objects, and performs a set of responsibility and accountability relations whereby the adequacy of ontological respecification and recognition can be assessed. Here then is a three-part scheme similar to the dealings by airport managers in our first example: activities each relating to the who, what, and how for managing mundane terror. MI5 articulate this three-part scheme first, by asserting that SMEs are a particular target for letter bombs. They follow up this statement of risk on the website by also e-mailing SMEs with the suggestion to inform all employees of ways to manage this threat (indeed our own university department received and distributed this advice to all members of staff). The instructions are set out in Box 8.1.

The first part of the MI5 advice attempts to establish the insecure ontology of letter bombs. We are told of the likely frequency of letter bombs— they 'have been a commonly used terrorist device'. Subsequently, we are told about the need for risk assessments in our organizations. We are then

---

BOX 8.1 LETTER BOMBS

Letter bombs, which include parcels, packages and anything delivered by post or courier, have been a commonly used terrorist device.

A properly conducted risk assessment should give you a good idea of the likely threat to your organisation and indicate precautions you need to take.

Letter bombs may be explosive or incendiary (the two most likely kinds), or conceivably chemical, biological or radiological. Anyone receiving a suspicious delivery is unlikely to know which type it is, so procedures should cater for every eventuality.

A letter bomb will probably have received fairly rough handling in the post and so is unlikely to detonate through being moved, but any attempt at opening it may set it off. Unless delivered by courier, it is unlikely to contain a timing device. (MI5, 2006)

---

offered a brief introduction to the kinds of precautions we might need to start thinking about: we need procedures for the handling of packages, we need to know if we should move the package, handle it roughly or delicately, and we need to look out for packages delivered by courier. Incorporated in this information are initial indicators of who should be taking responsibility and be accountable for managing the risk of letter bombs. Much attention is focused on managers of SMEs, their post rooms, and the post handling staff. Managers are expected to take responsibility (and future accountability for any failure to take responsibility) for ensuring post rooms and associated staff are in a position to take responsibility (and some delegated accountability) for handling letters and packages on behalf of the rest of the firm. In an otherwise ontologically uncertain situation (in which letters may or may not be bombs), this first move is intended to increase certainty. The specification of relations of responsibility and accountability offers a way in which ontologically insecure objects might be managed.

The second part of the MI5 advice focuses on separating out the letter bomb as a potential threat. The move is from who (managers, post room staff) to what (some of the possible characteristics of letter bombs). We are told that SMEs are at risk of being a terror target, that post rooms should take responsibility for managing this targeting, and that certain signs need to be looked out for. There is no discussion of which particular kinds of firms and organization might be targeted beyond the general category of SMEs, but much about the characteristics of a letter bomb. One effect of this is to imply that every SME is equally at risk and hence an appropriate recipient of advice. MI5 offers detailed advice to help recognize a letter bomb, set out in Box 8.2.

MI5 thus specifies in general terms that organizations might be at threat from letter bombs (the category SMEs), identifies those who should be accountable for managing the threat (managers and post rooms and post room staff), and separates out items of concern (the ontological respecification of ordinary letters as potential bombs).

BOX 8.2 INDICATORS OF A LETTER BOMB

It is unexpected or of unusual origin or from an unfamiliar sender
There is no return address or the address cannot be verified
It is poorly or inaccurately addressed, e.g. incorrect title, spelt wrongly, title but no name or addressed to an individual no longer with the company
The address has been printed unevenly or in an unusual way
The writing is in an unfamiliar foreign style
There are unusual postmarks or postage paid marks
A Jiffy bag, or similar padded envelope, has been used
It seems unusually heavy for its size. Most letters weigh up to about 30 g, whereas most effective letter bombs weigh 50–100 g and are 5 mm or more thick
It has more than the appropriate value of stamps for its size and weight
It is marked 'personal' or 'confidential'
It is oddly shaped or lopsided
The envelope flap is stuck down completely (a normal letter usually has an ungummed gap of 35 mm at the corners)
There is a pin-sized hole in the envelope or package wrapping
There is any unusual smell, including but not restricted to almonds, ammonia or marzipan
It has greasy or oily stains on the envelope
There is an additional inner envelope and it is tightly taped or tied (however, in some organisations sensitive material is sent in double envelopes as standard procedure).
(MI5, 2006)

The list is presumably intended as an information resource for lessening ontological uncertainty about these particular objects of mundane terror. Yet it is unclear how much the list accomplishes in making clear the difference between ordinary letters and letter bombs. For example, many listed features of possible letter bombs can be read as ordinary features of letters and packages in general: 'It is unexpected', 'There is no return address', a 'padded envelope has been used', 'It is marked 'personal' or 'confidential', and it is 'oddly shaped or lopsided'. Although these anti-terror instructions encourage widespread vigilance, at the same time the indicators of threat are so general as to constitute an extremely high likelihood of threat—perhaps too high for most SMEs to manage. For example, what would be the consequences if a small business treated every padded envelope it receives with high levels of suspicion?

Further, close inspection suggests that several of the listed attributes are in themselves ontologically uncertain. Who, for example, is to decide that 'writing is in an unfamiliar foreign style', 'It seems unusually heavy for its size', or that 'It has more than the appropriate value of stamps for its size and weight'. Just how foreign should a writing style appear before declaring a major incident? What counts as sufficient foreignness? Would the post room need to establish a consensus about what counts as a sufficiently foreign writing style? Or should managers be called in to arbitrate if writing appeared foreign? In addition, how easily can post room staff spot indicators of the bomb-like qualities of letters. In a busy post room, who would spot a pin hole in a package? Who would notice the sufficiently marzipan-like smell of a letter and decide it signalled a problem? Once again, the work required to respond adequately to the threat constituted by the instructions would appear to pose threats to the business itself. Letters are no longer just sorted by address, but separated, searched for pinholes, sniffed, weighed, their hand writing analysed, and so on. Consequently, although the list may be intended as definitive (or perhaps just adequate) guidance, it might also pose a problem for the operation of many businesses in that almost all objects are rendered ontologically insecure, almost all letters become potential bombs.

The list of attributes for noticing a possible letter bomb is lengthy and detailed. We are reminded of the detailed list of what can and cannot be recycled, as presented to householders in leaflets issued by the local council (Chapter 3). And it similarly poses two puzzles. On the one hand, close scrutiny of the list raises more questions than it answers, precisely because the specification of properties of objects is indeterminate. On the other hand, it leads us to ask: who exactly has the time to read these detailed specifications, absorb, and act on them? If such lists are not being read (in detail) nor being acted upon, what is their function? What does a list do if it does not list? One possible answer is that it performs accountability relations. The making and issuing of a list can be seen as fulfilling an obligation to try to change the situation, even if there is no evidence that the list is effective in doing so.

The third part of the MI5 website suggests appropriate actions on the part of those who come into contact with potential letter bombs (Box 8.3).

BOX 8.3 LETTER BOMB ACTIONS

Although any suspect item should be treated seriously, remember that the great majority will be false alarms and a few may be hoaxes. Try to ensure that your procedures, while effective, are not needlessly disruptive. Take the following into account in your planning:

Seek advice from your local police CTSA[a] on the threat and on defensive measures

Consider processing all incoming mail and deliveries at one point only. This should ideally be off-site or in a separate building, or at least in an area that can easily be isolated and in which deliveries can be handled without taking them through other parts of the building

Make sure that all staff who handle mail are briefed and trained. Include reception staff. Encourage regular correspondents to put their return address on each item

Ensure that all sources of incoming mail (e.g. Royal Mail, couriers, hand delivery) are included in your screening process

Ideally, post rooms should have independent air conditioning and alarm systems, as well as scanners and x-ray machines. However, while mail scanners may detect devices

---

for spreading chemical, biological and radiological (CBR) materials (e.g. explosive devices), they will not detect the CBR materials themselves. At present, no CBR detectors are consistently capable of identifying all hazards reliably. Post rooms should also have their own washing and shower facilities, including soap and detergent

Staff need to be aware of the usual pattern of deliveries and to be briefed of unusual deliveries. Train them to open post with letter openers (and with minimum movement), to keep hands away from noses and mouths and always to wash their hands afterwards. Staff should not blow into envelopes or shake them. Packages suspected of containing CBR material should ideally be placed in a double-sealed bag

Consider whether staff handling post need protective equipment such as latex gloves and face masks (seek advice from a qualified health and safety expert). Keep overalls and footwear available in case staff need to remove contaminated clothing

Make certain that post opening areas can be promptly evacuated. Rehearse evacuation procedures and routes, which should include washing facilities in which contaminated staff could be isolated and treated

Prepare signs for display to staff in the event of a suspected or actual attack.
(MI5, 2006)

---

[a] Counter-Terrorism Security Advisor.

Here we find that not only are objects (in this case letters and packages) respecified as part of a new classification (as potential objects of mundane terror) and not only should particular organizations (SME post rooms) assume responsibility for managing the threat, but also that those targeted should re-orient the organization's activities around the threat in very detailed and specific ways. As before, however, the list of recommended actions seems actually to encourage more of the ontological insecurity that the list purportedly intended to repair.

The first instruction is to avoid 'needlessly disruptive' measures, but what is the likelihood of an SME being able to carry out some of these actions without disruption? It is assumed that SMEs have the budget, time, energy, willingness, and staff to invest in making significant changes. For example, it seems unlikely that a small shop or a university department could easily install post rooms with 'independent air conditioning and alarm systems, as well as scanners and x-ray machines' or 'washing facilities in which contaminated staff could be isolated and treated'.

Some of the actions themselves appear to introduce more uncertainty. For example, when setting up a post room dedicated to the handling of potential letter bombs, SMEs should introduce scanners to detect dangerous material—particularly of a chemical, biological, or radiological (CBR) nature. But in the same instructions we are told: 'However, while mail scanners may detect devices for spreading chemical, biological and radiological (CBR) materials (e.g. explosive devices), they will not detect the CBR materials themselves. At present, no CBR detectors are consistently capable of identifying all hazards reliably. Post rooms should also have their own washing and shower facilities, including soap and detergent'.[9] Also, although we were previously told that sniffing packages was important, now we are told 'to keep hands away from noses' when handling potential letter bombs. And we are not told to what extent our problems would be solved by placing radioactive material into 'a double-sealed bag'.

Instead of making an uncertain ontology (could be a bomb) more certain (a means to eliminate the risk of a bomb), we appear to have an escalation and redistribution of uncertainty. Uncertainty is shifted from the originators of concerns about mundane terror (MI5) to a broad audience of organizations (SMEs) who are encouraged to adopt concerns about ontological uncertainty. Ontological uncertainty remains but is displaced to a new location. In striving to satisfy its own accountability demands, that is, in taking responsibility for terrorism, and providing the government with value for money by communicating advice to the business community, MI5 relocates ontological uncertainty in SMEs.

This relocation of ontological uncertainty can also lead to its escalation. One way to understand this is to look closely at the orthography used to express uncertainty. The source of mundane terror is the possibility that something very ordinary looking may actually turn out to be something very extraordinary. The problem is that one can (no longer) tell just by looking whether it is a harmless object or a life-threatening explosive. Typically, we use inverted commas to draw attention to the deceptive appearance of something, for example, the difference between a letter and a 'letter'. The quotation marks around the latter term draw attention to the active construction that has gone into the apprehension of a letter. They signal that someone or something has designated the thing as a letter when it might not actually be a letter. It merely appears to be a 'letter'. Similarly, a 'bomb' can be distinguished from a bomb by suggesting that the former is merely a representation of a bomb.

Thus, for example, if dealing with a letter that had been opened by security and found to be free from terror, we might want to refer to this as a letter 'bomb'. Alternatively, if we were to discuss a package that had exploded, we might shift the inverted commas and refer to this as a 'letter' bomb. The placing of the inverted commas indicates the focus and boundaries of our ontological concern. Either the bomb in letter 'bomb' or the letter in 'letter' bomb are marked as available for ontologically sceptical scrutiny, because the inverted commas denote that some agency has been at work in the object's designation. By contrast, the absence of inverted commas suggests that the description can be taken at face value. But to place inverted commas

---

[9] The suggestion seems to be that washing facilities are needed because of the inevitable uncertainty in assessing packages.

around only one term is a form of ontological gerrymandering (Woolgar and Pawluch, 1985). It implies that we know (and do not need to scrutinize) the limits and certainties of the ontology of the objects with which we are dealing (their letter-ness or bomb-ness). But MI5's instructions do little to reduce the uncertainty surrounding letter bombs. Indeed, they could be considered as effecting an accountability shift from MI5 to SMEs. In this example, we might be better to use more inverted commas rather than less: instead of letter 'bombs' or 'letter' bombs, in this instance we appear to have 'letter' 'bombs'. The double inverted commas emphasizes that this is not just a situation of uncertainty, but a situation in which deep ontological insecurity (just what is the nature of these objects and who should decide, using what means) has been extended to a wide range of different objects, people, and their organizations. Ontological insecurity derives from the lack of criteria for distinguishing between letters and letter bombs, coupled with not meeting expectations that the objects will be adequately handled.

8.5 Biometric Identity Cards

We noted in Chapter 7 that airport managers saw the incorporation of biometric data into passports as a way of constituting governable passengers and an orderly airport space. Between 2002 and 2010, a general enthusiasm for biometrics included a UK government drive to introduce biometric ID cards. At the time, these cards represented the latest example in a significant social history of branding the body (or its component parts) as a means to categorize, specify, and segregate populations.[10] In recent years, advances in biometric techniques (van der Ploeg, 2003) have led to claims that it is increasingly possible to constitute, corroborate, and mobilize identities (see also UK Home Office, 2005). These kinds of identity technologies have attained a pervasive resonance across Europe (in biometric passport developments) and beyond (for example, with biometric entry/exit points to the USA).

In the UK, the promise of advances in constituting bodies as digital identities initially moved forward the long-standing political debate about the introduction of national ID cards. Since the repeal of the last UK ID card after the Second World War, the debate had centred on the importance of identity, knowing who someone was, and being able to demonstrate one's own identity. The emergence of biometrics—in the form of iris scans, facial recognition systems, and fingerprinting technology—promised better ways of managing

---

[10] Other examples include tattooing, scarring, and haircutting as embodied branding (Schildkrout, 2004), fingerprinting (Cole, 1998), and phrenology (Allen, 1846) as indicators of category membership.

identity. In place of the restricted use of identity assessments for tackling criminal activity or border security, the Tony Blair and Gordon Brown Labour governments advocated the biometric ID card as a way to regulate access to, among other things, social welfare, medical treatment, air travel, and money. The digitization of biometric identity, it was argued, would enable the coupling of iris, fingerprint, or facial scan with, for example, credit rating, medical history, and criminal record. The introduction of national ID cards promised assessments of identity, which could include information about their history, interests, and status (medical, criminal, financial, citizenship).

The Labour government proclaimed that an ID card system was necessary 'to prepare the UK to meet the challenges of the 21st century' (Home Office, 2005). These challenges included:

- 'the fight against illegal working' by preventing employers employing staff who did not have the right to work in the UK and include a biometric work visa for non-permanent residents;

- 'immigration abuse' by making the UK less attractive for asylum seekers as, unlike some other EU states that had ID cards, many came to the UK and would disappear;

- ensuring free public services were 'only used by those entitled to them—preventing abuse such as "health tourism"';

- helping to 'protect people from identity theft' whereby victims had their identities stolen by others who may then use the identity for financial or other gain;

- 'the use of false and multiple identities' by terrorists and criminals.

Biometric ID cards were envisaged as a means of mundane governance: card use would be an everyday occurrence, biometric checks were to become routine and all kinds of actions—from getting money from a bank, accessing a government service, to getting on a plane—were to be redrawn through biometric constitution. We can understand the meeting of the above 'challenges' as an effort to reduce ontological insecurity. Various digital codes would apparently be used to reconstitute bodily attributes in records, compiled in a database, and later matched with the (actual) bodies to confirm their identity. Mundane terror arising from the use of multiple identities was a problem to be solved through the certainty of biometrics. In place of an uncertain, perhaps multiple body, biometrics could establish a certain singular body (and identity). However, moves to promote ID cards generated anxiety, expressed in the media and in campaigns against ID cards (see, for example, www.no2id.net). In response the Home Office carried out a variety of consultation exercises to reaffirm the opportunity to manage ontological insecurity—that multiple bodies and identities were a problem and that biometrics would work, that bodily information could be recorded, stored, and made to match bodies—and to emphasize that the technology would not generate further troubles.

One of these consultation exercises was carried out by the UK passport service.[11] This consultation did not publicize the ongoing pro- and anti-ID card arguments in the UK, nor did it mention the political positives and negatives that might be implicated in a future card scheme.[12] Instead, the 'consultation' process offered people the chance to take part in a biometric ID card trial at the end of which each person would be given an ID card (Figure 8.1) and the chance to answer ten multiple-choice questions. The 'consultation' thus provided the Home Office with data about the technical feasibility of the biometric ID card programme. It also offered interested members of the public a glimpse of the future under biometrics. The consultation included journalists, anti-ID card protestors, and even social scientists interested in this new form of mundane governance.

Dan took part in the consultation. In Leicester's main post office he was asked to sit down at a desk with a computer, monitor, and various other pieces of technological equipment. After a few moments he was approached by a member of the passport service staff:

OPERATIVE: OK, so we're going to record your biometric identity, take a photo, fingerprints, iris scan and facial recognition. None of this data will be kept after the trial but we will issue you with a card to take away. OK?

DAN: Yes.

OPERATIVE: OK. So first we'll take your picture. Look at the machine.

[I had been sat facing him, but now have to turn towards a silver box on the wall which has a black rectangle of reflective glass in it.]

OPERATIVE: Is that photo OK?

[A photo has appeared on his computer. It looks awful, but I don't say so.]

DAN: Yes.

OPERATIVE: Right, next we will have to record your face. Just look at the machine again.

DAN: Oh, I shouldn't smile or anything should I?

OPERATIVE: Do what you want.

[I seem to remember that on passport photos it was against the rules to smile, but I don't know if his flippant remark relates to this only being a trial or whether it really doesn't matter what I do with my face.]

---

[11] The UK passport service was originally part of the Home Office, but was rebranded, between 2008 and 2010, as the Identity and Passport Service, with responsibility for ID cards.

[12] These included who had control of and access to information on the databases, and issues of data security (see Neyland, 2009).

DAN: OK.

[2 or 3 seconds pass with me staring at the wall.]

OPERATIVE: OK that's your face recorded. Now we'll do your eyes.

DAN: Why do you record my eyes?

OPERATIVE: They are more accurate than fingerprints. Fingerprints use 12 to 16 points and your eyes use 240—your eye is more unique and your chance of having a matching iris with someone else is 17 billion to one so you shouldn't get a match. Fingerprints can only be measured by a maximum of about 34 points.

Although this seemed statistically reasonable (apart from the 17 billion people figure, presumably this number was just meant to sound big), Dan managed to upset the computer by being unable to align his eyes with the black box.

[I look into the machine and am told to follow its instructions. In the reflective glass, green circles appear around my eyes.]

MACHINE: Move back please.

DAN: Ooh. [I am surprised the machine is talking to me]

[I move my head back].

MACHINE: Move back please.

DAN: Oh.

[I move my whole body back.]

MACHINE: Look into the camera please.

[The machine appears to have lost track of me so I move much further forward].

MACHINE: Move back please.

OPERATIVE: Just move back an inch or so.

[He actually starts to direct my head into position—this is really surprising to me. Is he supposed to touch me? Is this the biometric future? Red squares flash on either side of the reflective glass and the green circles reappear around my eyes.]

OPERATIVE: OK we've got the first one, now we'll do the other. Just try to open your eyes nice and wide.

[I stare manically at the machine on the wall.]

OPERATIVE: OK. Now your fingerprints.

Dan had to place his fingers and then thumbs on a glass plate. His digits were recorded digitally. The operative said he had to check the results, during which Dan tried to strike up conversation:

DAN: Does it record my eye from the centre outwards or round in a circle?

OPERATIVE: I've no idea.

DAN: Is this your full-time job?

OPERATIVE: Yes for four months on secondment.

DAN: I imagine if everyone has to have one of these, you'll be busy.

OPERATIVE: Yes I should think so. Right that's done. You can move over to my colleague for verification.

DAN: Do you collect DNA?

OPERATIVE: We'd love to, but it is too invasive and in an airport you wouldn't have an easy way to collect DNA and match it.

At this point, a machine to the left of the operative produced a plastic ID card. The operative picked up the card, gave it a cursory glance, and handed it to his colleague. Before being told the results were OK, Dan was directed to another desk. The colleague entered the new card into a reader.

COLLEAGUE: OK this should only take a few moments. What we'll do is use one measure to see if it comes out on the computer. Do you want fingerprint, eye scan or facial recognition?

DAN: Oh eye scan please.

COLLEAGUE: OK, look into the machine in front of you and follow the instructions.

[The machine in front of me appears to be the same as the previous machine except it is on a metal stand, not fixed to the wall. Colleague puts my card with my picture on it in a machine—like the chip and pin readers in shops.]

MACHINE2:   Move back please.

[I remember Operative's advice and just move back an inch.]

MACHINE2:   Move to the right please.

[I can see the green circles on the reflective glass and try and line my eyes up with the circles. Before anything has apparently happened...]

COLLEAGUE: OK that's fine. Here's your card and this includes a chip with your biometric data. You can't actually use this for anything, but this is what a national ID card would look like.

DAN: Oh that's nice isn't it?

COLLEAGUE: Can you fill in the rest of the questions on the survey please?

As instructed, Dan ticked a few boxes in response to questions about whether or not he thought the cards were a good idea. It did not seem the consultation offered much information about the advantages and disadvantages of the ID cards. Perhaps this was an attempt to convey ontological certainty about the scheme. For Dan the whole experience had felt awkward. This was reflected in later published results that perpetuated the confusion between trial and consultation. Although the opening section of the report described it as a trial (Atos, 2005: 3), the next section suggested it was 'a consultation' and 'not a technology trial' (Atos, 2005: 3). The report included several statistical outcomes. For example, disabled participants had far greater trouble with biometric recording and testing (for example, face scanning worked for only 48 per cent of disabled participants compared to 68 per cent of others); people with large fingers or who had manual jobs had problems with fingerprint scanning. It took an average of eight minutes to record each person's biometrics, which figure corresponds to

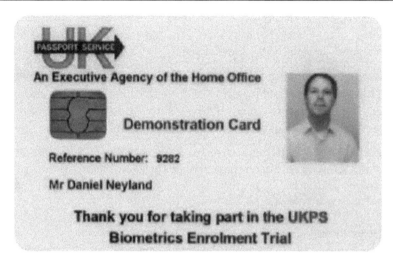

Figure 8.1. Dan's national biometric ID card

3820 years of working days effort needed to record the 59.6 million people in the UK, not to mention the immense effort needed to locate 59.6 million people in the right places at the right times to do the recording. (And this recording would need to be repeated every ten years.)[13] Other research on biometric trials has similarly resulted in failure to match biometrics back to the bodies from which they were recorded (see Introna and Wood, 2004). This research also suggests that larger databases have higher failure rates; and that the failure rate increases each year as bodies' age and computer-stored biometrics remain unchanged; and that certain ethnic groups (particularly people without high contrast skin colours) create more false matches than others.

Given that the government proposed recording biometrics with ten-year passport renewals, the inconvenience of biometric recording would only occur once a decade for each member of the UK population. However, occasions when the biometrics might need to be recalled and aligned with features of the body might prove more regularly problematic. These moments of proposed future identity recall appeared to offer a greater likelihood of change in day to day activities than ten-yearly recording of biometrics. Dan's bodily features were translated into a digital code and would have been stored on a database if the trial had instead been part of the actual introduction of ID cards. Matching these biometrics to Dan's bodily features would then have become part of the everyday mundane

---

[13] For more reflection on the trials see BBC (2005).

governance to which he was subject (for example, when coming into contact with the banking, social service, certain aspects of retail, and health sectors).

It would be possible to re-tell this as a straightforward tale of having one's body objectified and constituted as an identity for future assessments and checks. The end of such a story would be ontological certainty and identity singularity. This was the story the government would have liked to tell. But such a story both ignores the technical complexities revealed by the trial/consultation and takes no account of the complexity of mundane governance and ontological constitution.

As with the constitution of security ready passengers and letter bombs, the first aspect of the biometric ID card trial/consultation involved classification. In this case approximately 10,000 bodies (but if it had become a national scheme, closer to 60 million) had to be corralled and addressed, organized and co-ordinated, and rendered as a series of digital code to be maintained on computer servers and linked to other code (such as government databases) and bodies (which might or might not provide an enduring relation to the code). Dan felt he had to invest quite some effort to participate in the trial/consultation (he had made several attempts to register on the trial website, failing this he had made multiple phone calls, driven 80 miles, and participated in the awkward biometric recording and testing). Scaled up to a national scheme with biometric recording repeated every ten years, and testing of biometrics on (potentially) a daily basis, this would mean a significant transformation in the activities of the UK population.

In Chapter 3 we emphasized the importance of governance pairs (in that case recycling boxes and their households). Pairing was the second step involved in mundane governance in Dan's trial; his biometrics had to be successfully paired with his body. Once again, if this system had been scaled up to a national one, this pairing could have become a regular feature of everyday life. Generating this pair would then lead to attributions of responsibility and accountability if this was not just a trial. Recorded on databases accessed through the pair (of body and biometrics) would be information about the pair's recent history, health, activities, and financial transactions, for example. To introduce certainty into situations of potential mundane terror, the pair could be inscribed with various further classificatory schemes. To use the terminology of the airport managers, the pairing of body and biometrics could be classified in various ways on databases as 'clean' (and, therefore, requiring no particular scrutiny) or 'dirty' (and, therefore, in need of singling out for greater attention). Indeed, under government proposals for the use of ID cards, airports were a key location where such classifications would take place.

Producing a governance pair (biometrics and their bodies) and classification (clean or dirty) appeared ontologically certain and singular. However, the pair was not easy to produce and did not seem to hold together well in the trial. For Dan, recording and testing his eyes (that is, matching his eyes to the ones recorded) was cumbersome, time consuming, and confusing. Scaled up to the 20 million passengers who passed through the airport terminal each year, the production of ontologically singular and certain governance pairings might be a huge organizational burden.[14] Furthermore, the pairings seemed fragile. In the trial fewer than half the disabled participants could match their bodies to the biometrics they had just recorded and, among non-disabled participants, 32 per cent failed successfully to match their face to the biometric just recorded a few moments previously. In the airport terminal, this would lead to many of us being apprehended as uncertain entities. So, ironically, mundane terror might increase as a direct result of trying to impose certainty and singularity on bodies.

Is the example of biometric identity different from liquids and letter bombs? In the latter cases, the anticipated use of objects by terrorists led to scares about the insecurity of those objects. Is biometric identity different because uncertainty derives from the inability of the technology adequately to constitute certain governance pairs? No. The basic rationale for this third story of mundane terror is the anticipated use of bodies as terrorist threats. The insecurity then derives from a lack of certainty about identity. Are they or are they not terrorists, bombs, or hijackers?[15] As in the preceding examples, it is in anticipation of ontological insecurity (in this case, which of these bodies are bad?), that attempts are made to impose a new mechanism for the production of certainty and singularity. The Home Office justification for the scheme suggests that while we know that terrorist bodies are multiple, biometrics will provide the means to identify the shared, natural, common core of the singular body that is carried across this multiplicity. And it is the attempt to reassert ontological certainty and singularity that makes apparent the difficulties of governing into being such certainty—the (terrorist) body singular is always just out of reach. A deep sense of ontological insecurity is manifested in the move to highlight an initial uncertainty (difficult to identify terrorist bodies), which is then compounded rather than resolved by the introduction of a system which, although designed to relieve uncertainty, only seems to raise more questions. Introducing new governance pairs (biometrics and their bodies)

---

[14] One colleague suggested that the 'real' mundane terror would be subjecting the population to even more queues, even more bureaucratic processes than they currently had to endure.

[15] There are other uncertainties in broader renderings of the scheme: benefit cheat or not, eligible for this service or not, to be granted access to this bank account or not, etc.

to resolve uncertainties (bodily multiplicity), seems only to introduce new insecurities. Whose bodies, whose biometrics, and how to cope with mass multiplicity? The introduction and subsequent failure to manage an initial ontological uncertainty seemed only to engender a deeper sense of ontological insecurity.[16]

8.6 Analysis

We have argued for a greater understanding of the ways in which ordinary and everyday objects can become matters of concern. In particular, we explored the extent to which the phenomenon of mundane terror—whereby ordinary and everyday objects are called to account for the extent to which they might contribute to acts of terror—can be understood in terms of ontological insecurity. There are four key points to be drawn out.

First, we outlined the three-part procedure that characterizes mundane terror. The work done both by the airport terminal managers (to manage passenger objects of mundane terror as they move through the airport) and by MI5 (attempting to communicate management strategies for potential letter bombs to SMEs) involved initially constituting a particular target group as responsible for a possible terror threat (departing passengers, SMEs); then respecifying a particular class of object as a focal point of terror (sharps and water bottles, letters, and packages); and then tying the responsibilized and reclassified people and objects into new relations of accountability. This accomplishes the new ontological status for people, actions, and objects (do not carry liquid containers over 100 ml in hand luggage; do introduce new practices to the post room). The three-part procedure depends on this combination of constitution, responsibility, and accountability, drawing up classifications of objects of concern and people to be concerned, and figuring out appropriate paths of action to take. Whereas airport managers take steps to try to hold together the people responsible, objects of concern, and appropriate paths of action, MI5 shifted accountability to their target audience to decide whether and how to take on the suggested ontological transformation of people and things. In neither case is much punishment involved; most airport passengers who transgress the water bottle rule simply have bottles taken away and continue on their journey; SMEs carry on regardless

---

[16] As it turned out, the UK scheme to introduce biometric ID cards was itself beset by insecurities of cost. When the UK elected a new government with a cost-cutting agenda, the ID card scheme was one of its first targets. With cost estimates ranging from £5–£20 billion and concerns about the system's technical efficacy emerging from the results of the trial/consultation, the abandonment of the scheme came as little surprise.

of whether or not they have rebuilt their post rooms. There is an uneven distribution of further accountabilities with airport managers apparently more accountable to their board than are members of MI5 to the government, and hence more likely to be reprimanded for failing correctly and adequately to separate objects from their passengers, than are MI5 for not having their advice followed by SMEs.

Secondly, we suggested that the source of mundane terror is the inability to distinguish between a very ordinary object and one with anything but ordinary properties. The problem is precisely that the letter bomb looks just like a letter; that an ordinary everyday water bottle might turn out to be a highly explosive liquid. The ironic (in the technical sense) dimension of mundane terror is that the object turns out to be other than it appears, and this is what gives rise to ontological uncertainty. We noted how orthographic designations of this situation sometimes deploy inverted commas, to distinguish between entities that are to be taken as given and those (with inverted commas) presented as the upshot of some constituting work. We suggested that in general this distinction is untenable. That, as a matter of principle, we would not wish to treat any entity as given, and would prefer the wholesale use of inverted commas, at least metaphorically. Indeed, MI5's instructions suggest we are in no position to rest content with just occasional inverted commas. As we cannot know if we are dealing with a letter 'bomb' (preferable) or a 'letter' bomb (not so preferable) we must resolve to deal with 'letter' 'bombs'. In a similar manner, in the airport we should accept that the kinds of objects we are interrogating are 'water' 'bottles' or in the ID card example, 'terrorist' 'body/ies'.

Thirdly, the biometric ID card trial demonstrated the complexity of ontological uncertainty in relation to pairings of objects of mundane terror and particular bodies. In this example, the basic pairing at the centre of governance relations frequently failed to hold together. Although in the airport bodies were classified as either 'clean' (in need of no further attention) or 'dirty' (in need of further attention) and notional forms of accountability (assessments of the value, nature, intent, and likely future action of the body in question), in the biometric trial, these notional actions seemed difficult to accomplish. The failure of the pairing (biometrics and their bodies) to hold together during the trial and Dan's difficulty in dealing with the awkwardness of having his biometric eyes match his own eyes from which the biometrics had just been recorded, suggested that any subsequent questions (is this the body of a terrorist?; how should they be held to account?) were likely to be secondary to problems with getting the governance system to do the pairing adequately.

Fourthly, from these problems we can see that governance efforts in relation to these mundane terror episodes seemed to involve an escalation of ontological uncertainty. The moves to govern mundane terror appeared to involve an initial constitution of uncertainty. For example, the airport managers' leaflet (for dealing with sharps and water bottles), MI5's instructions (on how to deal with letter bombs), and the UK government's justification for attempting to introduce ID cards (the need to manage multiple identities used by terrorists), each introduce ontological uncertainty by emphasizing a particular kind of mundane terror. Coupled with the introduction of ontological uncertainty was the means to appear to manage the ontological uncertainty. Hence the leaflet established paths of action that would shift water bottles from uncertain to certain, MI5's instructions would reduce the terror threat faced by SMEs thus introducing ways to handle letter bombs, and biometrics would provide a means to reduce the body multiple to the body singular. This might have constituted a problem–solution pairing. However, this way of managing uncertainty seemed only to deepen ontological questions. The leaflet (and its apparent frequent failure), MI5's instructions (and the remaining need for double apostrophizing), and the ID card scheme (and its apparent failure to hold together the central pairing of biometrics and their bodies) each seemed to introduce and highlight, and fail to deal with, ontological uncertainty. This resulted in a kind of ontological escalation and amplification. What was introduced as a system to govern ontological questions in episodes of mundane terror only compounded uncertainty, leading to a deeper sense of ontological insecurity.

Escalation and amplification of ontological concerns seemed to derive from the explosion of questions and matters of concern that stemmed from the constitution of ontological uncertainty and a system for governing uncertainty through relations of accountability and responsibility. For example, in the airport terminal questions asked of 'water' 'bottles' were the basis for further multiple questions and concerns. What began as a question of the nature of objects rapidly transformed into broader questions about business models, the value of shares, the likelihood of a takeover, and the insecurity of people's jobs in the airport. These questions were not solely attributed to the 'water' 'bottle' scare, but the scare formed the occasion through which these concerns could be given clear articulation. Similarly, with the attempt to introduce ID cards, questions began with a focus on the uncertain nature of bodies and their identity. This rapidly proliferated into questions of who or what might count as secure, human rights, invasions of privacy, rights to freedom, technological capacity, the nanny state, and concerns about the impact of this proposed system on specific sectors of the population (for example, those with mental health problems). Instead of reducing the terrorist body multiple to a terrorist body singular, the introduction of security measures seemed to have the opposite effect.

8.7 Conclusion

The ontology of objects and their people is central to questions of certainty, insecurity, accountability, and responsibility in moments of terror. We considered three examples—airport managers' attempts to manage the apparent threat of sharp objects and water bottles, British intelligence attempts to help businesses manage the threat of letter bombs, and the UK government's failed attempts to introduce biometric ID cards to counter the threat of terrorism. In each case, uncertainty was constituted through the respecification of the ontologies of specific people and objects (passengers, terrorists, sharps/water bottles, letters, and objectified bodies), to shift accountability relations to specific audiences. In every case, these efforts ran into problems. Airport passengers still tried to carry sharp objects and water bottles through security, the instructions for dealing with letter bombs appear opaque, and the attempt to make ID cards generated new problems in trying to pair biometrics and their bodies. The result was that in place of new ontological certainties, accomplished through the distribution of new ways of orienting actions towards objects of concern, came an escalation and amplification of ontological concern. This escalation and amplification from ontological uncertainty to insecurity, resulted from attempts to make audiences aware of ontological uncertainty, followed by an apparent failure to introduce systems capable of governing the uncertainty.

In this chapter, we have shown how the phenomenon of mundane terror arises in virtue of a particular ontological constitution of objects and their people, specifically through the enactment of ontological insecurities. We also saw that opening ontological security/insecurity to public scrutiny can pose more questions than a governance system can easily resolve. We saw again (as in Chapter 3) the importance of governance pairings (objects and their people) and, in particular, the difficulties that arise when key governance pairings fail to hold together. We further illustrated the uncertainties of accomplishing evidence (as introduced in Chapter 4), for example, in airport managers' use of various proxies of passenger activity to stand as adequate explanations for why passengers act in certain ways. We have also built on the argument that mundane governance involves the active enactment of the structures of governance 'within which' governance takes place (Chapter 5) and that compliance in mundane governance is much more than straightforward acquiescence and assessment (Chapter 6). These previously noted difficulties in achieving mundane governance leads us to suggest that introducing heightened forms of accountability in relation to terror scares may even exacerbate the problems of accomplishing accountability, and encouraging targeted populations towards particular paths of action.

We have stressed some of the difficulties in achieving mundane governance, but have done so mainly from the perspective of what we can call the
operatives of mundane governance. We have thus discussed ontological insecurity as a property of systems of governance, emphasizing the responsibility
for constituting and attempting to manage ontological insecurities on the
part of airport staff, MI5, or the UK government's ID card scheme. An implication of this way of looking at mundane governance is that on those, albeit
rare, occasions where the operatives enjoy success, the effects of their efforts
follow straightforwardly. But we have already cautioned against this interpretation when demonstrating the myriad complexities associated with the idea
of compliance (Chapter 6). Against the notion that systems of governance
have straightforward effects or that they provide rationales for internalization by governed populations, we now turn to a more detailed consideration
of responses to mundane governance. In particular, in Chapter 9 we consider
the experiences of the subjects of mundane governance by examining examples of resistance and breakdown.

9

Disruption

9.1 Introduction

We have argued that mundane governance is not best understood as comprising an explicit rationale, a straightforward process of interiorizing, and a clear set of accountability relations. For example, in Chapter 3 households seemed unaware that the local council provided leaflets on how and what to recycle. In Chapter 4 the city council were not always sure what evidence of waste management they were collecting and why. In Chapter 5 the structures of governance involving national government, regional safety camera partnerships, and the handbook all slipped into the background when partnership managers made decisions. Similarly, drivers in Chapter 6 were not always aware of the rules with which they were officially expected to comply. Airport passengers managed to board planes in a haphazard manner and often in spite of wayfinding technologies in Chapter 7, and although airport managers were clear about liquids rules in Chapter 8, the same was not always the case for airport passengers. We have thus far used these slippages, negotiations, invocations, and moments of messiness to criticize existing approaches to governance and, in particular, to argue that mundane governance should be understood as the ongoing accomplishment of ontologies of governable people and things, spaces, processes, pairs, documents, and outcomes. But what of the putative subjects of mundane governance? We have seen how organizations articulate the terms of governance and accountability. But how do those designated as users, customers, accountees, the governed, drivers, households, and passengers (among other descriptions) themselves apprehend governance and accountability? This chapter examines the phenomenon of disruption as a further way of understanding the workings of situated ontology in mundane governance.

Disruption—especially in the form of the 'breaching experiments' of early ethnomethodology (Garfinkel, 1967)—is well known for its capacity to reveal the unnoticed, taken for granted basis of social order. For our purposes, the bases of social order are the ordinarily taken for granted, situated ontologies and corresponding relations of governance and accountability. So this chapter explores the idea that disruption in mundane governance can make available an articulation of the relations of governance and accountability. Precisely because they are usually taken for granted, these relations are not straightforwardly available to participants as pre-existing antecedent circumstances. Rather, it is in the acts of disruption that the artful enactment, constitution, display, or concealment of governance and accountability relations are brought to the fore.

In addition, our analysis of instances of disruption begins to address the question of why people put up with mundane governance. Recalling our grumpy old men in Chapter 1, we note their considerable irritation and frustration associated with the idea that ordinary stuff is increasingly controlling their lives. But their reaction did not take the form of, for example, organized resistance. Their response was to be grumpy. Similarly, we reported the disquiet of airport passengers at having to conform to the liquids rule (Chapter 7). Although they manifest considerable annoyance at the inconvenience, their reaction was not channelled into any kind of systematic co-ordinated challenge. So, in moments where governance breaks down or fails, or is successfully challenged or resisted, what is the reaction of the grumpies? In particular, what do these episodes tell us about the ways in which normally operating governance is understood? To what extent can disruptions shed light on the nature and extent to which the world in all its mundaneity is normally taken for granted?

This chapter explores the situated ontologies and relations of accountability in four examples of disruption of mundane governance. By disruption we mean to include instances of related phenomena: breakdown, failure, breach, challenge, contestation, and resistance. In each case, central and taken for granted aspects of mundane governance are disrupted. Of the three main substantive areas we have concentrated on in this book, perhaps the most dramatic forms of disruption have occurred in response to governance through speed cameras. For example, it is possible to find websites that celebrate, and offer guidance for, the destruction of speed cameras (for more on resistance to speed cameras, see Wells and Wills, 2009). Readers may be relieved to learn that we ourselves resisted the opportunity to engage in this particularly dramatic form of disruption. Rather, our focus is less on organized resistance to mundane governance, of which the sabotage of speed cameras was a rare example, than on more pervasive everyday forms of disruption. Our selection of these examples emerged, to a large extent, through the use of our happenstance methodology (see Chapter 10). That is, the examples arose as a result of our keeping a sceptical eye out for opportunities for trouble. The empirical examples are: (1) contesting recent airport regulations for carry on liquids; (2) interpretations and discussion around the failure of traffic light systems; (3) disputing parking fines; and (4) the speeding database.

Our aim is further to explore our central thesis, that governance and accountability are constitutively linked to the accomplished ontological status of the key entities involved, by looking at the ways in which these phenomena are brought to the fore in moments of disruption. We begin by considering disruption in theory.

9.2 Disruptions and Breaches

Garfinkel (1963, 1967) designed a series of breaching experiments where central features of social order would be revealed, as they were undermined. He suggested: 'In accounting for the persistence and continuity of the features of concerted actions, sociologists commonly select some set of stable features of an organisation of activities and ask for the variables that contribute to their stability' (1963: 187). Garfinkel (1963), however, recommended a distinct course of action: 'An alternative procedure would appear to be more economical: to start with a system with stable features and ask what can be done to make for trouble. The operations that one would have to perform to produce and sustain anomic features of perceived environments and disorganized interaction should tell us something about how social structures are ordinarily and routinely being maintained' (1963: 187).

Garfinkel deployed a variety of breaching experiments in which the conventions for social action would become apparent through participants' attempts to make sense of 'what had happened' in the course of what was later revealed to be an experiment. In deploying a variety of repair mechanisms for coming to terms with apparent breaches in social convention, participants would reveal the means by which their ordinary, everyday social actions were constituted and maintained.

For example, in one experiment Garfinkel asked students to return home and act as if they were lodgers in their own homes rather than as members of the family. Students were asked to maintain the task for as long as possible and report the outcomes. Students reported referring to their parents by their surnames rather than by more familiar terms, being polite at the dinner table, and talking to family members as if they were part of an economic relationship rather than a family. The students responded in various ways. Several students found the terms of the experiment particularly difficult to maintain in the face of questioning and of the disconcerted family members. Other students reported that the experiment revealed things about family members and partners that they had always suspected. Others reported the extremely short-lived nature of their experiments. The students detailed the ways in which participants in the experiments (both students and family members) first tried to figure out the breach in social order (What was going on? Why were individuals acting in this way?), and second, to repair the situation. Attempts at repair included coming up with rationales for why individuals were acting in the way they were (by suggesting, for example, that the son was obviously sick) and trying to get individuals to act in line with what other members of the social interaction now suggested was the norm (by articulating the ways in which family members were expected to act).

The breaches and repairs (or attempted repairs) offered opportunities to consider the social order of these forms of interaction. They made available the expectations that students were to act in particular ways as members of a family, which involved sitting in certain ways at the dinner table, addressing family members using certain terms, talking about particular subjects, and so on. In these articulations of the social order, clear reference was made to expectations as to how members of the social interaction should act. In our terms, the people, objects, relations, and actions of how family life ought to be accomplished, the evidential–moral–actionable order of family life, were constituted through the breach. What kinds of productive trouble can we make in relation to mundane governance and accountability? In what ways can trouble help illuminate the ontological constitution of the means, relations, objects, and people of governance? The following examples will address these questions.

9.3 The Water Bottle

We saw in Chapter 8 how ordinary objects in, for example, airport settings could become transformed into objects requiring various apparatuses of direction (leaflets, signs), assessment, accountability (security checks for assessing the adequacy of presentation of decoupling of people from things), and passage (from passenger to staff to bins). Ordinary objects could acquire an insecure ontology. A water bottle was transformed into a potential object of terror. The ontological status of ordinary objects turned out to be subject to a precise local choreography (cf Thompson, 2005). For example, on one occasion when Steve and Dan travelled from London Heathrow Airport, they went through security clearance, which meant having various of their liquids confiscated in the process. Steve then purchased a terror-free bottle of water in the departure lounge. But in making their way to the departure gate they managed to misread the signs (in the chaos of ongoing rebuilding works in terminal 1) and found themselves again the wrong ('dirty') side of another security check. At this point, the terror-free bottle of water was transformed into an object of potential terror and promptly confiscated. Evidently, ontologies can become insecure in virtue of a particular local history of passage and spatial alignment.

Overall, passengers seemed compliant with the new liquid (and other security) regulations, even though they were puzzled, annoyed, and frustrated by them. Many passengers continued trying to take oversize liquid containers through security checks, thereby causing queues while these containers were checked and removed. But, in general, a kind of compliance was accomplished: offending liquid containers were separated from their passengers. Many passengers had tales to tell about the absurdities to which the rules had given rise, for example, the confiscation of a perfectly good (and expensive) bottle of whisky, initially purchased at a remote airport by a connecting passenger, 'just because it was wrapped in the wrong plastic'. The perceived absurdity of the case draws its force from the evident ordinariness of the liquid in question. It was after all just a bottle of whisky. Very few of the passengers we asked could articulate a rationale for the new rules. Instead, they frequently offered caustic comments such as 'It gives them something to do, I suppose'.

But what happens when the (insecure) ontology is contested? Over the course of several flights to and from British airports, we took the opportunity to question the basis for the rule at the point where offending objects in hand luggage prompted investigation by the security clerk. In the following example, the offending items are canisters of shaving foam and deodorant.

[I myself pass through the detector without the alarm going off. But when my bag emerges from the other side of the x-ray machine it is taken off the conveyor belt and put to one side. The security clerk then places it in front of me on a separate table.]

CLERK: Is this yours?
STEVE: Yes.

[She passes an electronic wand over and around the bag.]

CLERK: Please will you open it?

[She passes the electronic wand inside the bag and moves it around inside. She removes my wash bag, unzips it herself, and removes the shaving foam and the deodorant.]

CLERK: I'm afraid you can't take these with you.
STEVE: Why not?
CLERK: You have to leave them here. Unless you want to go all around again to check in and have them put it in the hold? You'd have to go all round again, a lot of time?
STEVE: What happens to them?

CLERK: They are just left here.
STEVE: Why can't I take them?
CLERK: Because they are more than 100 ml. Any liquids more than 100 ml can't go through.
STEVE: Why's that?
CLERK: It's because they're more than 100 ml.
STEVE: Yes, I understand that, but what's the problem with more than 100 ml?
CLERK: It's the law you can't take more than 100 ml.
STEVE: But why can't you take more than 100 ml?
CLERK: I don't know, it's just the law, the DfT. Okay?
STEVE: Okay.
CLERK: Okay sir. Thank you.[1]

The exchange takes place at the front of a long line of following passengers, all anxious to get through the check as quickly as possible. The clerk does not want to delay things unless absolutely necessary. Steve also starts to feel the pressure just to accept the answer and move on. He is not only accountable to the clerk for his objects. There is a line behind him: they also survey who only stand and wait.[2]

In general, these exchanges were characterized by the passenger asking, and persisting in asking, the reason for the rule. What was it about the object that disqualified its passage through security? The security clerks tended to answer questions about the reason for the rule with a restatement of the rule. And the dissatisfied inquisitor tried again.

It seemed the persistent request for a reason for the rule was heard as seeking who or what was accountable for the regulation. The security clerk typically disavowed any personal responsibility. (And in one case the exasperated security clerk declared 'I have no idea why!') Instead, a typical response was to identify institutions (the law, the DfT) responsible for the regulation. On other occasions, the passenger's persistence was rewarded with being handed a leaflet.

In addition to these breaches through persistent questioning, planned as part of the field work, an inadvertent further breach was perpetrated. Consider the following excerpt from Steve's field notes:

On the return trip [from Schipol to Birmingham] I tried to set up my (by now) standard altercation with security clerks by secreting a (500 ml) plastic water

---

[1] These exchanges were reconstructed from notes written after the encounter. We made no attempt to audio record the exchanges, because we anticipated that details of the operation of mundane governance in this security context were highly sensitive. Our one attempt to photograph the process of hand luggage inspection incurred dramatic interventions by security staff, reprimanding us, and insisting that we deleted the images.

[2] With apologies to John Milton.

bottle in my carry on [luggage]. Since it contained barely 50 ml of water I thought I'd use this marginal object to challenge the rationale for the rule: 'containers of more than 100 ml capacity are prohibited'. To my disappointment, the offending item was not spotted, so it came with me in my carry on bag, on to the plane.

I then decided, since it was not a full flight, to 'interview' a random selection of passengers about their views on the new security rules. I ended each discussion by showing them my 500 ml plastic bottle with about 50 ml water in it. I had intended that this would be in the spirit of passenger bonhomie about the general absurdity of the rules, that we would agree how silly they were etc. Instead, the mood changed dramatically in each case. Each of my 'interviewees' looked anxiously from bottle to me and back again. Is this a scary object, I asked jokily. Yes, they said. It is very scary. They didn't know what was in there. One person said I seemed alright but maybe I was just a good actor. Another said my particular bottle may be okay but what about any others on the plane that had also got through undetected?

Steve was amazed that just by showing others the bottle (which action he could now see as 'revealing' the bottle or perhaps even as 'brandishing' it) generated a chilling turn in the interaction and a striking inversion of the tacit assumptions in the interaction up to that moment. He did not anticipate how intense the change in mood would be. In retrospect, this little venture seemed foolhardy if not stupid. But of course the sense of 'stupidity' directly reflects not appreciating what, after all, the object had become; that the bottle had transposed, in the eyes of his fellow passengers, from ordinary object to one of potential terror. Again, we see how the now insecure ontology of the water bottle arises in virtue of a particular local history of its passage and spatial alignment. The 'revelation' of the bottle to fellow passengers prompted further speculations about the nature of the passage and alignment of things and their people. All these are now also rendered potentially insecure: just what else could have accompanied whom else on to the plane?

9.4 Traffic Lights Failure

A common source of popular comment and complaint about disruption of the mundane centres on the failure of traffic lights. Motorists experience it as a nuisance. But in many accounts, the breakdown of traffic lights is reckoned to occasion an actual improvement in traffic flow. In these accounts, the irony of this outcome is played out against the alleged intentions of the authorities, which are portrayed as erroneous at best, or based on an unwarranted, overzealous urge to control the citizenry. The apparent fact that traffic flows more smoothly when traffic lights have failed is said to demonstrate that drivers are perfectly capable of controlling their own movement across busy interchanges, without the need for mundane technological governance. So traffic light failures, together with the attendant commentary on these situations, provide a further opportunity for understanding the ontological basis of disruption. To what extent does the discourse of breakdown depend on the redistribution of accountability relations, and on the reconstitution of the key objects at stake?

The internet contains a large genre of video clips of traffic moving through road junctions, traffic lights, and other kinds of traffic crossings. Many of these video clips, posted as short (approximately three minutes) clips on YouTube, have the quality of travellers' tales. That is, they are presented as demonstrations of curious things that are done in foreign places. The curiosity is all the more marked it seems, on account of the fact that these curious happenings in foreign places occur in relation to just those mundane objects—traffic lights—with which we (at home) are familiar. Thus, we find clips annotated with titles and comments such as 'strange traffic lights in Netherlands' (referring to a light system that deploys a physical barrier, which rises from the road surface under the car); or 'Imagine if your country has no traffic lights' (commenting on a clip of traffic movements in a street in Saigon). Curiosity about the operation and/or lack of lights is indexed by incredulous commentaries appended to the clips, for example: 'No traffic lights and yet they do just fine!!!'[3]

One clip shows traffic passing through a junction in St Petersburg, Russia, described as 'The most dangerous traffic light in th [sic] world (Russia)—a hiden [sic] camera shows us the most dangerous traffic light in the world. u would'nt wanna miss watching that...beleive [sic] me'.[4] It is not clear from the selection of fierce collisions shown in this clip that any traffic lights are working at this junction. However, one contributor tries to defend the operation of these traffic lights. 'RusMishania (16 hours ago): I live a couple blocks from there, and i got in a wreck there as well but they didn't have the cameras at [that time]...the traffic light there is perfect, almost all of those wrecks happened because somebody try to run a red light or the road is icy so you can't break'. In other words, the fault is not with the governing technology but with the deviant drivers who try to ignore the lights.

The rendered exoticism of the lack of lights (or of their curious operation) in strange places, plays upon the extent to which we tend to take them for

[3] Added 1 September 2007. An indeterminate Asian city: http://www.youtube.com/watch?v=8j8FI-jfw6o&feature=related

[4] Added: 15 July 2007. (http://www.youtube.com/watch?v=H2JFL1Sk21Y&feature=related

granted. It is helpful to recall that these most mundane and pervasive objects of traffic regulation have their own contingent history (McShane, 1999). The presence and absence of traffic lights in Oxford was a recurrent focus of controversial comment during the period of our study. For example, in December 2006 it was reported in the *Oxford Times* that a set of signals installed in the city centre two years previously to improve pedestrian safety at a cost of £40,000 was due to be removed (Sheldrick, 2006). The paper reported 'cycling and pedestrian groups, bus drivers and councillors all seem to agree the lights are a waste of time, space and money'. A city councillor Paul Sargent, is quoted as saying 'No one had the right to spend that amount of money on something so pointless...The junction is more dangerous with the lights, because people are not taking any notice of them. Buses and taxi drivers assume people are going to stop walking when they change, but they don't'.

By chance (and in keeping with the happenstance methodological sensibility that informs an immersed investigation of pervasive mundane phenomena) a colleague of ours (James Tansey) experienced a traffic lights failure in a road junction immediately outside the Said Business School in Oxford, and took the opportunity to video record the passage of the traffic during this time. At about 8.50 a.m. on 30 March 2006 he made a first video (three minutes forty-six seconds) using a web camera plugged into his laptop. About half an hour later, when the lights were working again, he made a second video (two minutes nineteen seconds). This disruption did not exactly follow the ethnomethodological experimental tradition; we did not in any way tamper with the lights. It was instead a serendipitous breach (the sudden removal of working lights), which we were able to take advantage of.

> James said: I took the video because I had to cycle across the junction from west to east to drop off my daughter at childcare. I noticed that it was much less congested that morning and it wasn't until I was halfway across that I noticed that the lights were out! Usually I find the whole cluster of intersections very frustrating because the cars cheat the lights, entering junction boxes and because there is no obvious pedestrian route across from the King Charles building to Said...the fact is that driving by car into the centre of Oxford is just a mess and some heavy congestion is inevitable. I was just surprised how smoothly the traffic was flowing without the lights.

James phoned a local newspaper (*Oxford Mail*) and emailed them the two video clips. They phoned to interview him within two hours and published a story the following day (Wilkinson, 2006):

> If you wondered why your car journey into Oxford was quicker yesterday morning, it may have been due to a traffic light failure at a key road junction...Road campaigners and traders believe the fault at traffic lights in Frideswide Square

which lasted for two hours through the rush-hour helped cut congestion for commuters. Video footage shows motorists passing smoothly through the square, where seven roads meet, during the blackout. But minutes after power was restored, traffic was queuing.

The report includes the views of 'many motorists' (who found their journeys along Botley Road into the city centre were quicker than normal), a local newsagent (who said lots of customers said they had never moved faster across the square), a traders' group (who believe the traffic lights should be replaced with a roundabout), a taxi driver (it was lovely to drive around here this morning), a police spokesperson (no accidents were reported during the period when the lights were out), and 'Said Business School lecturer' James Tansey (who 'filmed traffic easing through Frideswide Square and Hythe Bridge Street at 9.40am, above, yet the streets were congested half an hour later after the lights were repaired'). However, a spokesman for the local council said the lack of congestion was due to unusually light traffic.

> David Robertson, the county council cabinet member for transport, said the council could not judge the success of removing the traffic lights on one day's evidence. He added: 'Across Oxfordshire the flow of traffic was much better. We don't know what that reason is, it was not just Frideswide Square.'

The report of free flowing traffic engendered considerable popular local support, with many outraged condemnations of various traffic light installations around the city. Reports of subsequent breakdowns (for example, Gray, 2006) referred back to this same incident. An especially popular reference point for all these stories is a series of 'shared space' experiments in traffic management started several years previously in Drachten, the Netherlands (although our preliminary investigation suggests the outcome of these experiments is far less clear-cut than has been subsequently reported). The recurrent argument is that traffic lights are unnecessary since the failure and the longer-term Dutch experiments demonstrate that road users are perfectly capable of negotiating their way through complicated junctions without lights. It is said that those responsible for the lights, 'the Council', have imposed a form of nanny state. When left to their own devices, road users show they do not need governance by traffic lights.

In effect, then, the breakdown and its analysis is characterized by narratives organized around the redistribution of accountability. Importantly, the redistribution of accountability depends on the identification and mobilization of relevant entities. In the press coverage given here, drivers are prominent as the rightful bearers of accountability wrested from 'the council' and its agents (the traffic lights). Equally important, the whole disruption and its articulation is premised on the basis that traffic was indeed flowing smoothly without the lights.

9.5 Parking is Such Sweet Sorrow

Our third example is drawn from a further source of continual and popular anxiety for motorists—traffic wardens and parking fines. In a very brief perusal of stories about parking fines, we find controversy regarding the level of penalties,[5] the difficulties of payment, outrage about changes in regulations, which give parking wardens more power,[6] buses being given parking tickets while stopping to drop off passengers,[7] and the possibility that private companies in control of parking regulation are excessively penalizing motorists to increase their profits.[8] A recurrent theme in these stories is: which town or city has the 'worst' (that is, those who issue most tickets) traffic wardens?[9] We also find spoof articles lampooning the power of traffic wardens (for example, by suggesting that traffic wardens have x-ray vision)[10] and complaints from traffic wardens about being targeted by internet campaigns.[11] However, we are also told that problems with traffic wardens are not new, with stories about parking woe dating back at least forty years.[12]

In the course of our study, one notable case of parking disruption occurred in St Albans (an English town that does not routinely make the national news). Following a change in the law, English local authorities were able to outsource the job of traffic warden to private companies (under licence, on fixed-term contracts, as long as they matched various stipulations). Uniquely in St Albans, the local police force interpreted this to mean they were no longer required to enforce parking. In discussion with the locally elected political authority (the council), the police negotiated a three-year winding down period, at the end of which the police would no longer provide traffic wardens. But when in April 2004 the three years expired the council did not have a substitute team of traffic wardens in place, as a result of which there was no one to take over from the police and hence no one to enforce parking regulations.[13] Once word of this lawlessness spread, social order in St Albans rapidly collapsed. Drivers parked their vehicles 'anywhere'. They parked for

[5] http://icbirmingham.icnetwork.co.uk/0100news/0100localnews/tm_objectid=14353073& method=full&siteid=50002&headline=parking-tickets-double-in-city-name_page.html

[6] http://news.bbc.co.uk/1/hi/uk_politics/3367865.stm

[7] http://news.bbc.co.uk/1/hi/england/2808771.stm

[8] http://www.manchestereveningnews.co.uk/news/s/71/71856_250k_bill_to_oust_parking_ firm.html

[9] See, for example: http://news.bbc.co.uk/1/hi/england/2601411.stm and http://icbirmingham. icnetwork.co.uk/0100news/mercury/tm_objectid=14289245&method=full&siteid=50002& headline=parking-mad—name_page.html

[10] http://www.deadbrain.co.uk/news/article_2004_01_05_1929.php

[11] http://www.theregister.co.uk/2002/07/09/web_site_censored_over_pictures/

[12] http://news.bbc.co.uk/onthisday/hi/dates/stories/february/23/newsid_2518000/2518671. stm

[13] http://news.sky.com/skynews/Home/Sky-News-Archive/Article/200806413197382

as long as they liked, without regard for other drivers, pedestrians, and local businesses. The latter complained they could not access their own premises.[14] Parking enforcement signs were painted over, residents erected their own barriers to 'protect' the parking spaces in front of their homes, and a lively internet discussion ensued. Further problems were said to have emerged when the council realized that disregard for parking regulations was actually wearing out the yellow lines on the road, as vehicles were driving over and stopping for long periods on the lines. Despite the continued absence of traffic wardens, the council tried to repaint the lines, but failed because line-painting trucks could not navigate their way through the mass of 'illegally' parked cars.[15]

Although initial discussions considered that St Albans' residents might themselves come up with a way of controlling the parking, no form of self-mundane governance emerged. During one visit to the town, Dan encountered this breakdown in civilization as a practical impediment to ethnographic inquiry. He found it very difficult to get into or out of St Albans by car because most major routes were blocked by badly parked cars.[16] Local residents expressed diverse views of the situation:[17]

> VERUL: Millions starving throughout the world, and the residents of St Albans, the foundation stone of Christendom in Great Britain, are more concerned with people parking for free in their lovely yellow lined streets. How petty.
>
> ED: It is great, we have been parking on double yellows and no parking areas.
>
> BARBARA: I don't think that the reintroduction of traffic wardens will do much good because, unfortunately, anarchy has gained too strong a foothold.

Order of a kind was re-established when the council contracted with a private company for the training of a new team of traffic wardens, the repainting of yellow lines, a supply of new traffic warden uniforms, and new signs warning of the reintroduction of enforcement.[18] The disruption surfaces many of the taken for granted features of parking governance: drivers will park in certain spaces, for certain times; parking in other spaces and other times is inappropriate; appropriateness requires policing; in the absence of the policing, the allegedly 'true' (inappropriate) nature of people and parking is revealed; and

---

[14] See, for example: http://www.bbc.co.uk/threecounties/content/image_galleries/st_albans_parking_gallery.shtml and: http://www.bbc.co.uk/threecounties/content/articles/2004/09/09/st_albans_parking_feature.shtml

[15] http://www.bbc.co.uk/radio4/youandyours/index_20040816.shtml

[16] Dan later discovered that most journalists covering the story visited by train.

[17] Taken from an on-line discussion forum: http://www.bbc.co.uk/threecounties/content/articles/2004/10/04/st_albans_parking_attedants_arrive_feature.shtml

[18] http://www.bbc.co.uk/threecounties/content/articles/2004/10/04/st_albans_parking_attedants_arrive_feature.shtml

inappropriateness can become celebrated, at least by some citizen subjects, if it is limited geographically and temporally.

Media coverage of this incident combined humour with a generally negative attitude towards traffic wardens.[19] Even one story about wardens' own anxiety was cauched in mock outrage. In general the stories emphasized the undeserved, excessive, or incorrect issuing of penalties; bemoaned the failure of traffic wardens to listen to appeals or protests; claimed that traffic wardens go beyond the terms of their job; and condemned those in 'positions of power' who were presumed to be in charge of parking ticket related decisions. Sometimes this latter category was said to be private companies, sometimes a local elected political authority, and sometimes the target was more vague. The prevalence of negative attitudes towards wardens was re-emphasized when, in the aftermath of the reintroduction of traffic wardens, St Albans local residents quickly found voice in complaining about overzealous and unwarranted ticketing.

In his ethnography of traffic wardens, Richman (1983) suggests that: 'for most of the entrants street work was a new experience and they had to learn its ways, in all their manifestations: experiencing the discomforts of the inclement weather, detecting the hidden dimensions of the territorial rights which street users had carved out for themselves and, equally central, knowing how to ride out the hostility, sometimes violence, of motorists' (1983: 1). Richman explains negativity towards traffic wardens as resulting from uncertainty about the extent of their powers, varying levels of discretion and leniency, the particular ways in which individual wardens manage time (for example, how long is one hour in a time-restricted parking zone), willingness (or lack of it) in entering ongoing brokerage arrangements with persistent offenders, and 'fleeting and unpredictable relationships with motorists' (1983: 203). The primary aim of traffic wardens is to give 'good tickets' (1983: 60)—that is, tickets that withstand the challenges and potential challenges from offending motorists.

By chance an opportunity for disruption of the mundane governance associated with parking emerged when Dan returned to his car after work.

I left the University meeting and walked a few minutes to where I had parked the car. Imagine my surprise when I found a 'PENALTY CHARGE NOTICE' strapped to the windscreen with the instruction 'Do Not Ignore'. Immediately following this rule, I tore the notice off the windscreen (how could anyone ignore this notice when it blocks their view from driving?) whilst checking the sign next to the car. The sign said: '2 Hours No Return Within 2 Hours'. I had been parked for a

---

[19] http://www.bbc.co.uk/threecounties/content/image_galleries/st_albans_get_parking_attendants_gallery.shtml?1

maximum of one hour (maybe one and a half). I sat in the car and read the Notice. It stated the Penalty was for: 'Parked for longer than permitted'. I had already assumed this was the offence and read through the rest of the Notice to see how to appeal. There was information on 'easy ways to pay' (by cheque, by card, by post, on-line or in person), but nothing about how to appeal. In the small print after 'easy ways to pay' was a… Web Enquiry e-mail address. I decided to go home and send an e-mail.

Two initial features of this incident are noteworthy. First, in contrast with the popular vernacular, specifically terms such as 'traffic wardens' and 'parking tickets', the document affixed to the screen styles itself a 'PENALTY CHARGE NOTICE'. No mention of 'tickets'. Was this perhaps the beginning of a process of ontological respecification. The driver, car, relations of accountability, and forms of governance were imminently on their way to reconstitution in terms of a 'PENALTY' rather than a mere ticket. Second, although Dan, perhaps because he was innocent, expected, and looked for, the means to appeal, there was none. Orthographically, the intensity of the language of the (alleged) offence appeared to be ratcheted up (from ticket to PENALTY CHARGE NOTICE), whereas the opportunity to appeal appeared to be played down (a long, difficult to type e-mail address provided an uncertain indication of how it might be possible to contest the charge).

I got home and sent off an e-mail. Still furious to have got the ticket [PENALTY CHARGE NOTICE]. The e-mail included the phrases: 'The ticket states that my car (registration XXX) was 'Parked for longer than permitted'. This is not true.' and: 'I do not see how this is a parking offence.' Four days later, I received the following response on e-mail:

'Dear Mr Neyland
Thank you for your recent email regarding Penalty Charge Notice OX16582255. With reference to the above Penalty Charge Notice, it has been established that the Notice was issued incorrectly. The Notice has now been cancelled'.

The disruption seemed to have succeeded, but it was not clear why. We can only surmise that the initial configuration of driver, car, relation of accountability, and responsibility had turned out to have a fragile constitution. It had taken little time or effort to dismantle this particular constituency. However, six months later Dan's field notes contained the following:

I left work and walked the short distance to where I had parked the car. Imagine my surprise when I found a 'PENALTY CHARGE NOTICE' strapped to the windscreen with the instruction 'Do Not Ignore' … [I checked] the sign next to the car. The sign said: '2 Hours No Return Within 2 Hours'.

I had parked in a different parking bay further along the street for two hours earlier in the day and then moved the car to its current location for two hours. It was not clear that this had contravened the rule on the sign [I had not parked in the same place for longer than two hours and I had not returned to the same bay]. Another opportunity for disruption!

I went home and e-mailed another enquiry. I set out my case, explaining about the movement of the car and the two different bays. I received a response after twelve days:

'Dear Mr Neyland

Thank you for your recent correspondence regarding Penalty Charge Notice OX19102902.

Your vehicle was seen parked at the given location in excess of the permitted two hours... When parking your vehicle in a free bay, you are aware of the time restriction placed on you and it is then your responsibility to ensure you return within the permitted time.

The Parking Attendant recorded the location of your vehicle at 11.35 hours together with the position of the valves. When he next saw your vehicle at 14.32 hours the vehicle was *at the same location* and valve positions remain unchanged. The conclusion that could be drawn from this was that your vehicle had not been moved, had therefore over stayed the permitted time for that bay. This is the reason why Penalty Charge Notice was issued.

Having taken into consideration the circumstances as outlined in your letter, we believe that there are insufficient grounds for cancelling your ticket'.

The response emphasizes driver responsibility: traffic wardens (now described as parking attendants) are presented as merely recording failed responsibility on the part of the driver. The response is also characterized by a mixture of certainty and uncertainty. When describing the car, it specifies precise times and even the position of valves on the car tyres in relation to the kerb. Not much room for doubt there. But the use of less certain language, deploying phrases such as 'The conclusion which *could* be drawn', 'taken into consideration *the circumstances*', and 'we *believe*' (emphases added) all suggests the possibility of further 'enquiries'. The message included no guidance on how to make further 'enquiries', only repeating the instructions on 'easy ways to pay' contained in the original notice. Instead of diligently following the payment instructions, Dan wondered if further disruption might reveal more about the governance and accountability relations underpinning this exchange. And perhaps he would not have to pay the fine.

I sent another 'enquiry'. I used phrases such as: 'Sorry if there has been any confusion—please let me state again my case' and: 'Not only had the car moved, it was in a different parking space, in a different parking bay'. I was trying not to be too confrontational, despite feeling aggrieved by the ticket [PENALTY CHARGE NOTICE]. I received the following response the next day:

'Dear Mr Neyland

Thank you for your recent correspondence regarding Penalty Charge Notice OX19102902.

In view of the circumstances surrounding the issue of the above Notice, we are pleased to inform you that this Notice has been cancelled on this occasion'.

Although disruption had this time extended one further turn in interaction (an extra e-mail and response) the constitution of driver, car, relations of accountability and responsibility, and form of governance seemed no stronger than before. Dan began to ponder the possibility that any notice could be disassembled if one was sufficiently dedicated to persistent 'enquiring'. However, before these thoughts had the opportunity to develop:

I left the pub at 9.30 p.m. and walked the short distance to where I had parked the car. Imagine my [somewhat diminished sense of] surprise when I found a 'PENALTY CHARGE NOTICE' strapped to the windscreen with the instruction 'Do Not Ignore'... [I checked] the sign next to the car. The sign said: 'Permit holders [B] or 8 a.m.–6.30 p.m. one hour No return within one hour'. The PENALTY CHARGE NOTICE stated my offence as: 'Parked in a permit parking space without displaying a valid permit'. Was this true? I didn't have a permit, but the sign seemed to establish that between 8 a.m. and 6.30 p.m. I either needed a permit *or* I could park for one hour. But what about 9.30 p.m.? I sent off another 'enquiry'. I pointed out that other parking bays certainly allowed free parking outside the hours on the sign and asked: 'How are drivers supposed to know that the parking bays where I received a ticket operate on a different rule? I look forward to your response'. The response arrived three days later:

'Dear Mr Neyland

Thank you for your recent letter regarding Penalty Charge Notice OX17612839.

Your vehicle was seen parked in a Permit Holders Bay without displaying a valid parking permit...

If the restriction applied only between the hours 8am to 6.30pm then the sign would read:

'8am–6.30pm

Permit holders only

OR

1 hour

No return within 1 hour'

[instead of:

'Permit holders [B]

or

8am–6.30pm

1 hour

No return within 1 hour'.]

It is the responsibility of the driver to check the signs and restrictions when parking in a marked bay. Further advice and information on parking, signs and highway restrictions can be obtained from a copy of the 'Highway Code'. Having taken into consideration the circumstances as outlined in your letter, we believe that there are insufficient grounds for cancelling your ticket'.

The claim here is that the driver has indeed broken the rule. But, more than this, questions of what might count as following a rule (which have long bedevilled social science), are finessed by emphasizing the responsibility of drivers in decoding the semantics of the rule. Drivers are responsible for their actions, and the Highway Code is the ultimate source of accountability, responsibility, and rules to be followed. That is where drivers can find clear instructions of their accountability and responsibility, and how they ought to park. For the 'enquiry' team, the appropriate next action was clear: they again sent Dan instructions on 'easy ways to pay'. But shouldn't the sign itself bear a clear articulation of the rule, not the Highway Code? Isn't it odd that the *positioning* of time on the sign (rather than the time itself) is the key arbiter of whether or not drivers are fined?[20] Dan was further surprised that so much interpretive work was demanded of the driver. He or She was expected to know every small detail of the Highway Code, that the position of time on the sign was key, that this particular position of time on the sign meant that those without permits could not park in the evening, that other signs with time positioned differently meant that you could park for free in the evenings, and so on. Dan found the Highway Code online, read it and ordered an associated government publication 'Know Your Traffic Signs' and read this too (for research purposes). The next day Dan sent a further 'enquiry':

'Hello,
Many thanks for your prompt response to my previous enquiry...
I read through the Highway Code and the associated government publication 'Know Your Traffic Signs' after receiving your e-mail. I can not find any regulation which states that the positioning of time (rather than the time itself) on a parking sign is the key indicator for drivers for when they are or are not supposed to park. Or that the positioning of time on this particular sign results in a different parking rule from the next parking bay [in which drivers park for free in the evenings]. Could you point me in the direction of this regulation?'

Three days later, Dan received the following response:

'Dear Mr Neyland
Thank you for your recent letter regarding Penalty Charge Notice OX17612839.
As you are not satisfied with our decision your next course of action is to make a representation to Oxfordshire County Council. If payment is made at the discounted rate of £20.00 the Penalty Charge Notice account is closed. If the penalty remains unpaid after 28 days a "Notice to Owner" will be sent giving full

---

[20] The 'Enquiry' team suggested that the notice was issued because time is positioned in the middle rather than at the top of the sign post.

details of the grounds on which a representation can be made. The penalty at this stage is at the statutory rate of £40.00'.

This third response invokes more complexity in governance and account-ability. The initial PENALTY CHARGE NOTICE starts to constitute driver, car, parking, time, and place as the entities to be governed. An 'enquiry' may then attempt to set the terms for disassembling the initial constitution. However, the 'enquiry' team can resist such disassembly by reasserting the strength and validity of their evidence or, as in this case, by recourse to a different governance body. That is, making a 'representation' is directed to Oxfordshire County Council, rather than to the 'enquiry' team. What was an 'enquiry' had now become a 'representation'. This helps ratchet up the relations of governance. The stakes are also raised: if a representation is made, this will fall outside the twenty-eight days within which payment of a parking fine can be made at a discount rate of £20. So the complainant is warned that the move from an 'enquiry' to a 'representation' may cost an extra £20. Needless to say, this e-mail also included further 'easy ways to pay' instructions. To further pursue the disruption the driver is thus obliged to resist the 'easy ways to pay' and ignore the escalation of the costs in countering the work being done to hold together the constitution of driver, car, parking, time, and place. Dan persisted with his efforts at disassembly:

Eventually after waiting for about six weeks, I received the paperwork for making a representation to the [Oxfordshire County] Council. One of the forms includes a tick-box list of things I could make a representation about. I have to tick the 'other' box as I think my representation is questioning the validity [legality?] of the sign. I then have to write a letter explaining my case. Unsure of what to include, I basically offer a repeat of the exchange that I have already conducted through my previous enquiries. I include the stuff about Highway Code, Know Your Traffic Signs (etc).

Four months went by, before Dan finally received a response:

'Thank you for your recent correspondence regarding the above Penalty Charge Notice.
Due to a back log in correspondence the County Council have failed to consider your representation within a 3 month given deadline therefore I confirm that the Notice to Owner has been cancelled'.

What to make of this outcome? Is it a victory in disassembling the relations of governance and accountability through which the local council constituted and held together driver, car, parking, time, and place? After all, the penalty charge notice 'has been cancelled'. Yet this outcome is based on a technicality: the county council ran out of time. So it seems more like a defeat: the signs remain in place, drivers continue to be fined, and they continue to have to work hard to try to disrupt the ways in which they are constituted.

However, notwithstanding our own experiences and irritation with mundane governance, we recognize that we need to try to go beyond thinking in terms of victory or defeat. We want to go beyond apprehending mundane governance as good or evil, right or wrong, appropriate or inappropriate, as if the aim was simply a critique that governance had gone too far, that our lives were subject to too much petty bureaucracy, or that ours was now a nanny state, which our research might set right.

Our preferred alternative is to look to episodes of disruption for what they can tell us about the ways in which governance constitutes ontologies of people, things, actions, documents, processes, and penalties. This last example brings to light the specific work that accomplishes the ontological constitution of drivers, cars, parking bays and signs, times and places, valves on tyres, traffic wardens, and the notices they issue. Attempts to challenge and disassemble this ontological constitution reveals more of the accountability relations of which the preceding entities form a part (including the payment system and the 'enquiry' team), the language of notices and further forms of governance revealed in pursuit of further questioning of a penalty (in 'representations' to Oxford County Council) and the potential (not realized in this example) to go further in courts of law, and through invoking acts of law (such as the Road Traffic Act). The governance relations of parking penalties are intimately bound up with the ongoing constitution of drivers, cars, penalties, and signs. And it is through disruption—receiving several penalties, and persistently questioning the penalties—that these material relations can be brought to light.

9.6 Speeding Database

During 2008, the following email enjoyed widespread circulation in the UK:

> *Road Traffic Speeding Cameras*
> *Following the Government's Freedom of Information Act, you can now get access to speed camera offences registered in the last 12 months. Did you know that every time your car goes past a speed camera, even 1 MPH over the set limit, it is registered and put on a database??*
> *You only get a ticket if you are way over the limit or (this is the bit we didn't know) if you receive 20 near misses, you will be classed a serial offender and get a ticket the next time you go over the limit.*
> *This is why you hear of some people being done for 34 mph in a 30 zone, and others not being done for going at 39 mph. You can check if there is anything against your vehicle at the following address:—http://www.i-database.co.uk*
> *You will be asked for a password, but just click on the need a password link and you will be given one for future use. If there is any data on your vehicle, you can click on the camera window to see a copy of the photograph. This photo will come in handy if you challenge any charges.*

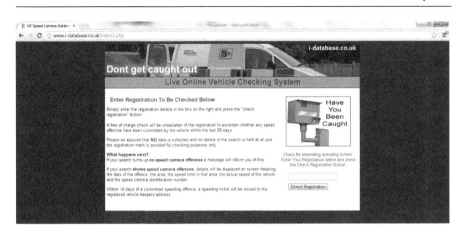

Figure 9.1. Don't Get Caught Out 1 (screen shot)

Figure 9.2. Don't Get Caught Out 2 (screen shot)

Following the link leads to the 'Live Online Vehicle Checking System' page (Figure 9.1) hosted by i-database.co.uk. Here drivers are invited to enter the registration number of their vehicle (say Y803 FBW), to check if any speeding offence information is held against that number. Entering the vehicle registration then leads to a page that states 'Vehicle Y803 FBW has recent speed offences registered against it', followed by detailed information of the offence including: the county, town, road, grid reference, camera reference, speed limit, recorded speed (written in red), and the date of the offence. In large capitals, the page declares: ACTIVE SPEED OFFENCE FOR Y803 FBW (Figure 9.2). To the right-hand side a button invites 'View Picture' with the caption 'Image Available. Click to View'.

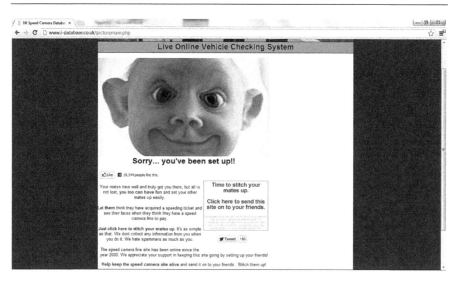

Figure 9.3. Don't Get Caught Out 3 (screen shot)

Upon clicking this button, drivers are disconcerted to find a large bizarre smiley doll/clown-like face staring out at them (Figure 9.3). The message is 'Yup you've been set up'. The putative offending driver learns he or she has been the subject of a spoof. The driver is invited in turn to pass the joke on: 'You can set also up your mates easily. Just click on the image on the right and fill in the mailer. It's a simple as that'.

Of particular interest are the many reactions of visitors to the site, their invited comments all recorded on a separate page. Some sample comments are:

'Brilliant'
'Enjoyed that very much'
'Nice one'
'Got me good and proper WELL DONE Fantastic!'
'Best laugh I have had in ages'
'you wankers u got me'
'basterds'
'I got caught to- Can I sit down and take my heart pills now please!!! phew......'
'OH MY GOD!! You got me good! Very funny.'
'Fell for it but made me laugh!!'
'Fantastic. Really thought it was genuine. A good laugh'
'sod you Paul! you really had me going there. but now I cant stop laughing!'
'Very good, I was just about to start ringing the police to say I hadn't been anywhere near Cambridge yesterday!'
'I actually went outside to check my number plate!! Very funny!!!'
'Got me. Fantastic!!! Looks really realistic. X'

The extraordinary degree of surprise is evident. All admit that they have been taken in by the spoof, and attest to the apparent realism of the set up. The spoof is interesting for our purposes because it evokes and plays on widespread fears about who knows what about whom. The framing of the initial email invokes the existence of a database of information about speeding offences, and cleverly suggests that although this information has always been out there, it is now possible to access it in virtue of the recent Freedom of Information Act. In the terms of our argument, a purportedly hidden mechanism for the processing of accountability—that is, the accountability of drivers for the speed of their vehicles—is now said to be revealed. This has the effect of putting in doubt the assumed relations of accountability. It is claimed that information (about you) is out there; indeed, that others know more about your object (and you) than you do.[21] The suggestion that photographic evidence is available is a clever touch. It invites the driver to see for themselves, it neatly mimics a key stage in the process of constructing the speeding driver (at the point where the penalty notice declares the availability of photographic evidence, see Chapter 5), and it compellingly invites the click that will lead to the 'reveal'.

Yet more interesting is that the putative offence rapidly and dramatically leads to the disruption of accountability networks and relations of which the driver is part. These further reactions each nominate the (potential) effect on spouses and parents of the driver:

'Had the wife worried'
'I got really worried my husband drives tha [sic] car & when I seen where the photo was meant 2 be taken I wondered what he'd been up to. Lol.'
'Brilliant—got all the family! My wife was in a right tizz since she'd never get to Middlesborough. I told her—"photos don't lie"—divorce proceedings under way!'
'I had my mother standing next to me when I loaded it so I panicked an shut the screen down thinking I had got caught out! Completely fell for it. Very amusing!'
'Blamed my hubby at first...went mad then looked at the picture lol...grovelling still now!'

Note that the concerns expressed here are not just to do with culpability for speeding. The revelation of hidden information is taken as the basis for questions about the whereabouts of the driver and thence about marital relationships. The last quote candidly reveals that the extent of alarm caused by

---

[21] This plays into an area of mundane governance not discussed directly in this book, namely, the ways in which information (especially hidden information) held about us is said to affect our everyday lives. In this case the primary object of mundane governance is the information, the situated ontologies include the information itself and the entities said to be responsible for gathering and holding the information, and the accountability relations turn on who should know what about whom and with what effect.

the spoof itself necessitated profuse apologies when the spoof was revealed. Visitors to the page are further encouraged to spread the joke, to send on the spurious email to others and thus to extend the sets of accountability relations thrown into doubt.

9.7 Analysis

What do all these different instances of disruption tell us?

First, it is clear that asking questions is itself a form of disruption. This is perhaps unsurprising given that persistent questioning was one of the original breaching experiments pursued by Garfinkel (1967). On the other hand, it is notable, partly because some of our situations, for example, the airport security check and the contestation of parking tickets, were occasions when questions were invited. Security clerks were available for discussion in the airport and parking penalty notices from the council included a contact email address. However, these occasions turned out to be set-piece interactions that were often scripted or tightly bound, such that questions from those governed were limited. Rather than causing a breakdown in interaction, persistent questioning tended to have one of two outcomes. It either led to a restatement of the rule, so that questions about the basis for the rule were met with restatements of the rule: a form of short circuiting of the chain of accountability relations whereby the rule is offered as the justification for the rule, and the subjects of mundane governance experience a kind of accountability loop. Or the proffered chain of accountability relations was ratcheted up, such that different sources of authority, external to the interaction, were invoked. Thus, in the water bottle example the security clerks would answer one or two rounds of questions, taking on the responsibility for re-emphasizing passengers' accountability. As questions persisted, the 'rules' in themselves or the 'DfT', were invoked as the arbiters of accountability. In the parking ticket example, the enquiry team responsible for managing tickets initially assumed responsibility for distributing and reaffirming accountability to drivers. However, as questions persisted, responsibility was directed to a higher authority—the county council. This continuous redirection had the effect of deferring final decisions on who was responsible for rule changes, and who might be the ultimate arbiter of accountability.

Second, although our argument throughout has focused on the ordinary, pervasive, and unexceptional—the mundane—our examples of disruption reveal moments of exotic dissonance. The breakdown of traffic lights, for example, or the different operation and practices surrounding traffic lights in other places, provided an interesting and sometimes exciting contrast with more familiar mundane people, objects, and practices. Drivers approaching traffic lights to find they were not working, reported a sense of frisson at suddenly having to take on the roles usually delegated to the technology. Similarly, Steve was intrigued that he managed to smuggle forbidden water on to a plane, to the extent that he found himself asking what turned out to be threatening questions of fellow passengers. Dan began to enjoy, if grudgingly, the arrival of yet another parking ticket as promising a further possible contestation. And those fooled by the spoof speed camera website expressed how exciting or brilliant they found the experience. The exotic dissonance of the ordinary-suddenly-rendered-unavailable, revealed aspects of the delegation and distribution of capacities for governance and accountability. Losing, evading, or finding inadequate the usual entities of mundane governance—airport security clerks, traffic lights, lines painted on roads, and signs signalling parking rules—required the redistribution and new constitutions of governance and accountability. While the traffic lights remained out of action, drivers could assume a form of responsibility, Steve became a perpetrator of terror (as far as some other passengers were concerned), and Dan found himself able to question the meaning of signs, and to reconstitute their capacity to operate as delegates of governance and accountability.

Third, however, the process of delegation is uncertain, and certainly not a smooth and universal response to losing, evading, or finding systems of governance inadequate. Thus, it never became clear in either the traffic light or parking example to what extent or in what sense drivers took on self-governance. It is unclear to what extent their actions were the same as the lost/replaced delegates of accountability. For every example whereby traffic (allegedly) flowed more smoothly in the absence of the governance delegate (the traffic lights breakdown), other examples (such as the absence of traffic wardens in St Albans) suggest that some of those with a newly acquired governance capacity revelled in new opportunities for ignoring the common good. In these latter instances, there occurred a breakdown of social and moral order rather than a new constitution of governance. Delegation is a rather unsatisfactory summary term for complex and uncertain shifts in accountability.

Fourth, the examples reveal aspects of the assembly and disassembly involved in constitutions of governance. The parking ticket farrago initially brings to attention the lack of durability in some constitutions of governance. Just sending an e-mail, without any explicit evidence to counter the penalty notice, effectively disassembled the constituency of driver, ticket, car, parking, sign, time, place, and relations of accountability and responsibility. Even the second parking ticket exhibited little durability, although slightly more was made of available evidence (such as the position of valves on tyres in relation to the kerb). This governance constituency collapsed through further pressing from the driver. The third parking ticket revealed perhaps the most durable governance constituency. But even this was eventually dissolved, even if through a technicality (the council ran out of time). Our other examples tell different kinds of stories of the durability of governance constituencies. For example, the traffic light breakdown can form the focus for assessments of the extent to which the constituency of drivers, cars, junctions, and driving practices endured (or even improved) despite the absence of the traffic lights as key delegates of accountability and responsibility. And the water bottles could be understood as the focal point for an inversion of the constitution of governance; it is the removal of and separation of bottles from their passengers that establishes the appropriate constituency of governance, rendered enduring by the intervention of security clerks.

Fifth, it was intriguing to see how the intensity and specificity of governance and accountability relations could be ratcheted up and down. In the first example, Steve's persistent questioning about the liquid containers was first met with a polite restatement of the rule (ratchet 1), then a more terse recourse to further restatement of the rule (ratchet 2), then the invocation of a higher authority—the DfT (ratchet 3), then Steve's realization that there was an impatient queue waiting for him to desist (ratchet 4). One could imagine that if Steve had persisted, further security resources might have been involved and from there who knows what kinds of governance relations might have come into play. Giving up the liquids and moving into the airport departure lounge immediately lessened the intensity of these governance relations. There was no sense in which, despite Steve's persistent questioning, this would be held against him in future similar moments of governance. In the parking ticket example, the intensity of governance relations was ratcheted up through the presentation of the ticket and its emphasis on paying quickly (ratchet 1); the response to the first enquiry and its reiteration of the evidence and need to pay (ratchet 2); the subsequent response, further restatement of evidence, suggestion that any further 'enquiry' would now have to be made as a 'representation' to a higher authority and that to do this would require paying a higher penalty (ratchet 3); and receiving the forms which required the driver to classify his representation and provide details of his case (ratchet 4). Although this 'representation' did not receive a response that clearly demonstrated answers to governance questions, the cancellation of the ticket did lead to a lessening of the intensity of governance relations. Whether or not this exercise has generated a record of Dan's contestations, to be held in consideration of any future contestations on his part, remains to be seen. Dan awaits further penalty notices. In the speeding database example, we see a similar arc of racheting. The intensity of the accountability relations gradually rises as the recipient of the spoof is presented with more and more evidence. The Freedom of Information Act now makes speeding data information available, there is a website where it can be accessed, the database responds to the vehicle registration number, details are provided of the time, location, and degree of the offence. The tension builds as more and more constituent elements are involved. The presented network of accountability relations is so convincing that subjects of the spoof begin to question their own memory of their whereabouts at the time of the alleged speeding offence, or start to become suspicious about the movements of their partners. The intensity of these governance relations dramatically disappears, to the visceral relief of all concerned, when the speeding database is revealed as a hoax.

Sixth, in each example, the particular constitution of governance and accountability relations was the result of occasioned forms of local history of passage and spatial alignment. The water bottles were questioned and separated from passengers according to where the bottles were being carried from and to; this passage contributed to constituting the ontology of the bottle and its contents. The governance pairing of cars and their drivers moving through the junction where traffic lights were temporarily not working, were understood as car drivers of a particular nature; the video was reported as an example of the ability of car drivers to self-govern and to accomplish governed driving better than expensive technological delegates. The nature of the car driver was the upshot of their positioning within a text of innocence (car drivers doing self-governance) and evil-doing (council spending on traffic lights). The local passage through the junction was the evidence upon which this ontology was based. Similarly, in the parking ticket example, the driver, car, and its particular passage of arrival, departure, and positioning within (parking) space(s) was the basis for constituting the nature of the pair.

Finally, moments of disruption provided insight into what counts as adequate repair to the disrupted relations of governance, so that they can either continue to function, return to normality, or be extensively reconstituted to achieve old functions in new ways. For example, attempts at repair occurred through the displacement of 'facts'. Thus, in media reports of the traffic light failure, the local council were quoted as saying: 'Across Oxfordshire the flow of traffic was much better'. In this case, the previously accepted fact—that traffic flowed smoothly *because* of the traffic light failure—is displaced. The traffic was now said to be flowing more smoothly everywhere, and everywhere includes the junction where the traffic lights had just happened to fail. Displacement is used here to try to re-establish the governance capacity of the delegate (traffic light) and the local authority (council). Attempts at repair also took place through use of 'evidence'. Hence Dan's 'enquiry' about the second parking notice was met with a response in which the position of valves on car tyres in relation to the kerb was invoked to demonstrate the adequacy of existing governance relations in the face of questions. Repair also took the form of dramatic reconstitution of governance systems. The reintroduction of social and moral order in St Albans entailed putting in place a contract for the provision of wardens, training of wardens, new uniforms for wardens, new signs, lines repainted on roads, stories carefully positioned by the local council in the local media, and the imposition of new penalties. The governance constituency was thereby rebuilt. These examples emphasize both the endurance of governance arrangements (that they can be repaired) and their fragility (despite the work to reconstitute order in St Albans, from the moment the first new penalty notice was issued, questions about the governance system could begin anew).

9.8 Conclusion

Our analysis of disruption in mundane governance—breakdown, failure, breach, challenge, contestation, resistance, and repair of governance and accountability relations—highlights the ways in which delegation and responsibility is managed and experienced. People and things are delegated governance capacities to be measured and assessed through accountability relations. Ordinary objects and the regulations associated with them, can give rise to considerable frustration, resentment, and controversy. Rules prohibiting carry on liquids come with no statement of their rationale. Exchanges with traffic wardens about the basis for parking regulations exhibit a circular structure, an accountability loop, whereby queries about the basis for the rule merely engender restatements of the rule. Traffic lights, like speed cameras, are seen as representing some hidden, removed, and anonymous authority. Just as with Plato's complaint about the absence of the author in the move from orality to literacy, ordinary objects are experienced as embodying the absence of their accountable author, or, more generally, as having links to accountable humans, which are unclear, hidden, or otherwise unavailable. The inability or failure to establish these links helps explain some of the frustration experienced by the regulating effects of ordinary objects and technologies. Grumpy old men do not know to whom or what they should direct their grumpiness.

Disruptions are a normal, taken for granted feature of governance relations. They demonstrate that relations of mundane governance are a continual ongoing accomplishment. The descent into chaos in St Albans is an example of the consequences when the continual work of ontological constitution and reconstitution ceases for a time. The scripted responses to airport passengers' questions about their liquid containers and repeated routine responses to driver 'enquiries' about parking notices, bring to the fore the ways in which relations of governance are frequently predicated upon preplanned exchanges, the execution of which ensures the continuation of the relations of governance. These preplanned exchanges appear largely durable.[22]

We have also noted in this chapter the ways in which disruptions instigate forms of repair. Mechanisms of repair both reveal forward planning (the anticipation of breaches and the need for repair), and continual shifts in relations of governance from ontologically robust to fragile and back again. Fragility is evident when persons and things are subject to ongoing, unsatisfactory, and circular processes of governance and accountability. It emerges when the recourse to evidence collapses or when questions about governance relations cannot be answered or when presumably key governance operatives (such as traffic wardens) are absent. The successful constitution of enduring governance and accountability relations depends on the appeal to what, after all, are the obvious ordinary properties of the mundane objects in question. That it is just-ordinary, that it is of the world, that is, mundane, is the basis for evaluations and assessments of courses of action in respect to the object.

In this chapter, we have argued for the importance of disruptions as a way to comprehend mundane governance. This has enabled us again to question the assumption that governance relations are characterized by fixed, monolithic, or even agential institutional arrangements. In the final concluding chapter, we draw together the strands of our argument as presented throughout, and use this to assess the likely futures of mundane governance.

---

[22] Except perhaps when subject to intense interrogation by Science and Technology Studies (STS) researchers.

10

Conclusions

10.1 Introduction

In this book, we have examined mundane governance in waste management, traffic regulation, and airports. We have suggested that accountability relations, modes of classification, evidence and moral orders, invoked structures, spaces, breakdowns and repairs, and forms of insecurity are all involved in the ontological constitution of the people, objects, processes, documents, technologies, finances, and regulations of mundane governance. Up until now these strands have been left somewhat loosely connected. Our first task in this conclusion is to draw some of these strands together. This will establish what we propose as a working schema for understanding mundane governance.

Having proposed this working schema, we warn against using it as a grand and overarching meta-statement of the nature of mundane governance and the way it works. Instead we set out the case that ours are partial and reflexive conclusions. The strands we draw together are thus intended as fragmentary stories, which gain a coherence through the narrative we constitute, but are only ever momentary snapshots in the continually changing landscape of mundane governance.

This leads us, in Section 10.2, to reflect on how our methodological sensibilities have helped us reach our conclusion. In proposing our particular understanding of mundane governance, we have drawn on and elaborated various contemporary themes in Science and Technology Studies (STS). Here we take the opportunity to comment on some of these theoretical issues, and indicate how our research might contribute to them.

Finally, further emphasizing the open-endedness of mundane governance, we consider the futures of mundane governance. In particular, we look at some changes already taking place in the substantive areas we have explored: in waste management, traffic regulation, and the spaces of airports. Mundane governance is a continually changing, moving, rolling phenomenon: every time we feel ready to complete our exposition, it seems, some new development emerges. So we consider how to address change as a defining feature of mundane governance.

10.2 Revisiting Narratives of Mundane Governance

We began our book by describing a ferment of mundane governance: the routines, processes, and outcomes of ordinary activities were newly opened to moral reclassification, everyday objects and people were being reclassified, the focus of indignation, and the target of legal action. We drew on a wide range of studies to help us make sense of it all: studies of accountability, governmentality, materiality, ontological multiplicity, evidence, space, the ordinary and everyday, objects, science, and technology. Yet delving into these literatures raised more questions than answers. What exactly are accountability relations? How are the ontologies of governance constituted? How do entities, objects, and things become of the world? Is it better to think that people and things are governed in spaces or that spaces are themselves governed into being? What is the import of noticing how objects are constitutively linked with their people? Through what processes are things and people continuously reclassified? These were some of the candidate questions for our exploration throughout the book.

We distinguished two main kinds of accountability. We argued for understanding accountability as a *mutual*, constitutive sense-making action. This contrasts with *organizational* accountability whereby accountable entities are taken as the basis for assessment. This distinction provided the basis for understanding the production of accountable material and for examining the processes through which people and things were called to account, whom or what was held to account, through what means, and with what outcomes.

In Chapter 3, we used materials from waste management to explore accountability in action. We showed how containers provide a form of classification, which constitutes the moral order of waste and thus accomplishes the order of the waste management centre. We showed how council-issued leaflets provide a classification scheme for the moral policing of household recycling. To clean, divide, and present the contents of a household recycling container, was to accomplish the moral order of the recycling container and thence the governance of the local household waste management system. Accountability relations policed these moral orders. Users of the waste management centre might be understood as the subjects of directed accountability, with multiple signs directing users to present adequate containment of their waste. The household leaflets might have operated similarly, constituting the nature of disposable items and a moral order for household recycling. The adequacy of containment 'presentation' could be considered a further aspect of the accountability relations between households and council. Yet the waste management centre, with its multitude of staff, containers, and signs, was characterized by continuing messiness. The wrong things were placed in the wrong containers, with staff employed to climb into containers to repair the inadequacy of centre users' presentation of containment. Further, none of the households in our research could remember receiving a leaflet setting out the ways they should present their waste. In the absence of formal accountability through which would-be recyclers might enact a rational for the moral constitution of their objects, users of the waste management centre and householders developed a range of ad-hoc, mutual forms of accountability, often with friends and family members. Instead of judging the adequacy of their presentation of containment in relation to a formal schema, erstwhile recyclers acted in line with their usual routines and practice, which seemed to have more or less worked on previous occasions.

What then to make of this messiness? In Chapter 4, we built on our analysis of accountability, classification, and ontologically moral constitution of governable people and things, by considering the place of evidence in mundane governance. We focused on the work of local authority in constituting evidence of the recycling habits of the local population. We found that the evidence, the 'facts' of recycling, could not be separated from its morality; that the move to constitute metrics for the actions of the local population was simultaneously evidential, moral, and actionable. The classification and accountability of waste, assessments of the adequacy of its presentation, and the governance of household actions is always and already a moral matter, and implies what appropriate actions might be taken. We looked more closely at how evidence became morally action-able, noting in particular how fleeting and discursive moral warrants accomplish the basis for action. However, moral warrants are not held by individuals nor do they endure over time. Instead, the moral warrant for translating the moral and evidential into further governance action often emerges in meetings and other moments of mutual accountability and requires swift action before they dissolve. We found that moral warrants dissolve more frequently than they are enacted. In Chapter 4, the long and arduous process of constituting the evidential and moral led to no further governance action.

Up until this point, we had argued that governance was a matter of the ontological constitution of a multitude of people and things. The messiness of the waste management centre and household recycling also suggested that ontological constitution was never settled nor clear-cut; the constitution of people and things was always subject to slippage, questions, challenges, redirections, and new methods or techniques for constitution. Are other areas of mundane governance less messy? In Chapter 5, we looked at mundane governance in speeding. Had our perception of mess in mundane governance resulted from being too close to the everyday practices of our subjects? Perhaps we needed to shift attention from individuals to the aggregates of governance? In Chapter 5, we examined the relationships between the authorities of governance, in particular, the governance system through which regional safety camera partnerships had been established across the UK, under the management of a national programme board, operated by the Department for Transport. We explored the ways in which safety camera partnerships were held accountable through a continuously updated set of annual guidelines (the handbook). These specified that partnerships must produce operational cases on the likely level of income they would generate annually from speeding drivers (caught by speed cameras), and how they would spend that income in line with the handbook criteria. Their operational cases would be assessed by the national board.

In place of the messiness of Chapters 3 and 4, we appeared to have identified an encompassing governance structure. Partnerships were held to account through a handbook (which set out numerous rules, ranging from the colour of speed cameras to the number of people who needed to be killed or seriously injured before the installation of a new camera could be justified), and a national structure oversaw the operation of governance. The identity of the key entities also appeared straightforward: drivers driving too fast were recorded by speed cameras and issued with penalty notices. However, on close engagement with the partnerships and those responsible for managing the programme board, it turned out that this governance structure did not straightforwardly pre-exist actions of governance. Instead, the partnerships attempted to bully the board into making changes, they looked out for what they could get away with, bent the rules, and pushed the parameters and extent of possible punishment. The partnerships were also busy trying out different interpretations of the handbook rules; for example, what counted as a speed-related death was constituted in different ways across the country, the appropriate speed at which to set a camera varied between partnerships, as did the extent to which the payment of penalty notices was pursued. So the governance 'structure' was not a monolithic, static, or agential feature of governance relations, far less a determining force. Instead, the governance structure was continuously enacted in different ways, according to particular moments of governance action, a specific case that a partnership made to justify a new speed camera, or to push for changes in governance practice. Nor did the handbook provide a singular form of accountability to which partnerships offered a compliant response. Despite a notionally standardized set of national guidelines, decisions were made and changed, and varied between partnerships. Structures and rules of governance were themselves subject to messy, ongoing ontological constitution.

The first five chapters of our book emphasize messiness in mundane governance. We make the point that mundane governance rarely operates in a smooth and linear manner. But this is not the concluding point of our argument. We brought to attention the moral orders and ontological constitutions, the means through which governance structures were invoked and classifications accomplished (and challenged, redirected, and questioned). In Chapter 6, we used our traffic management materials to investigate whether mundane governance works. Although we briefly considered the ways in which resources are constituted as evidential–moral–actionable to assess the extent to which governance works (for example, by establishing league tables of the best and worst performing speed cameras), we found it more compelling to investigate the means by which governance subjects are said to be compliant with governance.

We went out with drivers and studied the ways in which they accomplished driving. Through navigating a plethora of cameras, lines, signs, lanes, other road users, the invocations of past histories, what they had been told by friends, what they had seen on TV or read in newspapers, drivers actively constituted a sense of their driving, the objects and subjects of driving, and the roads along which they drove. Doing compliant driving involved constituting the rules to which they were being compliant along with an assessment (of sorts) of the extent of their compliance. What we noted was the complexity of these ongoing acts of constitution. Actively to make sense of even a brief stretch of road was to bring into being a broad range of entities, people, things, and folk sociologies, just in the moment of being recorded by us doing driving. On occasions drivers accomplished compliance through ongoing articulation work, which neatly drew together their statement of a driving rule (for example, how to enter and leave a road junction) and the driving they were doing. However, drivers also exempted themselves from such compliance work (either by driving in a manner they conceived as so cautious that they did not have to consider rules such as speed limits or through driving in a manner they conceived as reckless in the hope that 'everything would work out OK'). It was not possible to understand compliance as following a series of pre-existing rules (the rules were accomplished through the driving), neither was it possible to consider compliance as narrowly focused on accountability to other drivers (drivers were one of many potential accountability audiences, including cameras, signs, lines, and so on). We did not end our exploration of compliance there; instead, we took part in driver retraining in order to examine those specific set-piece moments where compliance was articulated. Driver retraining courses turned out to be occasions in which compliance involved the monotonous repetition of familiar messages about driving and driver accountability and responsibility, with responses rehearsed and rehashed as necessary and when called upon. Perhaps in virtue of the apparent obviousness of the ontologies they were asked to acknowledge and learn, some drivers on retraining courses expressed frustration, made jokes, and defied the governance relations offered to them.

We critically examined the idea of consistency as a way of assessing the extent to which driving could be recognized as compliant across times, places, actions, and different drivers. Our volunteer driver re-trainee failed to accomplish consistent compliance and soon faced a further speeding penalty despite the experience of the retraining course. Drivers in our videos of doing driving, provided myriad means to manage consistency between places, times, and what they conceived as a way to manage inconsistency in their driving. Doing consistency was an ongoing constitutive activity through which drivers accomplished a sense of what they were doing. In attempting to answer our question of whether or not governance works, it seemed that the terms for pursuing an answer were the means through which evidential and moral outputs would be brought into being. Hence a league table for the best and worst performing speed cameras provided a means to constitute the evidential and moral status of speed cameras across the UK. Our engagement with drivers doing driving and doing retraining offered a distinct take on this evidential constitution, by turning over to drivers the means to account for their actions as compliant and consistent. The huge variety in means for constituting the nature of driving, the extent and basis for judging compliance, and the actions through which drivers adjudged consistency, suggested that compliance, consistency, and the terms for assessing the degree to which governance works are all open to consideration as actions of ontological accomplishment.

In Chapter 7, we further switched attention by considering the spaces of airports as locales through which governance was accomplished. We drew together material from a guided tour of the airport terminal conducted by the managers of that terminal with a series of ethnographies completed by passengers seeking to catch planes. Accountability relations in the space of the airport were almost limitless in number and combination. For example, in seeking new wayfinding technologies, the airport managers presented their actions as accountable to the airport board (who might turn down a proposal on cost basis), architects and planners (who the managers invoked as seeking to protect the dignity of the airport's award winning architecture), passengers (who made representations to the managers through Passengers Service Group meetings), shareholders (who might put pressure on the board), government agencies (such as the Home Office and their invoked security expectations), and so on. On occasions these groups were combined such that initial plans drawn up by managers to introduce new signs to direct passengers were shelved in expectation that engineers would propose a cost too high to be accepted by the airport board and shareholders, that signs had to fit guidelines on font and size, that the signs might reduce airport income (by replacing or drawing attention away from advertising billboards), and that passengers had expressed more concern with TV screens than static signs. It proved almost impossible to distinguish between accountability relations according to our initial two-part scheme. Instead, the constitution of accountability relations, audiences, expectations, outcomes, and consequences for action were an ongoing feature of the airport and the terminal managers' jobs.

In place of any counter expectations that the airport terminal space accomplished governable and orderly transit of passengers or that passengers achieved an orderly transit through the space by drawing on the airport's wayfinding systems, we found a series of actions that accomplished more or less orderly spaces, transits, passengers, wayfinding systems, managers of terminals, and airport processes. That is, the wayfinding systems did not straightforwardly communicate a rationale for action to passengers who could pick up on and enact that rationale through their movements in the airport terminal. Instead, we found passengers actively attempting to accomplish a sense of wayfinding technologies, attempting to articulate ways in which the sense they had accomplished of the wayfinding technology adhered to the sense they were attempting to make of what they were trying to do, and a broad array of different activities that they accounted for as the purpose of their movement through the airport (from catching a plane, to shopping, joining a queue, finding a seat, looking for their lost husband, and so on). The space and its wayfinding technologies did not determine passenger actions. Instead, space as a more or less orderly, more or less sensible phenomenon was accomplished through walking, queuing, reading, questioning, changing direction, holding, and displaying various tokens of transit, displaying various objects at appropriate times and in appropriate manners. That the managers and staff of the terminal had to deal with a daily succession of lost and confused passengers or even people who were not trying to be passengers but were there to meet and greet friends or families but had got caught up in the classification of passengers who needed to act in certain ways, was treated as a normal and ordinary aspect of the airport space. To ensure that the space held together required ongoing actions to seek out new wayfinding technologies, to redirect the lost and confused, but also to bolster retail sales and to accomplish the airport business model.

In Chapters 8 and 9, we further developed our argument against the assumption that people, things, processes, relations, finances, documents, rules, regulations, laws, or technologies of mundane governance are stable and settled and straightforwardly accomplished governance. First, in Chapter 8, we considered entities that had—via particular passages through, and questions posed of, accountability relations—become ontologically insecure. We took water bottles and letter bombs as focal points for elaborating this insecurity. Water bottles were a recent candidate object of insecurity in airport governance and accountability relations that sought to constitute objects and their people as security ready. Letter bombs were a means through which businesses could take on responsibility for the management of terror. And yet objects and their passengers continually proved themselves to be security unready and the 'letter' 'bombs' and MI5's instructions for handling them proved impossible to operationalize. Indeed, it could be argued that actions to govern the insecure into being secure, constituted a broader, deeper, and more pervasive ontological insecurity than the insecure objects initially permitted. Hence to work to position letters as insecure (letter 'bombs'), without successful demarcation criteria and without feasible means to work up a demarcation (between letters and bombs), resulted in either treating all letters as if they were bombs ('letter' 'bombs') or ignoring the instructions to pay attention to letters (and risk invoking any manner of future accountability and responsibility failure). Second, in Chapter 9, we considered the ways in which relations of governance were disrupted, breached, and repaired. In particular, we looked again at water bottles and our attempts to carry liquids through security, at traffic management and the breakdown of traffic lights, at parking and our manoeuvres to challenge the status of parking tickets we had been issued, and at the spoof speeding database. This analysis drew attention to the ways in which the ontological constitution of the evidential and moral was not static, but could be open to ongoing challenge and restatement. We also suggested that the 'rules' of governance were often not available for deeper interrogation as representative of a governance rationale (even among those who formed part of governance set-ups, such as airport security clerks) beyond a restatement of the rules. We argued that repairs to governance relations were instructive for drawing attention to ongoing changes in governance. Finally, we suggested that breaches in governance relations are a normal and everyday feature of governance action; in none of our cases did governance operate smoothly, universally, in a stable manner, between distinct locations or people or technologies or documents or processes.

In sum, we have opened a space for considering mundane governance as situated ontology, as the practical constitution of matter, both in the evidential sense of bringing matter into being and in the sense of constituting what ought to matter, why, how, assessed by what means, using what kind of process, and so on. In this sense, the bin bag could be wrong in virtue of its particular passage of ontological constitution, evidential and moral ordering, accountability relations, their consequence, output, and disruption. Our argument about bin bags and other matters has focused on the mundane—in the twin sense of being every day and becoming of the world—and governance in respect to accountabilities, technologies, and ontologies. We have explored modes of accountability and the classifications, relations, disruptions, reorderings, and reinstatements that characterized our ethnographic pursuit of waste, traffic, and airport management. By looking at technologies and other material objects of governance, we have explored the means by which spaces, actions, and orders of governance are accomplished. And we have navigated ontological multiplicity and singularity, exploring the ways in which governance ontologies are constituted, the evidential and moral brought into being, and breaches, breakdowns, and repairs to governance constituencies made. In Section 10.3, we reflect on our own navigation of singularity and multiplicity.

10.3 Partial Takes and Coherent Accounts

Our story is partial (Strathern, 2004). It is an account comprising parts and wholes and holes. It presents our own ontological constitution of mundane governance. We tried to weave together some coherent narratives of mundane governance to address the key themes that emerged as the study developed. But without an account of our means of accounting, it seems to fall a little short. How did we bring mundane governance into being? What did we include and exclude? How did we make our decisions?

A particularly interesting aspect of researching the mundane is its inescapability. We started with the apprehension that the mundane concerned only the lesser things in life, but were astonished to realize how massively widespread are so-called trivial matters. There is neither news programme nor newspaper that does not in some way touch on the phenomenon we have been trying to study. There is no colleague nor friend who, upon hearing about our research, can resist providing their own tale of mundane governance: a problem they have had with their local council waste collection; the idiosyncrasies of the recycling system; a parking ticket that was in no way justified; the particularly idiotic placing of a speed camera; an airport experience involving an extraordinary new way of navigating the terminal. And, of course, we ourselves had similar experiences: in all these ways, we are already part of the phenomenon we are studying. We decided we should embrace rather than resist our *de facto* involvement with the mundane.

Partly because of this involvement, perhaps, we were frequently called upon to explain our 'position', by which is meant our political stance in relation to our subject matter. For example, to say that one is researching recycling is heard by many audiences, as we have now come to realize, as a commitment to the recycling cause, or to the environment or green endeavours broadly construed. To reveal something of one's acquired knowledge of the operations of speed cameras (even in the partial and self-deprecating manner to which we aspired) is to open oneself to questions as to what we know about speed cameras, how that might be useful, and where we stand on speed cameras.[1]

How did we draw together the stories we told? We have a sense that many elements of the stories still spill over the edges of our text.[2] Our selection of material was based on analytic themes we sought to pursue and how these might be illuminated. Hence, materials on waste management, traffic management, and airports were organized into narratives that could speak to themes of accountability and classification, constitution of the evidential and moral, the invocation of structures, compliance and consistency in governance actions, the spaces of governance, ontological insecurity, and resistance/disruption. But from where did these themes emerge? From the materials we gathered. So our decision protocol was inevitably circular; the materials appeared to recommend these themes, we selected materials further to explore these themes. We have some confidence in the choices that we made; many of the same themes could have been illustrated using different materials. For example, we drew upon the airport materials to analyse spaces of governance, but space also emerged as a theme in driving and waste management. We drew on waste management to illustrate accountability and classification, but these themes are also prevalent in airports and safety camera partnerships. We examined safety camera partnerships to develop the point about the active invocation of structures of governance, but such invocations were also apparent in waste management and the airport. Our narratives are partial, but the themes none the less recur with some frequency across the different substantive areas of our study.

At the same time that we grew confident in our emerging analytic themes, we were also aware that our argument was building toward multiplicity; at any moment it seemed that distinct governance stories could be told via objects, people, and pairings. For example, speed cameras were ontologically constituted in multiple ways as were drivers, roads, and vehicles. Following Mol (2002) we considered a variety of means to try to fashion an open text that draws attention to this multiplicity. And yet, throughout our study, ontological singularity has emerged as a key, central feature of mundane governance. Hence, although the bin bag could be read as a tale of multiplicity, a central characteristic of the story was that of singularity; that the singular entity admits one morally appropriate reading of the object, its owner, and its further relations. Governance was thus accomplished through this singularly constitutive

---

[1] In one particularly dramatic episode, the infamous tabloid newspaper the *News of the World* (before its demise) tried to obtain information from us to create an 'alternative map of speeding in the UK', that is, a map indicating in which areas of the country people could get away with driving at high speed. Despite their friendly overtures—we were told they would 'make it worth our while'—we declined their invitation to disseminate project information in this manner.

[2] We leave it to readers to assess the adequacy of our presentation of containment.

move. In place of various forms of textual experimentation (including multiple authorial voices, breaking up the text in different ways, reordering our earlier narratives in later chapters) we settled on policing our text by reference to our methodological sensibilities (discussed further).

Having developed a set of analytical themes and drawn together data to engage those themes, at the same time as embracing multiplicity and exploring distinct sensibilities, we also had to make decisions regarding areas to cut from the text. What did we omit from our study? There were many more objects of governance than we had space to analyse. For example, within the study of traffic management, multiple further documents relating to speed, assessment of the effectiveness of traffic management, and objects given to drivers to encourage road safety (for example, the speed awareness underpants and stress relief squeezable speed cameras that Dan collected but never tested) had to be omitted on the grounds of space and word limits. Similar decisions had to be taken regarding waste management and airport spaces. Furthermore, we cut out extended analysis of issues such as participatory accountability on the grounds that very little data emerged, which engaged this mode of accountability. The absence of participatory accountability—whereby subjects of governance might be invited to participate in and hence hold modes of governance to account—may have proven illustrative of the limits of accountability. But such an analysis would have been speculative as we had little material to support such an argument. Further analytical themes could also have been developed. For example, the recent STS focus on values, markets, and valuation (see, for example, Callon's work on markets and values, 1998, 2007, 2009; Dussauge *et al.*, forthcoming; Meadel and Rabehariosa, 2002; Milo and Muniesa, 2007) could have been brought to centre stage. However, value as a theme did not emerge as a central concern for research participants. This is one of several lines of future possible enquiry.

Further, although our focus has been on incorporating multiple voices, objects, processes, and so on, there has been a constraint on the number of accounts we could examine. For example, in our airport research, we mentioned the airport board, architects, and shareholders as accountability audiences constituted and given life by airport managers. To pursue these groups and others as empirical subjects proved beyond the limits of our study—the project would have been endless. Other groups with which we did engage—such as the Airport Passenger Service Group whose meetings formed part of the ethnography—only featured in the text in passing reference as the complexity of our chapters threatened to spiral out of control.

Our commitments, selections, edits, and cuts have posed a number of questions for us as authors of this text. To what degree can we talk of mundane governance when we simultaneously eschew the possibility of providing a single, final, complete theoretical account of mundane governance? How can we avoid falling into the trap of espousing a singular account of mundane governance? How can we draw on our methodological sensibilities as a means to police the writing of our account? We attempted to render our writing reflexively accountable to seven main sensibilities. First, we pursued a sustained focus on matters *ontological*. In place of a focus on questions of knowledge or representation, we have argued that the very nature of people and things is at stake in the governance activities we have analysed. Further, the nature of people and things is at once always and already both moral and evidential. Hence, the wrong bin bag is brought into being through carefully co-ordinated governance and accountability relations, which realize the moral, evidential, responsible, and accountable nature of the bin bag. This connects with our second sensibility, which has been to orient our research toward *constitution*. Here we have suggested that the political aspects of constitutions (as a more or less focused space within which to draw together rights (and wrongs) and relations of accountability) is important. The speeding driver is rendered thus through the funding, installation, and maintenance of speed cameras, the collection, reading, and processing of film, the issuing of penalties, decisions regarding annual operational cases, the invoked national structure of governance within which such cases will be assessed, attempts by regional partnerships to bend or break or ignore the rules of this structure, further decisions on how often to fill cameras with film, what counts as a speed-related death (to justify a camera), at what speed the camera ought to be set, how the notice issued to drivers should be designed, and how far non-payment of fines should be pursued. The constituency is complex, and yet accountability relations are carefully managed; hence, drivers are discouraged from asking questions of the evidence apparently demonstrating their guilt (through partial withholding of evidence) and are severely limited in opportunities for raising questions regarding the structure of governance. Thirdly, we have also paid close attention to the *reflexive* constitution of governance and accountability relations. Thus, much of the constitution of speeding drivers is brought into being through the actions of regional partnerships. Fourthly, our research work has been directed toward extensive *attention to detail* as a basis for elaborating the constitution work of mundane governance. Fifth, we have looked for ways to run a traditional ethnographic exotic-izing move (treating the ordinary as strange) alongside a mundane-izing move (investigating how things have become of the world), to confront things with what they have become. This has helped us to pose questions such as how can a bin bag be wrong? Sixth, alongside our more or less formal field sites, which required access negotiation, set entry and exit times, not to mention the collection of huge amounts of data for analysis, we also left space for a more *happenstance* methodology whereby we allowed some of the mundane features of our own lives, which appeared pertinent to our study, to find expression in our text (in, for example, driver retraining). Finally, and simultaneously, we have sought to retain an openness to the text. *Otherwise-ing* has become a key analytical move for us. In attempting to write this text, we have continually posed questions of our own writing. A commitment to the methodological sensibility 'it could be otherwise' has prompted us continually to ask ourselves: in what way, to whom, through what means, with what outcomes could our account be otherwise? This provided a satisfactorily unsettling basis for writing.

10.4 Outstanding Issues

Perhaps the most striking feature of dealing with the mundane is the hugely divergent ways in which it is apprehended. The mundane is at once mundane and profound; ordinary and extraordinary; inconsequential and highly political; unremarkable and the focus of great passion. So our central curiosity is: how is this done? How can something as lofty as governance happen in relation to ordinary things? What are these things and what exactly does 'in relation to' mean here? We have tried to disassemble the simplistic gloss that could be put on all this: that 'ordinary objects are ruling our lives'. Not much better is the formulation that our lives are regulated 'in relation to' ordinary objects and technologies. Again, we find ourselves needing to specify what these ordinary objects and technologies are, and again we need to consider what is involved in something being 'in relation to' something else.

We have argued for an understanding of mundane governance, which recognizes the importance of ontological constitution and enactment. The strength of our analysis, we have argued, depends on the extent to which we take mundaneity into account in terms of ontology. This focus, in turn, prompts five main themes for further elaboration and future inquiry. First, we have suggested an approach that entails a significant shift away from analysis in terms of either epistemology or (traditional) ontology. That is, we are advocating an approach that goes beyond both concerns about how we know entities (which are presumed already to exist) and the philosophical project of articulating theories of existence. As we have tried to show throughout, mundane governance depends on the localized, *in situ*, recursive enactment of ontologies. Recycling and waste disposal is about the achieved ontological relation between stuff and its householders; traffic regulation is about the ontological relations between the speed and position of vehicles and their drivers; airport passenger movement is about managing ontological relations between baggage and its accompanying passengers. In each case, we have suggested that ontological enactment goes beyond mere practices of representation (knowledge, epistemology) and yet does not simply derive from some inherently given properties (pure ontology). One way of expressing this is to say that we favour a form of inquiry, which asks how it is that entities (objects, persons, technologies) come to seem what they are. It remains to be seen how best to cash out this formulation without sliding back into either (closet) realism or (closet) constructivism or a (closet) compromise between the two.

Second, as noted in Chapter 2, the notion of ontological enactment might benefit from careful elaboration and development. Enactment is one of a cluster of related terms used to adduce a form of scepticism about essentialism, and about the notion that entities pre-exist our apprehension of them. As mentioned in Chapter 5, these terms can be arranged along a rough continuum from weak to strong scepticism: shaping, aggregating, affording, providing for, constructing, apprehending, performing, accomplishing, bringing into being, constituting, and enacting. Thus, 'shaping' connotes a relatively mild intervention in presumptions about the pre-existence of entities, and 'enacting' the most provocative. In this book we have tended to favour terms 'constituting' and 'enacting', in a bid to align ourselves with the more sceptical end of the continuum. More work is needed in teasing out the connotations and implications of these different uses.

Third, our central claim about mundane governance is that governance and accountability relations appear to flow from just the way the world is. Indeed, a summary way of speaking of the effectiveness of mundane governance (but see Chapter 6) is that it depends on accepting that things, objects, entities are just the way they are. That the existence and nature of an entity is taken for granted is crucial to the apprehension of what courses of action are appropriate in relation to it. At the same time, we are keen to avoid slipping (back) into essentialism and determinism. The vocabulary of affordances purportedly distinguishes itself from essentialism and determinism, but none the less implies an unsatisfactory compromise. It suggests that objects can give rise to behaviour albeit within a relatively open-ended set of possible outcomes. From a different perspective, Mol (2013) speaks of 'ontonorms', suggesting that the (ontology of the) enacted world provides norms for behaviour. Our parallel argument might be captured under the rubric of 'ontogovernance': the ontologies of the enacted world provide the basis for the practices of governance. Yet our claim that governance and accountability 'appear to flow from' enacted ontologies, offers a slightly more modified determinism, in part because it puts emphasis on the appearance of these effects. None the less, even our cautious approach to the problem retains connotations of essentialism and determinism. Is it ever possible to be rid of these?

In addition, our treatment of this issue is not always entirely consistent. Although we mostly speak of governance relations arising in virtue of enacted entities, at times we have used the inverse formulation: that govern-ance relations constitute ontologies. We think it not satisfactory to insist on one or other direction. By themselves, neither formulation—that relations constitute, or relations appear to flow from, ontologies—quite gets at the problem. So, for example, in the case of the wrong bin bag (Chapter 2), there are important ways in which governance relations appear to flow from what the bag appears to be (its wrongness), but governance relations are also cen-tral to establishing 'wrongness'. These governance relations also open the whole possibility that the governance relations themselves are wrong, which is a central thrust of the newspaper story.

How then to square the directional circle? One possibility is to think of gov-ernance operations in terms of a splitting and inversion model (Latour and Woolgar, 1979). In this model, scientific objects do not exist prior to, but in important ways are constituted through, the artful practices of discovery; the relationship is subsequently inverted so as to present the discovered object as antecedent to artful practices.[3] By analogy, perhaps, ontologies do not pre-cede the governance relations that constitute them. They are the upshot of governance relations but through a process of splitting and inversion, they come to stand as the things that give rise to appropriate behaviour.

Fourth, we need to clarify the status of our conclusion that mundane gov-ernance is characterized by messiness. It is easy to hear this as saying that mundane governance is *just* messy, *only* messy, or is *no more than* a muddle and mess. But we insist on the absence of these qualifiers (just, only, no more than)! We are not saying that governance is *just* a mess, we are saying that it *is* a mess! This is, of course, not intended as a criticism. It instead proposes that messiness is a constitutive feature of ontological constitution and gov-ernance relations. Indeed, some writers suggest that contingency and mess are endemic to organizations (Garfinkel, 1967: chapter 6) or functional for them (Weick, 1995). In the same vein, we are keen to resist the conventional requirement that we constitute our explorations in mundane governance as a set of stable findings, by imposing structure upon them and rendering them straightforwardly portable, in the manner of an immutable mobile. More important, we believe, are the puzzles and questions that our stories raise.

Fifth, we anticipate that other substantive areas might profitably be con-strued in terms of mundane governance, and worked through in terms of the schema we have developed. For example, food suggests itself as an ideal candidate for analysis in terms of mundane governance. Food is of course widespread. Whole varieties of behaviour are routinely aligned, contested, encouraged, or sanctioned in relation to food. And crucially, these activities

---

[3] For an application of this model to the use of methods in social science, see Law (2004).

and behaviours are made to follow on the grounds of what the food actually is, what it contains, what is its provenance, what good or harm it will do, who knows what about it, and so on. In other words, governance and accountability relations arise in virtue of its accomplished ontological status. Similarly, we imagine that information may be fruitfully analysed as a form of mundane governance. We saw (in Chapter 9) how information about speeding, the speeding database, was the subject of parody about the workings of mundane governance. Once again, it would be interesting to develop the argument that processes of governance and accountability arise in relation to the ontological constitution of information entities. Certain courses of action are said to follow, or are imagined might follow, from the constitution of who knows what about whom, what kinds of information are recorded, by whom, how is it gathered and stored, and so on. In each case we can ask what are the key entities, how are they constituted (enacted) and what accountability relations appear to stem from this. And, if broadly similar analytic frameworks can be worked through in relation to these different empirical examples, interesting questions arise about differences in resistance and breakdown. What do we make of the difference in challenges to the constituent ontologies? For example, why do food labelling systems seem to be much more the target of organized activity by, for example, consumer organizations, than is, for example, the airport liquids rule?

10.5 Futures of Mundane Governance

What of the future? As experienced by grumpy old men at least, mundane governance is on the rise, infiltrating and taking over more and more areas of life. Is this situation set to continue? What developments might diminish the widespread apprehension that 'ordinary objects are increasingly controlling our lives'? And, relatedly, which perspectives on mundane governance are likely to be more successful and more enduring than others?

Certainly, the people, objects, processes, finances, invoked structures, forms of evidence, moral orders and warrants, and relations of accountability are continually changing. Our three main areas of study exemplify this point. In recycling, the key governance pairing of boxes and their households has recently undergone revision and is now composed of larger wheelie bins and their households. What is and is not waste, what is and is not the appropriate presentation of the containment of waste and recycling, how and when collection occurs all continue to go through a process of change. Recycling is no longer sorted at the kerbside, but collected in singular containers and sorted at a later stage in the governance process. Waste is no longer collected weekly but fortnightly (at least for the moment; fortnightly collections continue to prove controversial and may change again). The governance of speeding drivers is still pursued through speed cameras, but the relationships between cameras, drivers, regional partnerships, and the national government Department for Transport continue to shift. For example, the invoked, challenged, and frequently modified governance structure of regional safety camera partnerships producing annual operational cases, assessed by a national board through which income was distributed, has been partly replaced by annual budget statements. The nature of evidential and moral actions has thus shifted. In the airport, the continuing challenge to maximize income from passengers through retail outlets at the same time as upholding the airport's coveted security record eventually brought such pressure to bear on the airport board that the managers lost their jobs, the airport was taken over, and new means were sought to increase income streams. The people involved in governance changed, but much of the confusion and messiness of airport passenger governance remains. Such changes appear to form central and continuous features of mundane governance. At no point does this ongoing change appear set to slow down.

In the UK at least, the overall organization of mundane governance is characterized by fragmentation and competition. In waste management and speeding governance, units of organization are in many respects set in competition with each other. Local councils compete in terms of percentage of waste in landfill, and have operated an exchange system of landfill credits. In our terms, this correlates with a disaggregation of ontologies. During our presentations of our research materials, we were frequently told of the different kinds of container that different local council councils across the country were using (a nylon green container here; a folding green coloured cardboard box there; an orange plastic box elsewhere). The lack of a standard ontology of container is mirrored by local variations in what counts as recyclable materials and what householder actions are appropriate. For example, households might be required to sort glass bottles according to colour in one location, but are asked not to sort by colour in recycling containers less than a mile away. These local variations reflect the changing and different contracts between local councils and collection agencies (for example, glass being recycled as bottles in one case, but as hardcore for road construction in the other). Similarly, as mentioned in Chapter 5, safety camera partnerships are organized as individual units each competing to generate revenue, one result of which is that the ontological pairing of speeding vehicle and driver is constituted differently in different geographical areas.[4]

---

[4] It was this that led to the putative media story about a 'postcode lottery' of speeding convictions (Chapter 5).

This lack of standardization goes hand in hand with the individuation and psychologization of the problems that mundane governance is meant to address. Fragmentation and competition are consistent with the definition of problems in terms of individual responsibility. Central government distributes accountability to individual councils, safety camera partnerships, and airports, which in turn make individual householders, drivers, and passengers accountable for their actions. This then reinforces distributions of accountability and responsibility organized around the particular figure of the individual. Rather than target the manufacturers of plastics and packaging, recycling policies are aimed at 'encouraging a recycling mentality'. Rather than restricting the production of fast cars, traffic management is organized around educating drivers.

At the time of writing, governmental discussions of mundane governance are characterized by concerns with financial crises, and the common political response, in many Western nations at least, is to implement austerity measures.[5] Within the series of proposed cutbacks, budget restrictions focus on forms of target setting, centralized government structures, town and city planning infrastructure, and government functions that provide oversight (either within government or quasi-independently) of government spending. In addition to reductions in decision-making authority and the budget for government-funded bodies with oversight functions, several smaller organizations have been abolished altogether.[6] These significant cutbacks not only exemplify the process of continual change in mundane governance, they also suggest that governance can at any moment be subject to sweeping reform.

These reforms appear to propose at least five kinds of change in mundane governance. First, the merging and consolidation of oversight functions (for example, with government ministers taking on responsibilities previously distributed among several agencies). Second, a reduction in the scope of oversight activity (particularly with regards to 'oversight' organizations issuing directives and becoming *de facto* policy makers). Third, the abolition of some organizations (such as the UK Audit Commission). Fourth, in the UK, the outsourcing of some functions of these organizations through competitive tendering processes brokered by, for example, the National Audit Office. Fifth, a stronger rhetorical emphasis on the citizenry holding government to account.

---

[5] Austerity drives have become a pervasive feature of European government and beyond following the economic crisis, which emerged in 2007 and 2008.

[6] For example, the UK government axed BECTA (British Educational Communications and Technology Agency) that had the role of ensuring value for money in educational IT procurement and the National Police Improvement Agency (NPIA).

Our aim here is not to decide the effectiveness or consequences of these proposals. It seems likely that accountability, transparency, choice, democracy, participation, localization, and reform will instantiate further messiness in governance. It could mean that cuts in government spending, coupled with less scrutiny of accountability, will effectively outsource mundane governance, leading to (cheaper) forms of citizen-led accountability. The talk is of: redistributions of accountability, from governmental architectures to transparency and participation; devolving the moral warrants for asking questions from quasi-autonomous government agencies to citizens; and bringing government departmental activity under greater scrutiny. Whether or not these particular outcomes will come to pass, is unclear. But change remains the enduring central characteristic of governance schemes, ontological constitutions, and the revocation or critique of governance. Hence, mundane governance is likely to continue to be characterized by a pervasive and ongoing ontological insecurity. Current reforms appear to signal a further expansion of the scope of change; we are all to become armchair auditors, to engage in the situated ontology of ordinary objects and entities, and to become increasingly part of the world of mundane governance.

References

Adey, P. (2009) Facing airport security: affect, biopolitics, and the preemptive securitisation of the mobile body. *Environment and Planning D: Society and Space* 27, 274–295.

Akrich, M. (1992) The de-scription of technical objects. In: Bijker, W.E. and Law, J. (Eds.) *Shaping Technology/Building Society: studies in sociotechnical change*, pp. 205–224. Cambridge, MA: MIT Press.

Allen, J.S. (1846) Phrenology examined. *Making of America Journal*. Available at: http://www.hti.umich.edu/

Amoore, L. and Hall, A. (2009) Taking people apart: digitised dissection and the body at the border. *Environment and Planning D: Society and Space* 27, 444–464.

Asch, S. (1951) Effects of group pressure upon the modification and distortion of judgment. In: Guetzkow, H. (Ed.) *Groups, Leadership and Men*. Pittsburgh, PA: Carnegie Press.

Atos (2005) *UK Passport Service Biometrics Enrolment—Report*. Available at: http://www.homeoffice.gov.uk

Barry, A. (2001) *Political Machines: governing a technological society*. London: Athlone Press.

BBC (2005) ID Trials Reveal Scan Problems. Available at: http://www.news.bbc.co.uk/1/hi/uk_politics/4580447.stm

BBC (2006a) Rubbish rage Radio 4 Broadcasting House 21 May 2006, downloaded from: http://www.bbc.co.uk/radio4/news/bh/ on 22-5-06 [starts at 9:21:10].

BBC (2006b) BBC Radio 4 Today Programme. http://www.bbc.co.uk/radio4/today/listenagain/zfriday_20060818.shtml 18-8-06 07.34am Edward Stourton's mention of a profound question of political philosophy at stake here, is at about 5.09 minutes in.

BBC (2006c) BBC Radio 4 *Today* programme (18 December 2006). Available at: http://www.bbc.co.uk/radio4/today/listenagain/monday.shtml

BBC White Paper (2006d) A Public Service For All. Available at: www.bbccharterreview.org.uk

Beaty, J. and Gwynne, S. (2004) *The Outlaw Bank*. Washington DC: Beard Books.

Benington, J. (Ed.) (2006) *Reforming Public Services*. London: National School of Government/The Stationery Office.

Benton-Short, L. (2007) Bollards, bunkers and barriers: securing the national mall in Washington, DC. *Environment and Planning D: Society and Space* 25, 424–446.

Bittner, E. (1965) The concept of organization. *Social Research* 32, 239–255.

Black, M. (1964) The gap between is and should. *The Philosophical Review* 73(2), 165–181.

Blowfield, M. and Murray, A. (2008) *Corporate Responsibility*. Oxford: Oxford University Press.

References

Bower, T. (1996) *Maxwell: The final verdict*. London: Harper Collins.

Bower, T. (1998) *Maxwell: The outsider*. London: Aurum Press.

Bowker, G. and Leigh Star, S. (2000) *Sorting Things Out—classification and its consequences*. London: MIT Press.

BRASS (2006) Is Waste Minimisation a Challenge Too Far?: The Experience of House-hold Waste Management and Purchasing in the UK Available at: www.brass.cf.ac.uk

Britanica online. Available at: http://www.britannica.com/

Brownson, R., Gurney, J., and Land, G. (1999) Evidence-based decision making in public health. *Journal of Public Health Management and Practice* 5(5), 86–97.

Bruun Jensen, C. 2010 *Ontologies for Developing Things*. Rotterdam: Sense Publications.

Cadman, C. (2010) How (not) to be governed: Foucault, critique and the political. *Environment and Planning D: Society and Space* 28, 539–556.

Callon, M. (1986) The sociology of an actor-network: the case of the electric vehicle. In: Callon, M., Law, J., and Rip, A. (Eds.) *Mapping the Dynamics of Science and Technology: Sociology of science in the real world*, pp. 19–34. London: Macmillan.

Callon, M. (1998) *The Laws of the Market*. Oxford: Blackwell.

Callon, M. (2007) An essay on the growing contribution of economic markets to the proliferation of the social. *Theory, Culture, Society* 24(7–8), 139–163.

Callon, M. (2009) Civilizing markets: carbon trading between in vitro and in vivo experiments. *Accounting, Organizations and Society* 34(3–4), 535–548.

Callon, M., Meadel, C., and Rabehariosa, V. (2002) The Economy of Qualities. *Economy and Society* 31(2), 194–217.

Callon, M., Millo, Y., and Muniesa, F. (2007) *Market Devices*. Oxford: Blackwell.

Canning, M. and O'Dwyer, B. (2001) Professional accounting bodies disciplinary procedures: accountable, transparent and in the public interest? *European Accounting Review* 10(4), 725–750.

Cassidy, J. (1995) The is-ought problem and the ground of economic ethics, *Humanomics* 11, 92–149.

Chappels, H. and Shove, E. (1999a) Bins and the history of waste relations. In Reader for Lancaster Summer School. Available at: http://www.comp.lancs.ac.uk/sociology/esf/bins.htm

Chappells, H. and Shove. E. (1999b) The dustbin: a study of domestic waste, household practices and utility services. *International Planning Studies* 4(2), 267–280.

Cochoy, F. (1998) Another discipline for the market economy: marketing as a performative knowledge and know-how for capitalism. In: Callon, M. (Ed.) *The Laws of the Market*, pp. 194–221. Oxford: Blackwell Publishers.

Cole, S. (1998) Witnessing identification: latent fingerprint evidence and expert knowledge. *Social Studies of Science* 28, 5–6.

Cole, S. (2002) *Suspect Identities: A history of fingerprinting and criminal identification*. Cambridge, MA: Harvard University Press.

Computer Weekly (2005) Sticky fingers could scupper UK ID card biometrics, warn experts, 13 October. http://www.computerweekly.com/Articles/2005/10/13/212301/sticky-fingers-could-scupper-uk-id-card-biometrics-warn.htm

Crabtree, A. (2000) Remarks on the social organisation of space and place. *Journal of Mundane Behavior* 1(1). Available at: http://mundanebehavior.org/index2.htm

Daemmreich, A. (1998) The evidence does not speak for itself: Expert witnesses and the organisation of DNA-typing companies. *Social Studies of Science* 28(5/6), 741–772.

Daily Express (2005) Front Page, Wednesday 20 April.

Dant, T. (2004) The driver car. *Theory, Culture and Society* 21(4–5), 61–79.

De Certeau, M. (1984) *The Practice of Everyday Life*. Berkeley, CA: University of California Press.

De Laet, M. and Mol, A (2000) The Zimbabwe bush pump: mechanics of a fluid technology. *Social Studies of Science* 30(2), 225–263.

DfT (2008) Road Safety Compliance Consultation, Available at: http://collections. europarchive.org/tna/20081223120624/http:/dft.gov.uk/consultations/open/ compliance/ (accessed 15 December, 2008).

Diprose, R. (2006) The political technology of RU486 paper presented at Stuff of Politics conference, Worcester College, University of Oxford, 7–10 December.

Dobrow, M., Goel, V., and Upshur, R. (2003) Evidence-based health policy: context and utilization. *Social Science & Medicine* 58, 207–217.

Douglas, M. (1984) *Purity and Danger*. London: Routledge.

Drew, P. (1990) Strategies in the contest between lawyer and witness in cross examination. In: Levi, J. and Graffam Walker, A. (Eds.) *Language in the Judicial Process*, pp. 39–64. New York: Plenum Press.

Drive Tech (2004) Speed Awareness. Handout at Oxfordshire Speed Awareness course.

Dumit, J. and Rabinow P. (2003) *Picturing Personhood: brain scans and biomedical identity (in-formation)*. Princeton, NJ: Princeton University Press.

Dussauge, I., Helgesson, C.-F. and Lee, F. (Eds.) (forthcoming) *Value Practices in the Life Sciences*. Oxford: Oxford University Press.

Ebbinghaus, H.D., Flum, J., and Thomas, W. (1984) *Mathematical Logic*. New York: Springer Verlag.

Elden, S. (2007) Governmentality, calculation and territory. *Environment and Planning D: Society and Space* 25, 562–580.

Emsley, C. (1993) 'Mother, what did policemen do when there werent any motors?' The law, the police and the regulation of motor traffic in England, 1900-1939. *The Historical Journal* 36(2), 357–381.

Encarta Dictionary (2006). Historically available from: http://www.encarta.com (Encarta was cancelled in 2009 by Microsoft).

Ericson, R., Doyle, A., and Barry, D. (2003) *Insurance as Governance*. University of Toronto Press, CA.

Espeland, W. and Sauder, M. (2007) Rankings and reactivity: How public measures recreate social worlds. *American Journal of Sociology* 113, 1–40.

Euben, P. (1996) Democratic accountability and comedic encounters Paper presented to conference on The Public Space and Democracy: theatricality, legitimacy, politics, University of California San Diego, 2–4 May.

Ferguson, J. and Gupta, A. (2002) Spatializing states: toward an ethnography of neoliberal governmentality. *American Ethnologist* 29(4), 981–1002.

Festinger, L. and Carlsmith, J.M. (1959) Cognitive consequences of forced compliance. *Journal of Abnormal and Social Psychology* 58, 203–210.

Flather, P. (2006) Introduction. In: *Restructuring Corporate Governance: the new European Agenda*, pp. 2–3. Oxford: The Europaeum.

References

Foucault, M. (orig 1966, re-published 2002) *The Order of Things*. London: Routledge.

Foucault, M. (orig 1967, re-published 2001) *Madness and Civilization*. London: Routledge.

Foucault, M. (1977) *Discipline and Punish*. London: Allen Lane.

Foucault, M. (1980) The eye of power. In: Gordon, C. (Ed.) *Power/Knowledge: Selected Interviews and Other Writings 1972-1977 by Michel Foucault*, pp. 146–165. Sussex: Harvester Press.

Garfinkel, H. (1963) A conception of and experiments with 'trust' as a condition of stable concerted actions. In: Harvey, O. (Ed.) *Motivation and Social Interaction* (New York: Ronald Press), pp. 197–238.

Garfinkel, H. (1967) *Studies in Ethnomethodology*. Englewood Cliffs, NJ: Prentice Hall.

Garfinkel, H. (1974) The origins of the term ethnomethodology. In Turner, R. (Ed.) *Ethnomethodology*, pp. 15–18. Harmondsworth: Penguin.

Garfinkel, H. (2002) Oxford: Ethnomethodology's Program: Working Out Durkheim's Aphorism Oxford: Rowman and Littlefield Publishers Inc.

Garfinkel, H. and Livingston, E. (2003) Phenomenal field properties of order in formatted queues and their neglected standing in the current situation of inquiry. *Visual Studies* 18, 21–28.

Geertz, C. (1973) *The Interpretation of Cultures*. New York: Basic Books.

Giddens, A. (1984) *The Constitution of Society: Outline of the theory of structuration*. Berkeley, CA: University of California Press.

Goffman, E. (1959) *The Presentation of Self in Everyday Life*. Harmondsworth: Penguin.

Goodwin, C. and Goodwin, M. (1996) Seeing as situated activity: formulating places. In: Engestrom, Y. and Middleton, D. (Eds.), *Cognition and Communication at Work*, pp. 61–95. New York: Cambridge University Press.

Gray, R. (1992) Accounting and environmentalism: An exploration of the challenge of gently accounting for accountability, transparency and sustainability. *Accounting, Organizations and Society* 17(5), 399–425.

Gray, C. (2006) Switch off lights for a jam free city. Christopher Gray finds a notorious road junction working much better without traffic control. *Oxford Times*, Weekend supplement (10 November, p. 32); also available at: http://www.theoxfordtimes.net/search/display.var.1012067.0.switch_off_lights_for_a_jamfree_city.php

Greenbaum, J. (2005) McDonalds Hot Coffee Lawsuit and Beyond: The Tort Reform Myth Machine Common Dreams.Org News Center (22 January 2005). Available at: http://www.commondreams.org/views05/0122-11.htm

Gregson, N. (2005) Throwaway Society? Truth is, we really care about getting rid of things. Available at: http://www.esrcsocietytoday.ac.uk

Grossman, E. (2006) *High Tech Trash: Digital Devices, Hidden Toxins and Human Health*. London: Island Press.

Guston, D.H. (1993) The essential tension in science and democracy. *Social Epistemology* 7, 47–60.

Guston, D.H. and Keniston, K. (Eds.) (1994) *The Fragile Contract*. Cambridge, MA: MIT Press.

Haraway, D. (1988) Situated knowledge. *Feminist Studies* 14(3), 575–599.

Hawkins, G. (2000) Plastic bags: Living with rubbish. *International Journal of Cultural Studies* 4, 5–23.

Hawkins, G. (2006) *The Ethics of Waste: how we relate to rubbish*. Lanham, MD: Rowman and Littlefield.

Heath, C. and Luff, P. (1999), Surveying the scene: The monitoring practices of staff in control rooms. In: Noyes, J. and Barnsby, M. (Eds.) *Proceedings of People in Control: An International Conference on Human Interfaces* in Control Rooms, Cockpits and Command Centres, pp. 1–6. Bath: University of Bath, IEE Press.

Hedgecoe, A., Rose, N., Rabinow, P., Bateson, P., Billinge, P., Morange, M., and Richards, M. (Eds.) (2004) *The Politics of Personalised Medicine: pharmacogenetics in the clinic.* Cambridge Studies in Society & the Life Sciences. Cambridge University Press.

Helgesson, C.-F. and Kjellberg, H. (2005) Macro-actors and the sounds of the silenced. In: Czarniawska, B. and Hernes, T. (Eds.) *Actor Network Theory and Organizing,* pp. 145–164. Malmö and Copenhagen: Liber and Copenhagen Business School Press).

Heritage, J. (1984) *Garfinkel and Ethnomethodology.* Cambridge: Polity Press.

Hertz, R. (1960) *Death and the Right Hand.* London: Cohen and West.

Hester, S. and Francis, D. (2003) Analysing visually available mundane order: a walk to the supermarket. *Visual Studies* 18, 36–46.

Hetherington, K. (2002) Second handedness: Consumption, disposal and absent presence. Available at: http://www.comp.lancs.ac.uk/sociology/soc097kh.html

Hine, C. (2000) *Virtual Ethnography.* London: Sage.

Hirsch, E. (1992) The long-term and the short-term of domestic consumption: An ethnographic case study. In: Silverstone, R. and Hirsch, E. (Eds.) *Consuming Technologies,* pp. 208–226. London: Routledge.

Home Office (2005) Identity Cards. Available at: http://www.archive2.official-documents.co.uk/document/cm63/6358/6358.pdf (accessed 7 March 2005).

Hopwood, A. (1998) Exploring the modern audit firm: An introduction. *Accounting, Organizations and Society* 23(5), 515–516.

Hubert, H. and Mauss, M. (1964) *Sacrifice.* London: Cohen and West.

Hume, D. (1979) *A Treatise of Human Nature.* London: John Noon.

Introna, L. and Wood, D. (2004) Picturing algorithmic surveillance: the politics of facial recognition systems. *Surveillance and Society* 2(2/3), 177–198.

Irwin, A. (1995) *Citizen Science.* London: Routledge.

Irwin, A. (2008) STS perspectives on scientific governance. In: Hackett, E.J, Amsterdamska, O., Lynch, M., and Wajcman, J. (Eds.) *The Handbook of Science and Technology Studies,* third edition, pp. 583–607. Cambridge, MA: MIT Press.

Jackson, W. (2009) *Completely Conkers: what drives you mad about modern Britain.* Chichester: Summersdale.

Jasanoff, S. (1998) The eye of everyman: Witnessing DNA in the Simpson trial. *Social Studies of Science* 28(5–6), 713–740.

Jasanoff, S. (2004a) The idiom of co-production. In: *States of Knowledge: the co-production of science and social order,* pp 1–12. London: Routledge.

Jeacle, I. and Walsh, E. (2002) From moral evaluation to rationalization: accounting and the shifting technologies of credit. *Accounting, Organizations and Society* 27: 737–761.

Jordan, K. and Lynch, M. (1998) The dissemination, standardisation and routinisation of a molecular biological technique. *Social Studies of Science* 28(5/6): 773–800.

Kitcher, P. (2001) *Science, Democracy and Truth.* Oxford: Oxford University Press.

Klauser, F. (2010) Splintering spheres of security: Peter Sloterdijk and the contemporary fortress city. *Environment and Planning D: Society and Space* 28, 326–340.

References

Kleinman, D. (Ed.) (2000) *Science, Technology and Democracy*. Albany, NY: State of New York University Press.

Lakoff, A. (2006) 'The political techniques of preparedness' paper presented at Stuff of Politics conference, Worcester College, University of Oxford, 7–10 December.

Latour, B. (1988a) Mixing humans and non-humans together. *Social Problems* 35(3), 298–310.

Latour, B. (1988b) Machines for machinations as well as for Machiavelli. In: Elliott, B. (Ed.) *Technology and Social Change*, pp. 20–43. Edinburgh: Edinburgh University Press.

Latour, B. (1988c) *The Pasteurization of France*. Cambridge, MA: Harvard University Press.

Latour, B. (1990) Drawing things together. In: Lynch, M. and Woolgar, S. (Eds.) *Representation in Scientific Practice*, pp. 19–68. Cambridge, MA: MIT Press.

Latour, B. (1991) Technology is society made durable. In: Law, J. (Ed.) *A Sociology of Monsters: essays on power, technology and domination*, pp. 103–131. London: Routledge.

Latour, B. (1992) Where are the missing masses? The sociology of a few mundane artifacts. In Bijker, W. and Law, J. (Eds.) *Shaping Technology, Building Society*, pp. 225–258. Boston, MA: MIT Press.

Latour, B. and Woolgar, S. (1979) *Laboratory Life: the social construction of scientific facts*. Beverly Hills: Sage.

Latour, B. and Woolgar, S. (1986) *Laboratory Life—The construction of scientific facts*, 2nd edn. Princeton, NJ: Princeton University Press.

Laurier, E. (2004) Doing office work on the motorway. *Theory, Culture and Society* 21(4–5), 261–277.

Law, J. (1996) Organizing accountabilities: ontology and the mode of accounting. In: Munro, R. and Mouritsen, J. (Eds.) *Accountability: power, ethos and the technologies of managing*, pp. 283–306. London: International Thomson Business Press.

Law, J. (2004) *After Method: Mess in social science research*. London: Routledge.

Law, J. and Mol, A. (1998) On metrics and fluids—notes on otherness. In: Chia, R. (Ed.), *Organised Worlds—Explorations in Technology and organisations with Robert Cooper*, pp. 20–38. London: Routledge.

Lee, J. (1984) Innocent victims and evil-doers. *Womens Studies International Forum* 7, 69–83.

Lefebvre, H. (1947) *Critique of Everyday Life*. London: Verso.

Livingston, E. (1987) *Making Sense of Ethnomethodology*. London: Routledge and Kegan Paul.

LSE Report (2005) The Identity Project: An Assessment of the UK Identity Card Bill and its Implications. Available at: http://www.lse.ac.uk/collections/pressAnd InformationOffice/PDF/IDreport.pdf

Luff, P. and Heath, C. (1993) System use and social organization: observations on human-computer interaction in an architectural practice. In: Button, G. (Ed.) *Technology in Working Order: studies of work, interaction and technology*, pp. 184–210. London: Routledge.

Lynch, M. (1998) The discursive production of uncertainty: The OJ Simpson 'Dream Team' and the sociology of knowledge machine. *Social Studies of Science* 28(5–6), 829–868.

Lynch, M. and McNally, R. (2005) Chains of custody: Visualization, representation and accountability in the processing of forensic DNA evidence. *Communication and Cognition* 38(3/4), 297–318.

MacKenzie, D. (2009) Making things the same: Gases, emission rights and the politics of carbon markets. *Accounting, Organisations and Society* 34, 440–455.

McLean, B. and Elkind, P. (2003) *The Smartest Guys in the Room*. New York: Penguin.

Mann, A., Mol, A., Satalkar, P., Savirani, A., Selim, N., Sur, M., and Yates-Doerr, E. (2011) Mixing methods, tasting fingers. *HAU: Journal of Ethnographic Theory* 1, 221–243.

McShane, C. (1999) The origins and globalization of traffic control signals. *Journal of Urban History*, 25(3): 379–404.

MI5 (2006) Available at: MI5 website http://www.mi5.gov.uk/output/Page45.html (accessed 3 March 2006).

Michael, M. (2006) *Technoscience and Everyday Life: the complex simplicities of the mundane*. Milton Keynes: Open University Press.

Milgram, S. (1974) *Obedience to Authority: An experimental view*. New York: Harper and Row.

Miller, P. (1992) Accounting and objectivity: the invention of calculable selves and calculable spaces. *Annals of Scholarship* 9(1/2), 61–86.

Miller, P. and O'Leary, T (1994) Governing the calculable person. In: Hopwood, A.G. and Miller, P. (Eds.) *Accounting as Social and Institutional Practice*, pp. 98–115. Cambridge: Cambridge University Press.

Mol, A. (2002) *The Body Multiple: ontology in medical practice*. London: Duke University Press.

Mol, A. (2011) This is My Body, Material Semiotic Investigations, Inaugural Lecture, Amsterdam, 15 December 2011.

Mol, A. (2013) Mind your plate! The ontonorms of Dutch dieting. *Social Studies of Science* 43, 379–396.

Mol, A. and Law, J. (1994) Regions, networks and fluids: Anaemia and social topology. *Social Studies of Science* 24: 641–671.

Munro, R. (1998) Disposal of the X gap: The production and consumption of accounting research and practical accounting systems. *Advances in Public Interest Accounting* 7, 139–159.

Neu, D. (2006) Accounting for Public Spaces. *Accounting, Organizations and Society* 31, (4/5), 391–414.

Neyland, D. (2008) *Organizational Ethnography*. London: Sage.

Neyland, D. (2009) Whos Who? The biometric future and the politics of identity. *European Journal of Criminology* 6(2), 135–155.

O'Neil, P.M. (1983) Ayn Rand and the is-ought problem. *Journal of Libertarian Studies*, II(1) 81–99.

Osborne, T. (2004) On mediators: intellectuals and the ideas trade in the knowledge society. *Economy and Society* 33(4), 430–447.

Osborne, T. and Rose, N. (1999) Governing cities: notes on the spatialisation of virtue. *Environment and Planning D: Society and Space* 17, 737–760.

Oxford Times (2005) Available from: http://www.oxfordtimes.co.uk/archive/2005/04/11/6557866.Our_love_affair_with_low_speed/

References

Pollner, M. (1974) *Mundane Reason*. Cambridge: Cambridge University Press.

Power, M. (1997) *The Audit Society*. Oxford: Oxford University Press.

Prior, A. (1960) The autonomy of ethics. *Australasian Journal of Philosophy* 38, 199–206.

Random House Dictionary of the English Language (1967) London: Random House Publishers.

Rappert, B. (1997) Users and social science research: Policy, problems and possibilities. *Sociological Research On-Line* 2 (3). Available at: http://www.socresonline.org.uk/socresonline/2/3/10.html

Rappert, B. (2001) The distribution and the resolution of the ambiguities of technology; or why Bobby cant spray. *Social Studies of Science* August, 557–592.

Rawls, A. (2002) Editor's introduction. In: Garfinkel, H. (Ed.) *Ethnomethodologys Program: working out Durkheims aphorism*, pp. 1–64. Oxford: Rowman and Littlefield.

Reno, J. (2011) Managing the experience of evidence: Englands experimental waste technologies and their immodest witnesses. *Science, Technology and Human Values* 36(6), 842–863.

Richman, J. (1983) *Traffic Wardens: An ethnography of street administration*. Manchester: Manchester University Press.

Rousseau, D. (2005) Is there such a thing as 'Evidence-Based Management?' *Academy of Management Review* 31(2), 256–269.

Rose, N. (1988) Calculable minds and manageable individuals. *History of the Human Sciences* 1, 179–200.

Rose, N. (1990) *Governing the Soul: the shaping of the private self*. London: Routledge.

Rose, N. (1996a) Governing 'advanced' liberal democracies. In: Barry, A., Osborne, T., and Rose N. (Eds.) *Foucault and Political Reason*, pp. 37–64. London: UCL Press.

Rose, N. (1996b) *Inventing Our Selves*. New York: Cambridge University Press.

Rose, N. (1999) *Governing the Soul: the shaping of the private self*. London: Free Association Books.

Rose, N. and Miller, P. (1992) Political power beyond the state: Problematics of government. *British Journal of Sociology* 43(2), 173–205.

Rose, N., O'Malley, P., and Valverde, M. (2006) Governmentality. *Annual Review of Law and Society* 2, 83–104.

Rubio, F. D. and Lezaun, J. (2011) Technology, legal knowledge and citizenship: on the care of Locked-in Syndrome patients. In: P. Baert and F. D. Rubio (Eds.) *The Politics of Knowledge*, pp. 58–78. London: Routledge.

Ryave, A. and Schenkein, J. (1974) Notes on the art of walking. In: Turner, R. (Ed.) *Ethnomethodology*, pp. 265–274. Harmondsworth, Middx: Penguin Books.

Sacks, H. (1972) Notes on police assessment of moral character. In: Sudnow, D. (Ed.) *Studies in Social Interaction*, pp. 280–293. New York: Free Press.

Saphores, J., Nixon, H., Ogunseitan, O., and Shapiro, A. (2006) Household willingness to recycle electronic waste. *Environment and Behaviour* 38(2), 183–208.

Schildkrout, E. (2004) Inscribing the body. *Annual Review of Anthropology* 33, 319–344.

Schurz, G. (1997) *The Is-Ought Problem: An investigation in philosophical logic*. Springer.

Searle, J.R. (1964) How to derive 'ought' from 'is'. *Philosophical Review* 73, 43–58.

Selznick, P. (1948) Foundations of the theory of organisation. *American Sociological Review* 13, 25–35.

Sharp, E. (2005) Community Waste Projects Are A Boost To Regeneration. Available at: www.esrcsocietytoday.ac.uk.

Sheldrick, G. (2006) £40,000 pounds lights face switch off OT. Available at: http://www.theoxfordtimes.net/search/display.var.1052006.0.40_000_lights_face_switchoff.php Friday 1 December.

Shove, E. (2003a) *Comfort, Cleanliness and Convenience: the social organisation of normality*. Oxford: Berg.

Shove, E. (2003b) Things in the making and things in action: A discussion of design, use and consumption (SBS STS seminar, 24 January).

Shove, E. and Southerton, D. (2000) Defrosting the freezer: from novelty to convenience. *Material Culture* 5(3), 301–319.

Shove, E., Pantzar, M., and Watson, M. (2012) *The Dynamics of Social Practice: Everyday life and how it changes*. London: Sage.

Sikka, P. (2001) Transparency and accountability of the professional accountancy bodies: some observations on the Canning and ODwyer paper. *European Accounting Review* 10(4), 751–762.

Singer, P. (1973) The triviality of the debate over 'is-ought' and the definition of 'moral'. *American Philosophical Quarterly* X, 1.

Singleton, V. and Michael, M. (1993) Actor-networks and ambivalence: general practitioners in the UK Cervical Screening Programme. *Social Studies of Science* 23, 227–264.

Smith, D. (1990) *Texts, Facts and Femininity: exploring the relations of ruling*. New York: Routledge.

Smith, D. (2001) Texts and the ontology of organisations and institutions. *Studies in Cultures, Organisations and Societies* 7(2), 159–198.

Star, S.L. (1991) Power, technologies and the phenomenology of conventions: on being allergic to onions. In: Law, J. (Ed.) *A Sociology of Monsters: essays on power, technology and domination*, pp. 26–56. Sociological Review Monograph. London: Routledge.

Stengers, I. (2006) Including non-humans: opening Pandoras box? Paper presented at Stuff of Politics conference, Worcester College University of Oxford, 7–10 December.

Strasser, S. (2000) *Waste and Want*. New York: Owl Books.

Strathern, M. (1999) The aesthetics of substance. In: *Property, Substance and Effect*, pp. 45–64. London: Athlone.

Strathern, M. (2000) Introduction. In: Strathern, M. (Ed.) *Audit Cultures: Anthropological studies in accountability, ethics and the academy*, pp. 1–18. London: Routledge.

Strathern, M. (2002) Abstraction and decontextualisation: An anthropological comment. In: Woolgar, S. (Ed.) *Virtual Society? Technology, cyberbole, reality*, pp. 302–313. Oxford: Oxford University Press.

Strathern, M. (2004) *Partial Connections*. Oxford: Rowman and Littlefield.

Suchman, L. (1993) Technologies of accountability: of lizards and aeroplanes. In: Button, G. (Ed.) *Technology in Working Order: studies of work, interaction and technology*, pp. 113–126. London: Routledge.

Thompson, C. (2004) *Making Parents: The ontological choreography of reproductive technologies*. Cambridge, MA: MIT Press.

Thompson, M. (1979) *Rubbish Theory*. Oxford: Oxford University Press.

References

Tucker, P. (1999) A Virtual Society for Sustainable Waste Management Planning. Available at: http://www.esrcsocietytoday.ac.uk

Van der Ploeg, I. (2003) Biometrics and privacy: A note on the politics of theorizing technology. *Information, Communication, Society* 6, 85–104.

Vaughan-Williams, N. (2010) The UK border security continuum: virtual biopolitics and the simulation of the sovereign ban. *Environment and Planning D: Society and Space* 28, 1071–1083.

Vrecko, S. (2006) Unpublished PhD thesis, Department of Sociology, London School of Economics.

Weick, K. (1995) *Sensemaking in Organizations*. London: Sage.

Wells, H. and Wills, D. (2009) Individualism and Identity Resistance to Speed Cameras in the UK. *Surveillance & Society* 6(3): 259–227.

Wieder, D. (1974) *Language and Social Reality: The case of telling the convict code*. Middlesex: Penguin Books.

Wilkinson, M. (2006) Traffic runs 'more smoothly without lights'. *Oxford Mail Online* (31 March). Available at: http://www.oxfordmail.net/search/display.var.711882.0.traffic_runs_more_smoothly_without_lights.php 10:41am Wednesday 22 March 2006.

Winner, L. (1986) Do artifacts have politics? In: Winner, L. (Ed.) *The Whale and the Reactor*, pp. 19–39. Chicago, IL: University of Chicago Press.

Woolf, P. (1994) Integrity and accountability in research. In: Guston, D.H. and Keniston, K. (Eds.) *The Fragile Contract*, pp. 82–100. Cambridge, MA: MIT Press.

Woolgar, S. (2002) *Virtual Society?* Oxford: Oxford University Press.

Woolgar, S. and Pawluch, D. (1985) Ontological gerrymandering: the anatomy of a social problems explanation. *Social Problems* 32(3), 214–227.

Wright, E.C. (1993) Non-compliance—or how many aunts has Matilda? *Lancet* 342, 909–913.

Wynne, B. (1989) Hazardous waste regulation in the UK and EEC comparison of risk management. *Third World Quarterly* 16(2).

Yaneva, A. (2012) *Mapping Controversies in Architecture*. Surrey: Ashgate.

Young, K., Ashby, D., Boaz, A., and Grayson, L. (2002) Social science and the evidence-based policy movement. *Social Policy and Society* 1(3), 215–224.

Index